Modernizing Enterprise CMS Using Pimcore

Discover techniques and best practices for creating custom websites with rich digital experiences

Daniele Fontani

Marco Guiducci

Francesco Minà

Packt>

BIRMINGHAM—MUMBAI

Modernizing Enterprise CMS Using Pimcore

Copyright © 2021 Packt Publishing

All rights reserved. No part of this book may be reproduced, stored in a retrieval system, or transmitted in any form or by any means, without the prior written permission of the publisher, except in the case of brief quotations embedded in critical articles or reviews.

Every effort has been made in the preparation of this book to ensure the accuracy of the information presented. However, the information contained in this book is sold without warranty, either express or implied. Neither the authors, nor Packt Publishing or its dealers and distributors, will be held liable for any damages caused or alleged to have been caused directly or indirectly by this book.

Packt Publishing has endeavored to provide trademark information about all of the companies and products mentioned in this book by the appropriate use of capitals. However, Packt Publishing cannot guarantee the accuracy of this information.

Publishing Product Manager: Pavan Ramchandani
Senior Editor: Hayden Edwards
Content Development Editor: Aamir Ahmed
Technical Editor: Shubham Sharma
Copy Editor: Safis Editing
Language Support Editor: Safis Editing
Project Coordinator: Manthan Patel
Proofreader: Safis Editing
Indexer: Tejal Daruwale Soni
Production Designer: Roshan Kawale

First published: July 2021

Production reference: 1090721

Published by Packt Publishing Ltd.
Livery Place
35 Livery Street
Birmingham
B3 2PB, UK.

ISBN 978-1-80107-540-4

www.packt.com

To the forests, which taught me the value of small things. To the climbs, which made me stronger. To everyone who told me it wasn't possible, because they gave me the motivation to go on.

– Daniele Fontani

This book is dedicated to my wife, who is the anchor that holds me steady, and who has always been by my side at all the important moments of my career. And to my son, who has just come to life, and who supported me in writing this book from the belly of his mother.

– Marco Guiducci

To Pongo, Pizzicottina, and the unforgettable Brina and Paco for bearing with me and making every day of my life special. I would be lost without you.

Finally, a special thanks to Daniele Fontani for his constant and priceless support and pulling me out of my comfort zone. A true friend and an immeasurable leader.

– Francesco Minà

Foreword

More than ten years have passed since Pimcore's conception. During this time, thousands of companies have embraced the Pimcore data and experience management revolution. So far, Pimcore has helped over 100,000 businesses deliver digital solutions and successfully perform digital transformations. We are proud to be able to offer Pimcore's Open-Source Community Edition to our whole ecosystem free of charge, complemented by an optional Enterprise Subscription. Pimcore is the point of conjunction between the marketing department, the development team, and the partner agency. Using Pimcore helps all parties to share the same vision, without friction, without getting lost in technicalities. Choosing the right digital platform in the right moment of its digital evolution is essential to business success today. So, learning how to build and deliver modern applications with Pimcore means that you are following the right path.

In this book, you will get the foundation of being autonomous in Pimcore development, starting from scratch and without any additional requirements. You will be led through the pillars of building a Pimcore solution. It will make you able to implement any kind of digital solution for your project, or for any customer project. This book will take you step-by-step through Pimcore, from the user perspective and as a developer. You will learn how to create web pages, manage and distribute digital assets, create golden records of your master data, and develop custom code.

After reading this book, you will be ready to start your next digital project and, with Pimcore, you will discover that regardless of the complexity of the project, there is always a solution.

Dietmar „Dietz" Rietsch

CEO and co-founder of the Pimcore company

Contributors

About the authors

Daniele Fontani is the CTO in Sintra Digital Business and has worked as a senior developer, team leader, and architect in a very large set of enterprise projects. He has a master's degree in robotic science and another master's degree in project management. His experience in technology extends to many technologies (Java, PHP, and .NET) and platforms (SharePoint, Liferay, and Pimcore) other than techniques (Agile, DevOps, and ALM). He is interested in Agile techniques, project management, and product development. He implemented DXP platforms for banks and worked in the loan industry as a team leader and software architect. In the pharma industry, he designed and developed retail portals for training and for the social engagement of retailers.

Linkedin: https://www.linkedin.com/in/daniele-fontani/

Website: https://www.danielefontani.it/

Twitter: https://twitter.com/zeppaman

Blog: https://daniele-fontani.medium.com/

I want to thank the coauthors of this book, the reviewers, the editors, and all the staff for making this book possible. I never felt alone.

Marco Guiducci is a certified Pimcore expert, team leader, and software engineer. He earned a master's degree in information science in 2017 with a thesis on AI, focused on semantic text analysis. Since then, he has taken his first steps as a developer. He fell in love with PHP and Pimcore. Now, Marco has matured with long-term experience, documented by public speaking and contributions to the Pimcore code base. Inside the Pimcore ecosystem, he is focused on the PIM/DAM/MDM strategy and has delivered a broad set of enterprise projects across the world. He has designed and delivered a lot of PIM solutions for enterprises using Pimcore, integrating with major e-commerce solutions such as Shopify, Magento, and Shopware. He has also delivered B2B portals and websites using Pimcore and other technical solutions.

Linkedin: https://www.linkedin.com/in/marco-guiducci/

I want to thank the people who have been close to me and supported me, especially my wife and my parents.

Francesco Minà started programming in 1997 and, since that time, has followed the most important trends in digital innovation. He graduated with a degree in industrial automation in 2010 with a thesis on informatic science, in which he built a box for sending profiled marketing messages to customers on their devices, anticipating what would become the norm a few years later with modern social networks and tools. During his professional life, Francesco has worked as a senior developer on Magento, WordPress, Pimcore, and other CMS solutions. He is a solution architect and team leader in a digital innovation company, where he delivers a complete solution based on Pimcore. Francesco is active as a public speaker and an open source contributor. He developed an open source solution for delivering WordPress plugins and presented it as a best practice at many developer conferences. He developed `erpselection.it`, the first Italian software selection network. Throughout his career, he has delivered portals and B2B applications for the fashion and logistics industries.

Linkedin: https://www.linkedin.com/in/francesco-mina/

I would like to thank my mother and my father for having me. They have done their best to raise a perfect child and, even if the result is not the best, I cannot imagine what life would be like without them. I love you.

About the reviewers

Christian Kemptner is the Marketing and Partner Manager at Pimcore. He has many years of experience in the successful online marketing of software products. In just 5 years, he has successfully helped Pimcore to build a global ecosystem of over 130 certified partner agencies and more than 100,000 customers.

Leonard Hirja is a father, husband, senior software architect, and Agile practitioner with over 6 years' active experience in the field. He's actively involved in e-commerce projects and automatic data integrations. He mostly specializes in backend architecture, and in the last couple of years he has also specialized in frontend technologies as a senior full-stack developer. His preferred technology stack is Laravel, Vue.JS, and Pimcore (with ShopCore).

Table of Contents

Preface

1
Introducing Pimcore

Why do you need more than a simple CMS?	2
Understanding the change in requirements	2
What is a DXP?	3
What is Pimcore?	5
Decoupling data from the UI	7
Unifying the user experience	7
Readying your company for the cloud	8
Discovering Pimcore's features	9
Data management	10
CMS and DXP	11
PIM	12
MDM	13
DAM	15
Digital commerce	17
Learning about Pimcore's benefits	18
Rapid innovation	19
Unmatched flexibility	19
A solid platform	19
Used by the masses	20
Web development is made easy	20
Learning about the benefits of using open source software	20
Speed and agility	21
Shared maintenance costs	21
Transparency and security	21
Cost-effectiveness	22
Community	22
Pimcore licensing	22
Summary	23

2
Setting Up Your Pimcore Development Environment

Technical requirements	26
Why use Docker?	26
For manual installation	27
Installing Pimcore from Composer (without Docker)	28
Installing Pimcore using Docker	31
The docker-compose file	32

The installation file	33	The bin folder	38
Starting Pimcore with Docker	35	The src folder	38
Exploring folder conventions	**36**	The var folder	38
		The vendor folder	39
The config folder	38	The public folder	39
The templates folder	38	**Summary**	**40**

3
Getting Started with Pimcore Admin UI

Technical requirements	**42**	Toolbar	49
Understanding the		Second tab bar	50
Pimcore Architecture	**42**	The opened document	51
Exploring the UI Components	**43**	**Inspecting the menus**	**51**
Sidebar Menu	45	File	52
Left sidebar	46	Tools	53
Main frame	46	Marketing	53
Right sidebar	47	Settings	53
Working with the grid		Search	54
component	**48**	**Summary**	**54**
First tab bar	49		

4
Creating Documents in Pimcore

Technical requirements	**56**	Implementing a simple layout	62
What is a document?	**56**	**Editing a document**	**66**
Creating a document	**58**	**Inheriting documents**	**71**
Creating a template	**60**	**Summary**	**75**
The Pimcore page design process	61		

5
Exploring Objects and Classes

Technical requirements	**78**	Designing different concepts	79
What is a Class?	**78**	No code required	79

Creating and Editing a Class Definition	80	Generic Relations	97
		Object Relations	98
Discovering Relevant Field Types	83	A Concrete Example of Relations	98
Layout Components	84	**Performing Data Entry**	**100**
Data Components	88	Creating Folders and Objects	100
Structured Components	92	Adding Object Variants	101
Understanding and Establishing Relations	96	Editing Classes and Objects	102
		Summary	**104**

6
Using Digital Asset Management

Technical requirements	106	**Image Editing and Enrichment**	**115**
What is a DAM?	106	Exploring the Image Editor	116
Characteristics of a DAM system	107	Defining Assets Metadata	117
Introducing Pimcore DAM features	109	Setting up Focal Points	119
Uploading and Relating Assets	**110**	**Defining and Using Thumbnails**	**120**
Uploading Assets	111	Defining thumbnails	120
Organizing Assets	112	Using Thumbnails	124
Relating Assets to Data Objects	113	**Summary**	**127**

7
Administrating Pimcore Sites

Technical requirements	130	Managing Perspectives	143
Installing a bundle	130	Importing and Exporting Pimcore settings	148
Exploring Users and Roles	136		
Setting Users and Roles	137	Using the Pimcore Console	152
A practical example of using users and roles	141	**Summary**	**155**

8
Creating Custom CMS Pages

Technical requirements	158	Select	188
Using the MVC Model	158	Multiselect	189
Controllers	159	Numeric	190
Views	163	Renderlet	190
Mastering Routing and URLs	176	Snippet	193
		Table	194
Using editables	182	Textarea	195
Checkbox	182	Video	196
Date	183	WYSIWYG	197
Relation (Many-To-One)	184	Using blocks	197
Relations (many-to-many relation)	185	Regular Blocks	197
Image	186	Scheduled Blocks	199
Input	187		
Link	187	Summary	200

9
Configuring Entities and Rendering Data

Technical requirements	202	Action for an article (ArticleAction)	213
Defining blog classes	202	Other Actions	215
Defining a BlogArticle class	203	Rendering blog views	216
Defining a BlogCategory class	204	Stylization and layout of HTML pages	
Defining a BlogAuthor class	205	with Bootstrap	217
Creating blog Users and Roles	207	Templating	219
Creating an Author Role	208	Inspecting the Article view	220
Creating Users	209	Rendering the Categories Widget	222
Putting it all together	210	Understanding Twig filters	224
Routing	211	Differences between Pimcore and WordPress	226
Editing the Controller for our blog	213	Summary	228

10
Creating Pimcore Bricks

Technical requirements	230	Implementing a contact form brick	239
Creating a bundle	230	Avoiding conflicts	245
What is a bundle?	231	Implementing a slideshow brick	246
Understanding how a Brick works	234	Using bricks and blocks for a general-purpose template	252
The class implementation	234	Summary	262
Templating	235		
Implementing a simple brick	236		

11
Finalizing the Website

Technical requirements	264	Using a multi-environment configuration	276
Making a Multisite in Pimcore	264	Using Environment variables	278
Making the bundles installable	268	Using environment variables for managing database connections	279
Installers	269		
Migrations	274	Summary	282

12
Implementing Product Information Management

Technical requirements	284	Creating an Event Listener	298
What is a PIM?	285	Managing different Product Types	301
Defining the Product Entity	286	Working with workflows	304
Creating product variants	290	Configuring a Custom Layout	304
Parent PHP class	292	Configuring a Pimcore workflow	306
Object Listing	294	Summary	310
Creating a new Variant	295		
Creating a Bundle Product	296		
Defining bundle products	296		

13
Implementing Master Data Management

Technical requirements	312	Using mutation queries	332
Turning Pimcore into MDM	312	Creating Objects	332
Implementing Data Quality	314	Updating objects	334
		Deleting Objects	335
Activating the Pimcore Datahub bundle	319	Creating a custom mutation	335
Creating a Datahub configuration	320	Defining custom reports	338
		Summary	342
Exposing entities	325		
Performing GraphQL queries	326		

14
Data Integration

Technical requirements	344	Limitations of Data Export	355
Importing Data	344	Limitations of Data Import	356
CSV File Preview	345	Creating a Custom Operator	357
Column Configuration	346	Implementing Custom Solutions	359
Resolver Settings	348	Adding custom buttons	359
CSV Settings	349	Creating Pimcore Commands	363
Save & Share	350		
		Configuring the Data Importer	365
Exporting Data	351	Summary	372
Limitations of Standard Functionalities	354	Why subscribe?	373

Other Books You May Enjoy
Index

Preface

Nowadays, digital innovation is a challenge for any medium-sized or large organization. This journey, also known as *digital transformation*, is not only related to technology but is guided by cultural and motivational pillars. Many managers or communication gurus will tell you that technology is not important and that it's just a commodity or a set of tools at the service of the company (marketing, sales, and suchlike). We believe that this approach is possible only if the technology you have chosen is genuinely able to support your business initiatives. In terms of starting to forget about technical issues and focusing on business only, we have to find a technical solution that works perfectly under all conditions that can scale and support the business as it grows. Following an extended period of research, we have found that this solution is called Pimcore.

Pimcore, in simple terms, is a technology facilitator that removes most of the operative friction between the mind and the hands of a company. Pimcore can act as a **PIM (Product Information Management)** system for distributing product information across the entire company or centralize essential data for the company (Master Data Management), allowing all other parties to consume it without any security risk.

Moreover, Pimcore is a powerful CMS engine that can manage a lot more than simple web pages. It is a very versatile solution that covers most of the problems you encounter every day. In this book, we will learn how to get the best out of Pimcore.

After reading this book, you will be able to do the following:

1. You will understand what Pimcore is and how it works. In fact, we believe that it isn't only a matter of which tool to use, but also to incorporate it perfectly into the big picture.
2. You will be able to create websites and portals, using Pimcore as a digital experience platform. This includes using the CMS engine, but also creating custom web MVC pages and reusable components.

3. You will be able to use the enterprise feature of Pimcore (PIM, DAM, MDM). You will learn how to collect data, incorporate it into a unified database, and share it with all potential consumers (apps, websites, legacy applications, and so on).
4. You will be able to install, maintain, and deploy a Pimcore website.

In simple terms, this book will lead you on a journey through theoretical and practical lessons to become a Pimcore developer!

Who this book is for

This book is designed to encourage you to learn about Pimcore in a straightforward manner. We will cover all the important topics to enable you to initiate and complete a real-world project. To reach this goal, we have developed a book that's not only a set of information but something that combines theory and practice. This pragmatic approach will teach you how Pimcore works and how to put your knowledge into practice without getting annoyed or barely being able to follow tutorials by asking you why you need to do that. In fact, the first chapters will introduce you to a high-level vision of Pimcore so that you are aware of all of its benefits, and then we will embark on a journey that will progressively uncover all the details of Pimcore step by step without introducing any excessive complexity.

This book is designed for any developer, CTO, or any other kind of technician wanting to deliver Pimcore-based solutions or is willing to build digital platforms to support their customers or their business on the digital transformation journey.

This book gradually introduces the most important concepts, so you do not require any special background. All you need to know in order to understand the book is the basics of the PHP language and some practices involving HTML and CSS.

What this book covers

Chapter 1, *Introducing Pimcore*, explains what Pimcore is. It introduces the main characteristics and describes how it works. This chapter introduces the tool to the reader and reveals all the features from a wide-angle point of view.

Chapter 2, *Setting Up Your Pimcore Development Environment*, covers the installation of Pimcore with a deep dive into setting up a local environment compatible with a source code repository.

Chapter 3, *Getting Started with Pimcore Admin UI*, explains how the admin UI works and how to find UIs for basic commands. This is useful for navigating the Pimcore menus and functionalities.

Chapter 4, *Creating Documents in Pimcore*, explains how to create Pimcore's documents and how to handle basic settings. This is a useful resource when it comes to editing documents and creating web pages.

Chapter 5, *Exploring Object and Classes*, explains how to create and manage Pimcore objects and classes. This step constitutes the basis for the majority of Pimcore tasks, such as creating complex websites.

Chapter 6, *Using Digital Asset Management*, explains how to manage assets in Pimcore using the DAM feature. This is important for uploading assets and spreading or integrating them inside web pages.

Chapter 7, *Administrating Pimcore Sites*, covers administration and maintenance routing. It explains how to install Pimcore sites and how to manage third-party add-ons. This is what you need to keep Pimcore up and running.

Chapter 8, *Creating Custom CMS Pages*, explains how to implement themes and prepare templates for custom CMS pages. Doing this is important when it comes to mastering the basics of custom web page building.

Chapter 9, *Configuring Entities and Rendering Data*, explains how to present data to the user in terms of implementing web pages. This is a real-world use case that helps to put into practice what you have learned so far.

Chapter 10, *Creating Pimcore Bricks*, explains how to create reusable components that can be configured by the user. This is the way to save you from a lot of work and simplify maintenance.

Chapter 11, *Finalizing the Website*, contains tips and tricks that save time and provide assistance in reusing a component on multiple projects.

Chapter 12, *Implementing Product Information Management*, shows the PIM configuration of Pimcore. It explains how to tune it for managing it as a PIM system. With this chapter, you can start using Pimcore as a PIM system.

Chapter 13, *Implementing Master Data Management*, explains how to expose data using GraphQL APIs. With this, you can activate this feature and start data integration.

Chapter 14, *Data Integration*, covers the data integration feature of Pimcore. This helps to implement a standard way of integrating with other systems without any development effort.

To get the most out of this book

Pimcore is a great platform, supported by many vendors and communities. This means that your application will always be hosted on an updated platform that will periodically release new features. This book is based on Pimcore X, and it is the latest version released at the time of publication, so by reading this book, you will be learning on the latest version available!

Pimcore X comes with many new features and an updated technology stack (Symfony 5, PHP 8, and ExtJS 7) that provides many performance improvements. Even though there are enormous changes between Pimcore X and the previous versions, most of the concepts you will learn reading this book will also be applicable to all the previous versions.

This book is designed for a seamless learning experience and doesn't require any relevant expertise other than basic PHP and HTML knowledge. In any case, any developer who has some experience with other platforms will be able to follow the instructions and understand the code. Moreover, we haven't introduced any paid or OS-related tools, and this makes this book available to all without any limitations:

Software/hardware covered in the book	OS requirements
Docker	Windows 10, macOS 10.4+, or Linux (any)
Visual Studio Code	OS X Yosemite (10.10+) Windows 7 (with .NET Framework 4.5.2), 8.0, 8.1, and 10 (32-bit and 64-bit); Linux (Debian): Ubuntu Desktop 16.04, Debian 9; Linux (Red Hat): Red Hat Enterprise Linux 7, CentOS 8, Fedora 24
LAMP Stack (*)	Apache >=2.4, PHP >=8.0, composer, MySQL 8.0+ or MariaDB 10.3+

All the items marked with (*) are only required if you do not choose to use Docker. In fact, we provide a Docker-based setup option that doesn't require anything other than Docker. All the dependencies will be managed automatically, so you won't have to worry about that. In any event, if you are going to follow the manual installation, you will also need all the tools marked with (*) installed on your local PC.

If you are using the digital version of this book, we advise you to type the code yourself or access the code via the GitHub repository (link available in the next section). Doing so will help you avoid any potential errors related to the copying and pasting of code.

Download the example code files

You can download the example code files for this book from GitHub at `https://github.com/PacktPublishing/Modernizing-Enterprise-CMS-using-Pimcore`. In case there's an update to the code, it will be updated on the existing GitHub repository.

We also have other code bundles from our rich catalog of books and videos available at `https://github.com/PacktPublishing/`. Check them out!

Download the color images

We also provide a PDF file that has color images of the screenshots/diagrams used in this book. You can download it here: `https://static.packt-cdn.com/downloads/9781801075404_ColorImages.pdf`.

Conventions used

There are a number of text conventions used throughout this book.

`Code in text`: Indicates code words in text, database table names, folder names, filenames, file extensions, pathnames, dummy URLs, user input, and Twitter handles. Here is an example: "Add a template to `/bundles/BlogBundle/Resources/views/Areas` called `view.html.twig`."

A block of code is set as follows:

```
<?php

use Pimcore\Bundle\BundleGeneratorBundle\
PimcoreBundleGeneratorBundle;

return [
    PimcoreBundleGeneratorBundle::class => ['all' => true],
];
```

When we wish to draw your attention to a particular part of a code block, the relevant lines or items are set in bold:

```
"autoload": {
    "psr-4": {
        "App\\": "src/",
        "BlogBundle\\": "bundles/BlogBundle/",
        "Pimcore\\Model\\DataObject\\": "var/classes/DataObject",
        "Pimcore\\Model\\Object\\": "var/classes/Object",
        "Website\\": "legacy/website/lib"
    }
},
```

Any command-line input or output is written as follows:

```
docker-compose exec php bash
```

Bold: Indicates a new term, an important word, or words that you see on screen. For example, words in menus or dialog boxes appear in the text like this. Here is an example: "Fill the form with data (it is a contact form, so the field meanings should be self-explanatory) and then click **Send**."

> **Tips or important notes**
> Appear like this.

Get in touch

Feedback from our readers is always welcome.

General feedback: If you have questions about any aspect of this book, mention the book title in the subject of your message and email us at customercare@packtpub.com.

Errata: Although we have taken every care to ensure the accuracy of our content, mistakes do happen. If you have found a mistake in this book, we would be grateful if you would report this to us. Please visit www.packtpub.com/support/errata, selecting your book, clicking on the Errata Submission Form link, and entering the details.

Piracy: If you come across any illegal copies of our works in any form on the internet, we would be grateful if you would provide us with the location address or website name. Please contact us at copyright@packt.com with a link to the material.

If you are interested in becoming an author: If there is a topic that you have expertise in and you are interested in either writing or contributing to a book, please visit `authors.packtpub.com`.

Reviews

Please leave a review. Once you have read and used this book, why not leave a review on the site that you purchased it from? Potential readers can then see and use your unbiased opinion to make purchase decisions, we at Packt can understand what you think about our products, and our authors can see your feedback on their book. Thank you!

For more information about Packt, please visit `packt.com`.

1
Introducing Pimcore

If you bought this book, you probably already have a rough idea of what Pimcore is. **Pimcore** is an open source, enterprise-grade **Digital eXperience Platform** (**DXP**) solution that aims to be the leader in its market segment. But what does this definition really mean? It sounds very vague as, too often in the IT world, buzzwords are used as filler when describing something. And that's why we have to explain what Pimcore is properly, not just telling you what it does but drilling down into the problems it solves.

Understanding the scenarios where the tools we are going to study will be employed is always an excellent way to proceed, especially when you want to learn Pimcore, a platform that will revolutionize your development experience.

In this chapter, we will explore the Pimcore platform, learning about the benefits and opportunities it offers and how it differs from other solutions.

The chapter is organized as follows:

- Why do you need more than a simple CMS?
- What is Pimcore?
- Discovering Pimcore's features
- Learning about Pimcore's benefits
- Learning about the benefits of using open source software

Why do you need more than a simple CMS?

In this section, we will learn about how the **Content Management System** (**CMS**) has evolved in recent years and what new requirements these changes have brought up. Understanding market trends and needs is fundamental to successfully adopting a CMS platform that will support our business or our customers' business for years to come. Learning about a tool such as Pimcore without fully understanding how it can be useful could be a waste of time, and you may lose a lot of technical opportunities that could solve your or your customers' problems.

So, let's introduce the problem that Pimcore solves. Then, it will be very easy to understand why Pimcore created this product in the way that it did and why we should adopt it.

Understanding the change in requirements

The first thing to accept is that there has been an evolution in the market. We are no longer satisfied with a tool that only builds a website. That was okay 10 years ago, but now, most companies have a more holistic approach to digital communication and want more. You don't have to be scared by this change; since the birth of the internet, we've seen many evolutions and things have become better and better. We simply have to follow the trends, or better, anticipate the trends.

Think of what has happened in the last 20 years. We started with the internet just producing static text content. It literally meant manually writing every single page and uploading it using a **File Transfer Protocol** (**FTP**) link, if you were lucky. We still remember when we were fighting with scripting languages to mix HTML, data, and Flash content just to render two or three pages for a simple website.

CMS was a very big leap forward. Managing dynamic content from the browser unlocked the opportunity of letting the final user manage their data, reducing the development effort required. That was a revolution, and many CMS solutions spread across the web. WordPress, Drupal, and other products became a must for creating websites. They were (and probably still are) good solutions for most scenarios, but we are here to enhance our tool range and be ready for what the market will ask of us tomorrow.

Now it's time to push the user experience to the next level, and we need a good tool to support this digital evolution.

What is a DXP?

The main topic to learn about to understand the market's current needs in terms of digital innovation is **DXP**. This acronym was coined by Gartner and is a way to describe a technical solution that can support the digital experience of a company. What a company should do, nowadays, is put the customer at the center of everything and use technology to power the delivery of the right content to the right person. Most of the companies that wanted to expand their business online started their digital transformations years ago. They created e-commerce sites to sell online and reached all their customers with the right products. They have had websites since the beginning of the internet (some have had more than one). Corporations can have a single global website, one per brand, or different websites based on the target market. They also have a portal, to give agents or third-party vendors access **Business-to-Business** (**B2B**) information.

All this segmentation is a nightmare: we have too many platforms, we have to keep them communicating with each other, we have to manage content in different GUIs, and we need multiple logins to do all this. This solution is not optimal, so warrants change.

But there is a more important reason for this change – we forgot the most important element in all of this: we missed the customer. While grappling with technologies and their evolution, we lost our focus on the thing that's most crucial. That's why we need a unique software solution to effectively manage all those problems we just described: that solution is the Digital eXperience Platform.

In the following figure, we can see how a DXP includes e-commerce, websites, and portals to create a unique experience:

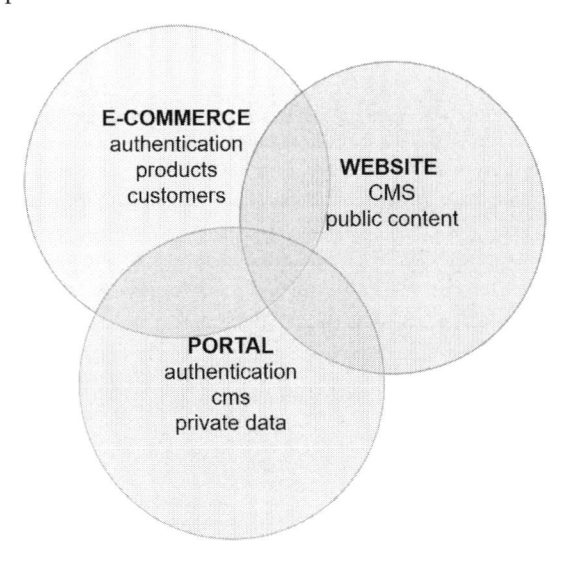

Figure 1.1: DXP diagram

As you can see in the preceding figure, the e-commerce and portal solutions have some things in common; for example, they share the same authentication system. We can also see that websites and portals create web content using the same CMS. Based on your experience, you may already understand that these three solutions need to share some features. Replicating them in separate platforms is redundant, but putting all the elements together in a single platform helps us to reduce complexity and avoid the duplication of data.

In simple terms, we are talking about having an integrated software framework that can implement a solution to all digital companies' needs. This will lead to engaging a broad set of users through all digital touchpoints.

Pimcore is that framework. The mission of Pimcore is to make technology an enabler for digital transformation and not an obstacle. The vision of Pimcore is very clear: using only one tool, we should be able to integrate all the other tools in the company and accelerate all processes.

Most companies have trouble finding data, or they have duplicated data across their system. This usually happens because, historically, these companies adopted many vertical solutions, and only later did they ask themselves how to integrate them. These isolated sets of data are called **silos**. A quick way to break down data silos is to create a central database with all the information that's needed and to facilitate delivery to the consumer through easy and transparent API protocols. This solution is called **Master Data Management** (**MDM**), and it's one of the features offered by Pimcore (we'll see this in *Chapter 6, Using Digital Asset Management*.

We always need to have central information, but often, this need becomes a pain point when we have to deal with product data. We might sell products across many channels, we might need to print information on them in physical catalogs, and we cannot have different information in different places about the same thing. The centralization of product management is called **Product Information Management** (**PIM**), and it is another feature of Pimcore. We will learn more about this later, but for now, keep in mind that growing companies have such needs.

Finally, we may want to centrally manage digital assets, such as videos, images, and other files. A system that collects and delivers digital assets is called a **Digital Asset Management** (**DAM**) system, and you have probably already guessed that Pimcore also covers this. We will learn more about this topic in the next section.

The Pimcore platform is the right tool for any company facing a digital experience transformation. Moreover, the digital experience transformation is not the only problem that such a company will face. That's why Pimcore is more than a PIM, CMS, MDM, and DAM put together. Pimcore is a solution to help us realize big changes in the digital experience of our customers.

In this section, you learned about the challenges that the most important companies are facing. Our duty, as technicians or consultants, is to help companies to look at their simple websites, come up with a more holistic vision of their digital communication, and support their needs with the right technical solution. In the next section, we will learn about what Pimcore is and why it is the right solution to this problem.

What is Pimcore?

When defining what Pimcore is, the first thing to take into account is the name itself. The name suggests that the PIM is the main part, but you shouldn't be taken in by appearances. Pimcore is a lot more than a PIM product.

We can describe Pimcore as a framework because it gives us all the tools we need to implement our projects. This second definition is not much more intuitive to understand than the first, but it gives us an important hint. Pimcore is a set of tools, but we cannot think of it as a library or some snippets. Pimcore is a set of collaborative tools; each tool can solve its own problem. It is not a product but a suite of products. The combination of all of them helps to design a complete digital solution. In this sense, Pimcore is a true DXP: a platform that enables developers to implement digital projects. This definition is a little bit vague, but it tells us that Pimcore gives us a very wide range of opportunities. We cannot merely say "Pimcore does this or that" because Pimcore can do everything.

Pimcore is a Swiss Army knife that allows developers to create any software solution. We have been talking about websites here, but Pimcore has other applications, such as delivering digital assets to a company or being the central database for all of a company's information. Pimcore offers many features out of the box, such as DAM, PIM, MDM, and **Datahub**, in a single package. We have already had a brief overview of what DAM, PIM, and MDM are, but there will be time to go deeper into these topics, including Datahub, in the coming chapters. So, don't worry if these definitions still seem high-level.

The important thing to know right now is that Pimcore lets you manage most data-related applications without writing a single line of code, as well as providing an out-of-the-box solid e-commerce framework.

This is the point where you should ask whether all that power is actually required. Do you really need the overhead of managing a complex platform like Pimcore to build your simple website? There are much easier solutions on the market for implementing a website. You can find a super-cheap CMS hosting provider, or use a site builder. These solutions are probably good for small companies, but not for medium to large organizations. Enterprises need to do more, and in this first chapter, you will learn about the opportunities you would be missing by using a simple CMS solution to implement your website.

If you are reading this book, you are looking for a CMS solution that is able to manage all scenarios, from the simplest to the most complex. And you don't want to implement 10 different tools to satisfy all the needs of your marketing department. Moreover, you do not want to pay for the cost of continuous re-platforming as your business grows. The technical solution for building an application must be a boost, something that gives you more benefits than doing things from scratch, but also something that doesn't limit constant change. You need the option of customizing each part of a website without compromises such as adding thousands of plugins and slowly but steadily losing control of the solution.

You may still think that Pimcore is a platform with a lot of features that you don't really need – that's understandable. Having a super-powered platform just to realize a simple website may seem like overkill. Sometimes it can be scary. Anyway, if you read the first section of this chapter again, you will agree that, sooner or later, you will need something more than a simple CMS and at that point, you will want to be able to scale without having to change your platform.

In the following sections, we will learn about the most relevant Pimcore characteristics. This will help you to understand why Pimcore can support your development in all scenarios, from a simple website to a complex corporate portal. Such characteristics include the following:

- Decoupling data from the UI
- Rendering content properly
- Being ready for the cloud

Let's take a look at these.

Decoupling data from the UI

The first characteristic of a modern CMS is the separation of the presentation layer from the data structure. Put simply, you have to add data on one side and then draw it from the other, without there being any dependency between the two layers.

With Pimcore, we have two options:

- Implement a fully decoupled solution (**Decoupled CMS**).
- Implement a **headless CMS** solution.

In the detached model, the separation between the business logic and the presentation layer can be achieved by detaching the data generated from the rendering process. In Pimcore, we have a **Model View Controller** (**MVC**) model where the **Twig** templating engine cannot elaborate on business logic. For anyone who is not an expert on MVC and Twig, MVC is a pattern for separating business logic (controller) from presentation (view) and data (model), while Twig is a PHP template engine.

The other option is to adopt a fully headless solution. In this case, we expose data using APIs and then render it with a modern **Single-Page Application** (**SPA**), such as a React website made static with Gatsby. This headless solution gives a strong separation between the various aspects (such as data definition and data presentation), and data exposed to the app can be used by other applications too.

The market offers many headless CMS solutions, but Pimcore comes out of the box with both solutions, headless and detached. So, you can manage simple websites using a standard detached approach, and this lets you create templates as usual, but without any mutual dependency between presentation and business logic. This keeps the design simple, and you will benefit from the advantages of decoupling, so you can refresh your website with little effort just by reimplementing the template.

Anyway, if you want to create an edge solution, you can do so with Pimcore. In fact, it comes with an out-of-the-box solution for exposing data in GraphQL format, and this is enough to transform it into a headless content provider. For those unfamiliar with it, GraphQL is a query language for APIs that describes data and reduces friction between the data producers and consumers.

Unifying the user experience

At the beginning of the CMS age, there was a division between interactive websites (also known as **web portals**) and institutional websites. That led to a division between CMS websites and portal solutions. As these CMS websites and portals had different needs, we became used to adopting different tools and maybe different teams of suppliers for each.

For example, in the past, creating a public website was quite simple, so having a simple CMS solution was okay. On the other hand, creating a portal was more complex, so we needed a highly customizable solution. But with the spread of digital technology, more and more companies started selling online, adding this new requirement. So, what was the solution? The companies simply took a tool from the market, installed it, and started to sell. This was a quick way to solve the problem of selling online, but it caused an issue: it added a third platform (e-commerce) to the CMS and portal. This often meant a new supplier, a new graphic interface, and a different user experience. In other words, it meant a situation where three systems were in different realms in terms of data and user experience. After a few years of fighting with data flows, integrations, and the replication of business logic across these environments, one day, advisors such as Gartner came up with a solution. They told us we had silos in our organization, that silos were bad, and that we should remove them. Moreover, the same advisors told us that commerce, portals, and content management are not different needs, but are all part of the same digital experience. The question is: if all those components are what the user wants, who can provide us with a tool to deliver them?

Pimcore does things differently from competitors. Its CMS engine manages public and private websites, so you can create reserved areas and portals as well as simple one-page company websites. Moreover, this solution keeps a link to the enterprise, adding some important components that help integration with all other pillars. This special configuration makes Pimcore an ideal platform for unifying the user experience by including in a single platform all the features you need to engage the user.

So, you can expand a website's functionality until you have encompassed the whole company, e-commerce included. In other words, you can adopt one tool and satisfy most of your digital needs.

Readying your company for the cloud

The ancient times when we bought physical servers are forgotten. We are now in the cloud age, and we want to take advantage of all the opportunities that this new world offers. However, we live in a complex world where, for many reasons, the cloud is not always an option. We may have to deal with sensitive data that has to be kept secure in a private data center, or our budget may only allow a cheap hosting provider. Each company has different requirements, but they all need to have a website. Having data on the cloud or on-premises shouldn't be a reason to adopt a digital platform. It has to support both of them natively.

As a developer, you don't want to serve different client targets with different tools. This would lead you to have to learn many different tools and use them at the same time; that's always hard if you want to maintain a deep specialization in one technology.

To use different products to serve different segments of the market, you will probably need different technologies and be a double-specialist. For human developers that work for a finite time each day, using too many technologies means having less specialization. The more technology you use, the less time you have to learn it well. We could find a few exceptions to this, but generally speaking, that's how it is.

Pimcore is different. It can serve everything from the simplest website to the most complex corporate one, thanks to its flexibility and its open source code, which delivers a complete solution for free. This agility is also reflected in its hosting aspects. Pimcore can be deployed as a simple PHP application just by uploading files via FTP to a cheap hosting service or a regular virtual machine, and it supports containerization natively.

In other words, as a container, Pimcore can be deployed on most **Platform as a Service** (**PaaS**) solutions, Docker, or Kubernetes, in the cloud or on-premises. So, the cloud is an opportunity, but not a requirement. You can deploy Pimcore to the cloud, implementing a solution that scales and stands up without human effort for monitoring and maintenance. If you feel confident with a different solution, or you simply don't need to scale, an easier solution is still an option with Pimcore.

Learning what Pimcore is is essential to understanding its capabilities and following along with the coming chapters. In fact, in the next section, we will start a deep dive into Pimcore's features, which would have been impossible without having discovered what Pimcore is already.

Discovering Pimcore's features

As we said earlier in this chapter, Pimcore comes out of the box with some huge features that make it the ideal platform for implementing simple and complex projects.

In this section, we will present the main features:

- Data management
- CMS and DXP
- PIM
- MDM
- DAM
- E-commerce
- Customer Data Platform (CDP)

Let's take a look at each one.

Data management

Data management is the root of all features in Pimcore. The data management feature aggregates any kind of data and distributes it across multiple channels. Compared to other solutions, Pimcore has the best data management system. It allows you to define data using the UI, and this is very good because you don't have to write a single line of code. You can stop messing about with database tables, field lengths, and data queries; all you need to do is simply open your browser, create your entities, and pick the fields you want. This feature is very similar to what can be found on low-code platforms or headless CMS, but with a boost.

Most data management tools have, as their unique goal, the data model definition. Such a solution gives us the ability to quickly define a data model and APIs but produces a UI that's hard to use for the regular user. Basically, you are very much limited to the standard data entry interface, so in most cases, you have to write a user UI from scratch. This is what the purely headless principle aims for: delegating all the rendering aspects outside the system. This is a good principle when designing an application for the final user (such as customers or portal users), but what if we need to allow an administrator or editor to enter content on our platform? For such internal users, Pimcore offers an administrative interface that can be customized when you define the data model.

In other words, when you add a field to a collection of items, such as when adding an SKU field for a product entity, you don't just define how the data is stored (uniqueness, field length, type of date, and so on) but also how this field will be presented to the user. For example, you can group fields in tabs or panels, or simply reorder them to create a good user experience for back-office users, without touching a single line of code. Moreover, Pimcore supports multi-language, so you can select which field is translated just by modeling the fields. This feature transforms Pimcore into the perfect headless CMS because it combines the flexibility of an admin backend that's ready to go with the power of a data API for building custom applications.

The first time that back-office users see the admin interface, many might feel a little bit lost, what with the thousands of features that the Pimcore admin interface offers. Just after a few minutes of playing with Pimcore, it will be clear what level of freedom you can reach with this tool. Thanks to the multi-tab environment, you can open multiple data tabs in the same window, easily cut and paste data from one place to another, and import\export data in seconds.

If this doesn't shock you, what we will tell you next will. All that data is made available by REST APIs; this is a native feature that doesn't require any development effort. This means that each one of the entities you model with the Pimcore interface is available through a REST API without any additional effort (since PimcoreX this feature will be available only as an Enterprise Subscription feature). You can make an HTTP call to put a row into a database or query a list of entities without writing a single line of code.

If you are still not shocked, we can mention the DataHub module again – you can turn on and expose your data to an external system, using the GraphQL standard for API modeling.

It's easy to see that, when you have the data layer managed, everything else that comes later will be easier.

CMS and DXP

Pimcore is defined on its website as "The Most Adaptive DXP Platform." Ask any developer working with Pimcore and they will confirm that you can probably do everything with it. Using this CMS, you can – other than realizing cool web pages – deliver a personalized digital experience to every customer at every touchpoint. Thanks to its CMS engine, Pimcore enables companies to implement their digital strategy effectively and spend more time and money on what really matters.

From a developer's point of view, Pimcore's DXP is an integrated framework for implementing any type of digital solution, be it a website or a portal. Moreover, it combines all the tools for implementing e-commerce, and you can turn your website or portal into a complete DXP solution. It's an API-driven approach to make a platform integrable with every system, and it helps to break down silos.

From the user's point of view, Pimcore is a natural extension of their creativity. The rich **What You See Is What You Get** (**WYSIWYG**) interface shows content as it will appear when published. So, you can enter data and build pages without any doubt about what the final result will be. Furthermore, you can create page templates that will drive the user through an assisted page composition. This process asks the editor to write only the content that is relevant, without wasting time changing styles or text positioning.

The component model lets you use a ton of widgets, all ready to be placed on the page and fully configurable. These widgets are called bricks and – as the name suggests – they build the web page. With the powerful template engine, you can render entities, such as articles or products, or you can define a custom template to be used to build non-standard pages from scratch.

What else is there to say? Using the integrated tools, you can preview the website while editing, and with the publishing workflow, you can save without the fear of breaking anything.

PIM

Thanks to its powerful data engine, Pimcore manages any type and any amount of data. What if you model a collection of items called "product" and you add a price inside the data model? Well, this makes Pimcore a PIM. This is not a joke. That is how simple working with Pimcore is. You can add a PIM to your company using your browser within a few minutes. After this 5-minute task, you have a unique database for all the products of your company. Thanks to the data integration capabilities of Pimcore, you can ingest data from any CSV files without writing any lines of code, or in any case, with very little effort. Job done.

Any other system in the company can integrate with you, and the marketing team will manage all products in unique central administration. Here they will define what products go in which channel, what languages are enabled for which market, and so on. So, even in this case, Pimcore gives us simplicity and a complete solution.

If we haven't convinced you yet, we could tell you about workflows. When you have approval processes or some business logic to add to product management, you can model that using Pimcore workflows. In the next figure, we have an architectural diagram that explains a PIM in action:

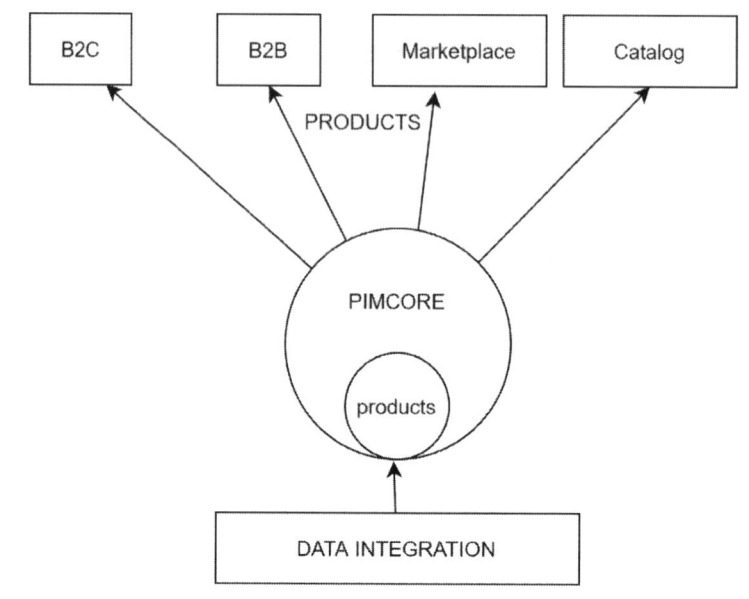

Figure 1.2: PIM architecture

The preceding figure shows how Pimcore, acting as a PIM, is the single source of truth for products, delivering to many consumers, such as B2B e-commerce, B2C e-commerce, Amazon or eBay marketplaces, or a simple printed catalog. As you can see in the diagram, thanks to the data integration layer, the Pimcore solution can be linked to an existing platform such as **Enterprise Resource Planning** (**ERP**).

PIM is a feature that you cannot miss from modern companies, and it is needed for scaling with multiple user touchpoints without duplicating information. It lets you keep control of product data and speed up your software integration. Also, in this case, Pimcore enables you to do this without any headaches, because this is a native feature that comes ready to be activated.

MDM

All that we have told you about PIM is cool, but it has one big limitation: it is related to products only. In fact, looking at your company's needs, you will discover that many other kinds of data need to be shared across the company and managed centrally. Orders, customers, and probably tons of other data are used from all sorts of applications by a company, and each time a project starts, you have to know where data is. But the problem is not related only to these few entities.

Using Pimcore, we can make information unique and central for all the golden records (information that is central for a company). This ability is out of the box, free, and with limited effort. How? Just by defining the data model and integrating it with the data masters, such as the CRM, ERP, or whatever owns the entity you want to move. Then, you can define an access policy for data, implementing all the logic you want. This is not just cool...it is super cool! With one tool and a few minutes, you can be ready to expose important data to all the company applications you need. Such a solution enables you to dominate your data (this mission is often called data governance).

This whole configuration is what we called MDM in the first section of this chapter. The main benefits of Pimcore's MDM are that it can manage the structure, but also the validation, versioning, and enrichment of elements. In fact, most entities have different attributes based on their destination. To explain what the benefits of MDM are, we could use any entity, but we will talk again about products. This is just because it is the most common scenario and we can understand it best. When reading the next paragraph, you can replace the word "product" with any other kind of data without changing the meaning (orders, customers, invoices, and so on).

Think about a product. Where did it start? This is a hard question, because we usually have an R&D team that works on a prototype, then somebody else approves it for market, and then we start selling it. Probably, in this flow, the first stage where we can talk about a concrete product is when the record enters the ERP, creating a product code. The product is owned by the ERP that manages product codes and prices. At this stage, you don't really need a lot more data. You have all that you need to produce a quote or an invoice. Furthermore, most technical solutions are not built to manage cool product information with multiple images and long descriptions. An ERP is a vertical solution and it does very well only with the set of things that are in its scope. It makes no sense to try to push it to do something different.

Well, what you need here is a data enrichment process. What normally happens, without a PIM or MDM, is that each user enhances data for what they need. So, you can have e-commerce that adds bigger images and long HTML descriptions, but that e-commerce provides information only for products sold in the **Business to Consumer** (**B2C**) channel. So, you have to do the same in the B2B portal for other products. That's why, in this example, a product is not managed centrally. Using Pimcore, products and any other entities can be translated and enriched with images, video, and attachments before being delivered to the consumer. This is the only way to dominate data and be able to put the bulk of your effort into the things that really matter to the company, such as implementing good applications instead of fighting with data.

In the following diagram, we see an architectural diagram of Pimcore acting as an MDM platform:

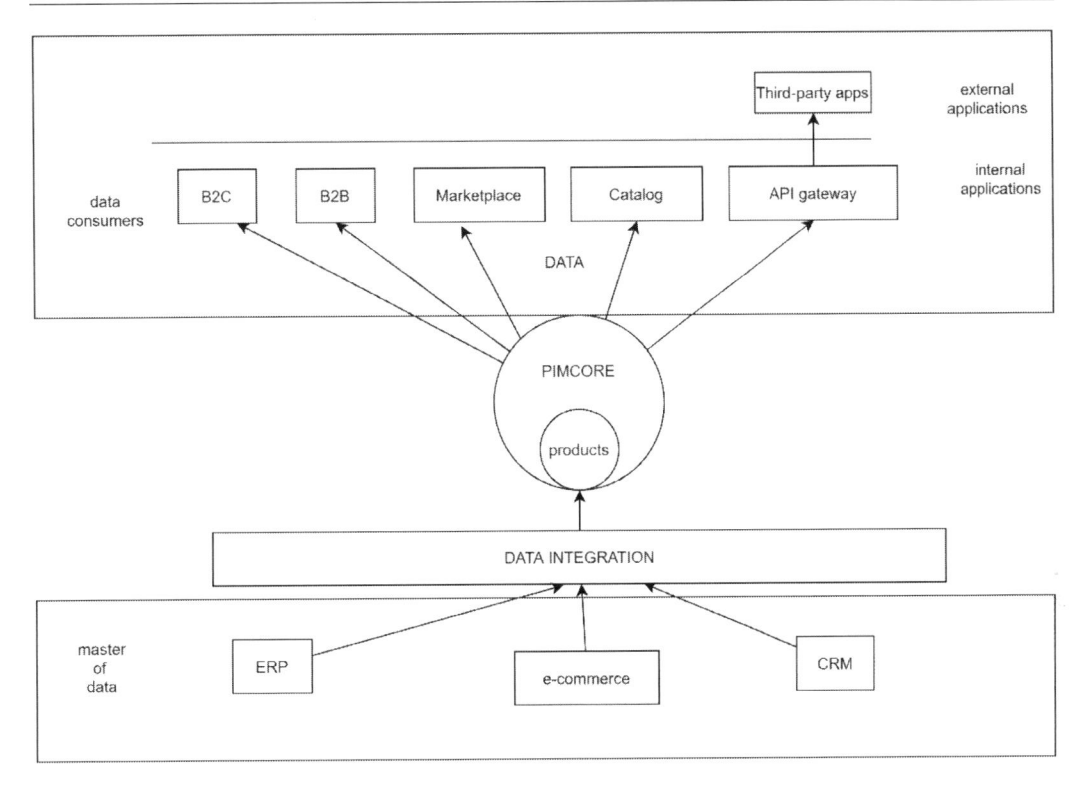

Figure 1.3: MDM architecture

In the preceding figure, you can see how Pimcore can integrate with many data owners (**ERP**, **e-commerce**, **CRM**). This step collects data through the data integration layer and makes it available to all of a company's applications (**Marketplace**, **Catalog**, **B2B** and **B2C** applications, or **Third-party** apps). Using an API gateway, which is a tool for exposing APIs in a safe way, we can also share APIs with suppliers or third-party applications.

MDM is one pillar of digital innovation. Without it, spreading data across an organization is a messy affair. Using Pimcore, you can manage data centrally, saving the time it would take to implement a custom solution or the money you would spend on expensive tools.

DAM

After having talked about products and data, it's clear that each company has to keep data in a single place, with a unique data model definition, and that they need to make sure that each consumer only receives and reads the information that they need. When talking about products and data here, we are talking about intangible data – not files, or images, or videos, or data that can be downloaded or sent in an attachment, but pure information.

Tangible data, such as files, videos, and images, are still important resources for a company. In a world where communication is becoming ever more digital, the digital asset is crucial, especially when you have to communicate the same piece of information through multiple channels.

You have probably guessed the solution to this: we can collect all this information inside Pimcore and then distribute it across the system. It is a very easy solution when you have it already up and running, but it provides a big leap forward for your company.

This solution is implemented by Pimcore. Pimcore's DAM software is a lot more than just a digital asset management application: it is a true digital transformation enabler. It is a consolidated digital media repository that provides a solid database of reusable digital assets and optimizes data dissemination and content search processes.

In the next diagram, we see Pimcore acting as DAM:

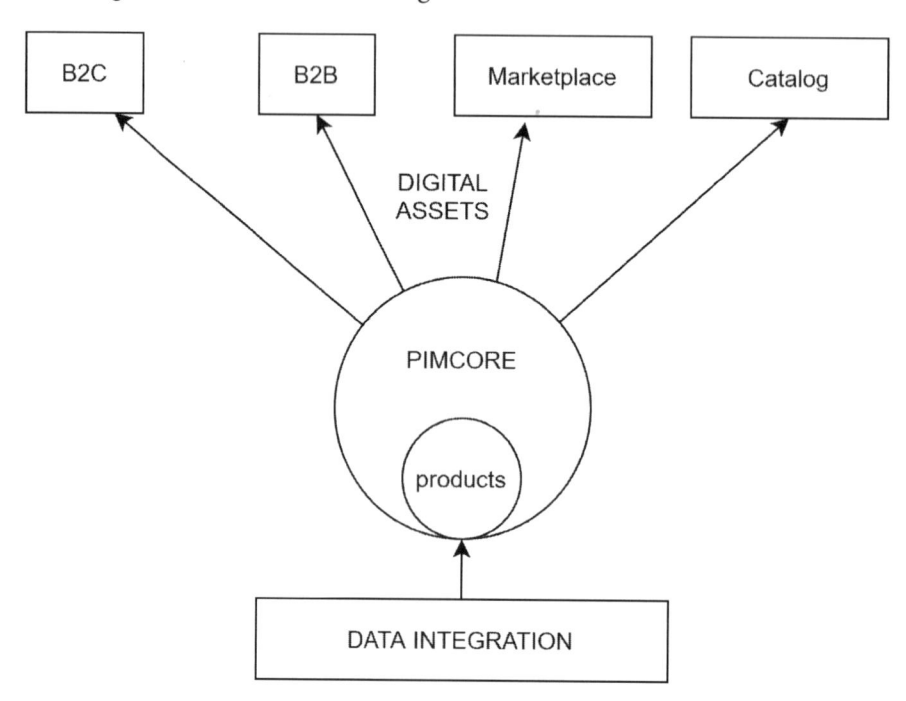

Figure 1.4: DAM architecture

In the preceding figure, Pimcore is the central point where all digital assets are stored. It delivers content to any consumer application that needs them.

Together with MDM and PIM, DAM is a must-have service in modern enterprises. It enables the distribution of media assets across the company. Here also, Pimcore is a powerful low-cost solution.

Digital commerce

Well, we understand that Pimcore is a very powerful platform for managing data and digital content in general and that it includes great CMS support. Now we need to discuss the e-commerce module.

In fact, a DXP needs this to embrace the full meaning of DXP: the fusion of portals, websites, and e-commerce. E-commerce nowadays is a huge market, and you are probably wondering why this feature was added to Pimcore.

Just think about what an e-commerce solution entails. The first element to talk about is the budget. Not all e-commerce systems are like Amazon or eBay, so we need to find the right solution based on what we need, but also on how much we can pay. Developers that were active when the e-commerce market started came from an on-premises, highly customizable era where a vertical open source solution such as the Magento e-commerce system was the standard. That solution was good because it let you customize each part of the process, but you had to host things yourself, taking on all the related risks, and the customization element required continuous maintenance. Therefore, the **Total Cost of Ownership** (**TCO**) was very high, and many companies moved to **Software as a Service** (**SaaS**) solutions, which come with fewer customization options but are free from maintenance and hosting responsibilities. This reduction of friction made e-commerce more democratic, but in many cases reduced the opportunities for the personalization of e-commerce. For many companies, the uniqueness of their service and the automation of the company's processes are crucial for e-commerce solutions. We're speaking mostly about the big players, but also a lot of start-ups got their success by thinking outside the box. The only difference is that a big player can land a mega-vendor solution, where cost grows exponentially but you get results to match. What about normal companies with a limited budget?

In this scenario, Pimcore fills the gap between fully managed SaaS solutions and mega-vendors. In fact, Pimcore comes with an e-commerce framework that is designed to speed up e-commerce development but doesn't introduce constraints or limitations. In addition, using a stable cloud-based solution, you can reach your low-maintenance-cost target and sleep peacefully during Black Friday, when availability is crucial.

The other advantage of using Pimcore as an e-commerce platform is that thanks to its multisite feature, it can handle B2B and B2C and obviously doesn't need any data integration, as there is PIM under the hood.

If you are not convinced yet, just read this shortlist of must-have features for an enterprise e-commerce solution that Pimcore happens to offer:

- Complicated pricing and product structures
- Complex availability computation
- Agile projects with evolving needs
- Individual design and checkouts
- Multiple catalogs, currencies, price lists, and product views
- Multiple frontend apps and flexible promotions

In the first three sections of this chapter, we have discovered what Pimcore is and we have looked at its features. This has been a great overview of the product, but we need to understand why we should use it in more detail. In the next section, we will learn about the benefits that the adoption of Pimcore brings.

Learning about Pimcore's benefits

The fact that Pimcore gives us great opportunities doesn't mean that it's definitely the right tool for you. You could assert that there are many other solutions on the market and that you could mix multiple solutions to achieve the same result. There are also many other mega-vendors selling integrated solutions. So, the question is, what are the benefits of Pimcore? In other words, what can it give us that is better than other solutions?

To avoid sectionalism, we decided to avoid direct comparisons. However, we want to give you all the tools you need to determine whether Pimcore is the right solution for you. In this section, you will discover the benefits of choosing Pimcore as a DXP solution, PIM, or CMS. With this information, you will be able to make a conclusion on your own.

In this section, you will discover the most important Pimcore benefits:

- Rapid innovation
- Unmatched flexibility
- A solid platform
- Used by the masses
- Easy web development

Let's take a look.

Rapid innovation

It is often not a question of cost, but of time. The market changes quickly, and every company needs to keep up with the times. The only option is to be ready for change. This leads us to rapid innovation. In many cases, having vertical tools, selecting software, and then activating a project is too slow a process. Maybe it is the best process, theoretically speaking, but it requires a lot of time and often is not in keeping with the market's trends and speed. You should be one step ahead of the market, planning investments before you need them, but this is not always feasible. Nobody has a crystal ball. And planning and spending in advance is a risk because you don't know what the future holds.

In this scenario, Pimcore is the right tool. This framework already has the most important components for enabling digital innovation and can be activated at any point, without any cost. This is the best approach for a start-up or growing company that makes timing their priority. Pimcore helps companies to start with small projects and build their target solution step by step, reducing the risk and rework. You can simply scale with your needs, or better, you can start your next idea faster and with less risk.

Unmatched flexibility

As we have already said, data management gives us unmatched flexibility. It helps in headless scenarios, regular CMS, or enterprise applications. Thanks to the extensible APIs system, there is no limit to the user's needs. Implementing a solution is just a matter of time, not feasibility. Plus, the cost in terms of resources and time implementing data management is reduced because it is all managed by a web UI.

A solid platform

Pimcore is a great tool supported by a great framework, **Symfony**. This PHP framework brings many advantages that make development easier:

- Strong modular division of code (into bundles)
- The separation between app and framework
- Dependency injection
- Tons of components and documentation
- The power of Composer for managing packages

The adoption of Symfony helps to create a standard code structure and speed up web application creation. Moreover, Symfony helps improve your application's performance by implementing a bytecode cache that works natively. Pimcore is fully written on top of Symfony, using it under the hood, and has the same fluid developer experience.

Used by the masses

The Pimcore platform is used by more than 100,000 companies in 56 countries. Its open source community has thousands of followers. Support from international funding ensures product development continuity, and new features come year by year. Pimcore has got many awards, including from the analysts Gartner and Forrester, the most important advisors in the market. This gives us extra confidence when betting on it.

Web development is made easy

When you leave the comfort zone of a web CMS, such as when adding web pages or blog articles, you often fall into situations where you need to code. This means, in most cases, defining the data structure, mapping it using an **Object-Relational Mapping** (**ORM**) tool, and finally interacting with data by implementing reading/saving routines. If you want to publish this functionality as web APIs, you may need to take additional steps.

The development process is composed of a small number of activities that each bring value, such as modeling your business logic and doing a lot of other repetitive tasks, including data modeling or exposing APIs. Such boring tasks need to be carried out because otherwise, your project will not work. Ideally, we would like to put our effort only into the tasks that give us real value. Automating what is automatable will save time and prevent human error.

Pimcore helps in this situation by doing all the repetitive stuff for you. All you need to do is just log into the browser, configure what you need, and then you are set with data management. All the time you save can be invested in more valuable things, such as providing a better experience for the user.

Now it should be clear what benefits Pimcore can bring to any company and why we should use it to boost digital transformation. Pimcore is our ally for everything from building a simple website to creating a complex application. In the next section, we will focus on Pimcore's licensing and how it can help us to reduce friction with its adoption.

Learning about the benefits of using open source software

Most people think that the best reason for using something that's open source is getting a software solution for free. The opportunity to get a product free of charge is appealing, but it shouldn't be the main motivation for selecting an open source product.

In this section, you will learn about the most important arguments for adopting open source software such as Pimcore and all the advantages of a Pimcore solution:

- Speed and agility
- Shared maintenance costs
- Transparency and security
- Cost-effectiveness
- Community
- Pimcore licensing

Let's take a look at each in turn.

Speed and agility

An open source product is ready to go. You can download and install it, and then you are ready to work with it. You can also test it without worrying about trials or cost explosions during the growth of your project. Open source software comes with a ton of plugins that allow you to activate features rapidly without development costs. Moreover, you have the source code, so if something doesn't work as you need it to, you can work on it.

Shared maintenance costs

The core of an open source project is maintained by the community. This has a big advantage over an approach where you build entire custom software from scratch and you need to maintain it yourself. With an open source project, you are responsible only for maintaining your customizations, which usually constitute a small layer on top of the platform. If you create software from scratch instead, you are responsible for the maintenance of 100% of the code. Moreover, if you develop a module that could be useful for the community, you can share it open source and the community can benefit from it.

Transparency and security

The source code is public. This means that not only can you see how it works, but also the rest of the world. As the user, you can trust open source software because such software will not contain tricks; otherwise, the community would have found them and rejected the project. Moreover, speaking about security, this transparency means any issues emerge rapidly and are resolved rapidly.

Cost-effectiveness

Starting with no fee, you can adopt an open source solution without any obligations and then scale it up. Many open source products have a "pro" version that has more features. Well, in this case, you only start paying once you have started to use the product, and the cost is sustainable for such a useful tool.

Community

Another important point is the community. It helps to provide documentation, test the product, and give answers to your questions. It would be impossible to compete with a community composed of thousands of members. There isn't any company in the world that can do this alone.

Pimcore licensing

The public version of Pimcore is called the **Community Edition** and is licensed using GNU General Public License (GPL-3). For an enterprise that needs wider support and additional features, Pimcore offers an enterprise license called **Pimcore Commercial License (PCL)**.

This solution makes Pimcore the perfect alternative to commercial enterprise solutions offered by mega-vendors. You aren't limited to buying software, and you won't face any vendor lock-in. Moreover, if you don't want to use a GPL license, you can simply avoid it, keeping full ownership of your code. This is useful if you are going to create a product based on Pimcore and you want to keep your **Intellectual Property (IP)** safe. In many cases, you can customize the product using modules from the community or third-party vendors.

Finally, the open source aspect means it's your choice as to whether you deploy on-premises or in the cloud. The cloud solution, supported by a number of SaaS offerings, helps to reduce costs and build a solution that has all the advantages of typical on-premises open source solutions (customization and ownership, for instance) and the advantages of the cloud (for example, low TOC and high performance).

For software companies who want to get the most out of Pimcore, and remove the legal constraints of the GPLv3 license, there is the **Pimcore Enterprise Subscription** option. This subscription unlocks all the commercial services and products, such as the Pimcore Enterprise Extensions (**Pimcore Experience Portals**, **Product Data Syndication**, and so on). The Enterprise subscription gives access to the **Long Term Support (LTS)** and **Service-Level Agreements (SLAs)**. In simple words, it adds special features that may save a lot of time (and money) in medium and large business scenarios, plus additional warranties with high-quality support.

To summarize all the benefits of open source in just one sentence, an open source solution is one that can be customized without any limits, where code is transparent and safe, that is available for free, and that still retains the benefits of the cloud.

Summary

In this chapter, we learned about what Pimcore is, not stopping at the definition but going deep into Pimcore's capabilities. Pimcore is a very flexible platform that can deliver many solutions without reinventing the wheel. By using it, you will experience the comfort of always having the right solution for your needs.

Pimcore comes with many interesting features (PIM, CMS, DAM, and MDM), and it is ready to use with a low-friction licensing model. Once you have adopted it to satisfy a single requirement, such as a CMS, you have all the other features available, and you can activate them as your needs evolve.

Now that this chapter is finished, you are ready to start the practical part. The first step will be to learn how to install and configure Pimcore on your PC. This lesson is very important for starting using Pimcore and being ready for all the lessons that will come later.

2
Setting Up Your Pimcore Development Environment

In the first chapter, we took a wide-angle overview of Pimcore. Now it's time to start getting our hands dirty with some code!

In this chapter, we will learn how to set up a development environment and start developing using Pimcore. This chapter is mandatory for having a working local environment and playing with Pimcore.

This chapter is organized as follows:

- Installing Pimcore from Composer (without Docker)
- Installing Pimcore using Docker
- Exploring folder conventions

Let's start our Pimcore setup!

Technical requirements

Writing code in Pimcore is very easy and does not require any paid tools. Despite the added value of most paid tools, we decided to use only free tools to make the content of this book available to you without any limitations.

You will require the following:

- Visual Studio Code as the **Integrated Development Environment** (**IDE**)
- A decent web browser (Chrome, Firefox, or Edge, for instance)
- Docker (optional, but strongly recommended)

Why use Docker?

If you use Docker, all the additional requirements (Apache, the necessary libraries, PHP, and so on) will be managed automatically. Moreover, using Docker removes any friction between development and the production environments, offering a virtual environment that's the same at all stages. That is why, nowadays, using Docker is the recommended approach for developing applications, an approach that we adopt in this book. And that is why we based this book's examples on this technology. For those of you who are not familiar with Docker, it is a system that can download (pull) a ready-to-go environment (container) and run it on your local PC. All the samples we will provide are wrapped in a `docker-compose` file (a file that lists and configures the container for you), so all you need to do is to activate the environment and Docker will download all the assets required and will start it transparently. So, even if you are not well-versed with Docker, all you need to know for the purpose of this book is the following:

- **Start your environment**: Inside the folder where the `docker-compose.yml` file is contained, run `docker-compose up`.
- **Stop your environment**: Press *Ctrl+C* on the terminal where Docker Compose was launched; this will stop everything.
- **Interact with the Pimcore container:** You can just run `docker-compose exec php <command>` for running a command inside the container named `php` (in our setup, this is the Pimcore one), or just enter the container with bash and launch whatever you want by means of `docker-compose exec php bash`.

For install Docker, which is available on Windows, Mac, and Linux, just navigate to the official documentation: `https://docs.docker.com/get-docker/`.

For manual installation

If you want to install Pimcore manually, you will have to configure your local machine (or server) and all its dependencies by hand. This is only if you're not using Docker, so if you want to use Docker, you can skip this section.

The only part of the book where we use this manual approach is in the following section, *Installing Pimcore with Composer (without Docker)*, where we will explain how to carry out a Pimcore installation from scratch.

For a manual installation, you need to install all the dependencies manually, including Composer, Apache, MySQL, PHP, and the PHP libraries. The prerequisites may change with the arrival of new Pimcore versions and technology updates. So, instead of adding a copy of the official system requirements of Pimcore, we have instead provided a link to the official page with the exact specifications: `https://pimcore.com/docs/pimcore/current/Development_Documentation/Installation_and_Upgrade/System_Requirements.html`.

> **Note**
> Pimcore supports MySQL and the MariaDB database engine, which is, in fact, a fork of MySQL. In this chapter, we refer to MySQL because it is the most common option. We used the official `docker-compose` file based on MariaDB. To avoid confusion, please consider MySQL and MariaDB as one and the same in this chapter.

All the source code is contained in the official GitHub repository for this book, which you can find at this URL: `https://github.com/PacktPublishing/Modernizing-Enterprise-CMS-using-Pimcore`. In this repository, you will find a folder for each chapter. Inside each folder, there will be a `Readme` file with all the instructions for running the code.

For those of you who are using Docker as the environment, there are no restrictions for you regarding the operating system. For Docker compatibility and system requirements, you can check the **Download** section of the official Docker website.

Installing Pimcore from Composer (without Docker)

Even though we encourage the use of Docker and the book is based on Docker containers, we should not fail to explain how to perform a vanilla installation. As you will learn after following all the steps, the process of installing Pimcore the vanilla way is basically the same as what is done internally by the Docker container. The most important difference is that using Docker, you do not have to grapple with the server, dependencies, and so on. This is because Pimcore is released through **Composer**, the PHP package manager. This makes the installation the same in all possible scenarios. If you are inside a Docker container, a virtual machine, or your PC, Composer is the same.

So, all you need to do to install Pimcore in your local environment is to run a few commands in the terminal after you have installed all the required dependencies mentioned in the *Technical requirements* section:

> **Note**
> This book uses a ready-to-use Docker container for this process. We are including this section to explain how a low-level installation of Pimcore works, but if you are interested in starting Pimcore quickly, you can skip this section and go to *Installing Pimcore using Docker*. Moreover, unlike Docker, using Composer in your local environment has a lot of dependencies (MySQL, Composer, and others) and needs complex PHP tuning. This is well covered by the Pimcore documentation and you can follow the official guidance for that. In this section, we will cover Pimcore's installation, assuming that you already have your environment set up and you just need to install Pimcore.

1. Create a folder in your filesystem. We assume that this folder is named `my-project`. There are no restrictions from Pimcore about where you can create that folder. It depends on your local settings (that is, it has to be accessible to your web server). For example, when using Apache, a common value is `/var/www/html`.

2. Run the following command:

   ```
   COMPOSER_MEMORY_LIMIT=-1 composer create-project Pimcore/skeleton my-project
   ```

This command will install the `Pimcore/skeleton` package in the `my-project` folder. This will also create a new folder in your filesystem, and the final path will be `/your/project/my-project`. Pimcore is available in two different releases: skeleton and demo. When starting a new project, it is recommended that you use the skeleton template, but if you want to see Pimcore's features, you can install the demo package to get a website with data that is ready to test. The process will take a moment, and you will see some console output that will display its progress.

3. If you do not have one yet, you will need to create a database. To do this, type the following command in your terminal:

```
mysql -u root -p -e "CREATE DATABASE project_database
  charset=utf8mb4;"
```

You can fine-tune the preceding command by changing the host, username, and password to fit your needs, or you can use a visual tool such as MySQL Workbench. You can also change the database name. The most important thing to remember is to use the right charset, `utf8mb4`, to fully support Unicode encoding.

4. Edit your Apache virtual host. It needs to point to the web folders inside `my-project`, so your Apache file should have the document root set as follows:

```
DocumentRoot /my/project/my-project/public
```

Note that Pimcore needs to be installed outside of the document root. So, if you installed it inside `my-project`, you cannot use this folder as the document root. This, besides causing functional issues, will expose you to security issues in terms of allowing access to protected content. A complete configuration for Apache can be found here: `https://pimcore.com/docs/pimcore/current/Development_Documentation/Installation_and_Upgrade/System_Setup_and_Hosting/Apache_Configuration.html`.

5. Set the filesystem permissions. The Apache user (or the Nginx user, depending on which web server you are using) will need to access all the files inside the Pimcore directory and will need additional write permission for the `/var` and `/public/var` folders. In most cases, this is done by entering the following code:

```
chown -R www-data .
chmod 764 ./var
chmod 764 ./public/var
```

Here, `chown` makes `www-data` (usually the group where the user that runs the web server belongs) the group owner of the Pimcore folder, and then `chmod` adds write permission to the required folders.

6. Navigate to the Pimcore directory and type the following command:

```
cd ./my-project
```

This will bring you to the `/your/project/my-project` directory.

7. Launch the Pimcore installation by typing the following command:

```
./vendor/bin/Pimcore-install --MySQL-host-socket=localhost --MySQL-username=yourusename --MySQL-password=yourpassword --MySQL-database=databasename
```

Here, `MySQL-host-socket` is the hostname of the MySQL database, `MySQL-username` and `MySQL-password` are the database credentials, and `MySQL-database` is the database name. This command will set up the Pimcore connection settings and will install Pimcore in the database. You will be prompted to choose the admin user for the Pimcore back office; we will choose `admin\pimcore` as a credential, but you can use whatever you want (although the use of simple passwords in your production environment is discouraged).

In the following screenshot, we can see the console output that we receive after launching the installation command:

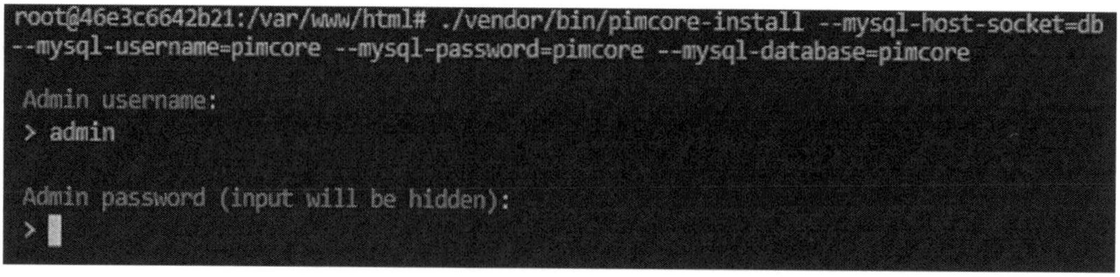

```
root@46e3c6642b21:/var/www/html# ./vendor/bin/pimcore-install --mysql-host-socket=db --mysql-username=pimcore --mysql-password=pimcore --mysql-database=pimcore

Admin username:
> admin

Admin password (input will be hidden):
>
```

Figure 2.1 – Pimcore installation and admin password prompt

8. You will be prompted to enter the username and password of the Pimcore administration user, and then you will be asked to confirm the installation.

9. The final step is to set up the maintenance job. Like many platforms, Pimcore needs to perform periodic maintenance tasks, such as log rotation and cleaning temporary or old data. Pimcore's guidelines ask us to execute this task every 5 minutes to make sure the environment is always efficient. To do this, we need to add a `cron` job. Type the following:

```
crontab -e
```

10. Then, enter the following content into `crontab`:

```
*/5 * * * * /your/project/bin/console maintenance
```

The configuration activates the maintenance job by running the `console` executable, with the `maintenance` parameter, which invokes the standard Pimcore maintenance job.

In this section, we introduced the Pimcore installation process. These instructions are quite easy to follow, but you need to have the hosting environment already installed. Installing Apache, MySQL, and configuring the network part is standard for most developers, but some system engineering knowledge is required that not all developers have (and maybe do not want to learn). Moreover, with this setup, you may have to replicate most of your jobs each time you set up a new project.

In the next section, we will learn how things are so much easier with Docker, seeing how you can do the same as what we achieved here (and maybe more) in just two commands.

Installing Pimcore using Docker

Docker is the leading solution for developing containerized applications, allowing developers to configure a virtual environment in their PC that can easily be transferred to a server and be used by the user. In fact, using Docker is the modern way to develop web applications. It accelerates the setup, reduces the friction between environments, and ensures an easy-to-use, replicable system.

Pimcore embraces Docker development and has released Docker images that are ready to be used. Moreover, it has released a `docker-compose` file that orchestrates all the containers needed to run Pimcore.

Using Docker, you will be able to set up and start Pimcore in minutes. Using the script provided in the GitHub repository for this book, most of the process is easy.

The first step is to clone the Pimcore repository and navigate to the `2. Setting up Pimcore Development Environment` folder. You can copy the files from there and paste them into your target folder. The files are as follows:

- `docker-compose.yml`: This contains the definition of the container; it is quite similar to the default Pimcore file.
- `install.sh`: This contains the installation script, which is an automated version of the installation steps from the official guide.

Let's see these two files and how we can use them.

The docker-compose file

The `docker-compose` file contains many container definitions for enabling all the required components. The first one is the `database` component:

```
db:
    image: mariadb:10.4
working_dir: /application
    command: [MySQLd, --character-set-server=utf8mb4,
--collation-server=utf8mb4_unicode_ci, --innodb-file-
format=Barracuda, --innodb-large-prefix=1, --innodb-file-per-
table=1]
    environment:
      - MYSQL_ROOT_PASSWORD=ROOT
      - MYSQL_DATABASE=pimcore
      - MYSQL_USER=pimcore
      - MYSQL_PASSWORD=pimcore
```

In the previous snippet, we have an instance of MariaDB tuned for Pimcore usage. Using the environment variables, we set the most important parameters of the database:

- The credentials of the root user: `MYSQL_ROOT_PASSWORD`
- The database name: `MYSQL_DATABASE`
- The credentials of the service user: `MYSQL_USER` and `MYSQL_PASSWORD`

With this configuration, we need to connect to the host database using Pimcore/Pimcore credentials.

The second container to take into account is the Pimcore container. Refer to the following code snippet from the `docker-compose` file:

```
php:
    image: Pimcore/Pimcore:PHP7.4-apache
    volumes:
      - .:/var/www/html:cached
    ports:
      - 80:80
      - 443:443
depends_on:
      - db
```

The name of this container is php because Pimcore relies on a PHP image. Using volume mapping, we mount the folder where the `docker-compose` file is located on the Pimcore directory inside the container.

The installation file

The installation file is just a set of commands that you should run individually, but condensed into a single script. This prevents any manual errors and reduces the effort needed to set up a new environment.

The script covers the following steps:

1. The first step is the Pimcore download. To do this, we need to add the following command to the script:

   ```
   COMPOSER_MEMORY_LIMIT=-1 composer create-project Pimcore/
   skeleton tmp
   ```

   The problem here is with the container image settings. It is created for listening to the `/var/www/html/public` folder, so the Pimcore installation must be done at the `/var/www/html/` level. The problem is that the Composer command will need a folder to download the files from. This will create a subfolder and necessitate a change to the default container settings. So, the most common approach is to download Pimcore in a temporary folder and then move the contents of the temporary folder to the standard Apache folder. This trick is done using the following commands:

   ```
   mv tmp/.[!.]* .
   mv tmp/* .
   rmdir tmp
   ```

2. Next, we need to fix the memory usage of PHP. Pimcore requires 512 MB for the installation process, and in most cases, the default value from PHP is not sufficient. What we will do in our script is increase the memory limit by changing the configuration files with the following commands:

   ```
   echo 'memory_limit = 512M' >>/usr/local/etc/php/conf.d/
   docker-php-memlimit.ini;
   service apache2 reload
   ```

3. Now we are ready to start the Pimcore installation. We will install Pimcore using the settings hardcoded into the `docker-compose` file. To do this, we need to add the following command to our script:

   ```
   ./vendor/bin/Pimcore-install --MySQL-host-socket=db
   --MySQL-username=Pimcore --MySQL-password=Pimcore
   --MySQL-database=Pimcore
   ```

4. Finally, we have to remember that all the commands we have launched so far have been done on behalf of the root user. So, all the files and folders created belong to the root user and group. The user running the web server will be different and will belong to the `www-data` group. This means that the web server cannot write or read the files, based on the `chmod` settings. That's why we need to reset permissions at the end of this process. The following line of code does that:

   ```
   chown -R www-data .
   ```

   This `chown` command adds the `www-data` group to the files and folders permission; this is enough to enable Pimcore to read and write files.

The final version of the script is as follows:

```
#!/bin/bash
#Pimcore download
COMPOSER_MEMORY_LIMIT=-1 composer create-project Pimcore/skeleton tmp
#trick for moving the files
mv tmp/.[!.]* .
mv tmp/* .
rmdirtmp

#increase the memory_limit to >= 512MB as required by Pimcore-install
echo 'memory_limit = 512M' >>/usr/local/etc/php/conf.d/Docker-php-memlimit.ini;
service apache2 reload

#run installer
./vendor/bin/Pimcore-install --MySQL-host-socket=db
--MySQL-username=Pimcore --MySQL-password=Pimcore --MySQL-database=Pimcore
```

```
# fix permission
chown -R www-data .
```

The preceding script is contained in the source code and is called `install.sh`. You can just copy and paste it to your source code directory and follow the instructions in the next section.

Starting Pimcore with Docker

Now that we have understood how Pimcore using Docker works, we can use our script to start Pimcore:

1. The first step is to navigate to the folder with the Pimcore setup files; in our case, the folder is called `/my/project`.

2. Open the terminal here and run the following command:

   ```
   docker-compose up
   ```

   This command activates the Docker environment. Because this command isn't launched with the `-d` parameter (run as daemon), if you close the console, the Docker environment will shut down. This console is helpful because it shows all the logs from the containers, including the Pimcore container.

3. Then, open another terminal and run the following command:

   ```
   docker-compose exec php bash install.sh
   ```

   This command will launch the `install.sh` script inside the container named `PHP`. The script will run all the instructions needed to install Pimcore. This command is only required the first time you run the container. Its purpose is just for installation.

4. Finally, open a web browser and enter the URL `http://localhost/`. You will see the standard Pimcore page, as indicated in the following screenshot:

Figure 2.2 – The Pimcore welcome page

5. Now we can test the credential used during the setup by visiting `http://localhost/admin` in the address bar. You will be redirected to the login page and you will be able to enter credentials and log in to the administrative section of Pimcore. The following screenshot shows the login page:

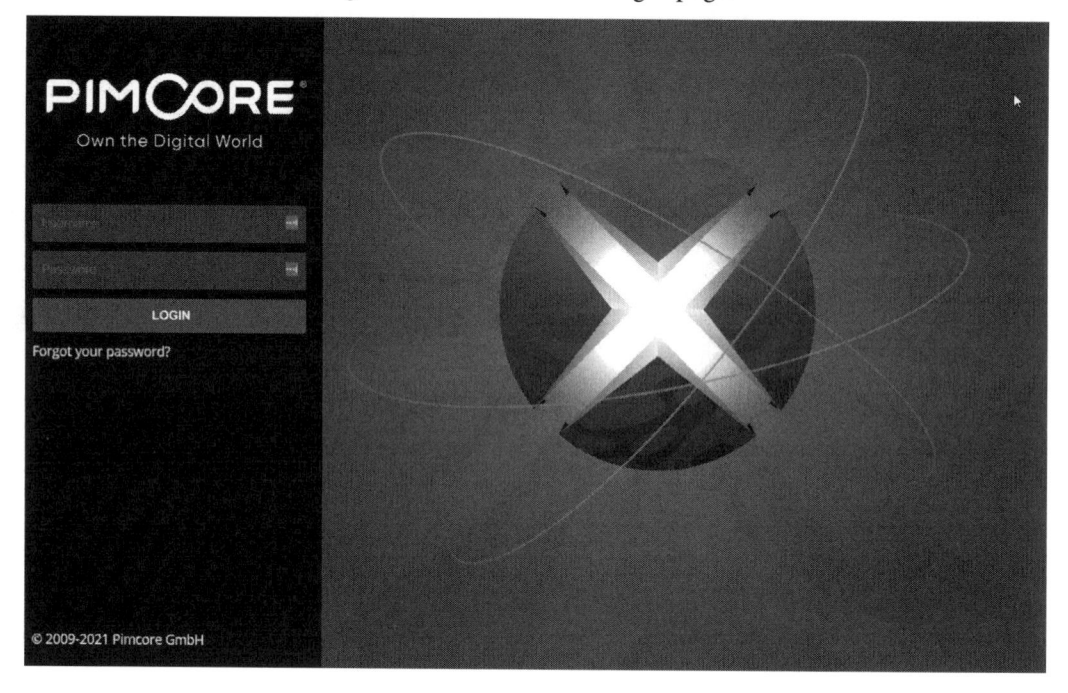

Figure 2.3 – The Pimcore login page

From now on, performing *Step 2* will be enough to run Pimcore!

What we learned in this section was how to install Pimcore using Docker in minutes. As you saw in the *Starting Pimcore with Docker* section, we just ran two commands and all the processes were set. This reduces the time and effort needed from hours (installing and configuring Apache, Redis, MySQL, and so on) to minutes. Now it's clear why we decided to use Docker in this book.

In the next section, we will enter the Pimcore folder structure and we will learn about what is inside each folder.

Exploring folder conventions

In the previous section, we downloaded and installed Pimcore on our PC. Before starting with Pimcore development, it's important to understand how the files are structured inside the filesystem.

Let's start by exploring our filesystem. In the following screenshot, we will see the Pimcore folder expanded:

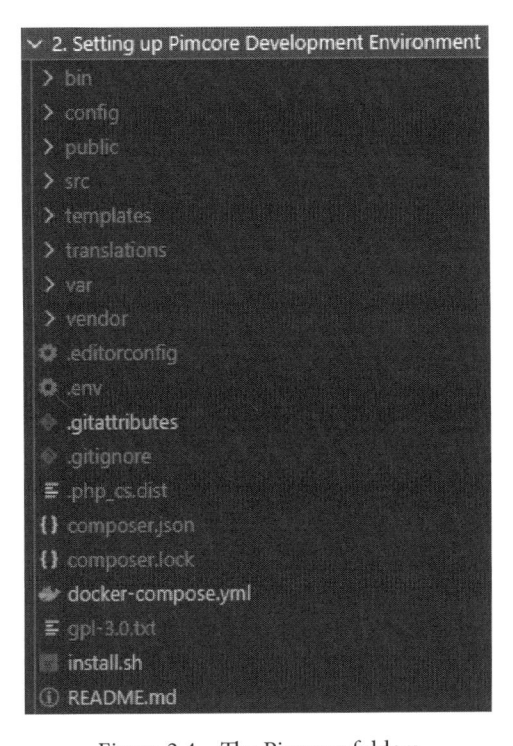

Figure 2.4 – The Pimcore folders

The Pimcore folder structure is very similar to the Symphony standard. Let's look at the first-level content:

- `bin`: This folder contains the executables.
- `config`: This folder contains the YAML configuration files.
- `src`: This folder contains the source code related to your project.
- `var`: This folder contains data saved from Pimcore, such as logs or cache data.
- `vendor`: This is the standard folder used by Composer to store application requirements.
- `public`: This is your document root.
- `templates`: This is the folder that contains all the template files.
- `translations`: This is the folder for translation files.

Let's look at these in detail, one by one.

The config folder

This contains all the YAML configuration files and settings. For example, inside `/config/local/database.yml`, you will find the connection settings for accessing the database. As an additional example, if you want to manage routing, override services, or tune security settings, you can go here and play with the configuration files (the `config.yml` file is the main configuration file and is usually split into submodules, such as `routing.yml`, `services.yml`, and `security.yml`).

The templates folder

This folder contains the templates. You can have one subdirectory for each bundle. Adding a file into the bundle folder will override the default template file shipped with the bundle. This override mechanism is a standard Symfony feature, and all you need to override a template file is to create a folder inside `templates` with the name of the bundle and then replicate the folder structure inside the bundle.

The bin folder

This folder contains the binaries. By default, it contains the console executables only, but you can add your own scripts here. The console executables form the program that we use to run maintenance jobs. Adding more jobs to Pimcore won't require you to create multiple executables; you will just need to run a command such as `./bin console <myjobname>`. That is why, in most cases, this folder doesn't contain anything more than the console file.

The src folder

Inside the `src` folder, you will also find the `Kernel.php` file, which represents your application kernel. The `Kernel` class is the main entry point of the Symfony application configuration, and as such, is stored in the `src/` directory.

The var folder

The `var` folder is designed to contain all the private Pimcore files and is divided into many subfolders, each one storing a different kind of file. This folder must be writable from the web server.

This folder is composed of the following subfolders:

- `application-logger`: Here, Pimcore saves the files from the application logger. The application logger is the system that traces events relevant to the application. Such logs are stored here and can be read from the Pimcore administrative interface.

- `cache`: This is the Symfony cache folder. Here you will find all the generated files.
- `classes`: This contains files related to classes. In fact, each class definition is stored in many files inside this folder.
- `config`: This contains the base settings files that are overridden and extended from the `app/config` structure.
- `email`: This stores the history of sent transactional emails.
- `installer`: This relates to the installer kernel. It contains cached data and other information related to the installer.
- `logs`: This folder contains the logs from Apache and PHP. It is related to the Docker installation.
- `recyclebin`: This contains the data deleted from the user.
- `tmp`: Used for temporary file storage, such as for creating dynamic minified JavaScript files.

The vendor folder

This folder is the standard Composer folder, so there isn't any real need to spend more time talking about it. The Pimcore core bundle is stored here just like any other package.

The public folder

This is the document root of your application, and it is exposed to the web. This folder is protected by a `.htaccess` file and implements some rewriting rules.

This folder is composed of the following subfolders:

- `bundles`: You will find a folder for each bundle; each of these subfolders has a symbolic link to the folder inside the bundle (so, `/src/bundlename` will be visible in `/public/bundlename`). This is because you can change the files inside the bundle and see the change without any copying or compilation having to take place.
- `var`: This contains the uploaded files: images, video files, or simple attachments.

This folder also contains the `index.php` file, which contains the PHP application where all requests are routed.

In this section, we learned how the folders and files of Pimcore are arranged inside the source code. This was important to cover so that you can use the source code samples without any difficulty. Now you won't be lost in *Chapter 4, Creating Documents in Pimcore*, when we will need this feature to start a working Pimcore's instance and view the examples shown in this book.

Summary

In this chapter, we learned how to install and start a Pimcore installation from scratch. Using Docker images, we reduced the complexity of the first installation, we made our environment independent from different operating systems, and we managed to speed up the setup time. Just by typing a few commands in the terminal, all the complex processes were done automatically. This is not only valid for a development environment, but also for production. Moreover, using a container will keep things easy if you would want to move to the cloud. Pimcore can also be installed in a regular environment by taking charge of all the dependency configurations.

In the following chapters, we will use this knowledge to run the examples provided in this book. Moreover, the installation script provided can be used as a quick start guide if you want to start a new project on your own and play in the real world with Pimcore. In the next chapter, we will discover the administration UI of Pimcore, and we will learn how to move between menu items. After this step, you will be able to navigate Pimcore's functionalities, which is fundamental for following the books' tutorials.

3
Getting Started with Pimcore Admin UI

In this chapter, we will examine all the components and menus of the Pimcore administration interface, the "control room" from which you can do most of the operations necessary for the management of your website. By reading this book, you will be able to build a site from scratch.

For getting your website completed, Pimcore allows you to create bundles, modify core components, or overwrite most of the parts that make it up (from controllers to models, from views to routing rules, and so on). All of these aspects will be explored later in the book, but you cannot tackle these topics without first learning how to move through the web interface as a user.

In particular, in this chapter, we will discover the most useful tools to configure your site and where to find them on the administration page.

In this chapter, we will cover the following topics:

- Understanding the Pimcore Architecture
- Exploring the UI Components
- Working with the grid component
- Inspecting the menus

So let's get started with a brief introduction to the Pimcore architecture.

Technical requirements

To follow the lessons in this chapter, you do not need more than a running Pimcore instance. You can just read through the chapter, but if you want to practice, you can open Pimcore and follow along.

All you need to do here is just follow the instructions in *Chapter 2, Setting Up Your Pimcore Development Environment*, for installing an empty Pimcore instance.

Once this is done, can just open your browser and type `http://localhost` and navigate around the UI.

Understanding the Pimcore Architecture

In this short section, we will look at a simplified outline of the Pimcore architecture, with particular attention paid to that part of the architecture that we will focus on in our discussion as we go through this chapter.

In the following diagram, we can take a look at the Pimcore architecture, and understand which part of Pimcore we will be focusing on in this chapter:

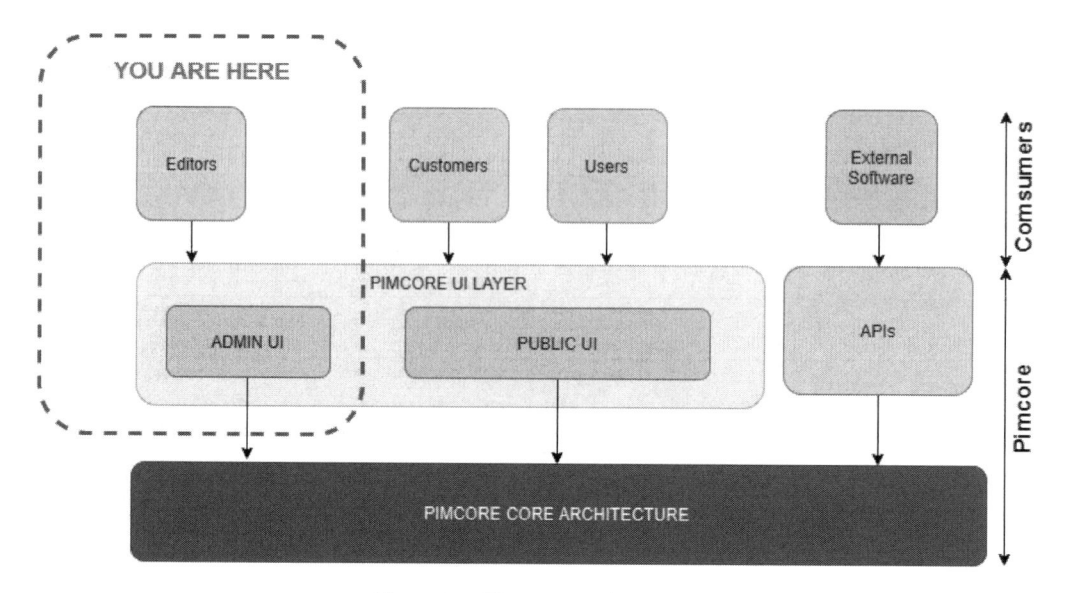

Figure 3.1: Pimcore Architecture

As you can see in the previous diagram, the starting point for our journey of discovering Pimcore is indicated by the dashed rectangle that contains the text: **YOU ARE HERE**.

Just to get an idea of how Pimcore is composed in all its parts, let's look at each aspect of the diagram; even if what we see is a simplified version of the Pimcore architecture, we can identify all the important parts of the platform. We won't go into detail on each part, but we can still describe them quickly.

The **PIMCORE UI LAYER** is the user interface layer, that is, the entry point for all interactions with the users. Inside we can identify two further aspects, the **ADMIN UI** and the **PUBLIC UI**: this division between public and private is necessary to keep the services related to the administration, usable only by users with administration roles, decoupled from public ones that all users can use.

APIs refers to the layer through which third-party software can access the Pimcore, interacting with its features and data; the possibilities of the iteration are many, such as importing data, updating data, exporting data, creating content, and so on. Access to all these operations within this layer is possible using communication protocols, such as a REST API or GraphQL, which expose their services in this part of Pimcore.

Finally, **PIMCORE CORE ARCHITECTURE** is the layer containing the business logic layer, the data models, the data access layer for database access, the templating engine for creating HTML pages – in other words, this is the core of Pimcore. Within the book, we will refer to this part as **Pimcore admin**, or the **Admin Page**, or even the **Pimcore Dashboard** in some cases.

Let's begin our journey through the administration of Pimcore, starting from the UI components.

Exploring the UI Components

Pimcore is a huge environment, supported by an equally important and extensive framework (Symfony), and this can be a bit confusing, especially for those new to Pimcore. But like all long journeys, we have to start with one step. Here's our first one. Let's log into the administration panel.

First of all, we need to access the Pimcore administration; to do this, we must log in to the administration page by visiting the page `yoursite.com/admin/`. Here is the first screen we are faced with, and we are welcomed by the Pimconaut, the Pimcore mascot:

Figure 3.2: Pimcore Administration Login Page (the image on this page changes from time to time)

Once logged in, we will be on the administration page, the Pimcore control room. In the next screenshot, we will see how the control room looks:

Figure 3.3 – Pimcore administration

As we can see, the Pimcore dashboard is divided into four parts that will be discussed in this section:

1. Sidebar Menu
2. Left Sidebar
3. Main frame
4. Right Sidebar

Let's take a look at each one now.

Sidebar Menu

The sidebar menu is the leftmost black bar you see. It contains two parts:

- The first part at the top contains all the actions necessary for the development and configuration of the platform, from languages to routing rules, and research to creating objects.
- The second part, at the bottom, contains information about the system and user, notifications, and the Pimcore logo.

Just above the lower section of the sidebar, the Symfony logo is visible. Symfony is the PHP framework on which Pimcore was developed; its engine in other words. Everything done on Pimcore goes through this framework. When you click on the Symfony logo, another thin toolbar appears at the bottom of the page, as can be seen in this screenshot:

Figure 3.4: Symfony Toolbar

This new menu contains some basic information about the system, such as memory usage, current user, Cache usage, or Database queries. Moving the mouse over it, some pop-up windows will appear with additional information, as shown in this next screenshot:

Figure 3.5: Symfony toolbar and additional details

When clicking on the items, a new page is loaded that contains more detailed information about each part of the system. If you need to have even more information than this about the system, you can click on one of the toolbar entries and a page will open where there is much more information about caches, logs, events, routines, and all the other parts of Symfony used by Pimcore.

Left sidebar

Always on the left, next to the menu sidebar, there is a second sidebar; this one contains shortcuts to documents, assets, and data objects. We will discuss them later in the following chapters, but they are the most common functionalities that we will use in creating beautiful Pimcore websites.

Main frame

The main frame is the central panel of the Pimcore admin interface. All elements that need to be changed are loaded here. In other words, this is the place where things related to the menu items are opened. The following is a screenshot of the main frame in action:

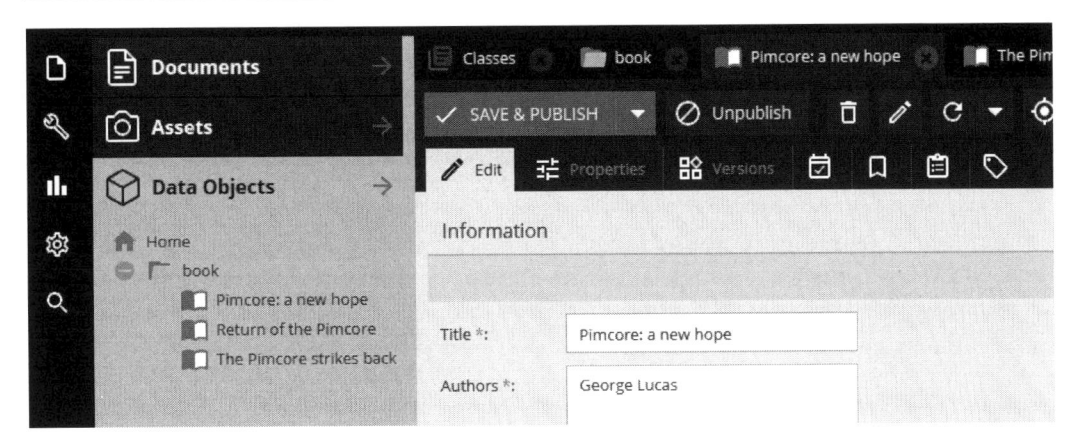

Figure 3.6: Pimcore administration with some tabs opened

As you can see in the previous screenshot, there are some documents opened, each in a separate tab. The main frame is, in other words, the container of all the configuration windows that will be open during our work on Pimcore.

Right sidebar

The sidebar on the right of the main frame is a place where you can move components of the left sidebar. This can be done easily by clicking on the arrow (see *Figure 3.3*). This layout is useful when you have to handle many items at once and you want to keep them under control. For example, you may want to navigate the pages and, at the same time, have the products ready to be used on the page. So you may use the right toolbar for showing data objects. We will learn how we can model product entities using data objects in *Chapter 5, Exploring Objects and Classes*.

Pimcore allows changing the sidebar configuration, including by adding menu items, which is often useful for quick access to specific features. In the case of e-commerce, for example, it might be useful to have shortcuts available for orders or customers. An example of these customization capabilities can be seen in the demo examples on the official Pimcore site: `https://demo.pimcore.fun/admin/`.

After this brief introduction about menus, we can see in detail all the elements we have just listed, starting from the main component of the Pimcore dashboard, the main frame. Any object opened from the sidebar (or the menu entries) is opened inside the main frame as a new tab. In other words, the main frame is a container for all the editing tabs, which the user can close one by one or all together just as you usually do with a browser.

Now that we're familiar with the UI components, we can go a little further, and start analyzing the other parts in detail, such as the grid component and menus. In the next section, we will move on to take a look at the grid component, where we will spend most of our time when working with Pimcore data.

Working with the grid component

In this session, we will analyze in detail how the grid component works. We will discover how to perform simple activities such as searches. Moreover, we will also understand what each of the functionalities of the main buttons present on the toolbar is.

First of all, let's take a look at the following screenshot, and see what the grid looks like during use:

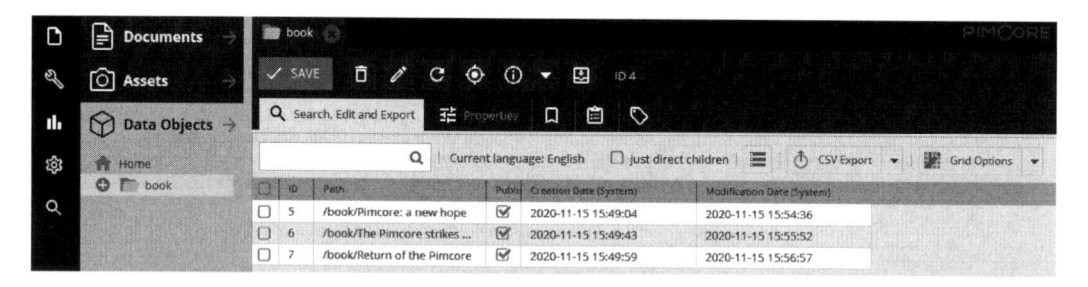

Figure 3.7: Grid component

As we can see from the preceding screenshot, there are at least four points of interest in this component:

1. The first tab bar with the opened entity, already seen before
2. The toolbar with buttons for the main actions
3. The second tab bar for a specific document
4. The opened document

We have listed the elements that make up the grid component seen in *Figure 3.7*, so now we can describe them in more detail, starting from the first.

First tab bar

This first element we have already seen and it does not need further explanation; you can refer back to the *Main frame* section if required.

Toolbar

Now let's see the toolbar, along with some of its action buttons.

Depending on the type of object we are modifying, and in some cases depending on the publishing state of the document itself, it is possible to have different buttons in this toolbar. In other words, the toolbar changes based on the element you are editing (that is, a document or object) and on its publishing status. For example, if we are editing a web page, depending on whether it is published or yet to be published, we will see the **SAVE** and **SAVE & PUBLISH** buttons or the **SAVE & PUBLISH** and **Unpublish** buttons.

The following screenshot shows a toolbar for different objects – for a folder, a web page, and then an object in a different state:

Figure 3.8: Toolbars displayed when editing folders, web page, and an object in a different state

As you can see in the previous screenshot, there are different numbers of buttons in the top toolbar – this is because the actions change dynamically depending on the type of object we are editing.

For example, the **SAVE & PUBLISH** button is always present in all elements that must be made visible, such as web pages or objects. For other elements of internal use, such as folders, it is not visible because it is not necessary.

In *Figure 3.8*, you can see some buttons inside a red rectangle. These three buttons, always present in the toolbar, are as follows (from left to right):

- **Reload**: Reloads the document (not the whole page).
- **Show in tree**: When you click this button, Pimcore identifies and selects the current object in the tree file on the left.
- **Info**: This button opens a modal window with some information about the document we are editing.

Now that we have seen the second element of the grid component, let's move to the next section, and analyze the third element of the four we have listed: the second tab bar.

Second tab bar

There is another tab bar, below the toolbar, which contains a variable number of tabs, each of which will display a set of properties for the object we are editing. Also, in this case, as we have just seen for the tab bar, the number and type of tabs change according to the object and its state when we are modifying it.

Depending on the element we are editing, whether it is a web page, an object, or a folder, the number of tabs changes along with their meanings. For example, as shown in *Figure 3.8*, if we are editing a web page, we will have the **SEO & Settings** and **Preview** tabs, while if we are editing an object, we can see the **Properties** tab.

In both cases, there is the **Versions** tab; if we open this tab, the contents will be shown, as can be seen in this screenshot:

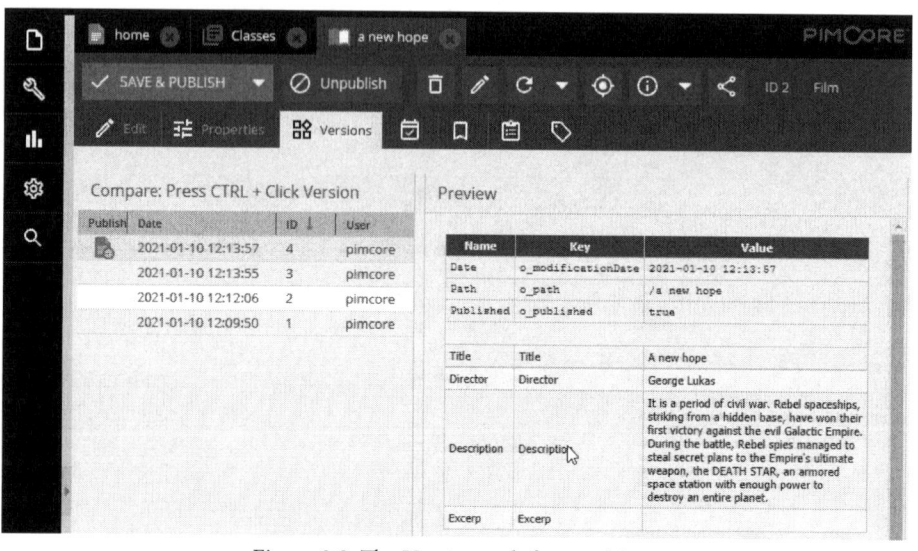

Figure 3.9: The Versions tab for an object

As we can see from this screenshot, the content of the **Versions** tab is exactly what we expected: all the information about the changes made to the object, the date when they were made, and who made them. By clicking on any version you can see how the document was previously, and by selecting two (*Ctrl* + click) you can see the differences between the two versions.

With this section, we have also described the third element of our list, the second tab bar. We can move on to the fourth and final item on our list, the opened document.

The opened document

This is the part where the content of the open tab is displayed. As you can imagine, it is the largest part of the whole component, because it contains all the properties and actions necessary to modify and configure the document.

For example, as we can see in *Figure 3.9*, the version tab divides this component into two parts: on the left, in a table, are displayed all the changes made to the document, while on the right, a preview of the selected changes is displayed.

Each tab will therefore contain different layouts and properties based on the document and what we are editing.

In this section, we have seen in detail the parts that make up the grid component, a fundamental tool for working with documents. The last part of this chapter is dedicated to the menus, which we are going to explore now.

Inspecting the menus

Now we will deal with the menus, which, as often happens, play a very important role due to the large number of actions that we find inside. We cannot look at them in detail one by one, so we will limit ourselves to discussing the scope of each menu and what we can do with the items we find inside it. This is essential for getting moving inside the Pimcore interface and following the lesson that we will learn in the next chapters.

All of the menus are shown in the following screenshot:

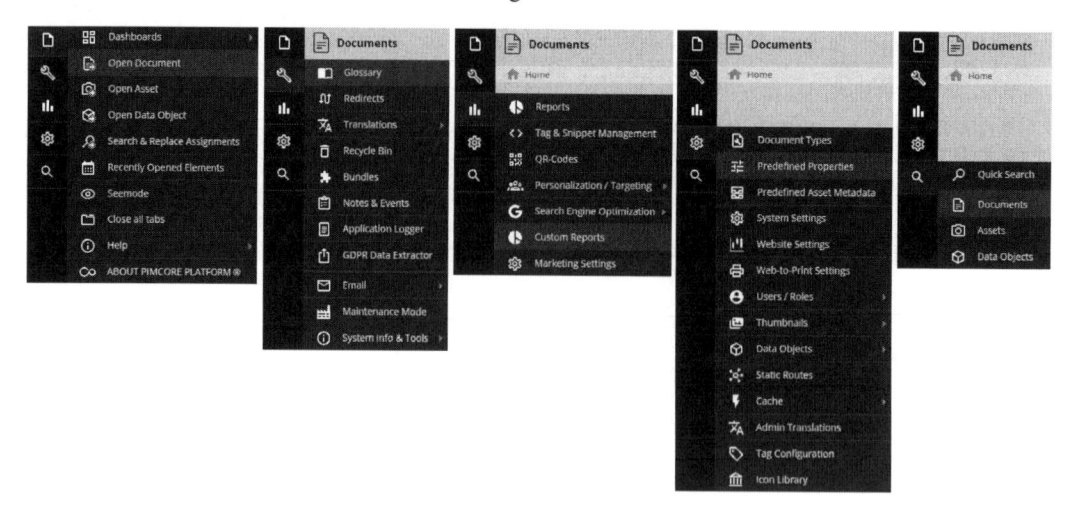

Figure 3.10: The Pimcore menus

From left to right, the menus are as follows:

- **File**
- **Tools**
- **Marketing**
- **Settings**
- **Search**

Clicking on the menu items opens a configuration page in the main frame as a new tab. However, there are menu items that contain a submenu (identifiable by the arrow on the right after the item), which appears when the mouse is moved over the item.

As we said, it is not possible to describe the functionality of each of the items in all menus, so let's now look at what the main commands we can find inside are.

File

The file menu, as we usually know, contains the actions to open documents (of various kinds), close all open tabs, navigate the Pimcore site to read the official documentation, or show the Pimcore information modal. There is also the shortcut for the dashboard page, where we can find some graphs that display the number of changes made in the last period, or the list of the last modified elements.

Tools

In this menu, we can find some useful tools for site management, such as redirects, site language management or emails sent, and the ability to send test emails. In addition to this, there are other ancillary features, such as notes and a useful link to the database administration page. In this menu, there is also some information about the system, such as the cache status or the PHP version in use.

Marketing

This menu is dedicated to marketing management, including features for search engine optimization, statistical reports, the configuration for analysis tools such as Google Tag Manager and Google Analytics, tools that those of you who work in web marketing know the importance of for monitoring visits to your website.

Settings

In this menu, we find all the actions necessary for the configuration of our site. It is possible, for example, to create and modify document types, general properties of objects, but also to manage users and their roles, configure the system in all its parts (time zone, default language, email settings, and so on), create static routes, and manage the cache or translations.

As we could have guessed, this is one of the most important menus, but it is not necessary to remember exactly which items it contains, we just need to remember that here we can find most of the configurations that we will have to do on our site from an administrative point of view. With practice and experience, we will be able to memorize all the functionalities of the various menus, although now this may seem like a distant goal.

Just to understand how many things can hide inside even just a menu item, here is the **System Settings** page:

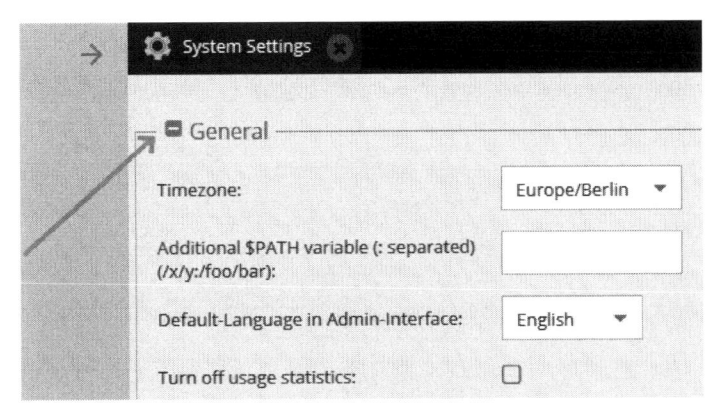

Figure 3.11: The System Settings page

As we can see, each section can be expanded by clicking on the + to access the configuration parameters of the section itself.

Search

Finally, in this last menu, you can find the shortcuts for the general search functionality, as well as for the specific search function for certain elements of the site such as assets, documents, and data objects.

In this section, we have seen what each of the menus are and the many features available in Pimcore. It was not possible to describe them individually, but we still discussed the most important items in the book, and we will leave the fun of exploring all the menu items that we have not described to you.

Summary

After reading this chapter, you now know how to move inside the Pimcore administration UI, where you can find the most important tools for Pimcore governance. We talked about the actions of the various menus, how to use the grid component, and what the main elements of the administration UI are. This is quite a large amount of information so far but it is essential for understanding what we will study in the next chapters.

Now that we are aware of how to navigate the most important of Pimcore's functionalities, we can move on to the next step, which is learning how to create documents using Pimcore.

4
Creating Documents in Pimcore

In the first three chapters, we provided an introduction to Pimcore and explained how to move around the admin interface. They were necessary steps because we now have the basics required to start learning how to use Pimcore for creating beautiful websites and solve all the digital innovation problems we introduced in the first chapter.

Now it is time to start facing some practical elements of Pimcore. We are going to introduce many topics throughout the coming chapters, with growing complexity, to master the entire Pimcore platform. In this chapter specifically, we will learn, step by step, how to create web pages using Pimcore.

In this chapter, we will cover the following topics:

- What is a document?
- Creating a document
- Creating a template
- Editing a document
- Inheriting documents

Learning about Pimcore documents will help you when it comes to building a simple website by defining your page format and designs.

Technical requirements

If you followed the instructions in *Chapter 2, Setting Up Your Pimcore Development Environment*, you should have a copy of the source code related to this book on your local machine.

So, all you need to do to run the demo connected with this chapter is clone the source code, navigate to the `4. Creating documents in Pimcore` folder, and start a Docker environment.

You can find all the code files for this chapter on GitHub here: https://github.com/PacktPublishing/Modernizing-Enterprise-CMS-using-Pimcore/tree/main/4.%20Creating%20documentes%20in%20Pimcore.

To start the code on your PC, just navigate to folder `4. Creating documents in Pimcore` and follow these instructions:

1. Run Docker with the following command:

   ```
   docker-compose up
   ```

2. Then, to restore all the settings from on your local, type this:

   ```
   docker-compose exec php bash restore.sh
   ```

3. Navigate to `http://localhost/admin` and log in with your admin/pimcore credentials.

Now you are ready to play with the demo related to this chapter!

What is a document?

Generally speaking, everybody uses documents every day. We deal with document specifications for our boss or our customer, we write documents to keep track of the changes in our software… but what is a document in Pimcore? In the context of information science, we are not referring to a paper sheet, but to a digital asset that contains unstructured information; in our case, a web page is a **document**. Documents are organized into a **document tree** that creates a hierarchy between elements. This structure of documents will represent the structure of the website. This may seem complicated to read, but it is very easy to put into practice.

In the following example, we have a simple website composed of a tree web:

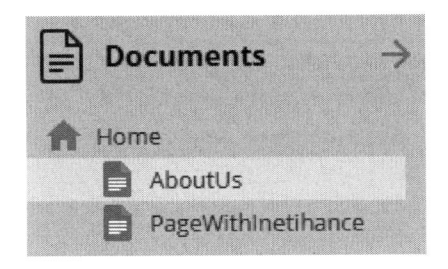

Figure 4.1: The document list

These are the pages we will create during this chapter and that will show all the document features.

We told you that a document could be any type of unstructured data container. Such containers can be very different, based on the kind of information found within them. To represent each document with the right amount of information, we need to classify documents using document types.

Pimcore offers many different document types that let you manage most of the use case you will face without any problems:

- **Page**: This is the typical web page. The path in the document tree defines the final URL.
- **Snippet**: As the word suggests, snippets are pieces of the document that can be embedded into pages for content reuse. We can also add snippets to snippets.
- **Link**: This is a raw web link that can be used inside a navigation tree.
- **Email**: This is a document that produces HTML content, such as pages, but also supports the sending of transactional emails, allowing you to define a sender and recipient.
- **Newsletter**: Very similar to email content but has some extra features to support usage as a newsletter (for instance, mass sending).
- **Hardlink**: Allows you to create internal links and alter the regular structure of the document.
- **Folder**: Like a folder on the filesystem of your PC, Pimcore folders contain multiple documents.
- **PrintPage**: Pages with some extra features for printing purposes, such as a **Generate PDF** button.
- **PrintContainer**: A container that organizes pages into a group to create a multi-page document that's ready for printing.

Not only does Pimcore come with document types out of the box, but you can also create your own.

In this first section of the chapter, we learned what documents in Pimcore are. This was useful for understanding what we are going to do next, as we will learn how to create a new document and implement a simple web page.

Creating a document

In this section, we will see how to create a document using Pimcore CMS. To do this, follow these steps:

1. Navigate to the document tree and right-click to activate the context menu.
2. Select **Add page** and then **Blank** (to create an empty page):

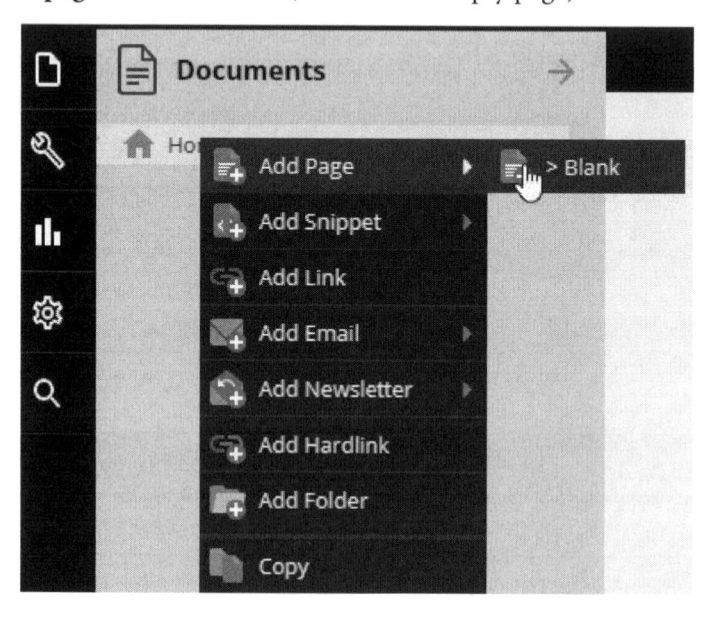

Figure 4.2: Adding a page in Pimcore

3. A modal popup called **Add page** will appear, with three parameters for you to complete. The **Title** parameter is the title of the page, the **Navigation** parameter is the name that will be used in the navigation menu, and **Key** is a unique key that you choose for the document:

Figure 4.3: Entering data for the page that we are creating

4. Click **OK** and you will see your **Home** page added to the menu tree:

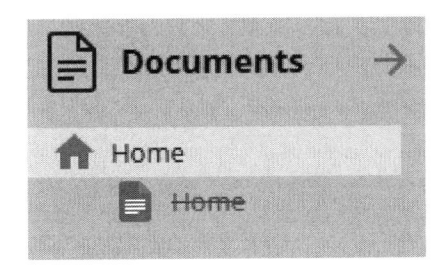

Figure 4.4: The page added in the tree menu

5. Click your newly created page, **Home**, and the page element will open the page in a new tab. The next figure shows the page editor:

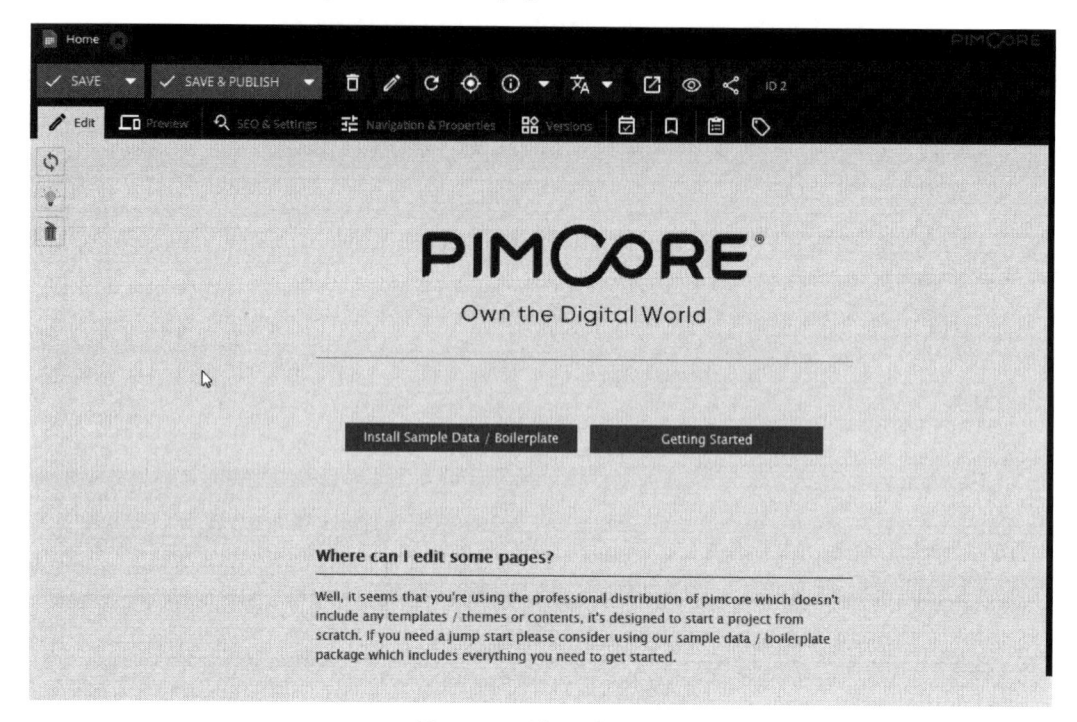

Figure 4.5: The web page

This page tells us that we have created a web page, but the site is empty because we don't have a template. This message may seem a little bit frustrating because, after all those steps, you are still not able to enter content without creating an HTML template. This may seem quite odd if you are used to ready-to-use solutions such as WordPress, where anybody can add content without needing to write a single line of code. This is because of the Pimcore philosophy, where there isn't any superstructure between you and the tool.

In the next section, we will learn how to create a simple template. For now, we can be satisfied that we have learned how to create web pages using documents.

Creating a template

The purpose of this chapter is to give you the basics for rendering a document properly. This is only one small part of Pimcore's rendering capabilities, and we go deeper into this topic in *Chapter 10, Creating Pimcore Bricks*, to discover all the secrets of rendering custom data. For now, we will focus only on the information we need to create simple websites.

The Pimcore page design process

The first concepts to introduce are templates and layouts. The **layout** is a generic page prototype where you can leave some placeholders that will be filled by **templates**. For example, you can have a layout page with two columns and two placeholders, one per column. On each page, you will be able to fill the content inside each placeholder. Such placeholders are called **Blocks** in Twig syntax, and you can define how many blocks you want.

In the following figure, you can see how the web page design process works:

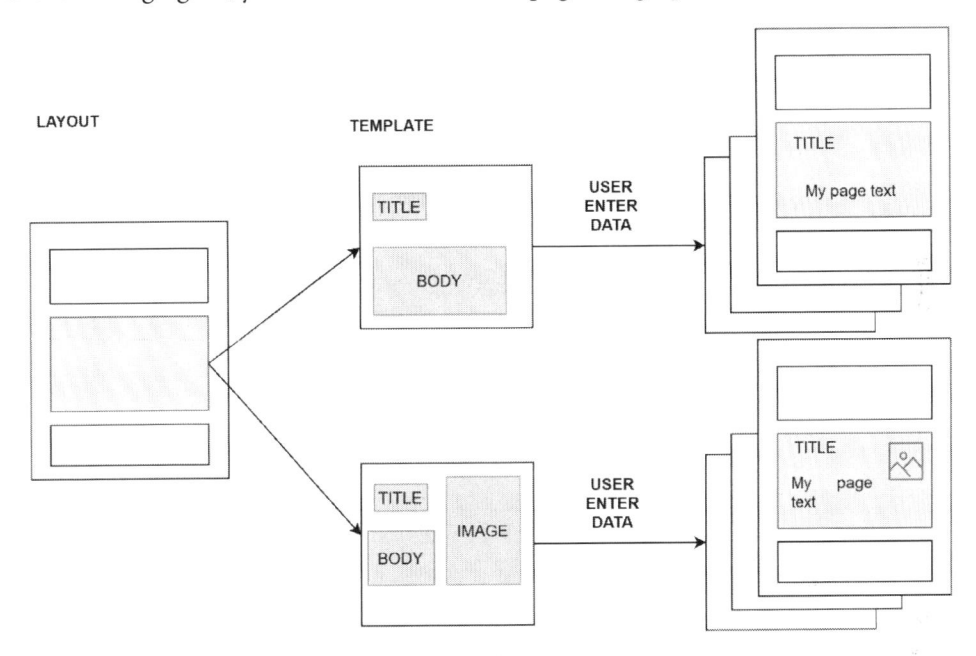

Figure 4.6: The template engine in action

Let's take a look at each stage:

- The first step is to define a **Layout**. This step must be done by a developer or someone that has mastered the HTML, CSS, and Twig templating languages. It is not complicated but requires you to access the source code and write down a file, and typically it cannot be done by the final user. At this stage, we will define the structure of the page; in the example, the number of rows/the common page parts are defined.
- Inside the layout, a space for the page implementation is left empty for the **Template**. Inside the template, the designer or the developer can add input that we filled by the user. In this manner, you can create the product page prototype and then the content manager can create many product pages.
- As the last step, the user will be able to enter data into the template placeholder. In this example, the user can enter a title, fill out the body text, and add images.

> **Note**
> Pimcore supports Twig or PHP templates. As stated in the official documentation, PHP templates are deprecated and will be retired with Pimcore X. That's why, even though many parts of the official Pimcore documentation show only PHP examples, we decided to base this book on the Twig template. We are aware that most PHP developers have been more comfortable with the plain PHP template, but it was hard to base a book on a deprecated feature.

In this section, we had an overview of Pimcore's templates; now it's time to learn how to create a template starting from scratch.

Implementing a simple layout

In this section, we will implement a simple layout that can be used to create web pages and build a website. As you will see, the process is easy and requires just a few steps to get a working template:

1. Firstly, we need to tell the system to use Twig files instead of the PHP template. Navigate to `/src/Controller` and open `DefaultController.php`. You just need to add an annotation to the `defaultAction` method inside the controller using `Template()`:

```php
<?php
namespace App\Controller;

use Pimcore\Controller\FrontendController;
use Symfony\Component\HttpFoundation\Request;
use Sensio\Bundle\FrameworkExtraBundle\Configuration\Template;

class DefaultController extends FrontendController
{
    /**
     * @Template()
     */
    public function defaultAction(Request $request)
    {
    }
}
```

In the next steps, we will learn how the layout engine works and how you can create templates for your Pimcore websites. This is very simple, as we need just some knowledge of HTML, CSS, and PHP to create structured websites.

2. At this point, we are ready to start creating a template. Navigate to /templates and create a file named layout.html.twig. The template engine behind Pimcore is Symfony, so most things that are valid for a generic Symphony project are also true for Pimcore. In the following example, we have a snippet of code that implements a Pimcore layout. You can copy this snippet into the layout.html.twig file or check the file provided in our demo:

```twig
<!DOCTYPE html>
<html lang="en">
<head>
<!-- head omitted -->
</head>
<body>
    <!--Navigation bar omitted   -->
{% block content %}
{% endblock %}
    <hr>
<!--footer bar omitted -->
</body>
</html>
```

As you can see in the previous code, a Pimcore layout is just an HTML file (or a Twig template) where you add the following snippet to create a place where the user will put content:

```twig
{% block content %}
{% endblock %}
```

Inside the template, you want to add all the common parts of your websites, such as menus, footers, and the page structure. Of course, you can use multiple layouts across different pages, even for the same website (for instance, tree columns versus a two-column layout).

3. The layout cannot be used by the final user, as it contains only the page structure definition. So, we will have to define a template. A template is another Twig file where you implement the blocks left empty in the layout. Navigate to /templates and create a folder named Default that contains a file named default.html.twig. Here, you have to extend the layout that we created in the previous step. To do so, add a simple template with a title, a subtitle, and a page body:

```twig
{% extends 'layout.html.Twig' %}
{% block content %}
    <!-- Page Header -->
    <header>
        <div class=»container»>
            <div class=»row»>
                <div class=»col-lg-8 col-md-10 mx-auto»>
                    <div class=»site-heading»>
                        <h1> {{ pimcore_input(<headline>, {<width>: 540}) }}</h1>
                        <span class=»subheading»> {{ pimcore_input(<subheading>, {<width>: 700}) }}</span>
                    </div>
                </div>
            </div>
        </div>
    </header>
    {{ pimcore_wysiwyg(<body>) }}
{% endblock %}
```

In this code block, we used simple HTML to define the page appearance and some Twig directives. The HTML page is composed of a header with an H1 title and a body. The highlighted parts are computed on the server side and will be rendered dynamically.

Let's take a moment to comment on each of them:

```
{% extends 'layout.html.twig' %}
```

This first statement links the template file to the parent layout. In this case, the template inherits the block from the `layout.html.twig` file.

The next statement indicates the beginning of the block of code that will fill the placeholder called `content` into the main layout file:

```
{% block content %}
```

4. Then, mixed with HTML, we have some special directives that allow the user to put content inside the template. Our goal is to remove any dependency from the developer during the editing (in other words, the user must be able to enter data by themselves). This can be done easily by using Pimcore **editables**. We will spend a lot of time in *Chapter 9, Configuring Entities and Rendering Data*, going deeper into the details of editables, but for now, just think of them as data placeholders.

In our example, we need plain text values for the text and title fields, so we used a standard input box. This part of the template is very easy because, in practice, we just have to invoke a function as follows:

```
{{ pimcore_input('headline', {'width': 540}) }}
```

The first argument of the function is the name on the input, `headline`, in this case. Then we can have many parameters; in this case, we use a fixed width during the editing.

To add HTML text, we do the same, but using a **What You See Is What You Get** (**WYSIWYG**) interface. This is quite similar to the previous case, as you can see in the next code snippet:

```
{{ pimcore_wysiwyg('body') }}
```

Now we are able to edit documents! In the next section, we will learn how to put data inside a template and how to iterate this process to implement a real website.

Editing a document

In this section, we will learn how to create and edit a document. As we told you, a document can be any of your CMS web pages, so just from this simple lesson, you will be able to create any kind of website. The process of editing a document is very easy, and we will explore it by completing some simple steps:

1. Open the admin panel and find **Home**, the page we created in the *What is a document?* section. By selecting it, you will open the web page in the main frame of the admin. As you can see in the next figure, we are going to edit the web page directly, and we will be using a mode called WYSIWYG, which is very useful because it makes the editor aware of what they are doing during the editing:

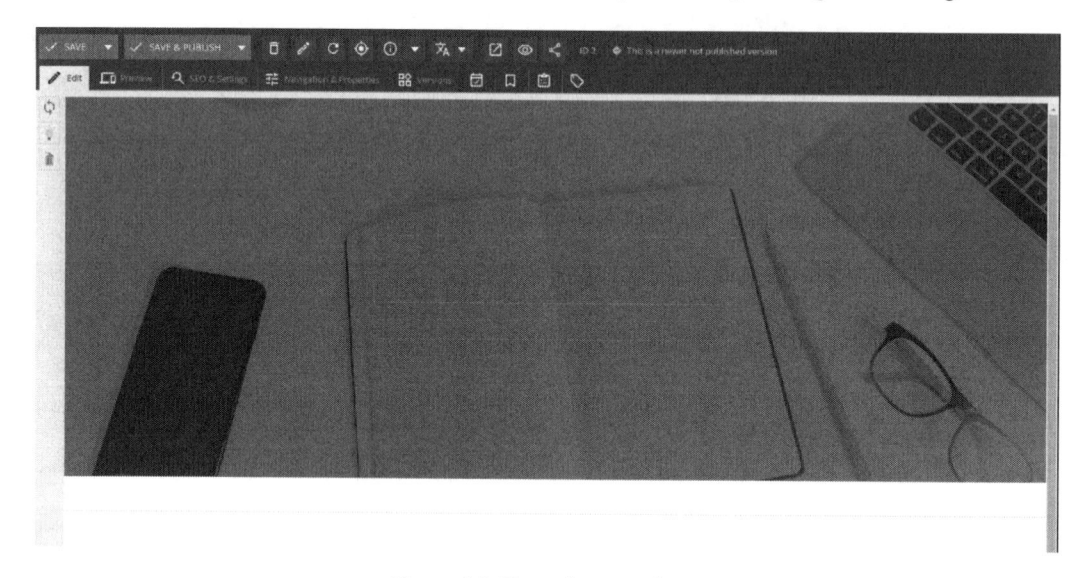

Figure 4.7: The web page editor

As you can see in the previous figure, we have some dotted areas, which are the placeholders that we added to the Twig template. These placeholders work like regular input boxes, so all you need to do is click on them and start entering text. In Pimcore, such items are called editables (as mentioned earlier).

2. Click the larger placeholder and type the words **Home Page**; you will see the editor being filled in while you are typing the characters. In the next figure, you can see the final result of filling in the **Title** field:

Figure 4.8: Writing the title

3. Click the second placeholder (the one just below the title). As in the previous case, clicking the editor will unlock the ability for you to write any text. The difference is that the **Title** field is a single-line editable box, whereas this field is an HTML editor; you can select text and then apply styles as you would in any word processor. In the next figure, you can see this in action:

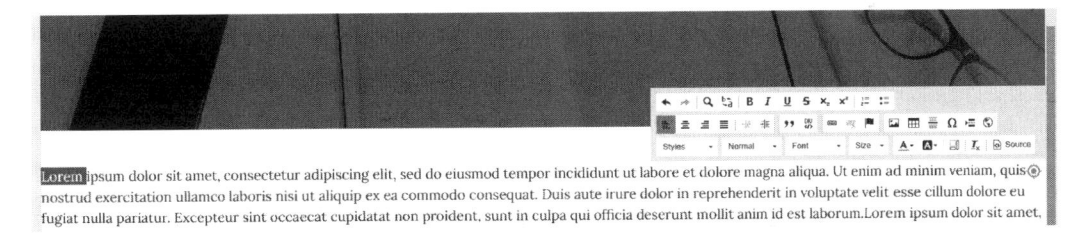

Figure 4.9: HTML editor in action

The previous figure shows the HTML text and the contextual menu that allows style settings for the text.

4. Once we have filled the editable parts of the document, the web page is done. We can publish it using the **Save and Publish** button in the toolbar.

5. Then, to view a preview of the page, just click the **Preview** button. In the next figure, we can see the preview tool in action. As you can see in the figure, we can choose the device to use for rendering the page (in this example, we are emulating a phone):

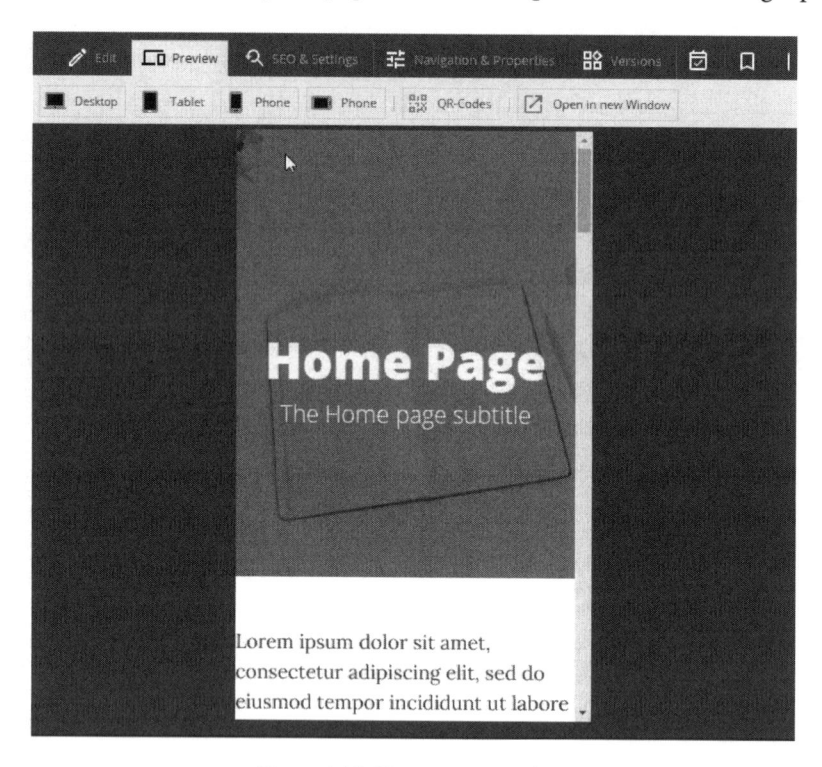

Figure 4.10: Document preview

6. Finally, we have to take care of search engine settings. Click the **SEO & Settings** tab to enter the panel where we can edit these settings. Here we can add a title, a description, and any metatags we want:

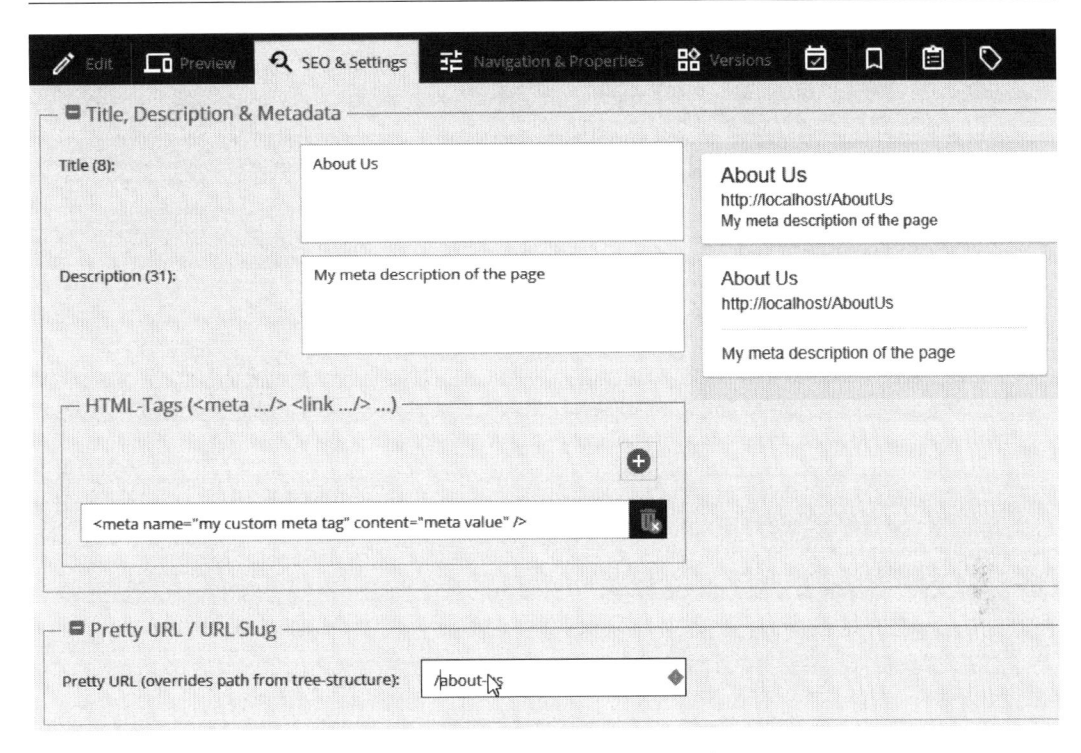

Figure 4.11: SEO & Settings panel

On the same page, you can see a Google preview of your web page, so you can be aware of how it will look for the user searching for your web page. In the last editable component, you can define a custom URL for the page. This setting overrides the normal page structure, so it is an absolute URL.

7. Finally, click the **Version** tab. You will see the history of a document, as shown in the following figure. Within the **Version** panel, you can access the history of the web pages and recover old versions in the case of errors:

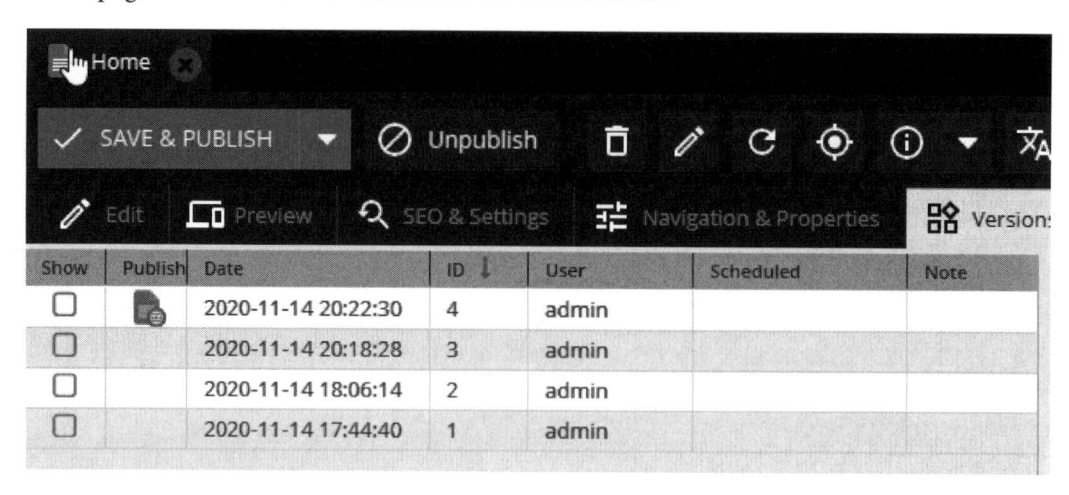

Figure 4.12: Version panel

Editing documents enables us to create simple websites. This is easy by simply defining a template and then putting information into it. We have learned that we can create document instances by creating different templates, and the user can autonomously manage them using a web interface. Replicating what we have done so far is enough for building simple websites.

However, things can get a bit more complicated. For example, let's say you want to create a website catalog containing a set of products to sell. Using what we have learned so far, you can create a catalog by adding a document template for the product page; then, you can create a product page and fill in the data. Now, imagine that each product had a variety of variants; these (child) variants share a lot of information with the original (parent) product. Creating multiple pages for these variants using the process we just covered would be time-consuming. Plus, if you copied and pasted data that is similar across all the product variants and then one piece of information changed, you would have to update each page individually. This example shows us how replicating data by copying and pasting information can lead to a website that is hard to maintain.

In the next section, we will learn how to reuse the content of a document to avoid data replication using document inheritance.

Inheriting documents

Document inheritance is a feature that lets you create a pre-filled document where you can override just the section you need. Think of this feature as a "template in a template." This feature is activated by setting the **Content Master Document** property in the document settings. This feature applies to every document type, and it is very useful for repetitive content, such as newsletters or technical documentation.

In the following steps, we will see how to take advantage of inheritance for reusing content and organizing website content better. We will create a simple product catalog with a product (here, t-shirts) with multiple variants (one variant per color), and each variant will have its web page.

Follow these steps to do this:

1. First of all, we have to create a template for a product page. So, let's create a file called `product.html.twig` inside `/templates/Default`. The process is very similar to the one followed in the *Editing a document* section, but this time we will have a more complex layout. In fact, we have to display product data, so we have to add more input. The next layout fragment displays the relevant part of the layout file:

    ```twig
    <div class="breadcrumb-item">Category:{{ pimcore_input('category') }}</div>
    <div ><h1>{{ pimcore_input('title', {'width': 540}) }}</h1></div>
    <div class="product-price"><span>€{{ pimcore_input('price') }}</span><strike><span style='color:black'>€{{ pimcore_input('originalprice') }}</span></strike></div>
    <div>Produced by: {{ pimcore_input('producer') }}</div>
    <div>Made in: {{ pimcore_input('origin') }}</div>
    ```

    Inside this code snippet, we have many inputs for adding all the product images (for example, `category`, `title`, `discounted price`, `price`, `producer`, and `origin`). We are now able of going into the Pimcore administrative interface and create a document item.

2. Create a page in the tree menu. In our example, we will create a page for t-shirts with some variants, so the page title will be **TShirt**. In our case, we created this page inside a **Products** menu item that is the root of our catalog. Then, you have to iterate the process, creating a sub-page for each color variant (**TShirt-Red**, **TShirt-Green**, and **TShirt-Yellow**). The final result is shown in the next figure:

Figure 4.13: The menu with products

3. Now double-click on the parent page, **TShirt**, and open the document.
4. Now hit **SEO & Settings**. Click on the **Template** dropdown and select **Default/default.html.twig**:

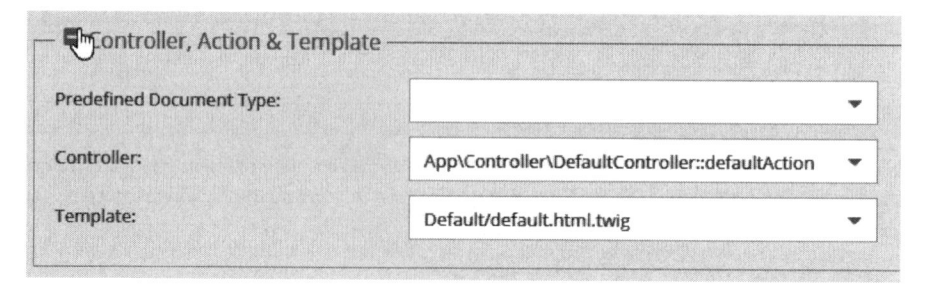

Figure 4.14: Selecting the product template

5. Repeat the previous step for all the child pages.

6. Enter data for each field we added in the template. The result should be something similar to what you see in the following figure:

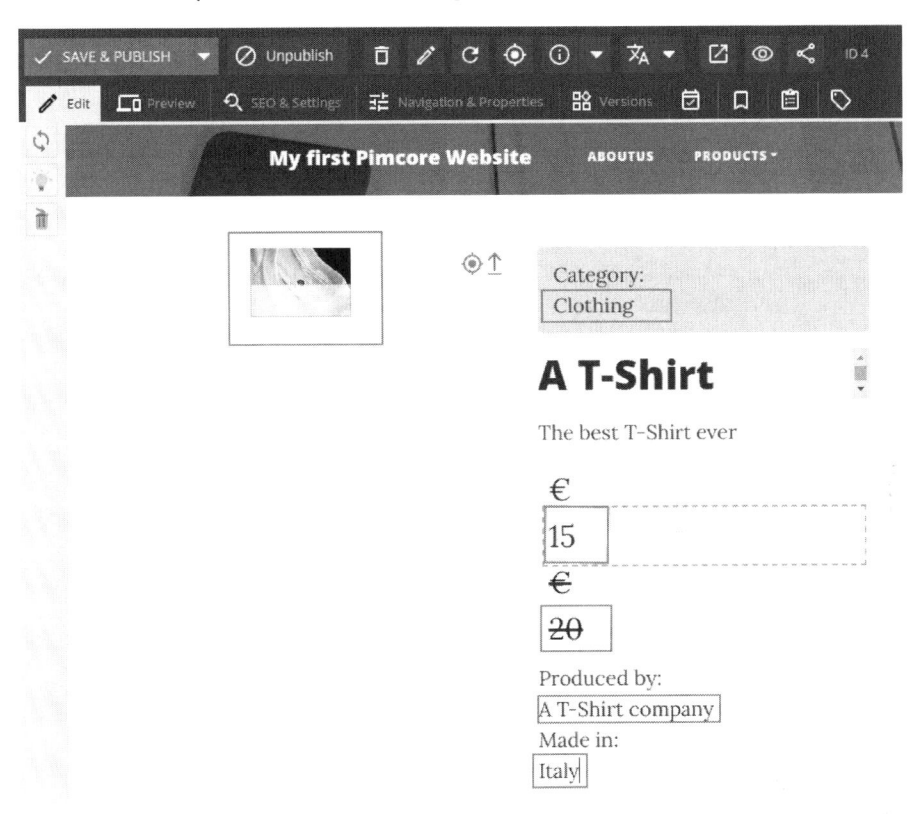

Figure 4.15: Editing the t-shirt product

Before editing a variant for the product that we created with these documents, we will assume that most of the information entered for this product will be the same for all the children. In fact, all products are just the same t-shirt, except for the color. Let's see in the next steps how to avoid data replication.

74   Creating Documents in Pimcore

7. Open the **TShirt** page and click on **SEO & Settings**. Then, drag and drop the **TShirt** page from the document tree to the **Content-Master Document** field:

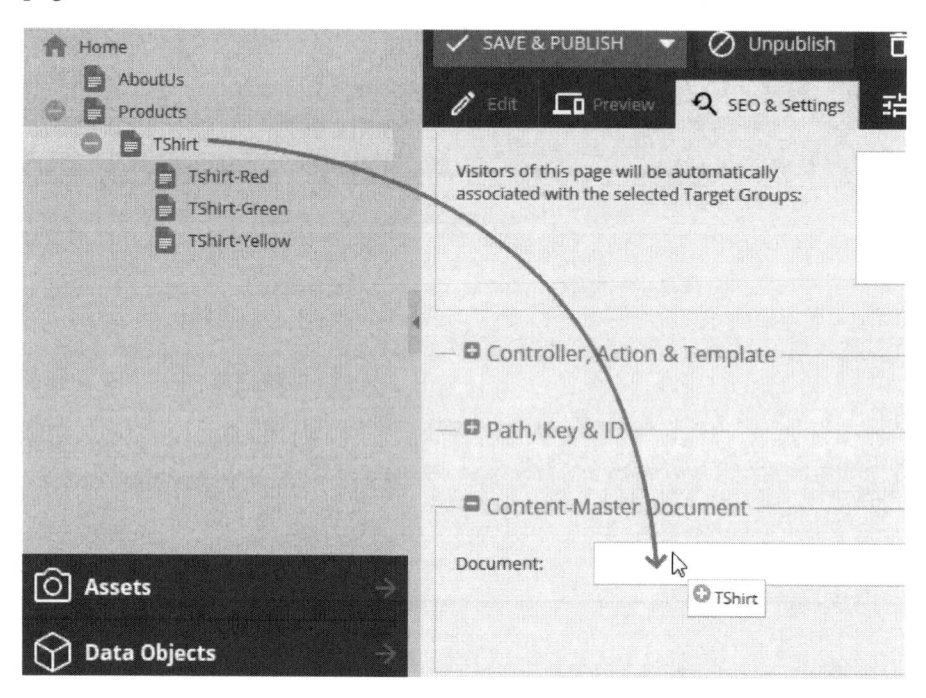

Figure 4.16: Drag and drop the parent document

8. After you click **Apply**, you will be prompted with the message: **Are you sure? All content will be lost**. When you confirm the operation, all the existing content on your page will be overridden from the inherited ones. Since the operation is completed, you now have all the editable components disabled. In the next figure, we can see how the page looks. As you can see, the placeholders are filled in automatically with the values from the parent page. You can see that the editable components are now disabled, and when you move the mouse over an editable area, a **Click right to overwrite** message appears:

Figure 4.17: Overwriting an inherited property

9. Right-click on the disabled editable; in this case, right-click **A T-Shirt**. This step unlocks the field and lets you change the default values for this page instance. In this case, we entered **A Red T-Shirt**:

Figure 4.18: After overwriting, the text is editable

In the previous figure, you can see that the product name was replaced. All the fields that are not inherited will reflect the changes from the parent document; so, if you change the price, this field will be updated in all the child pages. In that way, all common fields are entered once, and you replicate information only when you really need to.

10. Now, replicate *steps 6-8* for all the children of the **T-shirt** page tree.

In this section, we learned how to create a document by inheriting some data from a parent. This Pimcore feature lets us reuse information across a website. Using this inheritance feature, we avoided replicating common fields in the product hierarchy. This feature is another option for managing unstructured data in a more convenient way and avoiding data replication.

Summary

In this chapter, we learned how to create documents and how this feature enables us to create and manage very simple websites. The first thing we discovered, with respect to other CMS solutions, is that we don't have anything that's ready to use. Just to create the first web page, we needed to define some templates. This may seem like a waste of time, but it is in fact the opposite. Templates force you to work in a structured way from the beginning of the process. They force you to create editable web pages where the final user will be able to edit data without breaking the layout. This allows non-developers to master their content. It is what we called a detached approach in the first chapter.

If you have some experience in web development, you are probably wondering how far you can go with editables. Their flexibility can help you implement a huge amount of web pages, and you could theoretically go on and manage complex websites with them. The only limitation to this approach is that we are working with plain documents. Do you remember when we gave the definition of documents? We said that they are containers of unstructured information. That's the limitation. We can structure how information is distributed across the page, but this doesn't allow us to query or reuse data. We can create thousands of blogs or product pages with ease, but this is not enough. In fact, we will need to be more dynamic, by listing products on a category page or group blog articles by tag. You may want to implement these features using documents, but in spite of the power of Pimcore, in most cases, it will require a lot of effort, and you'll get a poor result. In fact, documents are good for rendering web pages but don't quite suit structured data or interactive content.

So, if you are wondering how to handle structured data, don't worry. In the next chapter, we will describe what data objects are and how to represent information in a structured way. This will be the basis for starting to manage data properly and render it without any duplication of content or source code.

5
Exploring Objects and Classes

In this chapter, we are going to see one of the main functionalities that Pimcore offers to us: the possibility of defining a personal and completely custom dataset for each project by creating classes and objects.

The big advantage of using Pimcore is that you can do everything through the user interface, without the need of writing a single line of code or to define complex database structures, changing or adding new attributes whenever you want. Pimcore will do all the magic, and you can update your dataset with no worries of running risky migrations on the database. Besides, you can export and import all class definitions to share them between different projects without the need for reinventing the wheel every time.

In the following sections, we will present class configuration, focusing on various field types that could be added to them, and how to concretely see these classes in action through data entry. If we've caught your curiosity, just go through this chapter to discover how simple it is to create and update your classes with Pimcore. The chapter structure is organized as follows:

- What is a Class?
- Creating and Editing a class definition
- Discovering Relevant Field Types
- Understanding and Establishing relations
- Performing Data Entry

By the end of this chapter, you will know how to create Pimcore classes and how to properly configure them to make the most of their potential.

Technical requirements

As you previously have done in *Chapter 4, Creating Documents in Pimcore*, all you need to run the demo connected with this chapter is to navigate to the `5. Object and Classes` folder on the official book repository and start a Docker environment.

To do so, just follow these instructions:

1. Run Docker with the following command:

   ```
   docker-compose up
   ```

2. Then, to restore all the settings on your local machine, just open a new shell and type the following:

   ```
   docker-compose exec php bash restore.sh
   ```

3. Navigate to `http://localhost/admin` and log in with your admin/pimcore credentials.

You can access the official book repository to get the source code through the following link:

`https://github.com/PacktPublishing/Modernizing-Enterprise-CMS-using-Pimcore/tree/main/5.%20Object%20and%20Classes`

Now you are ready to navigate the demo to discover all the aspects related to this chapter.

What is a Class?

In this section, you will learn what a class is in Pimcore and how it is useful for managing any kind of data. In the context of Object-Oriented-Programming, a **class** consists of a set of variables (or properties) suitable to represent a concept, methods to affect values, and the behavior of objects that instantiate the class itself.

Pimcore classes reflect this definition, but there is more. In the following sections, we will better understand how those classes work, and how they simplify our work on dataset development. In particular, we will see that despite the name, Pimcore is not limited to product information management; moreover, you will discover that no coding at all is needed to define classes.

Designing different concepts

As we already know, one of Pimcore's main features is product information management, so we are led to believe that everything revolves around the definition of a `Product` class. This is often true, of course, but it must not be seen as a limitation.

Think about a basic e-commerce structure: there will be the `Product` class, as we would expect, but maybe we want to categorize our products; we can think about creating a `Category` class to link to the product, instead of repeating the category's attributes in each one. We can apply the same reasoning on product materials or other attributes, gradually increasing the complexity of our structure as needed. And what if we need to implement a store locator for our e-commerce site? All we would need to do is create a `Store` class!

To be more generic, we can design every different kind of concept creating the respective class. That said, you can easily understand how simple it could be to design the dataset for your CMS. You just need to define classes for articles, authors, and so on and start to insert your data. Even better is the fact that you can do it without writing a single line of code.

No code required

You may think that defining these classes will require a lot of code development or database engineering, but you would be wrong. You just need to define your classes and their attributes, and Pimcore will do all the magic. To be more specific, we may say that every operation that we make on each of our classes affects a couple of PHP files that are needed to define the classes themselves.

The `definition` file contains a complex structure of arrays that represent class fields, all information regarding visual aspects, such as width, height, or CSS rules, and the spatial organization of these fields. This file contains all class attribute definitions, so it can be used to restore the class itself.

The `class` file, named after the class itself, contains all getters, setters, and other common methods that allow us to manipulate objects that will instantiate the class. This class can be referenced within the project and used to access class properties and create or update class instances.

Those come with flexible and dedicated database tables for each class and the relations between them. Once more, all this happens behind the scenes and so you will never have to worry about that; all you need to do is define the structure that reflects your needs.

In this section, we discovered what a class is and how anybody can configure it without any knowledge of code development. In the next section, we'll see how to create and edit a class definition.

Creating and Editing a Class Definition

Now that we know the basic definitions, in this section, we are ready to create our first class. To open up the class definition panel, go through **Settings | Data Objects | Classes**. Now, we can click on the **Add** button on the left side. In the following screenshot, we can see the class creation pop-up modal that appears:

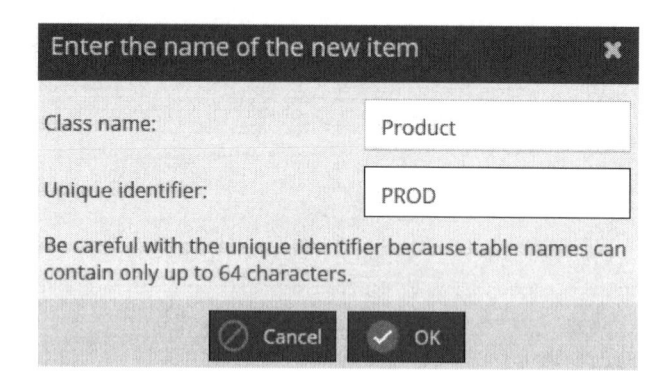

Figure 5.1: Creating a new class

In the popup that appears, we must define the following:

- **Class name**: The name of our class. Pay attention to avoid whitespaces.
- **Unique identifier**: A short string to identify the class uniquely. If we omit the identifier, the first available integer ID will be applied to the class. This identifier cannot be updated again.

Click on **OK** and the class will be created.

Now we need to define the general settings for the class. We will list all these settings, explaining their meanings and how to properly configure them. Remember that all settings are optional, and some may not be useful for your project.

In the following screenshot, we can see these settings with plausible values:

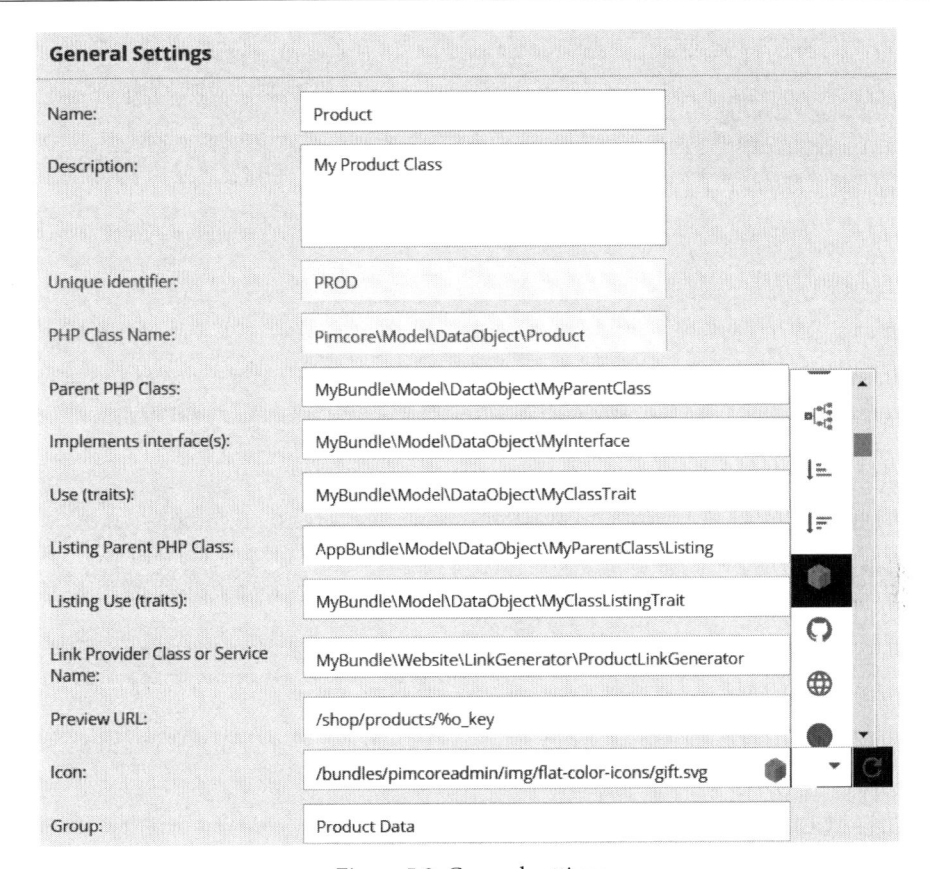

Figure 5.2: General settings

Let's now describe each property that we see in the preceding screenshot:

- **Description**: Just a description of your class. It has no other implications. It may be useful to transmit the purpose of the class in the case of remote collaboration.

- **Parent PHP Class**: A PHP class that you want your class to extend. It is crucial that, on the inheritance chain, the class extends the `Pimcore\Model\DataObject\Concrete` class, which contains common methods for all classes.

- **Implements interface(s)**: A comma-separated list of interfaces that you want your class to implement.

- **Use (traits)**: In PHP, traits are mechanisms for code reuse, which allows reducing some limitations given by single inheritance. In Pimcore, we could use traits to implement methods of the previous interface(s).

- **Listing Parent PHP Class**: We can also define a parent PHP class for the listing class. This class must extend the `Pimcore\Model\DataObject\Listing\Concrete` class.

- **Listing Use (traits)**: As we just mentioned, traits are a PHP paradigm of code development used to implement interface methods. The same concept is valid for class listing.

- **Link Provider Class or Service Name**: Link generation is a particular class used to dynamically generate web links for objects and is automatically called when objects are linked in documents or other link tags. It must extend the `AbstractProductLinkGenerator` class and implements the `LinkGeneratorInterface` interface. The link generator will receive the referenced object and additional data depending on the context.

- **Preview URL**: The preview URL is useful to generate a dynamic URL for the object directly on the class definition. You can use placeholders for each defined attribute of your class, in addition to common properties such as object ID or key. This feature became deprecated in the last version, and it is suggested to use **Link Provider Class**.

- **Icon**: You can choose a custom icon for your class from the icon list. If you prefer, there is the possibility to link your icons, providing the path to the icon itself. It is recommended to use SVG files.

- **Group**: This property is necessary to group your classes into folders in the class definitions tree. Classes with the same prefix word are automatically grouped even if no group is explicitly provided.

- **Allow Inheritance**: If checked, this property enables the inheritance among objects in a tree-structured way. Child objects could be instances of the same class or objects of a different class. If child objects belong to the same class as the parent object, they automatically inherit all data values from the parent object and can override them.

- **Allow Variants**: Object variants are a particular kind of inheritance. A variant's class cannot be chosen; it's forced to be the same as the parent object. We must note that, by default, variants are excluded from listing queries.

- **Show variants in tree**: This property allows you to see the variants in the object tree. If not enabled, variants are only shown in the appropriate tab inside the object edit modal.

- **Show App Logger Tab**: If enabled, the **Application Logger** tab is shown inside the object edit modal. In that tab, it's possible to read eventually created log events related to the object.
- **Enable grid locking**: This allows you to block some columns in the object grid views.
- **Encrypt Data**: This property enables the possibility to encrypt the object's data in the tables created to store information for the class.
- **Visibility of system properties**: This allows you to choose which attributes are shown by default in the grid view and the search view. These attributes are **Id**, **Key**, **Path**, **Published**, **Creation Date**, and **Modification date**. These properties are useful for grid filtering.
- **Composite Indices**: Pimcore allows you to create custom indices in tables that store the information of your class objects. You can choose the index name and the class attributes involved in it.

Once you have filled in these class properties, you must click on the **Save** button to apply them.

In this section, you learned how to create Pimcore classes. Then, you discovered what the main settings for a class are, and how to properly fill in these properties concerning your specific needs. Moreover, you have seen how to enable class inheritance. In the next section, we will present all the different kinds of components that can be attached to the class.

Discovering Relevant Field Types

In the previous section, we created our first class. The created class is just like an empty box of which, let's say, we have just established the shape and the dimensions. In this section, we will see how we can model our class, defining layout components and all different kinds of attributes. These concepts are crucial to properly configure your classes according to your needs. In particular, we will describe the two different kinds of attributes:

- The Layout Components
- The Data Components

Let's see both of these kinds of components in the following sections.

Layout Components

The layout components allow us to organize the class attributes through space. To better understand the usefulness of these components, let's think about a website structure. There are no rules that prevent putting all site information vertically on the page. All text, input fields, images, and related links, just listed one below the previous one. Sure, it's easy to create, but the reading experience for the user is quite a mess, don't you think?

Maybe it'd be better to group common information in different tabs or create a box with input fields that the user must fill in with the required information. Images can be grouped into a gallery, on the right-hand side, or we may want to expand or collapse certain information.

Well, class layout components are designed for just that purpose. You must add at least one layout component to the class to be allowed to add the class attributes; to add a layout component, just right-click on **General Settings** in your class definition.

Let's see the common characteristic of all kinds of components and the specific properties for each of them:

- **Name**: The component name will only be shown inside the class definition panel.
- **Region**: Combined with a parent layout component, this can be used to locate the component in different positions, using **North**, **West**, **Center**, **East**, and **South**.
- **Title**: The component title will be shown in object instances of the class. The position and style of the title depend on the specific component.
- **Width**: The width of the component in the object edit modal.
- **Height**: The height of the component in the object edit modal.
- **Collapsible**: If enabled, this makes the component collapsible by the user.
- **Collapsed**: If enabled, the component is collapsed by default on object opening.
- **CSS Style**: Consent to write custom CSS style rules for the component, such as a margin or floating position.
- **Border**: Adds a border to the element.

We can now have a specific look at each kind of layout component. In the following screenshot, we can see all the different types of layout components:

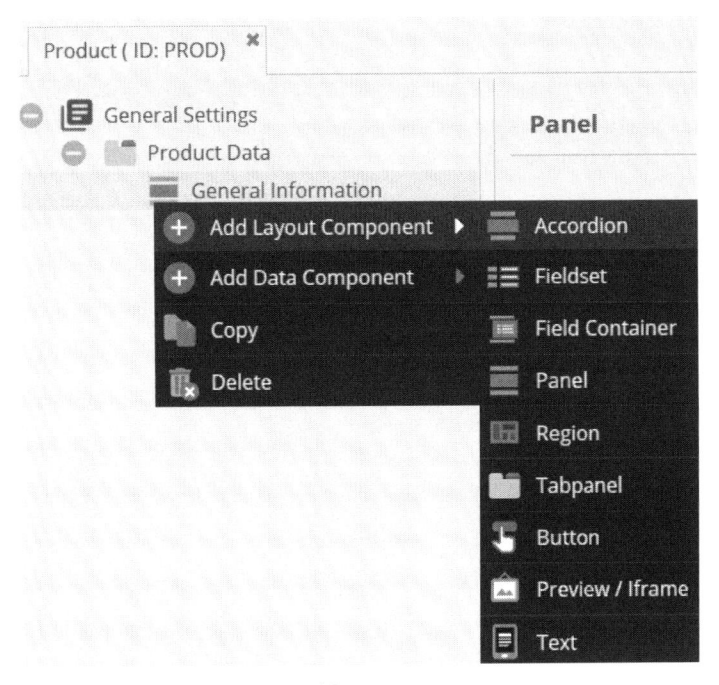

Figure 5.3: Add Layout Component

Let's describe the properties of each component in the following sections as shown in the screenshot.

Tabpanel

This component allows you to group different panels inside. Each panel will act as a tab in the object edit modal. Besides the common properties, for Tabpanel, you can specify the **Tab Position** property. This lets you choose in which position you want to put your tabs; possible values are **top** (default), **left**, **right**, and **bottom**.

Panel

A simple component that lets you add attributes inside. This component can be nested inside other components, such as Tabpanel and Region, and located in different positions.

For this component, we can specify these additional properties:

- **Layout**: If the **Fit** option is selected, all fields inside the panel will fit the screen dimension.
- **Label Width**: Sets the width of the panel label.
- **Icon**: Allows choosing a custom icon that will be shown at the left of the label.

Accordion

Similar to the Panel component, this component is designed to be collapsed and expanded as needed. This concept is often used for site development to let the user hide or show some extra information that may or may not be useful. For this component, there are no extra properties to add.

In the following screenshot, you will see the difference between panels and accordions:

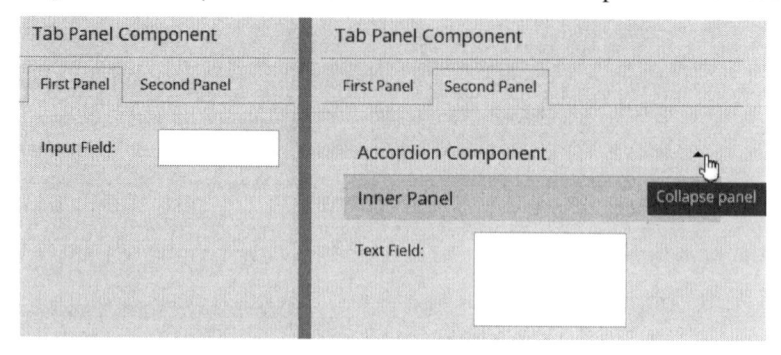

Figure 5.4: Panels and accordions

As you can see in the preceding screenshots, the panels are placed on top inside the **Tab Panel Component**. The accordion component contains other layout and data components and can be collapsed or expanded.

Region

This component is designed to contain only other layout components. If you add panels inside a region, you can organize them in the five fixed positions mentioned previously. Note that you must specify a fixed region height, or your region will not be shown. As for the panel, you can choose a custom icon.

Fieldset

This component just lets you add some data components inside of it, grouping them with a small border with a label on top. You can use it to group a list of similar fields that make sense if shown together. The only specific property that can be set is the label width.

Field Container

The behavior of a Field Container is similar to a Fieldset. The main difference is just that you can choose whether you want to group your fields vertically or horizontally, by properly selecting the **Layout** property.

In the following screenshot, you can see the difference between **Fieldset** and **Field Container**:

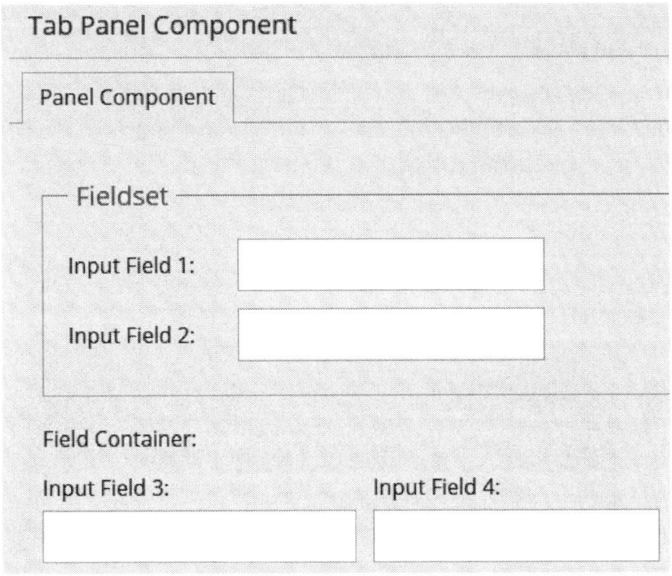

Figure 5.5: Fieldset and Field Container

As you can see in the preceding screenshot, the data components inside **Fieldset** are grouped inside a box vertically. **Field Container** does not have a designed border, and the inner components can be grouped horizontally.

Button

Allows you to add a custom button inside the object edit modal. The handler of the button must be defined in the component definition.

Text

This component is just a static text box that can be shown in the object edit modal. The HTML text inside the box can be directly defined in the class definition, or you can generate dynamic text specifying the class namespace in the **Custom Renderer Class** attribute.

Preview/Iframe

This component simply lets us render a custom Iframe inside our object edit modal. The Iframe URL must be a relative URL of action inside a controller that extends the `Pimcore\Controller\FrontendController` class.

88　Exploring Objects and Classes

Now that we have discovered all the options for the layout components, let's have a look at the data components.

Data Components

Data components are the concrete attributes of classes. There are tons of available attributes, grouped into different main types, that allow you to model your class according to your needs. In the following screenshot, you can see a panoramic of all types of data components:

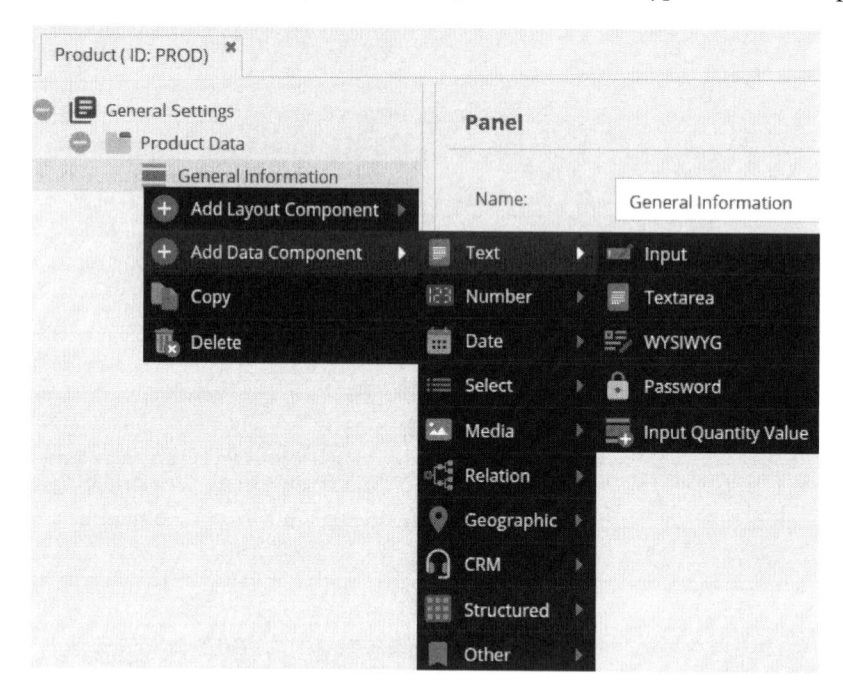

Figure 5.6: Add Data Component

As you can see in the preceding screenshot, there are 10 main data component types, which contain a different number of components. Each component type and every attribute have their specific properties, but all data components have a set of common properties that we explain here:

- **Name**: The name of the attribute. It cannot have spaces or special characters, because this is the name that will be used in the database table column and the PHP class.
- **Title**: The label of the attribute that will be shown in the object edit modal.
- **Tooltip**: Suggested text to explain the meaning of the attribute used to help the user.
- **Mandatory Field**: If checked, makes the attribute mandatory. An object cannot be published if all mandatory fields are not filled in.

- **Indexed**: If checked, creates an index for the field in the database tables.
- **Unique**: If checked, creates the unique constraint in the database tables.
- **Not Editable**: If checked, the attribute becomes read-only.
- **Invisible**: If checked, the attribute is not visible in the object edit modal.
- **Visible in Grid View**: If checked, the attribute is shown in the class' predefined grid.
- **Visible in Search Result**: If checked, the attribute is visible and searchable in the dedicated search modal for the class.
- **CSS Style**: As for layout components, consent to write custom CSS style rules for the component, such as margin or floating position.
- **Width**: The width of the component in pixels.
- **Height**: The height of the component in pixels.
- **Default value**: A lot of field types give the possibility to define a default value. If any value is typed for the field, the default value is saved. If inheritance is enabled for the class, this value is persisted in the database for its children.
- **Default value generator service**: Instead of setting a fixed default value directly on the component, there's the possibility to create a PHP class that dynamically calculates the default value. This class must implement the `\Pimcore\Model\DataObject\ClassDefinition\DefaultValueGeneratorInterface` class, and it is invoked once you open the object to perform the default value calculation.

Now that you have learned about the common properties of all kinds of data components, we will focus on each specific group of components to describe their peculiarities.

Text Components

This kind of component contains basic text input fields. All these components are quite similar and share all the common properties we mentioned before, but there are some differences:

- The **Input** component is the simplest text field. It's not possible to set the input height because it is meant to contain only one line. We can indeed show the character count and add a regular expression validation.
- The **Textarea** component is quite similar to the previous one but allows you to specify the height for your text. As the input component, it's possible to show the character count, bet we cannot add regular expressions.

- The **WYSIWYG** component, as the famous acronym suggests, allows you to insert and edit HTML-formatted text. It's possible to customize the editor configuration by providing a CKEditor configuration in the component definition.

- The **Password** component is an input text with hidden input characters. The column length cannot be chosen because contents are always hashed using the selected algorithm.

- The **Input Quantity Value** field is composed of value and measure units. We will look in depth into this concept in the following section regarding numeric fields.

Number Components

This section contains some simple numeric attributes.

The **Number** component is the simplest numeric field. It's possible to define the decimal size for the database column and the decimal precision for input values. Values can be restricted to be only integers or only unsigned. We can also specify minimum and maximum values.

The **Slider** component stores a numeric value but it renders a sliding cursor to select the value. By specifying min-max values and incremental steps, it's possible to define this slider component.

As mentioned before, the **Quantity Value** component consents to attach measure units to numeric fields, giving the possibility to define concepts such as prices, weights, and so on. To define your units, just go through **Settings | Data Object | Quantity Value** and simply add the units that you need. Units can be added and deleted at any moment, and every operation is auto-saved in the database. In the following screenshot, you will see the **QuantityValue** definition panel:

Abbreviation	Longname	Base Unit	Conversion Factor	Conversion Offset	Converter service
cm	Centimeters	m	0.01		
Kg	Kilograms	(Empty)			
m	Meters	(Empty)			
€	Euro	(Empty)			

Figure 5.7: Quantity value units

As you can see in the screenshot, different units can be related using a static conversion factor or by defining a converter service class; the second option could be useful for conversions that need a formula, such as temperature conversions.

Date Components

These components are designed to contain date and time values. Dates in the database can be stored as a timestamp or a date string.

Select Components

This kind of component lets you define different types of picklists. Some of them come with predefined options, such as **Country**, **Language**, and **User**. Instead, there are three types of custom picklists that we can define. For **Boolean Select**, we cannot define picklist values, but we can customize labels for the two states. **Select** is the most common component of this group. Picklist values can be added, removed, and ordered at any time. Values can be numbers or strings likewise. In the next screenshot, you will see how **Select** options are defined:

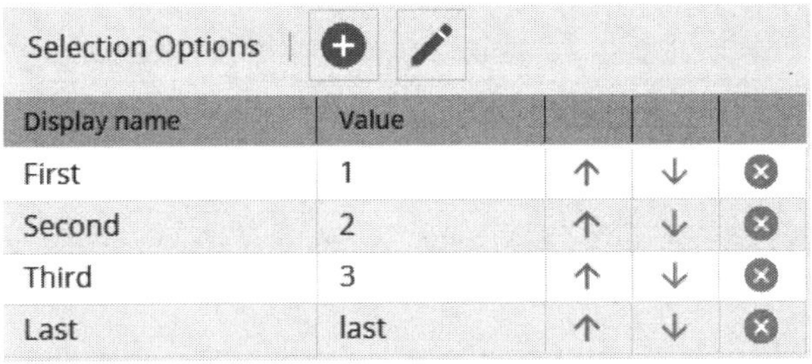

Display name	Value
First	1
Second	2
Third	3
Last	last

Figure 5.8: Select values

As you can see, we can define both the value and display name. Alternatively, you may also define a custom class to provide dynamic options for your field. The behavior of the **Multiselection** component is the same as the previous one, with the difference that we can select multiple values in objects.

Media Components

This set of components permits us to show media files in our class objects. We can link internal assets or external images, create galleries, and show video previews.

We will look into this part in depth in *Chapter 6, Using Digital Asset Management*.

Relation components

These components are used to establish relations between different classes or to link class objects to documents or assets. Note that for assets relations, the asset preview will not be shown in the object like the previously mentioned group of components. All kinds of relations may be many-to-one or many-to-many. For many-to-many object relations, we can choose which fields we want to show in the relation box. We may also use **Advanced relation components** to add custom metadata fields to the relationship.

We will have a look at relation details in the next section of this chapter.

Geographic Components

These particular kinds of fields allow us to search and put marks on a rendered map. You can add a simple geographic point or draw lines and polygons on the map. All points' latitude and longitude are stored in the database.

CRM Components

These components are designed to register customer information in Pimcore. We must pay attention that almost all these components, such as email, for example, have a fixed field name, so it's not possible to add this kind of component multiple times in the same class.

Other Components

This section contains a batch of mixed components.

There are simple components such as **Checkbox** and **Color**, or **Link** to external websites. We can then cite the **Encrypted Field** component, which allows storing encrypted values in the database as long as a secret key has been generated and properly configured.

We have mentioned all components apart from **Calculated Value**, because this particular kind of component is not intended to let the user input a value. By defining a PHP class that extends the `Pimcore\Model\DataObject\ClassDefinition\CalculatorClassInterface` interface, it's possible to dynamically calculate the value for the field, based on other object values. The calculated value is not stored in the database, but the calculation is made every time you open the object and every time the specific getter is invoked.

To summarize, throughout this section we described all different kinds of components. Firstly, we introduced all the common properties of all data components. We then listed different kinds of components, specifying eventual additional properties for each of them. In the next section, we describe a particular type of data component named structured components.

Structured Components

These particular kinds of components are designed to extend the class definition, defining structures or patterns with groups of attributes that can be attached to class objects.

We will see some of these components in action in future chapters regarding Product Information Management and Master Data Management features. Throughout this section, we will describe these components and when they are designed to be used.

Field-Collection

The most used component is **Field-Collection**. You can define your field collection in the same way that we explained for classes. Just go through **Settings | Data Objects | Field-Collection** and simply create a new one by adding layout and data components.

On your class definition, a **Field-Collection** component can allow one or more different **Field-Collection** types. In the class object instances, you can dynamically add multiple instances of the defined field collection to add the same group of attributes multiple times. This kind of component is useful when you have certain properties that can appear with different cardinality in various objects. In the following figure, you can see a schema that outlines how the **Field-Collection** works:

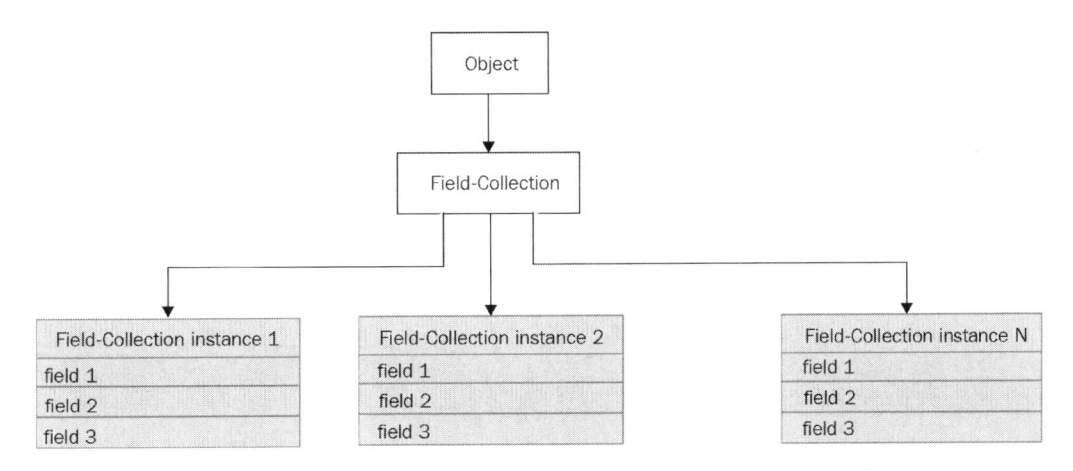

Figure 5.9: Field-Collection

As you can see in the preceding figure, we can add a **Field-Collection** component to the class definition. As we can do for the class definition, in the **Field-Collection** definition, we can add a set of layout and data components. In the class objects, you can add one or more instances of the same **Field-Collection**.

Objectbricks

With **Objectbricks**, unlike **Field-Collection**, objects can be extended without changing the class definition.

Think about a fashion company that wants to store information about their products. We can easily imagine that shirts and shoes will have different attributes. Sure, we could create two different classes for shirts and shoes, but you would need to define redundant fields for properties that are not shared between the two classes.

With **Objectbricks**, we just need to create little sets of attributes to describe specific fields and allow our class to dynamically add these bricks. As the name suggests, class objects can be composed of one or more bricks added to the common attributes.

Similar to classes and **Field-Collection**, just go through **Settings | Data Objects | Objectbricks** to define them. **Objectbricks** is inheritable between parent and child objects.

In the following figure, you can see a schema that illustrates how **Objectbricks** works:

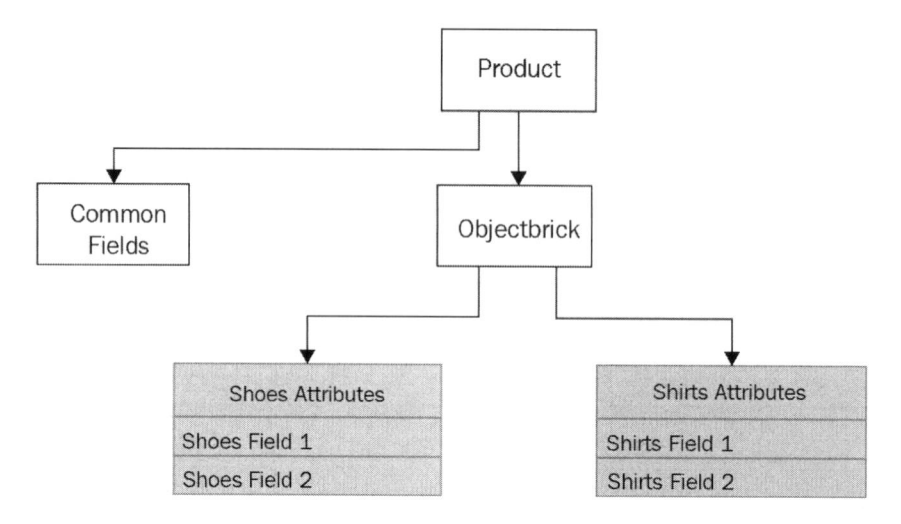

Figure 5.10: Objectbricks

As you can see in the preceding figure, we can add an **Objectbricks** component to the class definition. In the class instances, we can attach one or more bricks to add specific sets of components to the object itself, to give a categorization to the object.

Localized fields

We may also need to define attributes that should be translated into multiple languages within an object, such as titles and descriptions for a multilanguage site. Using the **Localized Fields** component, we just have to insert child components inside and configure languages in **System Settings**. In the following screenshot, we can see how the component is rendered on objects:

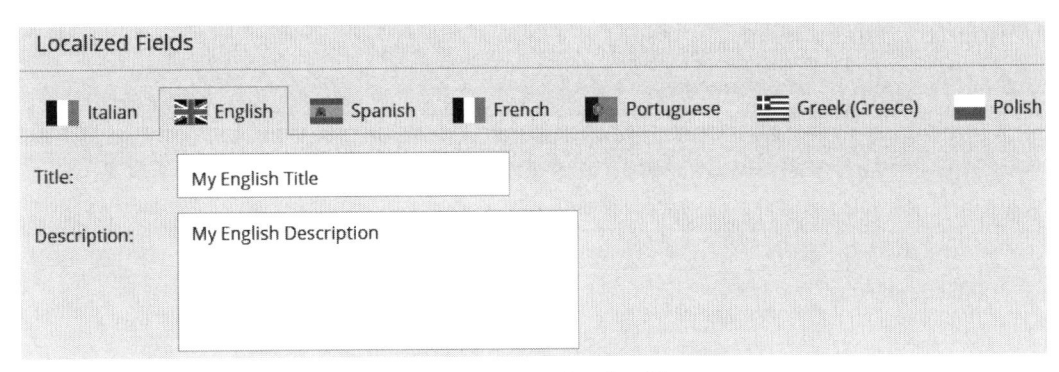

Figure 5.11: Localized Fields

As you can see, a specific tab is added in the component for each defined language.

Block

The **Block** component acts as a simple container for other data components. Similar to **Field-Collection**, an unlimited number of block elements can be created. The block data just gets serialized into a single database column. As a consequence, this container type is not suitable if you are planning to query the data.

Tables

Two other quite simple components are **Table** and **Structured Table**. In a **Table** component, you can dynamically add rows and columns inside objects, or define a fixed number of rows and columns in the component definition. In the database, values for tables are stored in a TEXT field, with column values separated by the pipe character. Structured tables respect the same principle, but rows and columns are always fixed and named.

Classification store

The final and most complex component is **Classification Store**. This component allows you to define a hierarchical key-value pairs structure to dynamically add groups of attributes to class object instances. To define a **Classification Store** component, go through **Settings | Data Objects | Classification Store**. To properly create a classification store, we must define the following:

- **Key Definitions**: Define keys for your classification store. All basic data components are available for that purpose. For each key, we can choose whether it should be mandatory or editable, and other standard properties.

- **Groups**: Select one or more keys to define groups. Within the group, you can define which keys are mandatory and define the order.
- **Group Collections**: Different groups can be grouped into collections. In the object edit modal, we can add one or more of the defined collections.

Now that you have discovered all kinds of data components, in the next section, we will focus on relations, looking in depth into component definitions and providing a concrete example of relations.

Understanding and Establishing Relations

In this section, we will look in depth into how to relate objects with other entities in Pimcore. As we have seen in the previous section, the first step is to add the appropriate fields onto our class to configure relations between two classes, or relations between classes and other entities (such as documents or assets). Here, you will see all the different kinds of relation components:

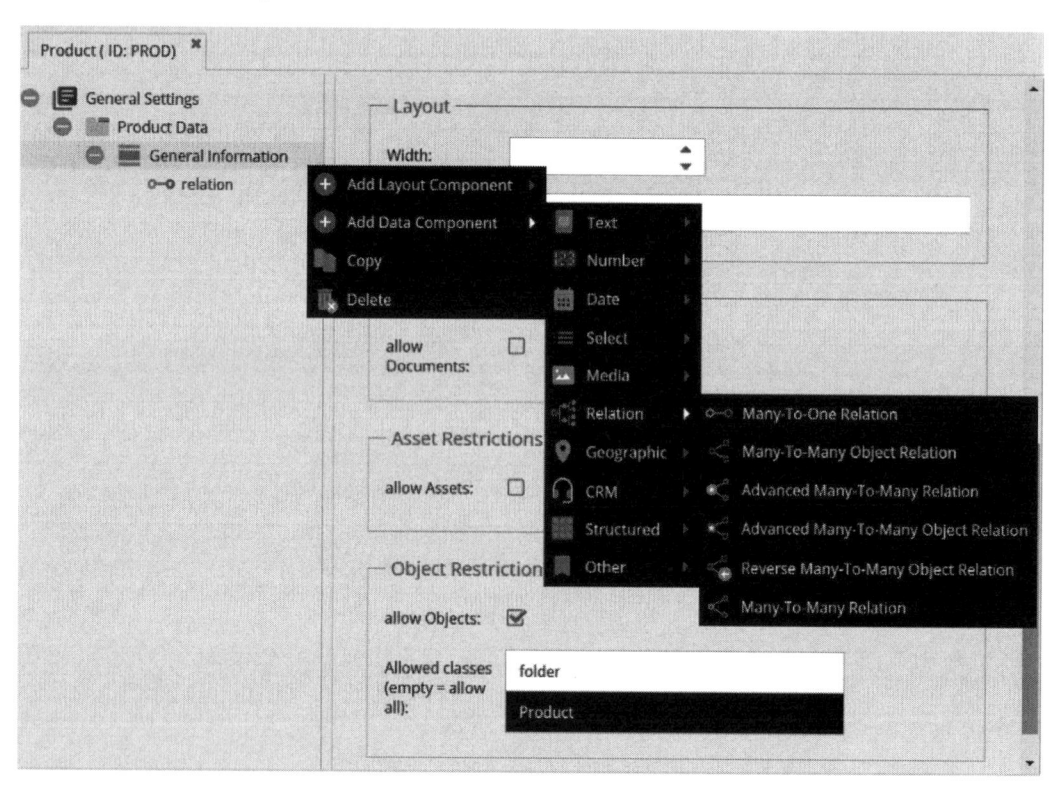

Figure 5.12: Relation components

As you may see, there are two main different types of relation fields, the generic relation fields that allow relating objects, documents, or assets, and specific relation fields for object classes. For each type, we can establish a many-to-one relation, many-to-many relation, or advanced many-to-many relation. The last one lets you define some additional metadata fields that can be attached to the relation instances.

In the following sections, we will focus on the two main types of relation components, which are as follows:

- **Generic Relations**: Relations between an object instance and other entities (this could include another object or instances of assets or documents).
- **Object Relations**: Specific relations between object instances.

Let's see the details of these different types of relations.

Generic Relations

The **Generic Relations** field allows relations between object instances and other previously created entities, which could be either other objects, documents, or assets. It's not possible to decide which properties of related entities we want to show on the object. For many-to-one relations, only the entity path is shown; for many-to-many relations, the ID and entity type are shown as additional information.

Besides, we can provide some limitations to the relation attribute, in particular, the following:

- For documents, we can specify which types are allowed in the relation. If none are selected, all types are allowed.
- For assets, we can specify which types are allowed in the relation. If no specific one is selected, all types are allowed. There is also the possibility to define an upload path for assets that could be directly uploaded through the object.
- For objects, we can specify which classes are allowed in the relation. If no specific one is selected, all classes are allowed.

In the next section, we will focus on the other kind of relation components, the ones specifically used to relate objects.

Object Relations

This kind of relationship is strictly limited to relations between objects. As for the previous group, there is the possibility to limit the relations to one or more classes. The main difference is that we can select which fields we want to show in the relationship within the object element. But if more than one class is selected, only common fields between the involved classes can be selected.

For advanced relations, we can define specific metadata fields for each relation. These fields could be created as one of the basic data types (**Text**, **Number**, **Boolean**, or **Select**) and will be added after the original object fields. Another particular component is **Reverse Many-To-Many Object Relation**. This component could only work if **Many-To-Many Object Relation** was previously configured.

In the following section, through a concrete example, we will see how to practically use relation components to connect objects of different classes.

A Concrete Example of Relations

To provide a concrete example, think about products and categories. We can specify a direct relation between a `Product` class and a `Category` class, and specify a reverse relation in the `Category` class that is related to the direct one. Let's first create a `Product` class. Follow the steps given here:

1. For the first component, add a tabpanel called `Product Data`.
2. Create a panel named `General Information` as a child of the previously created tabpanel component.
3. Add an input field for the product title and then save your class.
4. Create the `Category` class.
5. Then create the `Product` class. Here, create a new panel and add the **code** and **name** fields, and then save the class.
6. Now, come back to the product class and add a many-to-many relation component to relate the `Product` and `Category` classes.
7. On the relation, specify that you want to show **code** and **name** properties, and save the class again.
8. Now, we can add a reverse relation component to the `Category` class. To add this component, we just need to define the class and field for the original relation. Set this component as not editable, to make the reverse relation completely automatic.

In the following screenshot, we can see the final result:

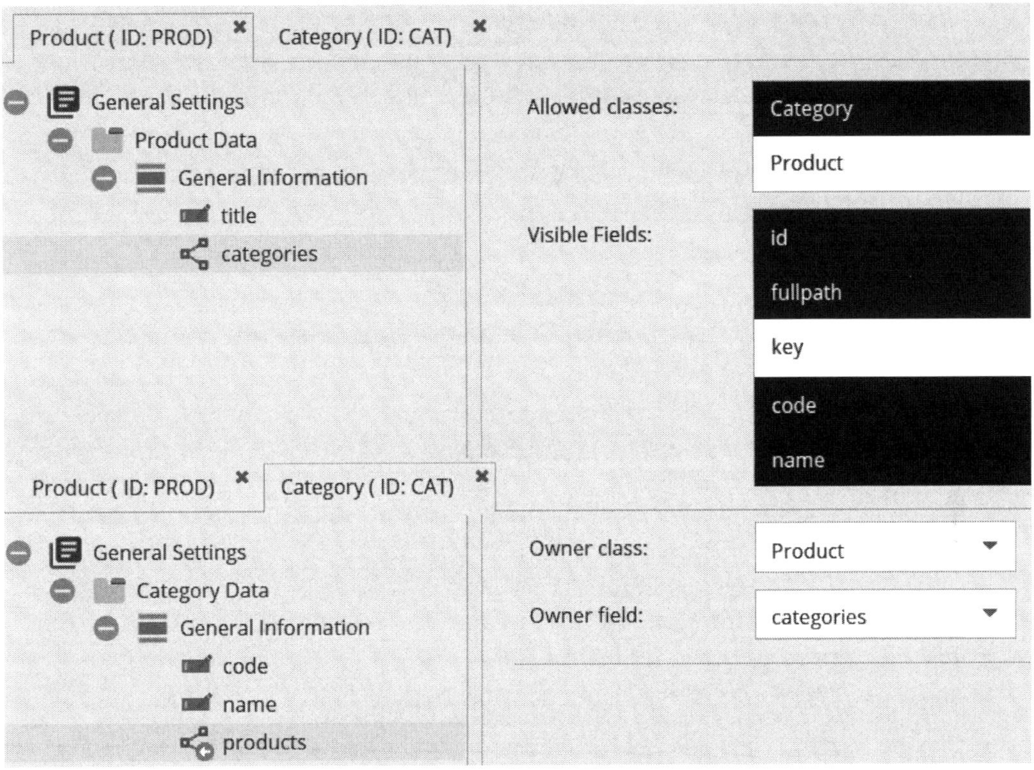

Figure 5.13: Reverse Many-To-Many Object Relation

In the preceding screenshot, you can see how the configured components appear. On the left side, we can see the components that appear in the class configuration tree. On the right side, there are some specific settings of the defined components. On top of that, we can see the many-to-many relation component that relates the `Product` class with the `Category` class. On the bottom, the reverse relation is shown.

In this section, you learned how to relate classes with other entities. In the next section, we will see how these defined relations are reflected in object data entry.

Performing Data Entry

In this section, we will check how class definitions are reflected in concrete object instances, discovering how to create Pimcore objects and perform data entry to fill their information. We will see how to easily create folders and objects, how to relate them, and how to create object variants. Then we will discover how easy and fast it is to add new attributes or edit some existing ones, paying attention to this last point to avoid the loss of data.

Creating Folders and Objects

In Pimcore, unlike what you might think, folders are just instances of a common base class for which we are not able to add custom attributes. It's not mandatory to create folders; think of it just as a helping feature to organize your objects semantically as you do on your PC desktop. Different folders can be nested in a tree structure. To create your first folder, follow the steps given here:

1. Open the **Data Objects** section on the main left panel, and right-click the **Home** element.

2. Select **Add Folder** and type your folder name. As you may see when hovering on that element, Home is a special folder object with **Id** equal to 1. This component cannot be deleted, and it will be the root element for the whole tree structure.

3. Having said that, let's create a Products folder and a Categories folder. Once again, this naming is just needed to separate concepts, but it's not mandatory. You can create all objects within a unique folder, or as direct children of the Home component itself.

4. Right-click on the created folders to add objects inside them, choosing the class and adding the object name. Note that these names are just keys that appear in the tree structure and must be unique within the same folder, but they are completely unrelated to any class data property.

5. With this information, let's create a Product object. As previously defined in the class definition, an input field for the product title can be filled. The relation with categories cannot be done yet, because we need to create categories first.

6. Replicate the previous actions to add a couple of category objects in the dedicated folder, and fill in the information for them. You will see that it will not be possible to select a related product since we have a reverse relation.

7. Switch back to the product and click on the search button in the relation component to select the created categories, and save the product.

8. Refresh the category objects, and see how the relation with the product appears. The result is shown in the following figure:

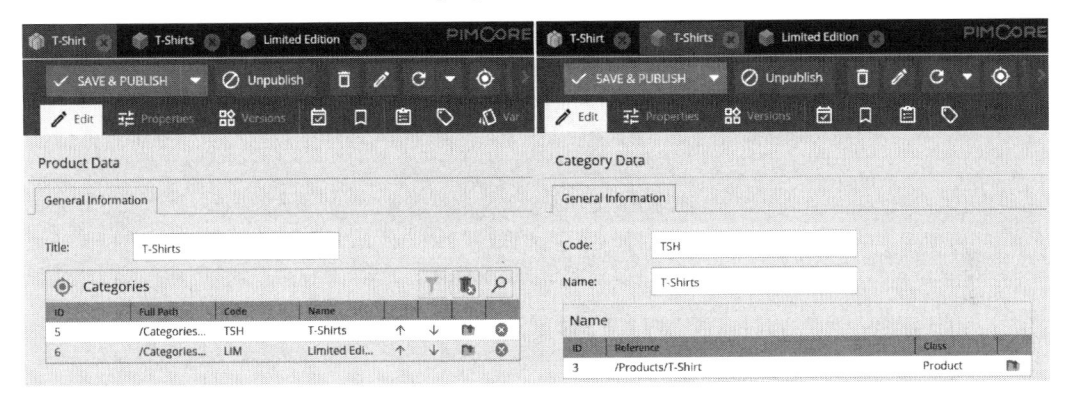

Figure 5.14: Object relations

In the preceding figure, we see clearly how objects are mutually related. As you may see in the direct relation component, the categories attribute that we required in the component configuration is shown in the relation.

In the next section, you will learn how inheritance work and how to add object variants.

Adding Object Variants

If enabled in the class definition, it's possible to add variants for the created objects. To create a variant, just right-click on the previously created object, select **Add Variant**, and type the variant name.

The variants inherit all values from parent properties. As you will see in the following screenshot, inherited values appear as read-only, but it's possible to override the value on variants:

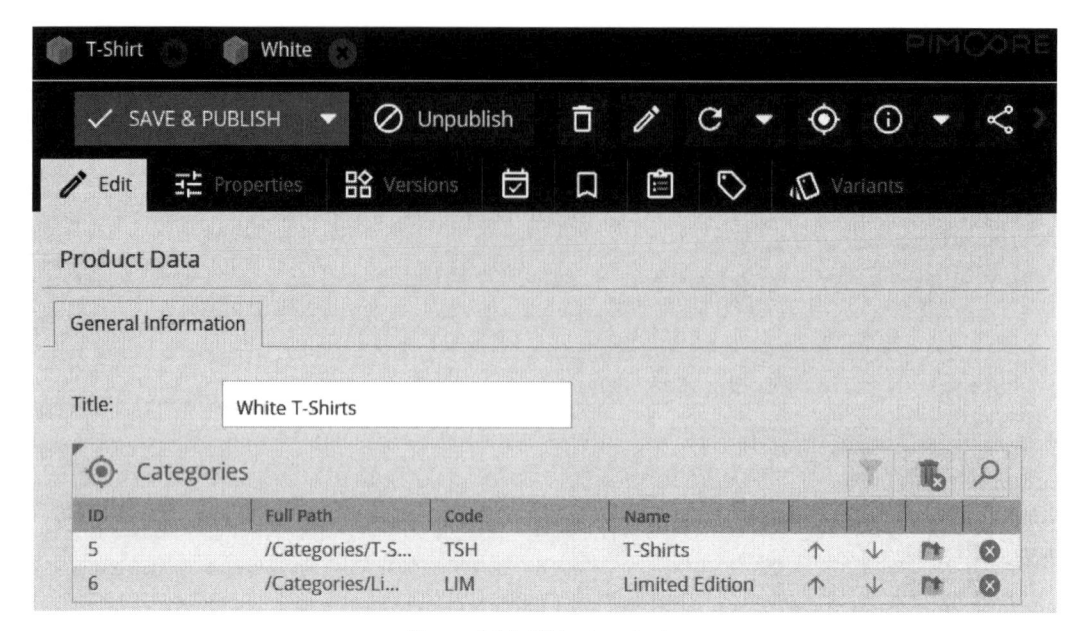

Figure 5.15: Object variants

Variants appear in the object tree structure like other objects, but for each object, it is possible to easily access variants by clicking on the opposite button in the object toolbar.

Editing Classes and Objects

In the *Creating and Editing a Class Definition* section, we saw how easy it is to create a class and add some data components. One big advantage of using Pimcore is that this can be done incrementally since we can add new components or edit existing ones at any time.

Every operation on a class is reflected in the corresponding PHP class and, above all, in the database tables. For these reasons, editing data components could be dangerous and lead, in the worst scenario, to the loss of data. Obviously, if an input component is converted into a relation component, or if a checkbox becomes an image component, loss of data is expected. This is not our focus, but we will point our attention to apparently safe operations that are not safe at all because they could lead to irreversible loss of data. These are covered in the following sections.

Text To Number

Converting a numeric component into a text one will never lead to loss of data because it just alters the database column from decimal to text, and decimal values are valid input for a text column. The opposite flow is not valid at the same. In this scenario, we have three possible cases:

- If the field value is a valid number, the data will be safe.
- If the field value is a mixed number with text, only the "numeric" part is left, removing all content after the first encountered letter or whitespace.
- If the field value is text, the converted value becomes 0.

Let's now see what the risks of changing data types between different kinds of numeric fields are.

Number to QuantityValue

We may think that this operation has no risks because we are just attaching a unit of measure to our numeric value, but this is quite false.

Indeed, in object tables, the original numeric column is dropped with the inevitable loss of data, and two new columns are created. In particular, given a certain "fieldname," we have the following columns:

- `fieldname__value`
- `fieldname__unit`

For this reason, modifying numeric components to `QuantityValue` is discouraged.

Moving a Component to LocalizedFields

If we move a component into LocalizedFields, data of the component is lost. This happens because the database column is dropped from the main object table and created in the specific localized table for each defined language.

In this section, we described different aspects of data entry. Firstly, you learned how to create folders and objects on the object tree, and how to create object variants. Then, you discovered how to prevent data loss during class definition editing, avoiding risky operations on changing component types.

Summary

In this chapter, we learned about the concept of classes. In Pimcore, a class represents the definition of a concept, such as a product or a category. We can add both layout and data components to model our classes and integrate them at any time, along with adding or editing their properties.

We learned that to define a class, it's not necessary to write any code or to create database tables, because Pimcore does all the magic updating the code and database every time you make a change on the class.

We know it's possible to create a custom PHP class that can be extended by one or more classes; this could be useful to add class methods to be used in development. With the same principle, it's possible to define rules to provide default values for class fields or calculate values for particular kinds of components.

We also learned how we can relate different classes, or link assets and documents to class objects using a particular kind of component, and how to define inheritance rules for classes. Then we learned about data entry and how it is made simple by the easy-to-use Pimcore interface; every change in the class definition is immediately reflected on the objects; you just need to refresh.

In the next chapter, we will discover the DAM Pimcore feature, and how it helps us to manage multimedia contents and prepare them for distribution.

6
Using Digital Asset Management

In the previous chapter, you learned what a Pimcore class is and how to create object instances for defined classes.

In this chapter, we will focus on **Digital Asset Management** (**DAM**), which is one of the main Pimcore features. This feature doesn't just let you upload your images like a storage platform, but it also helps you to categorize, elaborate, and version images and, in general, any kind of file, and distribute them across different channels. The chapter is organized as follows:

- What is a DAM?
- Uploading and Relating Assets
- Editing Images
- How to Create Thumbnails

After starting with an explanation of what a DAM is, we will then introduce the Pimcore DAM features. Then, we will discover how to upload digital assets on Pimcore and how to relate them to objects. A specific focus on images will follow, to let you see how images can be edited or enhanced inside Pimcore, and then we'll explore how easy it is to create different thumbnails.

Technical requirements

As you have previously done in *Chapter 5, Exploring Objects and Classes*, all you need to run the demo connected with this chapter is to navigate to the `6. Using Digital Asset Management` folder in the official book repository and start a Docker environment.

To do so, just follow these instructions:

1. Run Docker with the following command:

   ```
   docker-compose up
   ```

2. Then, to restore all the settings on your local machine, just open a new shell and type this:

   ```
   docker-compose exec php bash install.sh
   ```

3. Navigate to `http://localhost/admin` and log in with your admin/pimcore credentials.

You can access the official book repository to get the source code using the following link:

https://github.com/PacktPublishing/Modernizing-Enterprise-CMS-using-Pimcore/tree/main/6.%20Using%20Digital%20Asset%20Management

Now you are ready to navigate the demo to discover all the aspects related to this chapter.

What is a DAM?

In this section, you will learn about the concepts of Digital Asset Management. DAM software is an integrated system designed for the centralized strategic management of media content. It is the software that allows you to create, organize, and distribute content across different channels such as websites and applications and increase the effectiveness of communication.

Now that we know the academic definition, let's see what DAM software is useful for and what its main features are. As the name suggests, DAM revolves around *Digital Assets*; this concept is not intended to be restricted to images or videos but involves all kinds of digital files, such as documents and audio recordings.

So, given the digital assets, let's now move on to the *Management* part of the definition. The management of digital assets is not just intended to organize assets in several folders like on the desktop of your PC; of course, in DAM systems, and thus also in Pimcore, we will always find the concept of folders, but this is just the starting point for structured organization. When it comes to management, DAM is all about being able to search for assets through indexes, share assets between users, and keep track of versioning, with the ability to define workflows to support the life cycle of an asset.

In this section, we will first look at the common characteristics of all DAM systems, then we will present the specific features of the Pimcore DAM system.

Characteristics of a DAM system

Let's see what characteristics must be present in every DAM system.

Organization

As we mentioned before, organization is one of the key aspects of asset management. The first thing that we must consider is creating folders and subfolders in a hierarchical structure. The folder paradigm has become a widespread concept in many different kinds of software and is crucial to organizing content.

However, this in itself is not enough, so it is required to have features to improve content organization, such as categorization through tags or other properties and advanced research methods for filtering and searching for content.

Content Enrichment

Every digital asset is, after all, a digital file. Every file has content that must be shown or downloaded, but there may be the need to provide some information to describe the asset or its content; we can think of these pieces of information as asset metadata.

In very common scenarios, metadata is used to provide an alternative view of a digital asset without showing its content. Let's take images, for example – it is good practice to use an alternative tag on websites to describe visual content with a short piece of text, in case there are connection problems or to improve accessibility for the visually impaired.

In addition to being used to improve accessibility, the correct design of metadata is useful to improve SEO, because it increases site indexing on search engines.

Sharing and Access Control

The use of a DAM system is important to centralize assets information and to share assets between all users that need a copy of an image. Sending and receiving assets through different kinds of distribution channels, such as emails or shared hosting services, is a heavy and dangerous operation because we risk losing files among the hundreds of other received emails or overriding someone else's changes if we upload a modified file in a shared folder.

In a DAM system, every user has its account, and appropriate rules can be defined for file sharing or to limit seeing or modifying assets for certain users or all users with a specific role. These rules could prevent, for example, accidental file deletions.

Versioning

Connected to the previous characteristic, it's important to maintain versioning for digital assets. Every user that has access to an asset in write mode can potentially update it to a new version. Versioning allows you to keep a history of asset changes over time, recording users who have made changes. This concept is useful to implement workflows and moderate the process of asset creation through different approval phases.

Assets Distribution

In modern scenarios, the same assets may be used in different contexts that require different specifications. Thinking about an image, it could be required to be shown on a website and maybe on the corresponding app, and also to be placed in a paper catalog. It seems clear that, for different targets, different image sizing could be required.

To serve this need, different croppings are usually manually created from the same original image. This practice leads to chaos because a lot of different versions must be maintained for the same image; if the original image changes, all croppings must be created again. Modern DAM systems circumvent this problem by letting you upload a high-quality version of the image and define rules to create croppings at runtime when they are needed.

To summarize, in this section, you learned the common characteristics of DAM systems. All these characteristics are implemented on the Pimcore DAM system, and in the next section, we will introduce the Pimcore DAM system, presenting its main features.

Introducing Pimcore DAM features

Previously, we presented the definition of DAM, introducing the main characteristics that a DAM system should have. In this section, we will introduce the Pimcore DAM component and briefly present its main features to discover Pimcore's DAM potential.

Asset Organization

As for object management, Pimcore's user-friendly interface helps users with asset organization. The use of a folder structure to store assets and the ability to search and filter through the grid component, combined with multi-tabbing navigation, makes asset management easy and fast. You can use the simple search options and work within an asset's tree structure, or utilize a grid view to filter by tags, metadata, and other properties that help you to organize the assets.

Pimcore offers a highly flexible and configurable metadata management system. It's possible to define metadata for each specific asset or, if needed, to define common metadata properties that will be attached to all assets automatically.

Pimcore's DAM software supports Office document formats, including Word, Excel, PowerPoint, and PDF. In addition to open source functionalities, enterprise features let you connect Pimcore to Adobe Creative Cloud applications and Microsoft Office software without leaving the application.

Image and Video Conversion

As we mentioned previously, one of the key aspects of DAM is the ability to distribute content among different channels. Those channels could be heterogeneous in terms of target size or media format, and this requires you to produce different versions of the same image or video.

Instead of uploading a bunch of different versions for the same asset, Pimcore gives the ability to upload just a high-definition version and to dynamically generate optimized versions for each target, through an integrated transformation pipeline to convert and transform your files. You will learn more about creating image thumbnails in the final section of this chapter.

The original and transformed images can be served as public links or eventually via content distribution networks or Pimcore integrated APIs. Pimcore's DAM software also provides transformations of images for offline and print channels in the right quality and format.

Users Rights and Permissions

One of the key aspects of DAM is the ability to share assets between different users, so it is important to define sharing rules. In Pimcore, there is the ability to create different users and roles. In the following figure, you will see how to configure rights for users and roles:

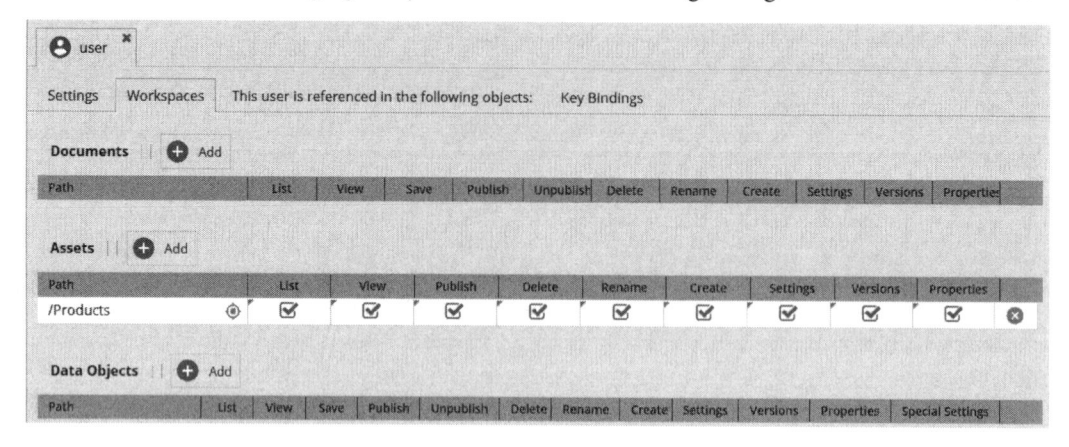

Figure 6.1: User rights and permissions

As you can see in the preceding figure, for each asset folder it's possible to let the user view a list of assets and open each of them. In the same way, the user can have the right to create, edit, or delete assets and alter their settings or properties. The same principle can be applied to documents and object folders. In *Chapter 7, Administrating Pimcore Sites*, you will learn more about users and role management.

To summarize, in this section, you learned about the main characteristics of DAM systems, with an introduction to Pimcore's DAM features. In the following sections, you will see some of these functionalities in action and discover how to use them. In the following section, we will see how to create assets and how to relate them to created objects.

Uploading and Relating Assets

In the previous section, we presented the characteristics of DAM systems, introducing some of Pimcore's specific features. In this section, we are going to see how to upload assets in Pimcore, and then we will see how assets are organized and how to relate assets to existing objects, introducing the various media components for object classes.

Uploading Assets

In this section, we will start discovering how to upload assets in Pimcore. To upload a file, you just need to right-click on an asset folder and hover over the **Add Asset(s)** option to expand the menu. As you can see in the following figure, assets can be uploaded from different kinds of sources:

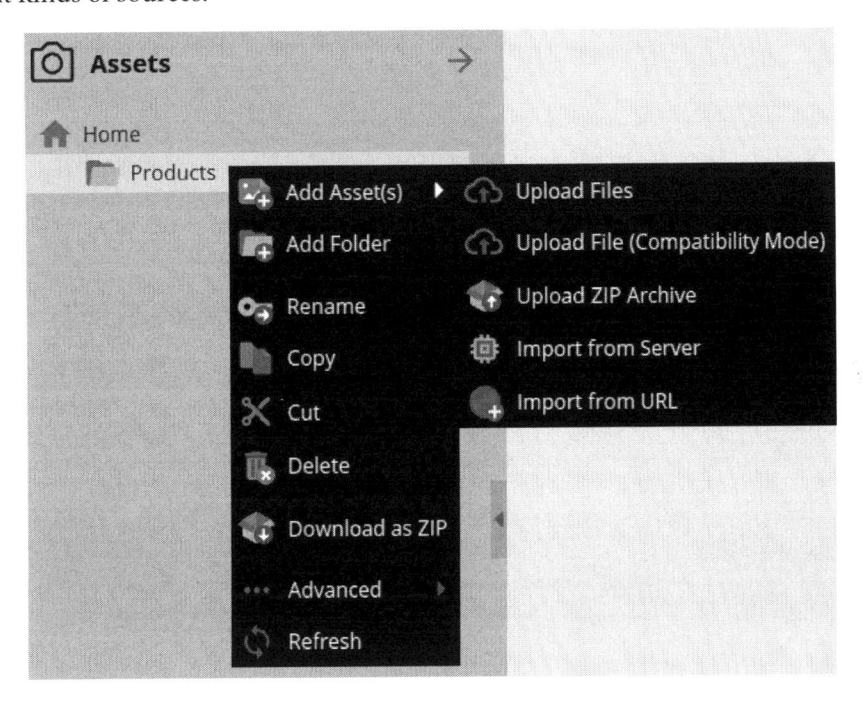

Figure 6.2: Uploading Assets

Let's describe the different methods that are shown in the figure:

- **Upload Files**: This is the standard file upload form, which allows uploading more than 200 file formats. Multiple files can be uploaded together, and they don't need to be of the same type. Images are the most common kind of assets, but also PDF and other Office documents are used. Pimcore can render preview images for most file types.

- **Upload File (Compatibility Mode)**: For older browsers, the previous functionality may not work. If that's the case, you must use this method to upload a single file.

- **Upload ZIP Archive**: This method lets you upload a ZIP file containing your assets. The ZIP file will be automatically unpackaged during the import.

- **Import from Server**: With the previous methods, files must be uploaded by your local filesystem. This functionality lets you select files that are stored within the Pimcore hosting server filesystem. This could be especially useful if files are shared through, for example, an SFTP folder.

- **Import from URL**: Instead of uploading physical files, there's the ability to upload assets just by pasting an external URL. Here, the asset name is extracted by the URL itself.

For each uploaded asset, there is the ability to upload a new version at any time. Ensure that only the standard upload method can be used to upload new versions. Let's now have a look at how to organize uploaded assets.

Organizing Assets

In this section, we will see how assets are organized within a folder and how to list and filter them. Unlike the case with objects folders, for the assets folders, we have two different tabs: the **Preview** tab just shows, as the name suggests, the preview images of the various assets, alphabetically ordered. The **List** tab shows, in turn, a small preview image and the list of asset properties. In the following figure, you will see how this tab looks:

Figure 6.3: Assets list

Looking at the figure, you will notice that, unlike what was shown for object grids in the *Working with the grid component* section of *Chapter 3, Getting Started with Pimcore Admin UI*, there are some extra functionalities. Above the grid, we can see the **only unreferenced** checkbox; if checked, only assets that are not related to objects or documents are shown. Nearby, you can see a button that lets you download the selected items as a ZIP file. Last but not least, to the left of the grid we can find a collapsible section that allows the filtering of assets by tags assigned to the assets. It's important to point out that only assets to which all the selected tags are linked will be shown in the grid.

Let's now have a look at how to relate assets, introducing the various kinds of media components.

Relating Assets to Data Objects

In this section, we will see how to practically relate assets to objects. Firstly, we will present the different kinds of media components that can be attached to classes, explaining the peculiarities of each one. Then, we will see how to upload, search, or drag assets directly on the object. In the following figure, you can see the various kinds of media components:

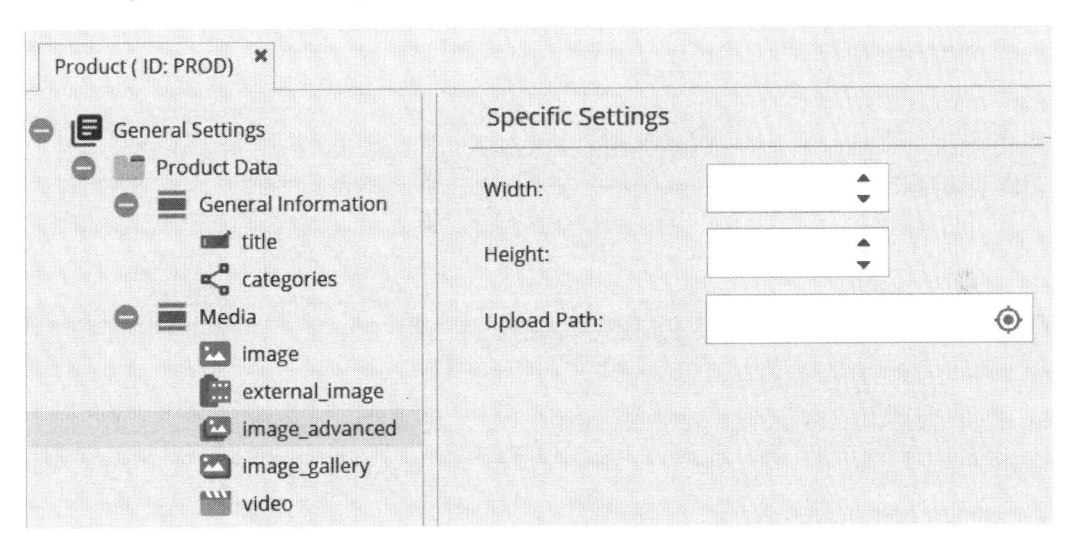

Figure 6.4: Media components in the Data Object Class Editor

Let's describe each field that is shown in the figure:

- **Image**: Allows you to attach an image to an object. As you can see in the previous figure, it's possible to set the component's width and height and to define an upload path for assets that are uploaded directly through the component. The defined path of folders and subfolders will be created at the first upload (if they were not previously created in the asset folders tree).

- **External Image**: Lets you link an external image by providing the image URL, instead of linking a physical asset. In the component settings, you can set the width and height of the image preview.
- **Image Advanced**: This is an extension of a simple **Image** component; this allows you to define and render hotspots, markers, and cropping on the uploaded image. For each hotspot or marker, we can set a name and eventually add one or more pieces of metadata, which could be textual information or relations with other assets, objects, or documents.
- **Image Gallery**: As the name suggests, this component allows you to add an unlimited number of images to create an image gallery, which can be sorted at any time. There is no control over which images are already present in the gallery, so you can potentially add the same image to the gallery multiple times. For each image in the gallery, we can add hotspots and markers as for the previous component.
- **Video**: This allows you to attach a video to the object. This video can be a physical asset previously uploaded on Pimcore, or an external video. For external videos, you must only attach the video ID; the allowed platforms are YouTube, Vimeo, and Dailymotion. For internal video assets, we can attach a poster image by dragging an existing image asset, and provide a title and the description.

Now that we have presented the various media components, let's see how to relate an image to an object. The different ways to make this operation are shown in the following figure:

Figure 6.5: Image relation

As shown in the figure, there are three ways to relate an image in the component:

- **Direct upload**: Upon clicking on the upload icon, the standard upload form will open, letting you upload a file from your filesystem.
- **Search**: Upon clicking on the search icon, a search modal will open, letting you select an image from the previously uploaded ones.
- **Drag and drop**: Just drag and drop an image from the asset tree to attach to the component.

Once the image is attached, you can open the asset directly from the component.

To summarize, in this section, you learned how to upload assets in Pimcore, with a particular focus on different upload methods. Then, you saw how to organize assets in folders and how to filter them to perform searching. In the last part of this section, you discovered the different kinds of media components and how to attach images to those components.

In the next section, we will have a look at the Pimcore internal image editor, and we will see how to enrich images by adding metadata.

Image Editing and Enrichment

In the previous section, you learned how to upload assets on Pimcore and how to relate them to objects. In this section, we will present the Pimcore-integrated image editor and how to perform product enrichment by creating metadata for images. After that, we will see how to set up a focal point for an image.

Exploring the Image Editor

Pimcore integrates a web-based component for image editing. Based on *miniPaint*, the image editor is essential for simple manipulation tasks such as color corrections and cropping. In the following figure, you can see how this editor looks:

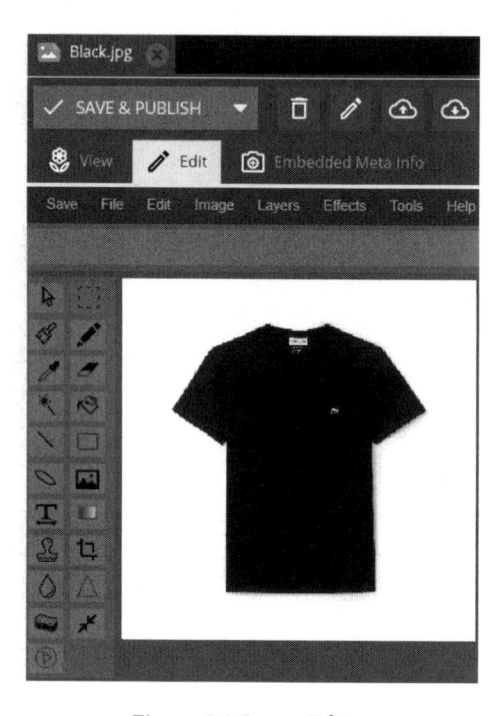

Figure 6.6: Image Editor

As you can see in the figure, in the left menu we find all the common tools of image editors, such as pencil, eraser, text, and so on. Then, in the top toolbar, we can access other features:

- **Save**: This lets you save changes to the image.
- **File**: This lets you upload a new image to replace the current one.
- **Edit**: Here you can find methods to copy and paste a selected area or to undo changes.
- **Image**: Here you can find methods to zoom and resize the image and functions to flip and rotate it. Moreover, there are corrective functions to adjust color brightness and contrast and the tool to get the image palette and histogram.
- **Layers**: Here you can find methods to create and manage different layers of the image.

- **Effects**: Here you can add effects/filters to the image, for example, the **Black & White** filter.
- **Tools**: In this menu, you can find some advanced functions for color replacement, border creation, and calculating key points on the image.

Now that we have explored the image editor, we will see how to define asset metadata.

Defining Assets Metadata

In this section, we will discover how to define metadata for assets. Typically, metadata is used to enhance asset information to describe content without showing it; this could be useful for scenarios in which the content cannot be shown due to poor connection or for accessibility reasons. With images, for example, it is good practice to use an alternative tag on websites to describe the visual content in a short bit of text.

In Pimcore, it's possible to create predefined metadata that could be applied to every asset. You can open the metadata definitions panel through **Settings | Predefined Asset Metadata**. The following figure shows the metadata properties and the different types of metadata that can be created:

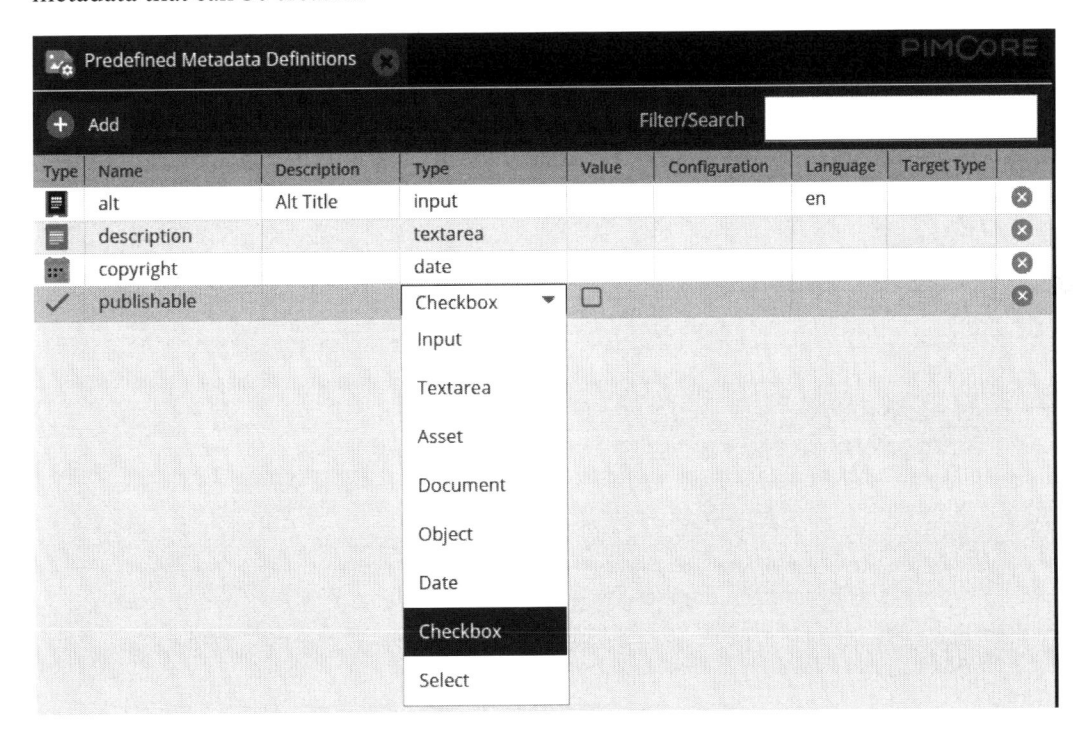

Figure 6.7: Predefined Metadata Definitions

118   Using Digital Asset Management

Let's look at the various properties that we can see in the figure:

- **Name**: The name of the metadata property (there are no unique constraints for this field).

- **Description**: An optional description of the metadata.

- **Type**: We can define simple metadata types such as **Input**, **Textarea**, **Date**, **Checkbox**, and **Select**. As a more complex option, there is the ability to link **Object**, **Document**, or another asset as metadata.

- **Value**: For each metadata, it's possible to define a default value. The type of this value reflects the previously defined type.

- **Configuration**: For select metadata, in this property, we must specify the options that could be selected for the metadata. These options must be comma-separated.

- **Language**: This specifies the language of the metadata.

- **Target Type**: We can specify whether certain metadata is restricted to a specific type of asset. If none is selected, the metadata can be applied to all kinds of assets.

To define new metadata, you just need to click on the **Add** button; all changes are autosaved without the need to click a button.

The predefined metadata can be attached to assets. You can do this by clicking on the **Custom Metadata** tab in the asset window, as you can see in the following figure:

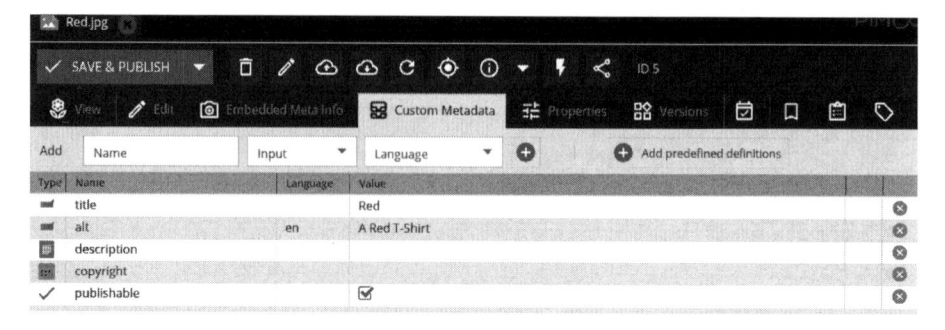

Figure 6.8: Asset Metadata

As you can see in the figure, for each asset, it's possible to create custom metadata. For each bit of metadata, we can define the value and specify the language. The previously created metadata can be attached to the asset by clicking on the **Add predefined definitions** button.

Now that you have learned how to create asset metadata, let's see how to set up focal points in Pimcore images.

Setting up Focal Points

In this section, you will learn how to set up focal points for images. This property can be configured in the image editor by clicking the **Set Focal Point** button, which you can see in the following figure:

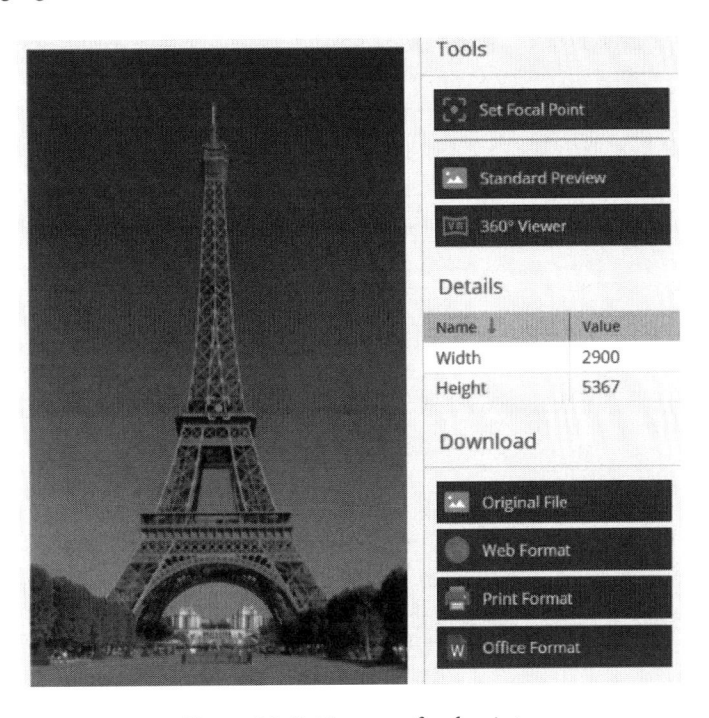

Figure 6.9: Setting up a focal point

As you can see in the previous figure, clicking the previously mentioned button will add a marker to the image. The focal point is placed in the middle of the image by default, but you can drag it to move it to the desired place.

As you will learn in the next section, the focal point can be used to dynamically create image thumbnails to ensure that the focus of the image is on the focal point.

To summarize, in this section, you learned how to edit images through the integrated editor. Then, you learned how to create predefined metadata and how to attach metadata to assets to enrich them, and how to set up focal points on images. In the next section, you will learn how to create images and video thumbnails and how they can be used to distribute assets across different mediums.

Defining and Using Thumbnails

In the previous section, you discovered how to edit images using the internal editor and how to create metadata for assets. In this section, you will learn how to define thumbnails for images and videos in order to distribute them across different platforms.

In a lot of scenarios, the same images must be shown both on a website and a mobile app, and this requires different resizing due to different spatial content organization and the different shapes and sizes of various devices' screens. Uploading different versions of the image as different assets is not the best solution, because if we want to make a change to the original image, we must resize all the images again.

To avoid this problem, Pimcore provides the ability to define transformation rules to dynamically create different thumbnails both for images and videos. We can therefore upload a high-definition version of the assets and define rules to create smaller resizing.

In this section, we will first see how to define rules for thumbnail creation. Then, we will discover how to practically require them on templates and how to dynamically generate public URLs. The physical thumbnail file will be automatically created by Pimcore when a certain thumbnail is requested for the first time.

Defining thumbnails

To define thumbnail generation rules for images, just go to **Settings | Thumbnails | Image Thumbnails**. In the tab that opens, click on the **Add** button, fill in the thumbnail name, and click **Ok** to create a new thumbnail definition.

In the following figure, you can see how the thumbnail definition panel appears:

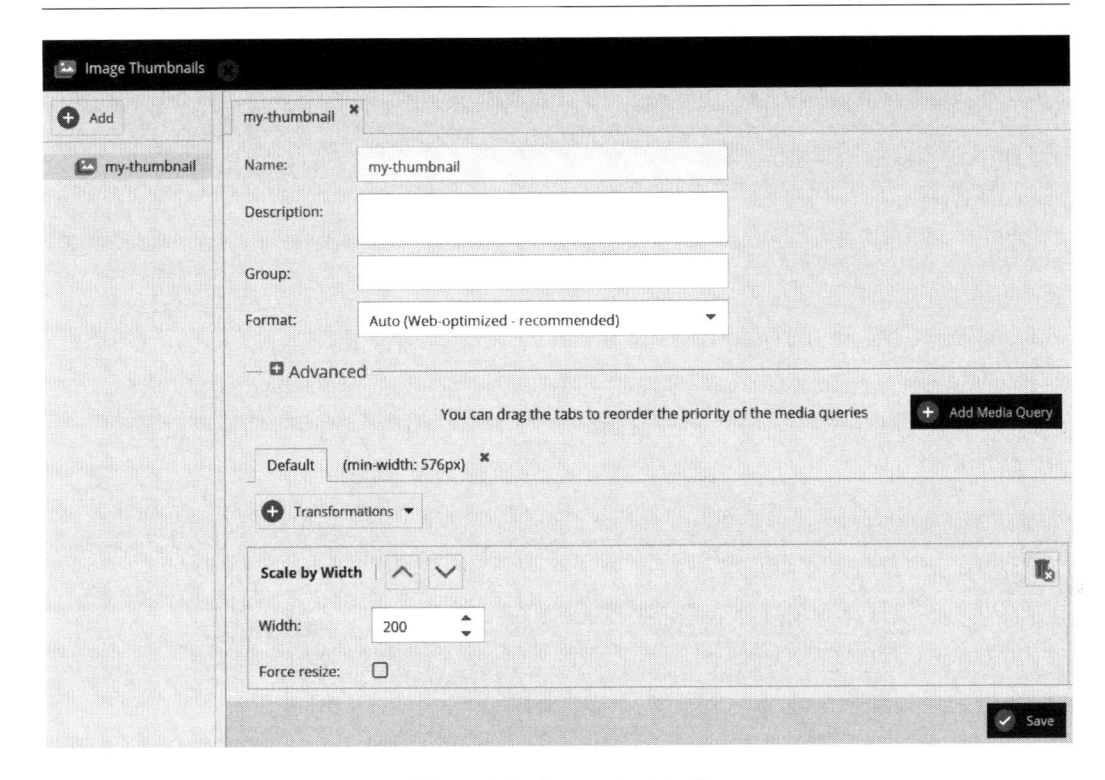

Figure 6.10: Image thumbnail

As you can see in the previous figure, the thumbnail definition name is the one that was defined on creation; this name acts as a unique identifier within the thumbnail definitions, and it's not possible to rename a thumbnail definition. Thus, we can add a description for the thumbnail and group multiple thumbnails in a folder.

The first relevant property is the output format. We can choose to keep the original image format, to produce a web-optimized image, or we can force the output format to be PNG, JPG, GIF, or TIFF. In the **Advanced** settings, we can set extra properties to define the image quality and resolution for JPEG and print formats.

At the bottom of the screen, you can see the **Transformations** definitions pipeline. For each thumbnail, we can define one or more transformations, which will be performed in the defined order from top to bottom. You can choose from a large set of transformations to perform cropping, resizing, rotating, or color filtering. In the previous image, for example, we have defined a transformation to scale the image by width, giving the maximum width in pixels and maintaining the image ratio. If we enable the **Force resize** checkbox, we force the generation of a thumbnail with the desired width; this also works when the original image is smaller than this width. Besides, it's possible to apply different transformations for different media queries, to dynamically adapt the image aspect based on screen size.

Once you have defined the transformation pipeline, just click on **Save** to persist the thumbnail definition.

What has been said for image thumbnails is also valid for video thumbnails. In the following figure, you can see how a video thumbnail definition appears:

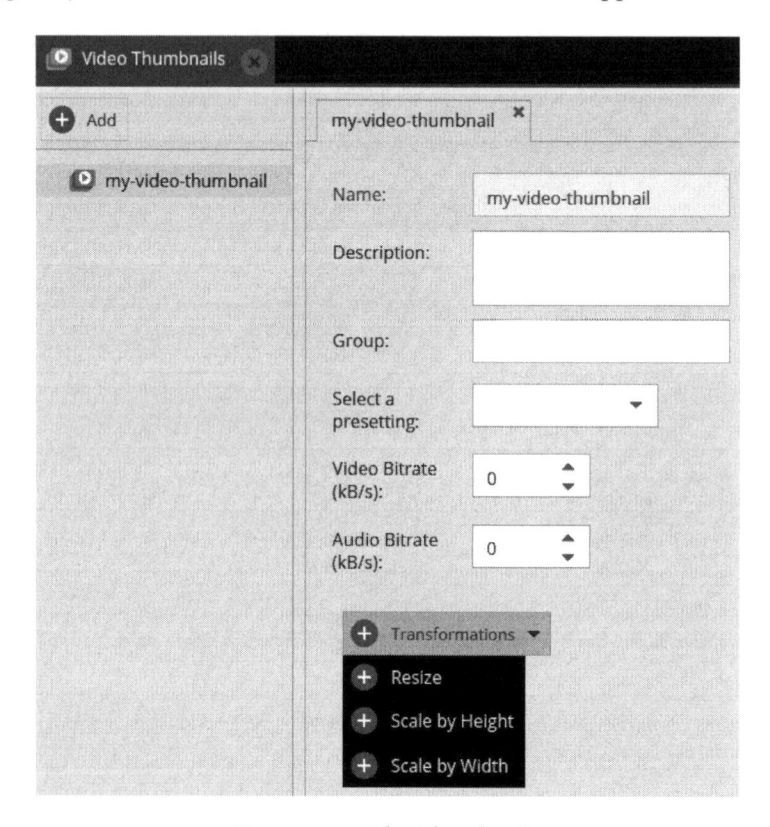

Figure 6.11: Video Thumbnails

As you can see in the figure, there are a limited number of possible settings for videos compared to images. Basically, for video thumbnails, we can define bitrates and scaling operations.

Now that you have learned how to create thumbnail definitions, let's have a look at how to define a thumbnail that uses an image's focal point.

Focal point on thumbnails

In the *Setting up focal points* subsection of the *Image Editing and Enrichment* section, you learned how to set up focal points for images.

As mentioned in that subsection, focal points can be used to define a particular kind of thumbnail transformation. In the following figure, you can see how to set up this transformation:

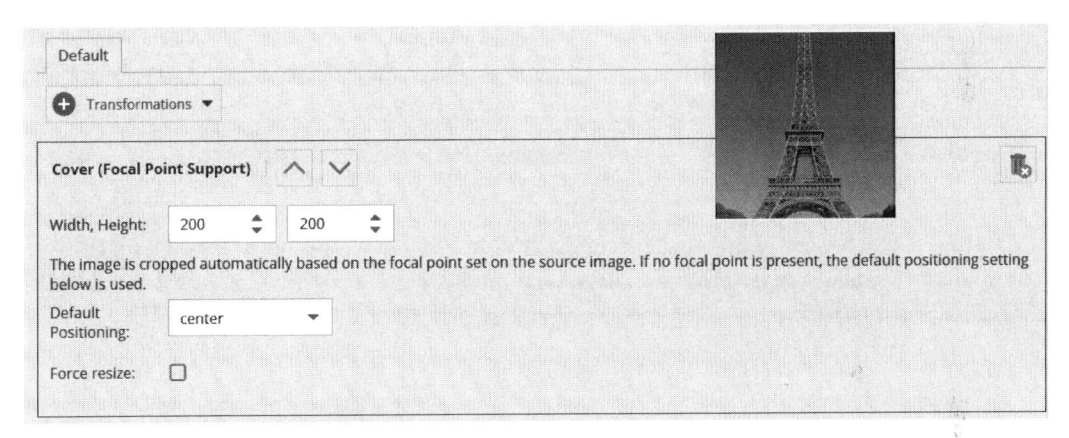

Figure 6.12: Thumbnail Cover Transformation

As you can see in the previous figure, you can add a **Cover** transformation, which supports the usage of the focal points. This kind of transformation will create a cropped image centered by the focal point. The size of this thumbnail is defined through the **Width** and **Height** parameters.

If no focal points are set for the image, the **Default Positioning** parameter will let you create a cropped image placed in the defined position.

In the next section, we will see how to invoke thumbnails on templates and how to dynamically generate a public thumbnail URL.

Using Thumbnails

In the previous section, you learned how to define thumbnails for images and videos. In this section, we will see how these thumbnails can be used in template and backend development. Then, we will show you how to dynamically generate public URLs to retrieve thumbnails in external applications.

Usage Examples

Let's show some code tips to explain how to use thumbnails. First of all, you need to get an instance of an asset; this lets you call the `getThumbnail` method, as we will show you here:

```php
<?php
    use Pimcore\Model\Asset\Image;

    $image = Image::getByPath("/Path/To/The/Image.jpg");

    $myThumbnail= $image->getThumbnail("my-thumbnail");
?>
```

In the previous code snippet, we can see how to retrieve an image thumbnail given the name of a previously created thumbnail definition. This method also permits the creation of a custom thumbnail definition on the fly, passing the thumbnail configuration as an input, as we can see in the following snippet:

```php
<?php
    use Pimcore\Model\Asset\Image;

    $image = Image::getByPath("/Path/To/The/Image.jpg");

    $customThumbnail = $image->getThumbnail(["width" => 500,
    "format" => "png"]);
?>
```

As we can see, we can create a custom thumbnail by setting basic configuration options like `width` and `format`.

The retrieved thumbnail can be placed in HTML templates. As we can see in the following snippet, one option is to set the source property for an image tag:

```
<img src="{{ image.thumbnail('my-thumbnail').path }}" />
```

The `getPath` method retrieves the filesystem path and can be used to set the image tag source; this method is called automatically if omitted because it's called by the implicit `__toString` function.

As an alternative, we have the option to let the thumbnail generate the HTML tag itself:

```
{{ image.thumbnail('my-thumbnail').html({'class' => 'my-css-class', 'alt' => 'The image alt text'}) }}
```

The `getHtml` method returns the image HTML tag; as an input of this method, we can pass an array of properties that will be applied to the tag. This could be useful to dynamically add a CSS class or data properties such as alternate text.

If you are using media queries in your thumbnail configuration, the `getHtml` method will return a picture HTML tag instead. If you want to require the image tag for a specific format, you can use the `getMedia` function, as you can see in the following code snippet:

```
{{ image.thumbnail('my-thumbnail').getMedia("(min-width: 576px)").html}}
```

The defined image thumbnail definitions can also be used to show a preview image of a video when we need to insert a video asset in a template. In the following snippet, we can see how to acquire these snapshots:

```
<?php
    use Pimcore\Model\Asset\Video;

$asset = Video::getById(123);

    echo $asset->getImageThumbnail("my-thumbnail");
    echo $asset->getImageThumbnail(["width" => 250], 20);
?>
```

As we can see in the code, the `getImageThumbnail` method accepts a thumbnail definition name or an inline configuration as an input. As a second parameter, we can specify which second of the video we want to take a snapshot of.

All these examples show how to use assets internally, but every asset in Pimcore has also a public URL, and the same goes for thumbnails. Let's see how to dynamically generate a thumbnail URL given asset information.

Downloading Thumbnails

Pimcore thumbnails are dynamically generated the first time they are requested for download or when they have to be shown on a page. To make a thumbnail downloadable from the asset details panel, you must check the **List as option in download section on image detail view** flag on the thumbnail definition. As we can see in the following figure, all thumbnails with this option enabled are listed in the **Download Thumbnail** dropdown on the detail view of an asset:

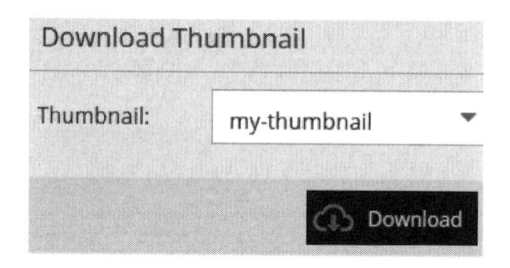

Figure 6.13: Download Thumbnail

To download a thumbnail, you just need to select the desired thumbnail definition from the dropdown that you can see in the figure and click the **Download** button.

Thumbnails can be also accessed and downloaded through a web browser by their public URLs. These URLs come with a fixed rule to define them. Let's look at the following example URL:

```
https://your-pimcore-url.com/Path/To/The/image-thumb__123__my-thumbnail/Image.jpg
```

Let's explain all the parts that compose the previous URL:

- **https://your-pimcore-url.com**: This is the base URL of your Pimcore installation.
- **Path/To/The**: This is the path of folders and subfolders in which the image is contained.
- **image-thumb**: This is a fixed part of the URL to specify that you require a thumbnail.

- **123**: The ID of the asset. It's preceded and followed by two underscores.
- **my-thumbnail**: The name of the thumbnail definition.
- **Image.jpg**: The name of the image.

Using this pattern, you can dynamically generate public URLs for all the thumbnail definitions starting from the image path and ID.

To summarize, in this section, you learned how to define different thumbnails for images and videos by defining a pipeline of transformation rules. Then, you saw some code examples showing how to practically use thumbnails during development. In the last part, you discovered how to dynamically generate the public URL for a thumbnail to make it downloadable.

Summary

In this chapter, we introduced Pimcore's **Digital Asset Management** (**DAM**) feature. After defining the common characteristics of all DAM systems, we presented how these characteristics are implemented in Pimcore.

We then learned how to upload assets in Pimcore, selecting various formats of files from different kinds of sources, which could be offline or online. Then, we learned how to organize assets using folders and tags and how to relate assets to objects. In particular, we presented the different data components that can be used to attach assets to objects.

After that, we saw how to edit images through the integrated editor and how to enhance image content by defining metadata for them. In particular, we learned how to create predefined metadata definitions and how to define custom metadata for each asset.

We then focused on asset distribution, learning how to create thumbnail definitions for images and videos. We saw how to practically use thumbnails in development, showing some code snippets, and how to dynamically generate public URLs for thumbnails.

In the next chapter, we will cover the administration of Pimcore sites, explaining how to install third parties' plugins and how to manage users and roles.

7
Administrating Pimcore Sites

In the previous chapter, we learned how to manage images, thumbnails, and assets in Pimcore, using the DAM feature. In this chapter, we will start by seeing how it is possible to enhance Pimcore features through the use of bundles, which are packages created by the Pimcore team or by third-party developers and can be easily installed.

Another fundamental feature that cannot be missed is the organization of users and their permissions. To limit the functionality of the site in the administration and content management sections, we will learn how roles are created, how permissions are created for roles, and how they are assigned to users.

We will also see how it is possible to import and export the settings of our Pimcore installation to other environments. Finally, we will get a little familiar with the Pimcore console, a powerful and useful tool to be able to execute commands, without having to access the web administration panel.

We will cover the following topics in this chapter:

- Installing a bundle
- Exploring Users and Roles
- Managing perspectives

- Importing and Exporting Pimcore settings
- Using the Pimcore Console

By the end of this chapter, we will have learned how to add functionality to our site by installing bundles, configure access to users with different roles and permissions, import and export settings and classes, and use the Pimcore console via the command line.

Technical requirements

To follow this chapter, the only requirement is to have an up and running Pimcore installation and be able to access it via the command line.

If you have installed Pimcore with Docker, just run these simple instructions:

1. Run Docker with the following command:

   ```
   docker-compose up
   ```

2. It is possible, but not necessary, to restore the local installation settings by running this command:

   ```
   docker-compose exec php bash restore.sh
   ```

Navigate to `http://localhost/admin` and log in with your admin/pimcore credentials.

Now you are ready to put into practice all the aspects related to this chapter.

Installing a bundle

In this section, we will see how you can add features to Pimcore with the use of bundles. We will then see what a bundle is and how to install it in a few simple steps.

Pimcore offers many features already pre-installed and ready to use, but while these may be sufficient for our needs, it is possible to need additional features that are not available in Pimcore. No problem, because the framework provides a quick and easy way to install new features. Adding functionality to the framework is done by installing packages, or **bundles** in the Pimcore world, just like in other systems, where they can be identified as plugins, modules, or add-ons. A bundle, in other words, is a package that contains additional components or features that will increase the functionality of Pimcore.

Installing a bundle

Installing a bundle is a relatively easy operation; let's proceed step by step.

The first thing to do is to identify a bundle to install according to our needs. There's a dedicated page for this on the official Pimcore site, where you can find a large number of bundles, many created by the Pimcore development team and others by third-party developers. This is the link to this page, which is called the Pimcore Marketplace: `https://Pimcore.com/en/developers/marketplace`.

We can see how the marketplace looks in the following screenshot:

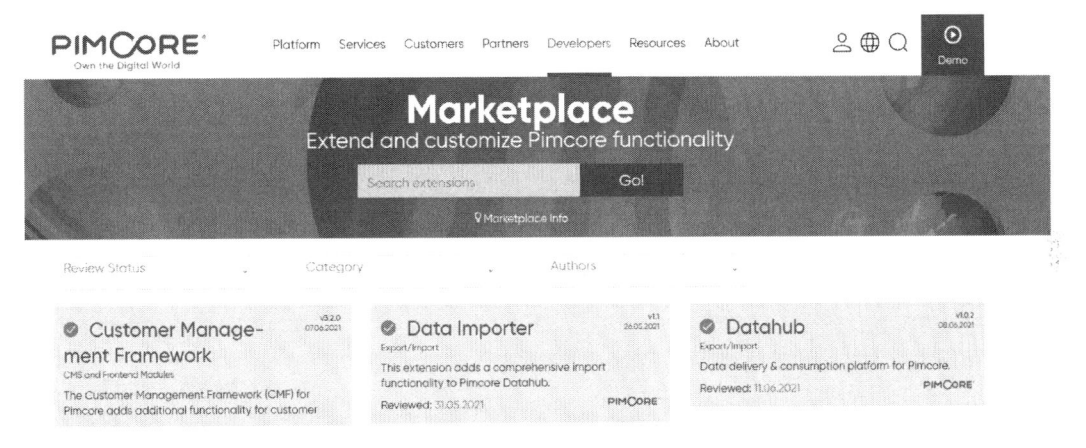

Figure 7.1: Pimcore Marketplace

As we can see in the previous screenshot, it is possible to do a search and filter the search results.

Now we just have to look for what we need. For this chapter, we can assume we need a bundle that allows us to generate continuous numbers. Even if the bundle we are going to install will not add many features to our Pimcore installation, the procedure remains valid for every bundle that we will have to install, regardless of its features.

After a simple search, we found a bundle that will be right for us. The bundle is called **Number Sequence Generator**, developed by the Pimcore team. In the next screenshot, we see what the page looks like with the search carried out and the results:

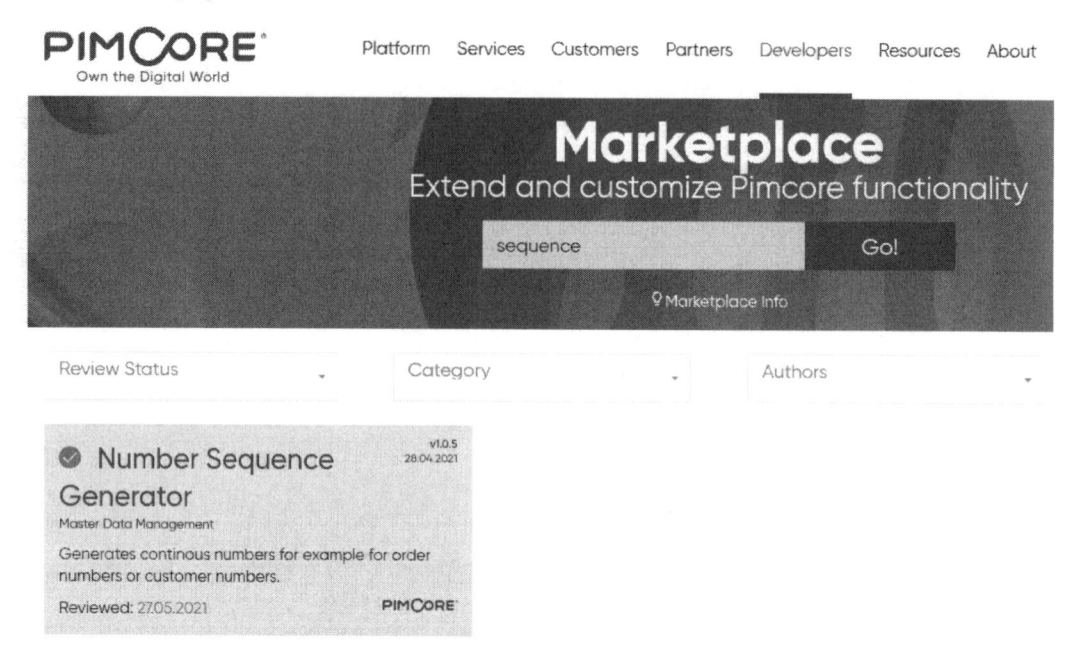

Figure 7.2: The Pimcore Marketplace page with a search performed

As we can see in the preceding screenshot, we got a list of results with our search. The search results are represented with cards, where we can read a brief description of the features that we will introduce with the installation of the bundle. There is also other useful information, such as the version number, category, name of the developer, whether it is a reviewed version, and when it was last reviewed.

Now, just click on the bundle and go to the details page. Among all the additional information that we find on the page, click on the **GET IT NOW** button. This is a link that will send us to the bundle's source code page.

So, let's go a bit further and begin with the installation procedure. It's nothing complicated, but compared to other plugin installation systems, such as WordPress or other similar systems, it requires some additional steps. So, get ready to get your hands a little dirty, and follow these steps:

1. Locate and open the `composer.json` file in the source file repository. In our case, the file looks like this:

```
{
    "name": "Pimcore/number-sequence-generator",
    "license": "GPL-3.0+",
    "type": "Pimcore-bundle",
    "config": {
        "sort-packages": true
    },
    ...
}
```

While familiarity with the `composer.json` file is certainly useful, in this case, the only thing we are interested in is retrieving the bundle name to install it. We find this by scrolling up the file to the `"name"` property.

Now that we know the name of the bundle to install, we need to execute one simple command, and `compose` will do everything for us. To do this, we need to access our command-line installation. If you do not use Docker, just open a shell on the machine where Pimcore is installed. Otherwise, you first need to access the container where Pimcore runs.

2. To do that, type the following command:

```
docker-compose ps
```

The output of this command shows a list of all the Docker images up and running on the machine, formatted as a table; we are interested in the second column, NAME, related to the Pimcore image.

3. Once you have recovered the container ID of the image where Pimcore runs, type this command:

```
docker-compose exec   xxxxxxxxxxx bash
```

Here, xxxxxxxxxxxx is the container ID retrieved from the previous command.

4. Once you are in, run this command:

```
composer require pimcore/number-sequence-generator
```

The preceding command produces some lines of output in the console where it was run because `composer` downloads and installs the packages needed to add the new bundle. The output of the command can be longer or shorter, depending on the number of packages that need to be installed or whether they are already installed and need to be updated. At the end of the process, the last few lines in the console should look like this:

```
... (previous console log lines)
Trying to install assets as relative symbolic links.
--- --------------------------------------- ------------------
        Bundle                                Method / Error
--- --------------------------------------- ------------------
        FOSJsRoutingBundle                    relative symlink
... (some other bundles)
--- --------------------------------------- ------------------
 [OK] All assets were successfully installed.
```

If the installation was successful, we will have installed a new bundle in our Pimcore. We just have to go and configure it.

By following the **Tools | Bundles** menus, you can access the bundle configuration page. In the next screenshot, we see what this page looks like:

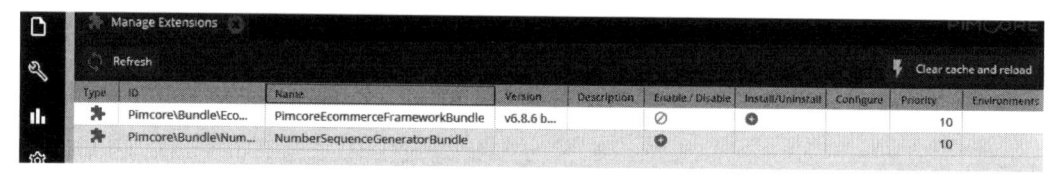

Figure 7.3: The Pimcore bundle management page

As we can see in the preceding screenshot, we have two bundles installed; the one on the second line is the bundle we just installed.

Before completing the installation of the bundle, let's stop for a moment and analyze the columns that we see in the table in *Figure 7.3*.

We can see that there are two types of columns:

- **Information columns**, which include **ID**, **Name**, **Version**, and **Description**.

- **Action columns**, which contain action buttons. In particular, the two columns that are of interest to us are the **Enable/Disable** and **Install/Uninstall** columns, and their action buttons.

First of all, we need to enable the bundle. To do that, click on the + icon in the **Enable / Disable** column, and proceed to enable the bundle. This action will take a few seconds, and when it is finished, a modal will appear on the screen, indicating that the enabling operation was successful.

Now we are ready to install the bundle. Before moving on to this step, we need to clear the cache. You can do this easily by clicking on the button at the top right: **Clear cache and reload**. The cache cleaning operation is necessary because Pimcore extensively uses caches for different types of data, including bundle files and their configurations. It is not recommended to complete the operation without first clearing the cache and then reloading the page.

After clearing the cache and Pimcore has reloaded, we can return to the bundle management page to verify the correct status of the bundle.

Now that we have enabled the bundle, an icon with + appears in the **Install/Uninstall** column, as shown in the following screenshot:

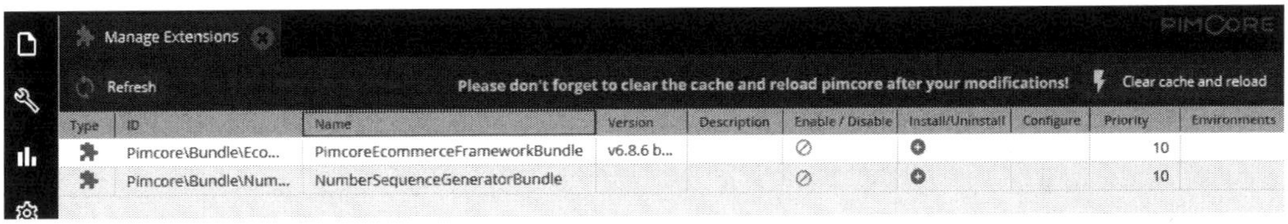

Figure 7.4: The Pimcore bundle after being enabled

As we can see from the preceding screenshot, it is now possible to click on the + icon in the **Install/Uninstall** column of the new bundle to start the installation process.

As for the enabling action, the system notifies us of the result of the operation through a modal containing some information on the operation that was just completed.

Once again, Pimcore reminds us that we need to clear the cache and reload Pimcore. Let's do this for the last time, and the bundle installation is complete.

Now that we have successfully installed the new bundle, we can take advantage of its features. The bundle we have chosen for this chapter allows us to generate continuous numbers, for example, for order numbers or customer numbers. We will not see how this feature works in detail because the purpose of this section is to learn how to install and manage bundles.

In the next section, we're going to see how users and roles are created, and how a user can be profiled to limit access to content.

Exploring Users and Roles

In this section, we will see how we can manage users and their permissions, to limit the functionality of the site in the administration and content management sections. We will see how roles and permissions are created and how they are assigned to users.

During the creation of a site, we often have to manage different parts with different importance. In addition to this, it is possible to differentiate the work we do in the organization. The administration part of the site is important and concerns the creation or editing of contents.

Generally, the part concerning the maintenance and management of the site is the responsibility of the administrator. Thus, tasks such as managing languages, configuring routing rules, or creating users and installing bundles are done by expert users who have the required skills and knowledge, and the privileges to do such actions are dependent on the administrators. The content, on the other hand, is often the responsibility of other people such as the **users**, often defined as editors or publishers. Once we become aware that the management and maintenance of a site pass through several users, we can therefore take another step and define some basic notions that concern the rules of *who does what*.

As we have already mentioned, there are different types of users: in our example, we talked about administrators, who manage the configuration parts of the site, and editors or publishers, who enter the content. This distinction, although valid, is however limited because just as in a real company, where there are many people with many different tasks and responsibilities, even on a site, there can be many users with many different roles and responsibilities.

So, how do we distinguish the users who access the site, and above all, how can we allow these users to be able to see and modify certain information that we want them to work on? The answer to this question is simple: through roles.

But what are roles? A **role** is essentially a set of permissions. If we wanted to create a role for a publisher, referring to the previous example, we would have to put within this role the permissions to create and modify content such as web pages, products of a shop, or articles of a blog. Once the role has been created, it will be possible to give this role to one or more users of the site, effectively allowing these users to do the actions that the role allows.

Setting Users and Roles

In Pimcore, as well as in almost all systems that allow access to multiple people, it is possible to create users and roles and to relate the two entities. For this purpose, there are dedicated sections in the Pimcore **Settings** menu: **Users** and **Roles**.

Following the **Settings | Users** menu, Pimcore opens a page with a list of registered users. On this page, we can delete, modify, or create new users. To open the role management page instead, simply follow the link in the **Settings | Roles** menu. Here, we will find the list of roles created in the system, and the possibility of modifying, deleting, or creating new ones.

By clicking on a user, the **Configuration** tab will open, where you can add or change information such as **Firstname** and **Lastname**, **Email**, and **Language**, as shown in the following screenshot:

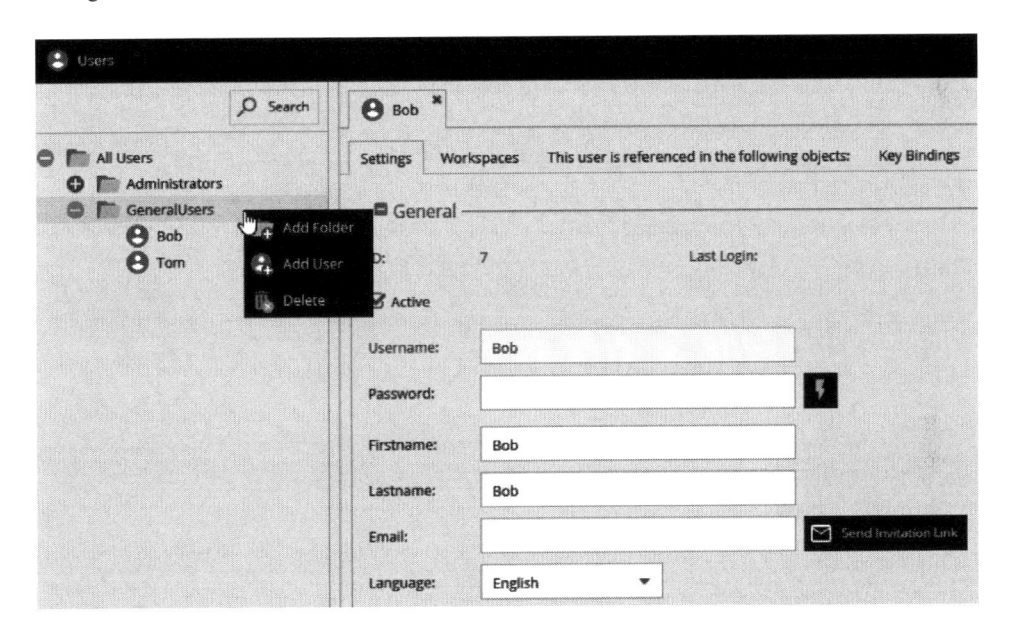

Figure 7.5 – Administration pages for users

In the previous screenshot, we can see the user administration page; by right-clicking the left menu, a pop-up context menu will appear where you can create or delete a user. The role administration page has the same layout and functionality as the user administration page.

In Pimcore, there are two levels of user permissions:

- Permissions on system components
- Permissions on data elements (assets, objects, and documents)

Permissions can be granted to roles or individual users. It is not mandatory to use roles; permissions can be granted to users directly instead. However, it is advised to use roles if there is a larger user group to manage. In the **User/Role** settings tab, inside the **Permission** section, it can be decided which permissions are granted to that user or role. An individual user has a few more general settings than the role.

So, let's see how to assign permissions to users. Take a look at how the user configuration page is defined. As you can see in *Figure 7.5*, the page is divided into four tabs. Describing them all in detail would take a long time and is beyond the scope of this chapter. For our purpose, we will keep the focus on the **Settings** and **Workspaces** tabs.

In particular, the **Settings** tab is divided into sections:

- **General**: Configures the account user
- **Admin**: Grants administrator role to the user
- **Permission**: Sets which system role to grant to the user
- **Allowed types to create**: Selects the classes allowed to be created
- **Editor Settings**: Selects the language for the user
- **Shared Translation Settings**: Manages shared translations

So, let's start with the configuration of user settings. By clicking on the + icon, you discover the various configurations for each section, as we can see in the following screenshot:

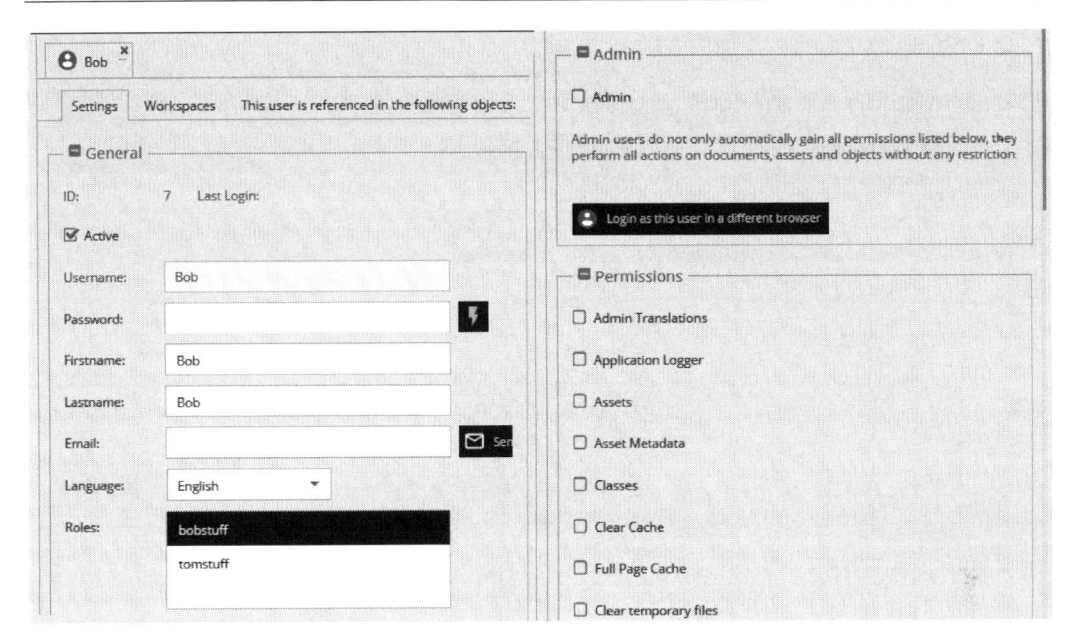

Figure 7.6: User administration page: sections inside the Settings tab

As we can see from the previous screenshot, the **General** section contains all the user information, such as username and password, image, and roles. The **Admin** section, on the other hand, contains only a checkbox that, if selected, will grant administrator privileges for the user; that is, they will have full control of Pimcore. The third section, **Permissions**, is a long list of checkboxes, each of which identifies particular permission to perform operations on Pimcore.

Let's check out some of these items and their meaning:

- **Assets**: Makes the assets tree visible.
- **Classes**: Makes the object classes editor visible (user can create and modify object classes).
- **Clear Cache**: Defines whether a user may clear the Pimcore cache.
- **Clear Temporary Files**: Defines whether a user may delete temporary system files.
- **Documents**: Makes the documents tree visible.
- **Document Types**: Allows the user to create and modify predefined document types.
- **Emails**: The user sees the email history.
- **Extensions**: Specifies whether a user is allowed to download, install, and manage the extension.

- **Objects**: Makes the object's tree visible.
- **Recycle Bin**: The user has access to the recycle bin.
- **Redirects**: The user can create and modify redirects.
- **System Settings**: The user has access to system settings.
- **Translations**: Defines whether a user may view and edit website translations.
- **Users**: Defines whether a user may manage other users' settings and system permissions.
- **Website Settings**: The user can create and modify website settings.

Therefore, by selecting some of these checkboxes, it is possible to configure the permissions of a user (or for a role, the configuration section is identical) according to the needs. These permissions are the Pimcore system permissions.

There are also other permissions that can be configured from the **Workspaces** tab, which looks like this:

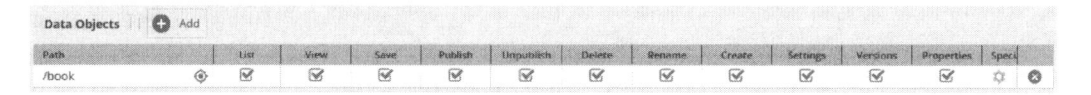

Figure 7.7: Managing user permissions on data elements (assets, objects, and documents)

As we can see in the preceding screenshot, a user's access can be restricted on an element basis. This can be done by defining workspaces for a user or role. Provided that a user may generally access documents, it can be specified what a user/role may or may not do with each document or workspace. The same is true for objects and assets.

The user permissions based on the elements are identified by a column, as can be seen in *Figure 7.7*. We can summarize some of them:

- **List**: The element can be listed in a tree.
- **View**: The element can be opened.
- **Save**: The element can be saved (save button visible).
- **Publish**: The element can be published (publish button visible).
- **Create**: New child elements can be created (does not exist for assets).
- **Delete**: The element can be deleted.
- **Versions**: Makes the **Versions** tab available.

Now that we have seen all the components needed to configure and use users and roles, let's move on to a simple practical example.

A practical example of using users and roles

Now that we have a clear idea of how to configure users and roles, let's take a simple practical example.

For this example, we created two users, **Tom** and **Bob**, and two roles, **tomstuff** and **bobstuff**. Let's assign **Tom** the **tomstuff** role and **Bob** the **bobstuff** role. This is possible by going to the **General** section of the **User Configuration** menu (*Figure 7.6*) and selecting the appropriate role in the **Roles** box.

What we need to do now is to select the permissions for each role. This can be done from the group called **Permissions** inside the **Settings** tab (see *Figure 7.6*):

- For **tomstuff**, we selected **Notes & Events | System Settings | Users | Admin Translation | Object**.
- For **bobstuff**, we selected **Recycle Bin | Static Routes | Clear Cache | Object**.

These are permissions concerning the Pimcore configurations and settings. Now let's set the permissions for the contents. We have created two classes: `Book` and `Film`. Class creation is fully described in *Chapter 5*, *Exploring Objects and Classes*. We assigned the **tomstuff** role permissions to manage the books, while **bobstuff** was given permissions to manage the films. This can be done from the **Workspace** tab, as seen in *Figure 7.7*.

Now that the configuration is completed, let's log in with the two users; in the next screenshot, we can see what the administration looks like by logging in as Tom:

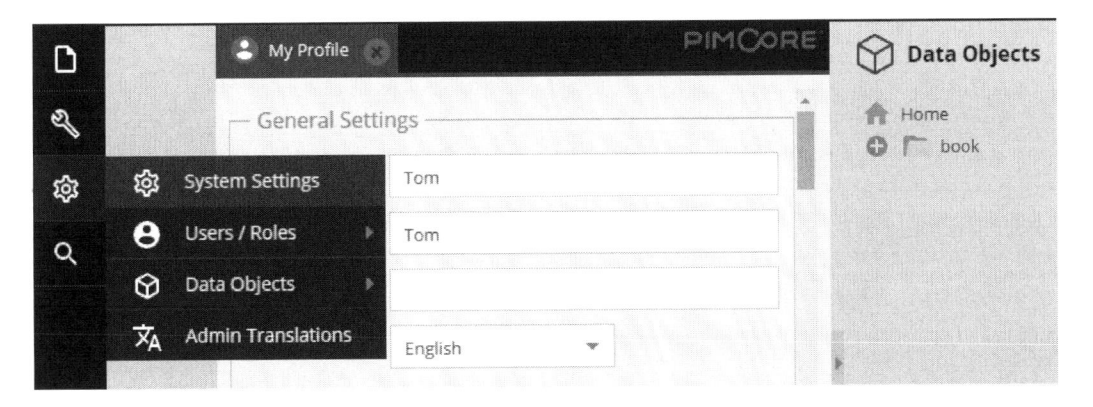

Figure 7.8 – Administration page for Tom

As we can see in the previous screenshot, only some menu items are accessible for Tom, under the permissions of the user's role. We can also see that Tom can only manage book objects, as we specified in the workspace of the **tomstuff** role. In the next screenshot, instead, we can see what the administration looks like for Bob:

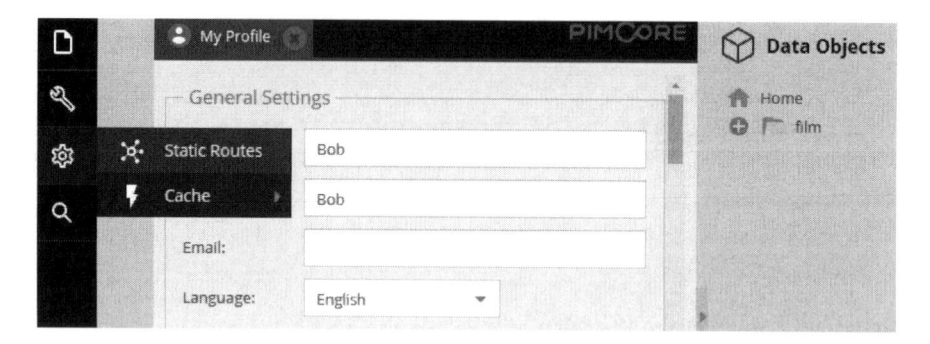

Figure 7.9: Administration page for Bob

Again, in this screenshot, we can see how the menus are limited for Bob, and how it is possible to manage only the film objects.

As we can see from the preceding screenshot, the context menus of the Pimcore administration are different according to the user and their roles. In particular, we can verify that only the actions related to the assigned permissions are visible; everything else is not accessible. Even for the contents, the two users are only enabled for the classes that are accessible through their role; in particular, Tom can manage books, while Bob can manage films.

What we have just seen in this section is a possible solution to the problem of limiting access to certain users based on roles, and it is possible to achieve this without having to write the code, simply by configuring users, roles, and permissions, from the Pimcore administration page.

Pimcore, however, offers a much more complete system for creating special views that is much more complete and configurable than what we have just seen. This Pimcore feature is called **perspectives**, that is, views created and configured ad hoc for specific users. So, let's see how a perspective can be created, how it is configured, and what the final result will be in our Pimcore.

Managing Perspectives

As we saw in the previous section, it is possible to limit access to Pimcore features by configuring users and roles. We also mentioned, at the end of the previous section, that there is a feature in Pimcore that allows you to obtain the same result, namely the perspective. While the preceding is completely true, there is one important difference to keep in mind: while using permissions on users and roles restricts access to data, perspectives are not intended to be used to restrict access to data. So, although the end result may seem similar, they are two very different things in terms of security. Our advice is to use both, so as to have a perfect result both from the administrative backend side as well as from the security side.

So, let's see how we can create a perspective. The simplest way is to use the bundle developed by the Pimcore dev team. This bundle provides an editor for Pimcore that allows us to do the following:

- Add/remove/edit custom views
- Add/remove/edit perspectives

It also allows us to configure most of the possible configuration options directly in the user interface.

The bundle page can be reached at this address: `https://github.com/pimcore/perspective-editor`.

As we have seen in the *Installing a bundle* section of this chapter, to install a bundle it will be enough to follow a few simple steps. We will not explain again how to install the bundle, but as we have already seen, we have to ask a composer to add the bundle to the solution, with the following command:

```
composer require pimcore/perspective-editor
```

144   Administrating Pimcore Sites

After installing and activating the bundle on Pimcore, we are ready to use this new feature, starting from the new menu item that we find under **Settings | Perspectives / Views**, as you can see in the following screenshot:

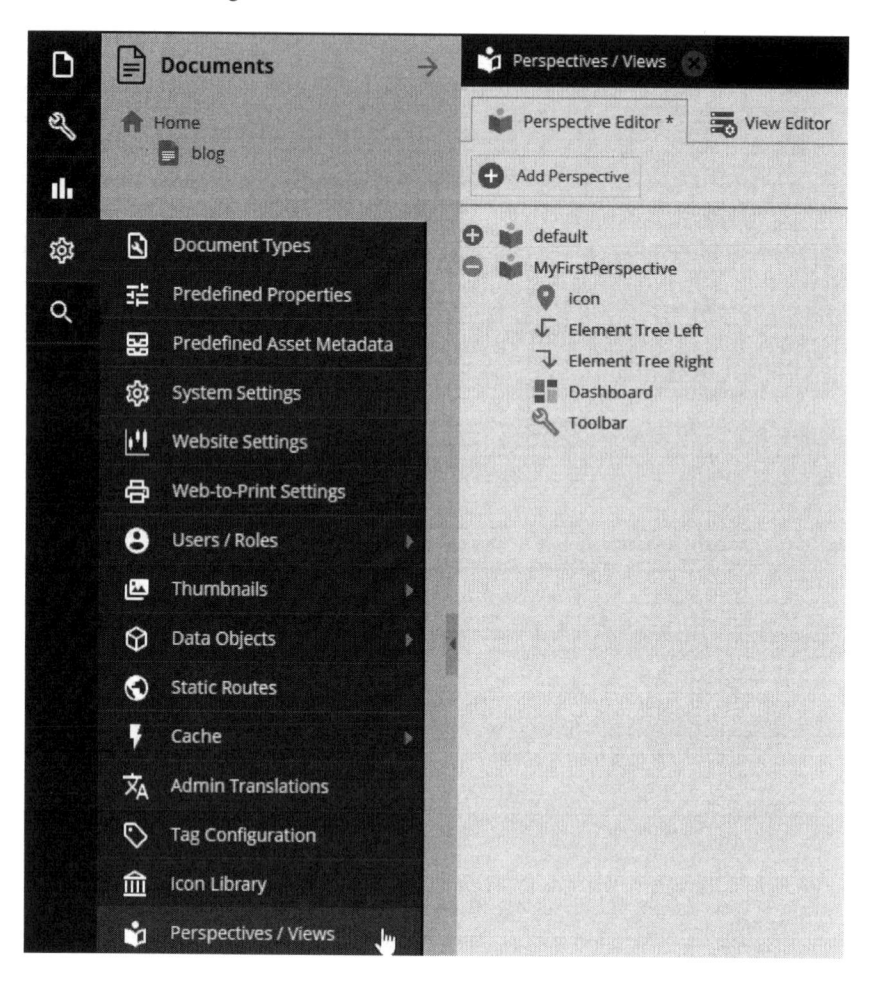

Figure 7.10: Perspectives / Views Menu item and the Perspectives edit page

As you can see in the previous screenshot, there is a default perspective, which can be changed at will. But in order not to touch the default perspective, let's go and create a new one. By clicking on the **Add Perspective** button, a modal will open, which will allow us to enter only the name of the new perspective. We will call our new perspective `MyFirstPerspective`.

As you can also see in *Figure 7.10*, we have five fields in a perspective, and they are as follows:

- **icon**: You can select an icon for the perspective.
- **Element Tree Left**: Within this element, it is possible to add one or more of the following elements: **Document**, **Asset**, **Object**, or **Custom View**. The added items will be displayed on the left column of the Pimcore admin interface.
- **Element Tree Right**: This is the same as the preceding item just described, but the items will be displayed on the right column.
- **Dashboard**: By selecting this element, you would be able to decide which elements can be allowed or forbidden in the dashboard. It is also possible to create new dashboards and, for each one, it is possible to decide which elements it is composed of.
- **Toolbar**: Through a list of checkboxes, grouped by menu, it is possible to choose whether or not to display a menu, but also to decide which items for a menu should be visible or not. In other words, through this element, it is possible to enable or hide the menu items of the Pimcore administration, and even hide entire menus.

As we have seen, in the two items, **Element Tree Right** and **Element Tree Left**, it is possible to add one or more of the document, asset, or object elements. In the next screenshot, we see how to add the document element:

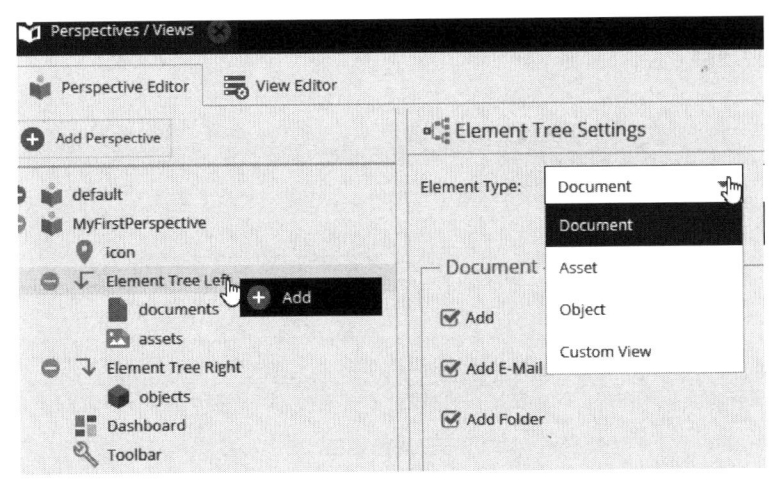

Figure 7.11: Perspective Menu item: add document element tree left

As we can see in the preceding screenshot, for our view we have decided to add a document and asset elements in the left column and an object in the right column. Once you have decided which elements to put where, by selecting each of these elements, it will be possible to decide, through a list of checkboxes, which elements of the contextual menu should be visible for each element. Let's take, for example, the document element, as seen in the following screenshot:

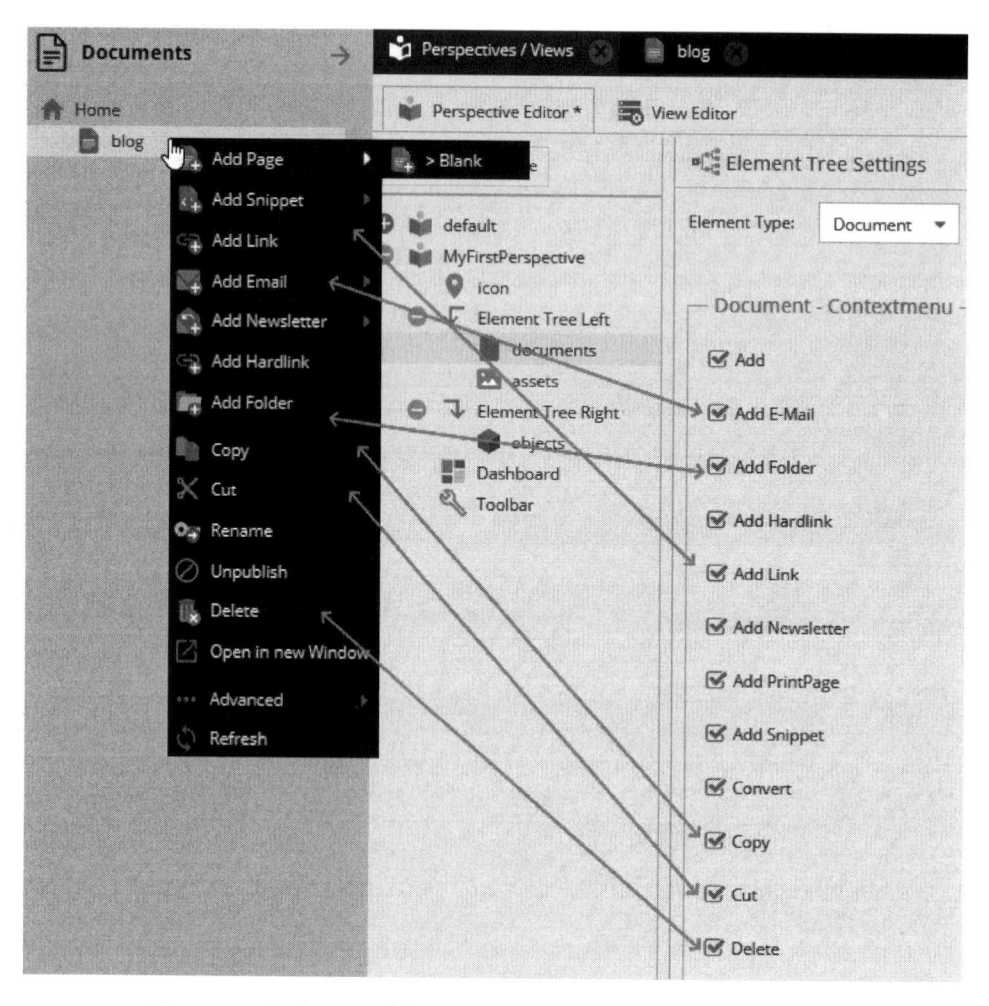

Figure 7.12: Definition of the context menu for the document element

As we can see from the previous screenshot, it is possible to select which context menu items we want to display.

As for the elements of the columns, just seen, through the **Toolbar** element, it is possible to decide which menus to show or hide, or it is possible to decide which items of a menu or submenu we want to hide. All menus are grouped, and in each group there is a list of checkboxes that act on the menu item, displaying or hiding it. For better understanding, let's take a look at the following screenshot, relating to the settings menu:

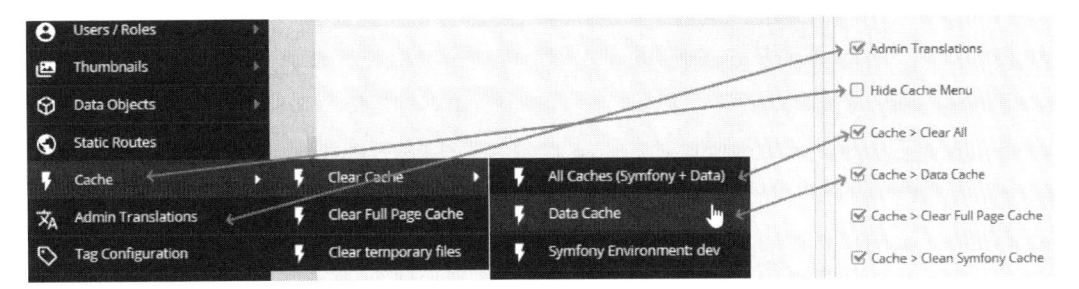

Figure 7.13: Selection of items to be displayed in the settings menu

As we can see in the preceding screenshot, each menu item is a group, which can be expanded, revealing the list of checkboxes that identify the various menu items. Each checkbox list group has **Hide xxx Menu** as its first entry, where **xxx** is the name of the menu. If we select this item, the menu will be hidden, and subsequent ticks will not be considered.

Once all parts of the perspectives are defined, the perspective item will appear in the file menu, and inside it will be possible to select our new perspective, as we can see in the following figure:

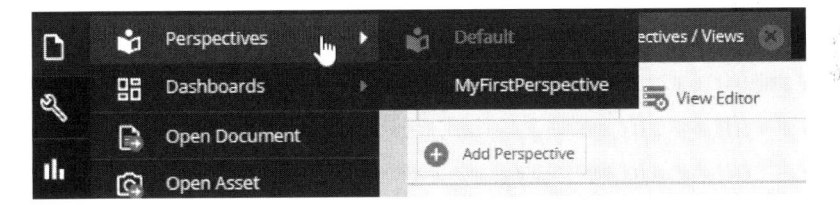

Figure 7.14: File menu with the list of perspectives

As we can see in the preceding figure, in the new menu item called **Perspectives**, inside the file menu, there are two items: the default perspective and our new perspective, **MyFirstPerspective**.

Once our perspective is configured as we want, we can associate it to users or roles. This can be done directly in the user or role settings, as we can see in the following figure:

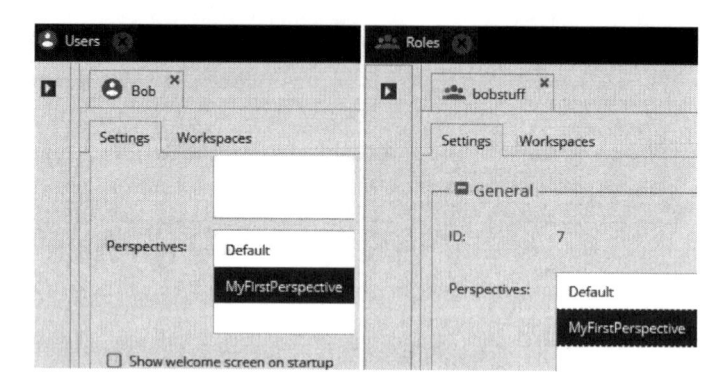

Figure 7.15: Configuration of the perspective for users and roles

As we can see from the preceding screenshot, the selection of the perspective for users and roles is extremely simple: just select the desired perspective from the list and save the settings. We have thus seen how users and roles are managed in Pimcore, and how to create and configure perspectives to be associated with each user or role. In the next section, we will see a very useful feature concerning the maintenance of Pimcore: the import/export of Pimcore settings.

Importing and Exporting Pimcore settings

In this section, we will see how it is possible to export the settings of our Pimcore installation and import them into other environments, a fundamental functionality when we have to work in different environments, such as for development, testing, or production.

As we saw in *Chapter 5, Exploring Objects and Classes*, when we talked about classes and objects, we learned how to create new entities and use them for our purposes. All the work we do is somehow trapped inside Pimcore, like in a kind of a box. This is completely normal, and when developing a new website, we are used to referring to the various environments, development, testing, staging, and so on, where we have made our changes. The doubt therefore arises: if I work in the development environment, for example, how can I transfer the work done in other environments?

Well, having a tool that allows us to export the work done in a Pimcore installation, to be able to import it into another installation, becomes a necessary, if not indispensable, benefit.

To clarify, let's take a simple example taking the two classes we initially created: `Book` and `Film`. If we want to export one of the two classes, or both, to be able to import them into another Pimcore installation in another environment, we can go to the class editing page and click the **Export** button in the bottom button bar, as you can see in the following screenshot:

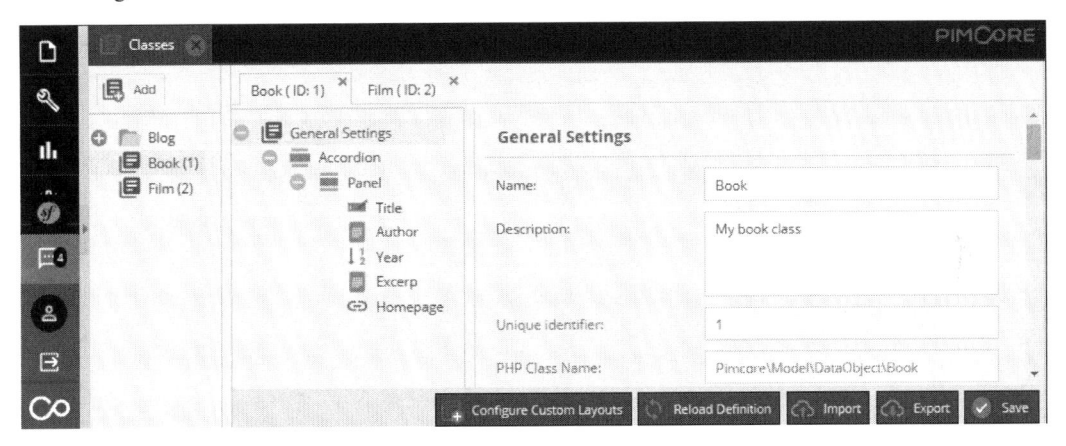

Figure 7.16 Class edit page, with the Import/Export buttons

As we can see, the **Export** button is exactly what we need. Just click on **Export** and Pimcore will generate a JSON file containing all the necessary information to be able to import it later on in another Pimcore environment. Once it has been exported, all we have to do is access the Pimcore installation where we want to import our class, create it, and then import the previously extracted file using the **Import** button, as shown in *Figure 7.16*.

But this is only part of the solution. Let's imagine we have hundreds of classes; exporting and importing them one by one could be a long job, and we could forget some classes along the way. To solve this problem, navigate to **Settings | Data Objects** and we find two items: **Bulk Export** and **Bulk Import**. After clicking on **Bulk Export**, a modal like this will appear:

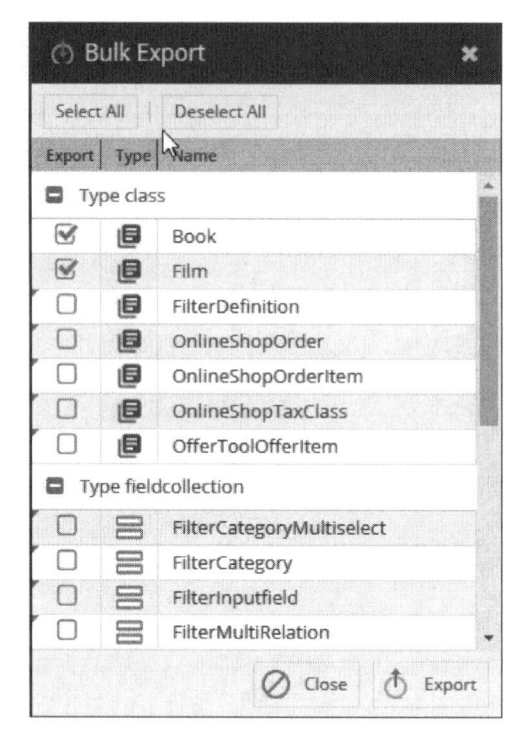

Figure 7.17: Bulk export

As we can see, it is possible to select from the list of classes the ones that we want to export.

Also, if you have created or edited **field-collections** or **bricks**, you can export these. **Field-collections** and **bricks** are internal Pimcore objects that can be added or modified. The management pages of these entities can be found by following the menu items: **Data Objects | field-collections** and **Data Object | bricks**. These two objects are described in *Chapter 5, Exploring Objects and Classes*. For our example, we select only the two classes: `Book` and `Film`.

Once we have selected what we want to extract by clicking on **Export**, Pimcore generates a JSON file containing all the information necessary to import all the elements in another environment. Finally, you can use the **Bulk Import** command to reload the exported file containing all the exported entities.

The import happens in two steps, as follows:

1. Select the JSON file generated during the export. Using the following modal, load the JSON file that was generated during the export stage, which you now want to import:

Figure 7.18: Select local file

2. Decide what we want to import from this file. In our example, we selected the two classes we want to import – **Book** and **Film** – from the following modal:

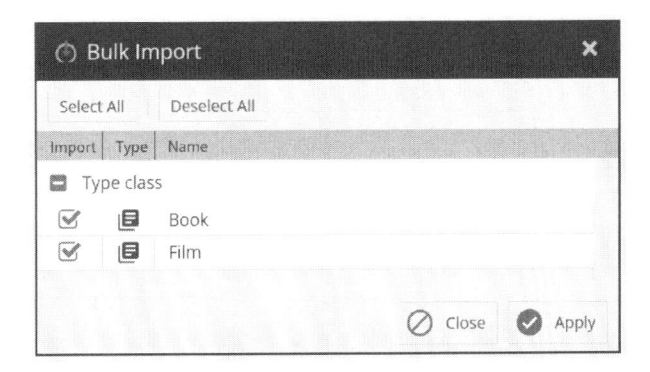

Figure 7.19: Select object to import

As you can see in the previous screenshot, Pimcore shows us the list of all the objects that we can import, related to the file we have uploaded. So, let's select what we want to import. Once we have decided, just click on **Apply**, and Pimcore will do the rest.

At this point in the chapter, we have seen how to install a bundle, how to manage users and roles, and also how we transfer our work between various Pimcore installations. We have done all these activities from the web admin interface that Pimcore makes available to us. But there is also another way to be able to make changes to Pimcore, without having to go through the administration page: using the Pimcore console tool.

Using the Pimcore Console

In this section, we will get a little familiar with the Pimcore console, a powerful and useful tool to be able to execute commands without having to access the web administration panel.

The **Pimcore Console** can be described as a command-line interface that allows you to install, configure, and maintain your Pimcore using only the terminal. The main goal is to provide a tool for the actions that can normally be performed through the administrative area.

As Pimcore's admin interface is so beautiful and easy to use, the natural question is: why should you use a command-line interface? There are two main reasons:

- **The keyboard is faster than the mouse**: For advanced users, typing a command can be an order of magnitude faster than pressing a button in a web browser.
- **Scripting**: You can put several commands in a text file and have it run automatically.

Using a console instead of using the web interface is much faster because it eliminates all the dead time for loading the page and all its components. The console acts directly on the Pimcore core, making the command execution much faster.

So, the first step to using the console is to get on board the machine where Pimcore is running, or inside the Docker container (for more on Docker, see the *Installing a bundle* section in this chapter to get commands to execute to access the container), and run this command to get a list of available commands:

```
./bin/console list
```

The output of this command is very long because many commands can be executed from the console. Let's look at the partial output of the command list:

Using the Pimcore Console   153

```
root@70c669c32f55:/var/www/html# ./bin/console list
Pimcore v6.8.6 (env: dev, debug: true)

Usage:
  command [options] [arguments]

Options:
  -h, --help                   Display this help message
  -q, --quiet                  Do not output any message
  -V, --version                Display this application version
      --ansi                   Force ANSI output
      --no-ansi                Disable ANSI output
  -n, --no-interaction         Do not ask any interactive question
      --ignore-maintenance-mode  Set this flag to force execution in maintenance mode
      --maintenance-mode       Set this flag to force maintenance mode while this task runs
  -e, --env=ENV                The Environment name. [default: "dev"]
      --no-debug               Switches off debug mode.
  -v|vv|vvv, --verbose         Increase the verbosity of messages: 1 for normal output, 2 for mo

Available commands:
  about                        Displays information about the current project
  help                         Displays help for a command
  list                         Lists commands
 assets
  assets:install               Installs bundles web assets under a public dir
 cache
  cache:clear                  Clears the cache
  cache:pool:clear             Clears cache pools
          ... other commands ...
  lint:yaml                    Lints a file and outputs encountered errors
 pimcore
  pimcore:bundle:disable       Disables a bundle
  pimcore:bundle:enable        Enables a bundle
  pimcore:bundle:install       Installs a bundle
  pimcore:bundle:list          Lists all pimcore bundles and their enabled/ins
  pimcore:bundle:uninstall     Uninstalls a bundle
  pimcore:bundle:update        Updates a bundle
          ... other commands ...
```

Figure 7.20: The partial output of the Pimcore console

As we can see in the preceding screenshot, the first part of the output contains useful information about the options for the Pimcore console, and beneath that is the list of the available commands (which for convenience we have cut out in *Figure 7.20*). Even if the list is very long, the logic for executing commands is always the same: we just have to understand how a command is structured and how to execute it.

Inside the **Options** section, we can see some parameters that we can pass before each command. For example, if we want as much information as possible when executing a command, we just add -vvv in front of the command. If, on the other hand, we don't want any information to be output to the console, just add the -q parameter before the command.

All commands are divided into **namespaces**. In other words, a namespace is a label that groups multiple commands. So, all cache-related commands will start with the `cache` namespace, the Pimcore core commands will start with the `pimcore` namespace, and so on.

To see the list of all commands for each namespace, you can run the `list` command followed by the namespace. For example, to get all the cache-related commands, we run the `list` command followed by the `cache` namespace:

```
./bin/console list cache
```

The output will be the list of all available commands to execute on the Pimcore cache.

Some namespaces are composed of several elements, concatenated by a colon, so if we want to identify the list of commands available for Pimcore bundles, we must execute the following command:

```
./bin/console list pimcore:bundle
```

Now that we are familiar with the console commands, let's try running a couple of commands as an exercise. At the beginning of the chapter, we installed a bundle, then we activated it from the web interface. Let's now try to run the same commands but using the console.

First of all, we need to identify which bundles are available in our Pimcore installation by running the following command:

```
./bin/console pimcore:bundle:list
```

The output of this command is shown in the following screenshot:

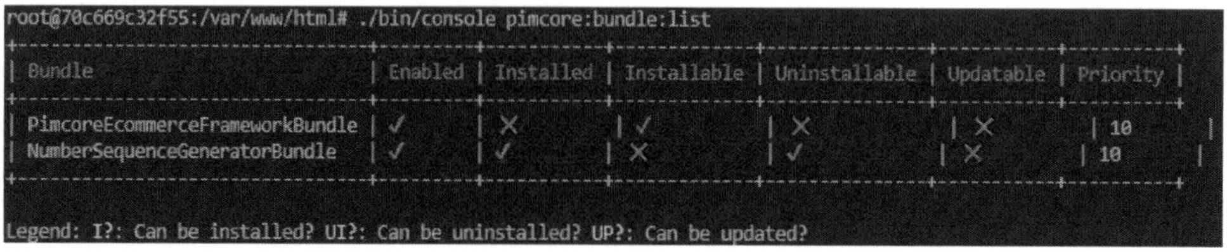

Figure 7.21: The output of the command to get the bundle available in our Pimcore installation

As we can see from this screenshot, the bundle we installed at the beginning of the chapter is enabled. Now let's try to disable it by running the following command:

```
./bin/console pimcore:bundle:disable
 NumberSequenceGeneratorBundle
```

As we can see, at the bottom of the command we have added as a parameter the name of the bundle we want to act on: `NumberSequenceGeneratorBundle`.

We now execute the command again:

```
./bin/console pimcore:bundle:list
```

The output will now look like this:

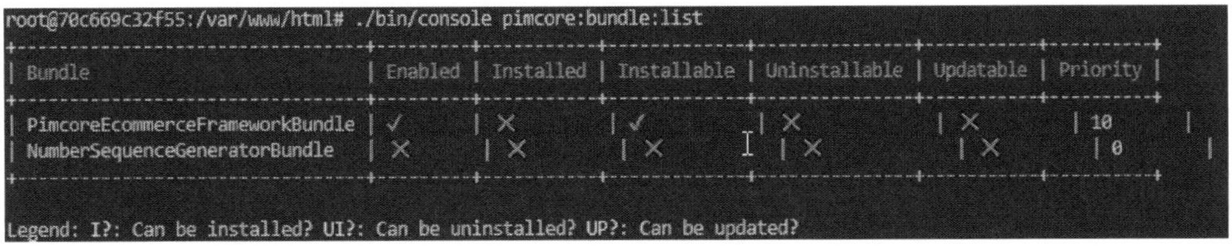

Figure 7.22: The output of the command to get the bundle available in our Pimcore installation

As we can see, the bundle is now completely uninstalled.

So, we saw how simple it is to execute a command using the Pimcore console. The other thing that makes the console very useful is in the execution of scheduled scripts, in which it is possible to execute several commands in sequence. For example, you can write a script that cleans up the cache and the mail logs, and have this script run every morning, for example, through a scheduler, such as **crontab** on **Unix systems**.

We leave you the freedom to try other commands, to become familiar with the Pimcore console, and to understand its potential.

Summary

In this chapter, we learned how it is possible to enhance Pimcore features through the use of bundles, and how they can easily be installed and managed.

We learned how to organize the site's users and their permissions, to limit the functionality of the site in the administration and content management sections, and how to create and configure perspectives, as well as associating them with users or roles.

We also learned how to import and export the settings of our Pimcore installation to other environments.

Finally, we learned how to use the Pimcore console, a powerful and useful tool to be able to execute commands, without having to access the web administration panel.

All these new skills acquired while reading this chapter will allow us to configure our site in the best way, to achieve the aim of creating a site that satisfies all our needs, and even a little of our pleasures.

Now that we have become familiar with all the tools that Pimcore offers us, it is time to get our hands dirty. After this chapter, we will begin to put into practice everything we have seen in the previous chapters, with the aim of creating a site, with blogs, static pages, and a products catalog. For this, in the next chapter, we begin by creating custom CMS pages.

8
Creating Custom CMS Pages

In the previous chapters, we learned how to create documents and objects and implement very simple websites using such features.

In this chapter, we will have a deep dive into the creation of custom CMS pages. In fact, if you are templating a document or creating a standalone page, you have many tools that make the development experience in Pimcore great for you. This chapter will cover many aspects that are fundamental for a full overview of Pimcore's CMS capabilities; such features are basic tools for creating custom web pages, which we have combined to discuss user inputs and templates for creating content.

The chapter is structured as follows:

- Using the MVC Model
- Using Editables
- Using Blocks

Let's see Pimcore in action!

Technical requirements

As with the previous chapters, there is a demo that you can find in our GitHub repository, which you can find here: `https://github.com/PacktPublishing/Modernizing-Enterprise-CMS-using-Pimcore`.

All you need to do to run the demo connected with this chapter is to clone it and navigate to the `8. Creating Custom CMS Pages` folder and start the Docker environment.

To do so, just follow these instructions:

1. Run Docker with the following command:

   ```
   docker-compose up
   ```

2. Then, to restore all the settings from on your local machine, type the following:

   ```
   docker-compose exec php bash restore.sh
   ```

3. Navigate to `http://localhost/admin` and log in with your admin/pimcore credentials.

What you will get with this setup is the following:

- A class definition called `MyObject`
- Two instances of the class, `My Item 1` and `My Item 2`
- The **Editables** page, a page with a demo of editables (see *Using Editables*)
- The **Template** page, a page with a demo of the templating helpers (see *Using the MVC model*)
- A thumbnail preset called `MyThumbnails`

Now you are ready to play with the demo related to this chapter!

Using the MVC Model

In this section, we will learn how the **MVC (Model View Controller)** model works and how to use it for creating a standalone web page that works outside the document scope. This is very important for covering all possible needs that you may encounter on your path with Pimcore as a Content Management System.

The MVC principle is very easy. When a URL matches a set of rules (**Routing**), a controller class is activated and this will compute data (**Model**) using certain business logic (**Controller**). The data is then sent to the **View** that implements the presentation logic and shows content to the user.

In this section, we will cover the most important concepts relating to building embedded web pages using the MVC pattern:

- Controllers
- Views (template helpers)
- Routing

Let's see them in detail.

Controllers

Pimcore **Controllers** implement the "C" part of the MVC pattern. Controllers are responsible for business logic or, in simpler words, are the part of your source code that reads, manipulates, and prepares data to be passed to the presentation layers (views). It is good practice to keep all the reusable logic in service classes, but the point that connects presentation with the business layer is, in fact, the controller element.

Pimcore offers an abstract class (`FrontendController`) that can be used as a base for your controller implementation. This simply means that all your controllers will usually inherit from the frontend controller. The naming convention of your files will follow the generic Symfony rules. In a simple scenario where you use Symfony's standards for your website, you will have the following rules:

- **Controller class name**: `/src/Controller/[Controller].php`
- **View filename**: `/templates/[Controller]/[action].html.twig`

Inside controllers, you can create any action you want. Each action is responsible for a single functionality and is linked to a URL. We usually create a controller for each topic or homogeneous group or function (that is, `CustomerController`, which manages all the customer's features). If you invoke a controller omitting the action name, `default` will be used.

As we explained in *Chapter 4, Creating Documents in Pimcore*, we can choose a controller for each document and Pimcore comes out with a ready-to-go controller called `DefaultController`. We can create controllers that are unrelated to documents and simply implement custom web pages.

Creating Custom CMS Pages

Inside controllers, you can access some special variables that can help you to define how to build the desired output:

- `$this->document`: If you are working on a document, this is the document that you are manipulating.
- `$this->editmode`: Indicates whether you are in edit mode or not, and can be used for diversifying the output based on the case. This applies when you are working with documents.

In the next sections, you will find some examples of controller actions that cover all the most common use cases.

Passing data to a view

The following example is an action that adds a variable into the view with a value. In this case, the value is just text, but imagine that you could use the input from `$request` for computing data and add a more complex data object:

```php
public function dataAction(Request $request)
{
    $input=$request->get('data');
    return array(
            'content' =>$input
        );
}
```

Setting HTTP headers

Another requirement that we may have is to set some HTTP headers. If these values are fixed, you can add them using an annotation, or you can access and programmatically alter the response object using the `addResponseHeader` helper:

```php
/**
 * @ResponseHeader("X-Foo", values={"123456", "98765"})
 */
public function headerAction(Request $request)
{
    $response = new Response();
    // using code:
    $response->headers->set('X-Foo', 'bar');
```

```
        return $response;
    }
```

The previous code adds three values for the same header: the first two from the annotation, and the other from the piece of code inside the method.

Specifying the template path

If you are scared about the fixed conventions of templating, we will reassure you with the next example. In the following snippet, we will override the normal template path by setting it manually:

```
    public function differentPathAction()
    {
        return $this->render("Default/default.html.twig",
["foo" => "bar"]);
    }
```

Alternatively, you can manually specify the template path to the `@Template()` annotation and just return the data, as in the following snippet:

```
/**
 * @Template(Default/default.html.twig)
 */
public function differentPathAction()
{
    return return ["foo" => "bar"];
}
```

Generating JSON output

Even though Pimcore comes with a powerful API engine and **Datahub Change this throughout the chapter** lets you make anything using **GraphQL**, you may need to produce APIs manually. This scenario is easy to manage with controllers and the `json` function. In the next example, you will see how to create a `json` response starting from plain data:

```
    public function jsonAction(Request $request)
    {
        return $this->json(array('key' => 'value'));
    }
```

This outputs the `json` serialization of data as the body of the response and sets the content type to `application/json`.

For all other cases

As a final fallback, if none of the standard solutions offered by Pimcore will satisfy your needs, there is the bare option to create a Symfony response object manually and return it to the MVC engine. Using this option, you will be free to set all response parameters, for `mime` type to the raw content without any limitation. In the next example, we will return fixed text:

```php
public function customAction(Request $request)
{
    return new Response("Just some text");
}
```

The previous block of code returns a response with text content as an example. Given the `Request` object, you can implement all the code you want and then produce a custom `Response`.

All the preceding actions are intended to be contained in a `controller` class like this:

```php
<?php

namespace App\Controller;

use Pimcore\Controller\FrontendController;
use Symfony\Component\HttpFoundation\Request;
use Symfony\Component\HttpFoundation\Response;
use Pimcore\Controller\Configuration\ResponseHeader;

class MyController extends FrontendController
{
    // Add your actions here
}
```

This set of samples is not exhaustive but contains the most important features and is a great starting point. You can find more details in the official documentation: https://pimcore.com/docs/pimcore/current/Development_Documentation/MVC/index.html.

Views

This section covers the "V" component of the MVC pattern. **Views** are the components that receive data and render it by implementing presentation logic. A views file can be written using Twig or a PHP template but, as we told you in *Chapter 4, Creating Documents in Pimcore*, we will focus only on the Twig solution, which allows a more strict separation between business and presentation logic and makes Pimcore a real detached CMS. The downside of this solution is that the logic that you can implement in a Twig file is limited as it forces you to implement all the business logic in the controller. This strict separation may seem limiting at the beginning, but when you are confident with the pattern, you will agree that it's more clean, reusable, and maintainable. Other than all the platform-specific features, called **helpers**, Pimcore's Twig files support all the standard features of Twig.

Here is a list of the most important Pimcore helpers.

pimcore_object

In the following code, we loaded an object by its `id` (in our case, 2) and we displayed the `Title` property:

```
{% set myObject = pimcore_object(2) %}
{{ myObject.getTitle() }}
```

Our object has a `Title` property accessed by the standard `getTitle` method, so the value will be printed.

pimcore_document

In the next snippet, we have loaded a document and printed the title:

```
{% set myDoc = pimcore_document(3) %}
title: {{ myDoc.getTitle}} </br>
url: {{ myDoc}}
```

The `myDoc` element is Pimcore's document and all its properties can be accessed.

pimcore_asset

This helper loads an asset that can be used in the template. In the next example, we loaded one asset and we displayed the `filename` and `url`:

```
{% set myDoc = pimcore_asset(2) %}
url: {{ myDoc}} <br>
filename: {{ myDoc.getFilename}}
```

Alternatively, you can find an asset by its path, using the following shortcut:

```
{% set asset = asset('/path/to/image.jpg') %}
```

As usual, the assigned variable can be used in the template file for implementing any presentation logic.

Render controller output

This function calls an arbitrary action and prints the result. In the next example, we used the `/custom/json` example and we rendered the output, passing `items=11` as the parameter:

```
{{ render(controller('App\\Controller\\
CustomController::jsonAction', { items: 11 }))
}}
```

The parameter order is action, controller, bundle, and parameters.

pimcore_cache

Pimcore's cache simply implements an in-template caching functionality. You can use this to cache some parts of the HTML page directly in the template, independent of the other global definable caching functionality. This can be useful for templates that need a lot of calculation or require a huge amount of objects (such as navigations, and so on). In the next block of code, we will see caching in action:

```
{% set cache = pimcore_cache("cache_key", 60, true) %}
{% if not cache.start() %}
    <h1>If you refresh the page this date will remain the
    same</h1>
    {{ 'now'|date('y-m-d') }} v{{ 'now'|date('U') }}
    {% do cache.end() %}
{% endif %}
```

The parameter order is the name of the key, the timeout in seconds, and an optional flag for forcing the cache in admin mode.

pimcore_device

The `pimcore_device` function helps when implementing adaptive designs. The next piece of code displays the usage of this helper in a template snippet:

```
{% if pimcore_device().isPhone() %}
    I'm a phone
{% elseif pimcore_device().isTablet() %}
    I'm a table
{% elseif pimcore_device().isDesktop() %}
    I'm a desktop device
{% endif %}
```

If you are running this script on your PC, the output will be **I'm a desktop device**.

Request

From the default Symfony objects, you can access the request data. This can be done using the `app.request` item that contains all the information that we need. In the next example, we used this method to get the "_dc" URL parameter that you usually have in a page preview:

```
{{ app.request.get("_dc") }}
```

This is just a sample, and you can access all the request parameters. You can look at the official documentation for more information, here: `https://symfony.com/doc/current/templates.html#the-app-global-variable`.

Glossary

This helper replaces glossary terms with links. The glossary module is a powerful tool, making internal and external linking easy and smart, and which Pimcore has out of the box. As an example, you can connect the word "Pimcore" with the official website, so that each time you use it in HTML, it will be replaced with a link to the website. The `pimcore_glossary` helper will be used by this helper to render links. To test this feature, follow these steps:

1. Go to **Tools** | **Glossary**.
2. Click **Add**.

3. Enter the term `PIMcore` in the **Text** column and then the link to the page in the **Link** column. In this example, we added PIMcore and CMS words with the related links. In the next screenshot, you will find the result:

Figure 8.1: Glossary terms

4. Now the glossary is set and we can use it on any web page using the `pimcoreglossary` helper. We can do this by placing the following snippet in a web page template:

```
{% pimcoreglossary %}
    My content PIMCore loves CMS
{% endpimcoreglossary %}
```

In the previous snippet, we surround the text with the `glossary` function. Because we defined the words **PIMcore** and **CMS** inside the glossary, they will be transformed into a link on the web page. This is the final result:

Glossary

My content PIMCore loves CMS

Figure 8.2: The glossary helper in action

This was a simple example to explain the concept, but it shows how powerful this feature is.

pimcore_placeholder

This helper adds custom placeholders into the template. The next snippet defines a placeholder called `myplaceholder`, which is configured for building an H3 tag surrounding the "`My content`" value:

```
{% do  pimcore_placeholder('myplaceholder')
.setPrefix("<h3>")
.setPostfix("</h3>")
.set("My content") %}
{# Print placeholder #}
{{ pimcore_placeholder('myplaceholder') }}
```

The output of this is `<h3>My content</h3>`.

pimcore_head_link

This helper collects a list of head links (stylesheet or any other `head link` tag) and prints them on the head section of the web page. Based on the presentation logic, the links are collected (you may or may not include a file based on some special conditions) and then printed once.

In the following example, the snippets append a favicon (favorite icon – the logos you see in browser tabs when you surf websites) to the link list:

```
{% do  pimcore_head_link({'rel' : 'icon', 'href' : '/img/favicon.ico'},"APPEND")  %}
{# Print head links#}
{{ pimcore_head_link()}}
```

In the example, we appended a favicon to the list. Using the correct configuration of `pimcore_head_link`, we can also define the order using relative inclusion (for example, add x file after y file).

pimcore_head_meta

This helper prints HTTP meta tags. It can collect a set of items that will be printed once in the header section. In the next block of code, like in the `HeadLink` helper, the data is collected and printed to the function by the final call:

```
{% do pimcore_head_meta().appendName('description', 'My SEO description for my awesome page') %}
```

```
{# adding addictional properties #}
{% do pimcore_head_meta().setProperty('og:title', 'my article title') %}
{# Print tags #}
{{ pimcore_head_meta() }}
```

pimcore_head_script

This is the same as `HeadLink` and `Style`, but for a JavaScript file. The next block of code adds a script to the list and then prints it on the page:

```
{% do pimcore_head_script().appendFile("/myscript.js") %}
{# Print tags #}
{{ pimcore_head_script() }}
```

pimcore_head_style

This helper manages inline styles. It is like `HeadLink`, but with inline scripts. In the next piece of code, we add a file called `ie.css` with conditional wrapping that, in this case, limits the CSS action to Internet Explorer before version 11:

```
{% do pimcore_head_style().appendStyle("ie.css", {'conditional': 'lt IE 11'}) %}
{# Print tags #}
{{ pimcore_head_style() }}
```

pimcore_head_title

Creates and save the HTML document's `<title>` for later retrieval and output. The following script adds the special `title` tag into the page:

```
{% do pimcore_head_title('My first part') %}
{# Print tags #}
{{ pimcore_head_title() }}
```

pimcore_inc

This helper includes a Pimcore document in the page. In the next snippet, we see how the `MySnippet` document is rendered and added to the page:

```
{{ pimcore_inc('/MySnippet') }}
```

pimcore_inline_script

This helper adds inline scripts to a page. The usage is very similar to `HeadScript`, but intended for inline usage. The next piece of code adds `myscript.js` to the list and then prints it on the page:

```
{% do pimcore_inline_script().appendFile("/myscript.js") %}
{# Print tags #}
{{ pimcore_inline_script() | raw }}
```

Navigation

This helper is responsible for generating and adding a navigation menu. In the next piece of code, you will find an example that prints a menu based on the document hierarchy:

```
{% set mainNavStartNode = document.getProperty('mainNavStartNode') %}
{% set navigation = pimcore_build_nav({
    active: document,
    root: mainNavStartNode
}) %}
{# Print tags #}
{{ pimcore_render_nav(navigation) }}
```

In the snippet, it rendered a menu that starts from `mainNavStartNode`, which is the root document, and uses the current document as the active one.

You can refer to the official documentation for more information on `navigation`: https://pimcore.com/docs/pimcore/current/Development_Documentation/Documents/Navigation.html.

include

This helper directly includes a template inside the page. Look at the following script:

```
{{ include("Default/include.html.twig", {'par':'value'}) }}
```

This script includes the `Default/include.html.twig` template, where you can use the set of parameters passed as the input.

Translations

This is a Symfony feature integrated within Pimcore's engine. With the pipe filter, you can transform text using the translations database and replace the original text with the translated version. To do this, do the following:

1. Create a document and assign a template to it.
2. Add the following snippet to the template:

   ```
   {% set message ="my-test-key" %}
   {{ message|trans }}
   ```

   This script sets a variable with a string value (`my-test-key`) and then prints it using the `trans` filter.

3. After the first usage of the label, an entry will be created in your backend, and you will be able to set a value for each language. Go to **Tools | Shared Translations**. Set the value of the label for each language by entering data into the table:

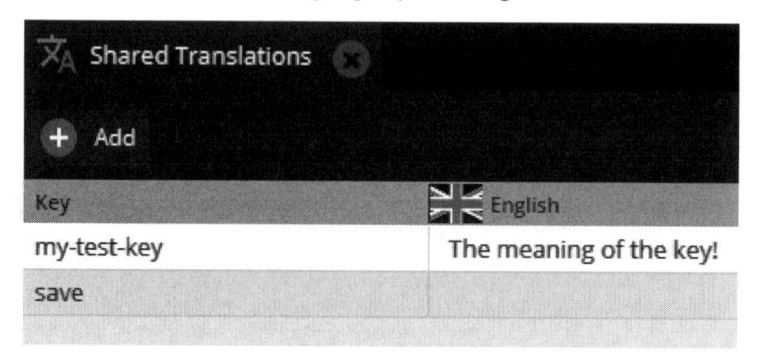

Figure 8.3: The Shared Translations panel

4. Open the web page and see the translated text.

The translation functionality is very useful and easy to manage with its visual interface.

Website config

Pimcore has a bucket of configuration keys that are easily editable via the web interface. You can add them from **Settings** | **Website Settings** and then you can insert the value into the template or controller. To do this, do the following:

1. Create a document and assign a template.
2. Open the website settings administration from **Settings** | **Website Settings**.
3. Enter a key for your settings in the top editing bar and choose the **Text** option.
4. Click the + button and the value will be displayed in the table. You will be able to edit it just by entering text into the grid. In the next screenshot, you will see the final result. In this example, we added a key called **mykey** with the value **My Value**:

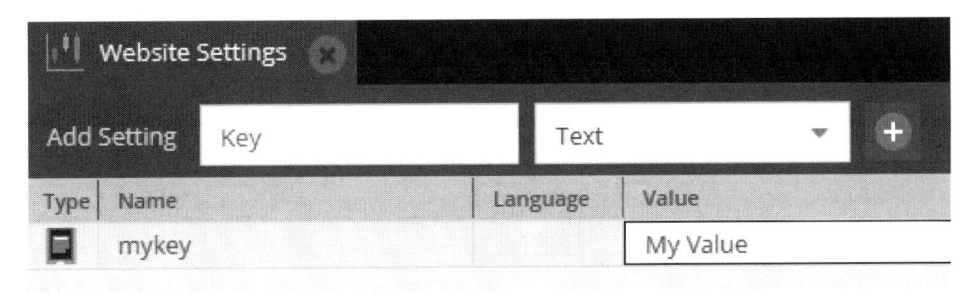

Figure 8.4: The Website Settings panel

5. Now add the following snippet to the template:

```
{{ pimcore_website_config('mykey') }}
```

Using the preceding code, you will get `MyValue` as the result of the helper.

The visual editing of settings is very useful because it lets us create configurable templates and websites that can be easily managed centrally.

instanceof

The `instanceof` construct is useful for checking whether an object is of a given type. In the next piece of code, we will check whether an asset instance is of type `Image` or not:

```
{% if item is instanceof('\\Pimcore\\Model\\Asset\\Image') %}
    {# print the image #}
{% elseif is instanceof('\\Pimcore\\Model\\Asset\\Video) %}
    {# print the video #}
{% endif %}
```

This feature is important because you can alter the code flow so it either completes or doesn't complete a task based on the object type. In the previous example, we get an object that could be a video or an image, and we can display it properly based on the type.

Thumbnails

When you are working with images, printing them at the right size is fundamental. The Pimcore thumbnail feature helps a lot with templating. What we can do is to define the asset thumbnails from the administration; you should have already discovered this topic in *Chapter 5, Exploring Objects and Classes*. Let's see this feature in action in a few simple steps:

1. Create a web page and assign a template to it.
2. Go to **Settings | Thumbnails | Image Thumbnails**.
3. Add a thumbnail configuration with the settings shown in the following screenshot:

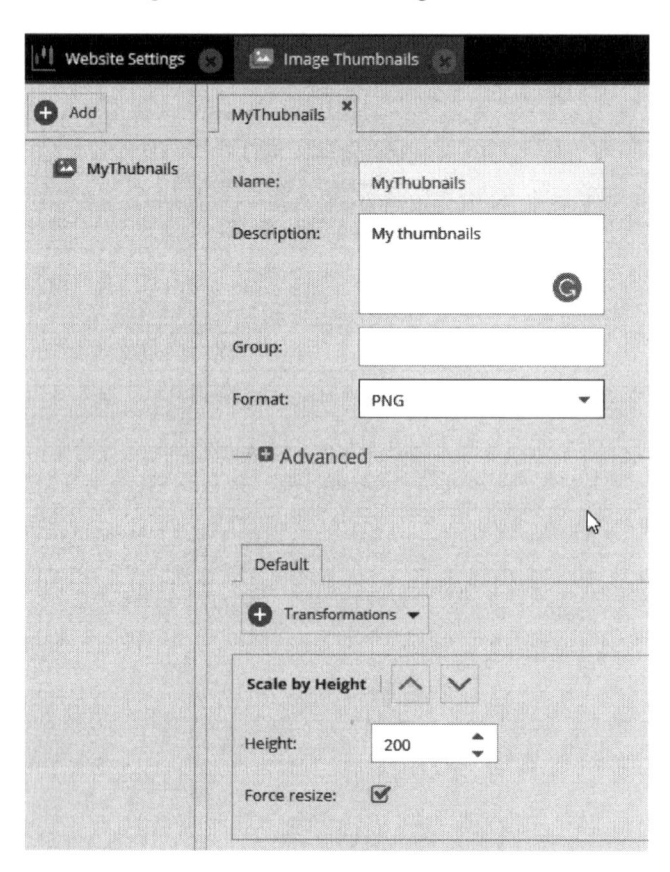

Figure 8.5: The thumbnail settings

We used the **PNG** format, and we set **Scale by Height** to **200**. Now the images that we will upload will have a proper thumbnail.

4. Upload an image into the **DAM** section. Right-click in the **Assets** section of the menu and choose the **Upload Files** option:

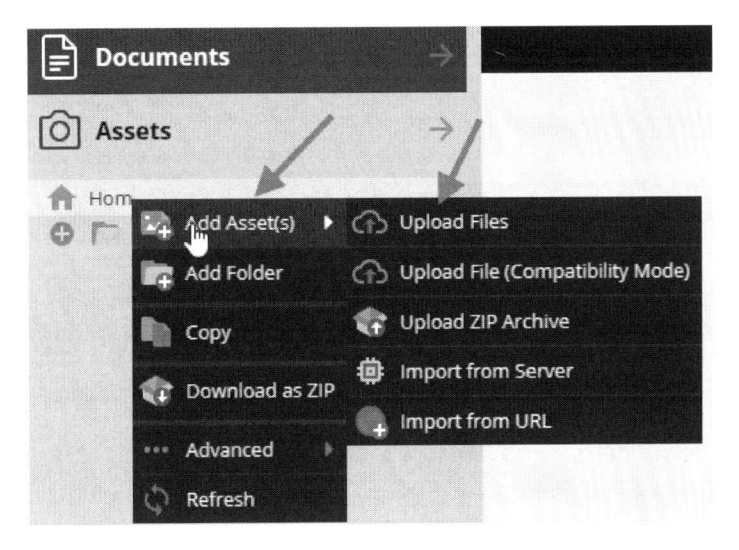

Figure 8.6: Uploading an image

5. The demo example already ships a Pimcore logo image with ID 2. To get a thumbnail, you just have to get the asset by path or ID, then render it. The next snippet does that. Copy the snippet to the template:

```
{% set asset = pimcore_asset(2) %}
{{ asset.getThumbnail('MyThubnails').getHtml() | raw }}
```

The scripts get the thumbnail (the files generated at the first usage) for the image and print the image tag to the document.

6. The next example gets an on-the-fly thumbnail without having a configuration defined. Copy this code to the template and see the result:

```
{{ asset.getThumbnail({
    width: 50,
    format: 'png'
}).getHtml() | raw }}
```

This example is quite similar to the previous one but uses settings that are not predefined by a thumbnail configuration.

That whole list of functions covers the set of features that Pimcore offers to us out of the box. In addition, you will have all the default Symfony functions, which you can discover using the official documentation: https://symfony.com/doc/current/reference/twig_reference.html.

But what should you do if neither Pimcore nor Symfony implements what you need? The easier solution, if we are talking about business logic, is to manipulate data inside the controller, and produce a clean output for the view. In some cases, we may need to implement some complex presentation logic that is hard to manage with Twig syntax. Moreover, we do not want to move this logic to the controller (where it will be easy to implement) because it will create coupling between the template and controller, and this is not what we want (do you remember when we talked about the benefits of a detached solution in *Chapter 1, Introducing Pimcore*?). The solution to the problem of implementing complex presentation logic inside templates is provided in the next section where we will see how to add methods to the template engine and implement reusable helpers for our project.

Implementing your own template helper

In the previous section, we learned how to use template helpers to generate dynamic content. Now it is time to learn how to extend the template helper system and add your own function inside the set. In the next example, we will create a template helper that will display the current date and time in a given format. You may object that the Twig templating already offers a feature more or less like this, but remember that this is an example to explain the template helper extension, so it is better to keep our case study as simple as possible. Now, follow the next steps:

1. Create a file in /src/Templating/Helper/Timestamp.php.
2. Then copy the following snippet inside the Timestamp.php file:

```php
<?php
...
class Timestamp extends AbstractExtension
{
    public function getFunctions()
    {
        return [
            new TwigFunction('timestamp', [$this,
                'timestamp']),
```

```
        ];
    }
    public function timestamp(String $format)
    {
        echo date($format);
    }
}
```

getFunctions is a special function that lists all the helper extensions exposed from this extension. In our case, we have one function, called timestamp. This function computes a textual date representation based on the format that's received from the user. This function is mapped to a command called timestamp and can be used inside the template engine. For simplicity, I used for the helper name the function that computes the result, but you can choose your own.

3. Register the snippet using the YAML configuration. Open the /config/services.yml file and add the following:

```
Services:
    ...
    App\Templating\Helper\Timestamp:
        public: true
        tags:
            - { name: templating.helper, alias: timestamp}
```

4. Now the timestamp helper is registered inside the templating engine, so we can call it inside our Twig files. Copy the following piece of code:

```
{{ timestamp("Y-m-d") }}
```

You will get something similar to 2020-11-03.

In this section, we learned how to add functionality to the template engine. This is good for reusing code and overcomes the Twig syntax limitations. In the next section, we will learn how to master routing rules to connect URLs with controllers.

Mastering Routing and URLs

The last step of mastering custom pages is routing. We learned in *Chapter 4, Creating Documents in Pimcore*, that each document has a path that can be changed by the document editing interface. What if we are not working with documents, but with custom pages? In this section, we will learn about the options that Pimcore offers, which are the following:

- **Hardcoded Routes**, as per Symfony standard.
- **Static Routes**, configurable routes that can be changed by the admin interface.
- **Redirects**, which can set HTTP redirection using a nice admin interface. For those who are not familiar with redirection, imagine it as a way to redirect the browser from one URL to another. This is very common when a page changes its URL or we have to move a website from one domain to another.

Let's look at them in detail.

Hardcoded routes

To add a route, there isn't anything more complex than adding it to the configuration. These settings are contained inside the `routing.yml` file, and these rules follow the Symfony standard that you can find here: https://symfony.com/doc/current/routing.html.

In the next code fragment, we can see an example of a rule:

```
custom_rule:
    path:        /custom/actionname/{parameter}
    controller:  App\Controller\CustomController:myaction
    defaults:
        parameter: "my default value"
```

The most relevant settings for our purpose are the following:

- name: The rule has a name that must be unique; in our example, it is `custom_rule`.
- `path`: This is the path that the rule is listening on; this can contain regular expressions and fetch parameters (in our case, `parameter`).

controller: This is the controller, including the action name; it supports the Symfony syntax. In the case that you write `App\Controller\CustomController:myaction`, you will activate `myaction` inside the `CustomController` controller of the application.

- For each parameter, you can give a default value in the case the parameter was optional.

Note that even if we used names with an understandable naming convention, you could define any rule as you want. The parameter inside the URL (or query path) is parsed and delivered to the action.

If you prefer, the second option is to use routing as an annotation of the controller's actions. The equivalent of the previous rule is the following:

```
/**
 * @Route("/custom/actionname/{parameter}", name="custom_rule")
 */
public function myaction(string $parameter)
{
    // ...
}
```

The routing rule is bidirectional, so it can both produce a URL from the parameter values and give the parameters values from a URL. For example, consider that you have the `/product/{id}` rule for the product URL. If the user enters `/product/5` in the browser, the routing engine is able to tell you that the ID parameter is 5. On the other hand, you can ask the engine to generate a URL for the product with ID 5 and you will get back `/product/5`. In simple words, you can build the URL automatically from the rule name and parameter. This is easy to do with the path helper:

```
{{% pimcore_path('custom_rule', {'parameter': 67}); }}
```

This will generate the full URL, `/custom/actionname/67`.

Configurable routes

The hardcoded rules used in the previous section are a good solution but are static, and you need access to the source code to understand or change them. The other solution offered by Pimcore is to define them visually, using the admin UI. Under **Settings | Static Routes**, you can find a table where you can enter all values of a routing rule (including the name, pattern, parameter names, and building rules). This makes rule management very easy and you can monitor how many rules you have and their configuration without accessing the source code.

You can follow these steps to see this method in action:

1. Create a controller caller, `CustomController`.
2. Add an action called `data` into the controller, similar to this:

   ```
   /**
    * @Template()
    */
   public function dataAction(Request $request)
   {
       $input=$request->get('data');
       $content = "data to show $input";
       return array(
           'content' => $content,
       );
   }
   ```

   This code will take the `data` parameter from the URL and will pass it to the view using the `content` variable.

3. Create a view in the controller folder called `data.html.Twig` and add the following code inside:

   ```
   {{ content }}
   ```

   This script will print the `content` variable.

4. Open the **Static Routes** section, where we can see the **Static Routes** table:

Using the MVC Model

Name	Pattern	Reverse	Bundle(optional)	Controller	Action	Variables	Defaults
custom	/\/custom_data\/(.*)?\//	/custom_data/%data/		@AppBundl...	data	data,	empty

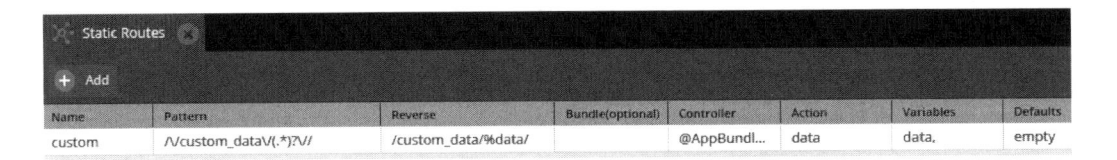

Figure 8.7: The Static Routes admin

In this editor, we can add rules. Each column lets you set the parameter, so enter the values in the previous figure using the following instructions:

- **Name**: The name of the rule. Hardcoded case is needed for computing reverse URLs. Enter `custom`.

- **Pattern**: The regular expression that matches the URL managed by this rule. It can contain many placeholders, and each one is parsed and saved to a variable. Enter `/\/custom_data\/(.*)\//`. Note that `\/` is for escaping the `/` char in the regular expression, so a URL such as `/custom_data/anything/` will be matched. The parameter matched by the selector `(.*)` is the `anything` part.

- **Controller**: The controller that is used by the URL. Click on the cell and choose `CustomController`.

- **Action**: The action that is used by the URL. Click on it and choose `data`.

- **Reverse**: The rule that generates a URL from the rule name and parameter. Enter `/custom_data/%data/`. With this value, the routing engine will be able to generate the URL, `/custom_data/value/`, if you use use the editable, `{{% pimcore_path('custom', {'data': 'value'}); %}}`.

- **Variables**: A comma-separated list that is used when fetching parameters. It is positional, so the first regex placeholder value takes the first value in the list, and so on. Enter `data`. This will mean that the value of `(.*)` will be named `data`.

- **Defaults**: A list with default data for optional parameters. Enter `empty`. In this case, if the parameter will be omitted, the parameter data will have the text `empty` as its value.

5. Open your browser and navigate to `http://localhost/custom_data/myvalue`. You will see the `myvalue` parameter printed on the page.

Similar to the previous example, we can generate a URL using a rule name and parameters with the template helper.

The settings that you edited through the admin UI are saved in a PHP configuration file (`var/config/staticroutes.php`), so it's also possible to edit the code directly or save them by committing it to a Git repository. The next piece of code shows what we obtained by adding the previous rules:

```php
<?php
return [
    1 => [
        "id" => 1,
        "name" => "custom",
        "pattern" => "/\\/custom_data\\/(.*)?\\//",
        "reverse" => "/custom_data/%data/",
        "module" => NULL,
        "controller" => "@App\\Controller\\CustomController:dataAction",
        "variables" => "data,",
        "defaults" => "empty",
    ]
];
```

Configurable routes are very useful when you want to keep URL routing flexible, letting the user choose the paths at runtime. This is essential for matching specification changes from the customer about URLs (maybe due to the SEO requirement changes) without touching a single line of code.

Redirects

Redirects are a useful feature of Pimcore for directing the user to the correct pages – whether it be for marketing URLs, for redirects after a website's relaunch, or redirects for moved documents.

The process for creating a redirect is very simple. Just follow these steps:

1. Navigate to **System | Redirects**. This menu opens a table similar to this one:

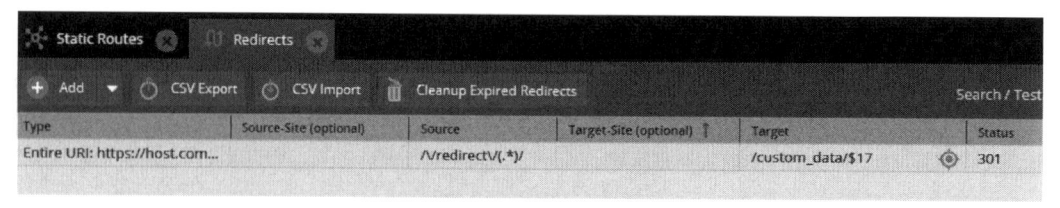

Figure 8.8: The Redirects table

2. Click the **Add** button. You will be prompted with the following popup:

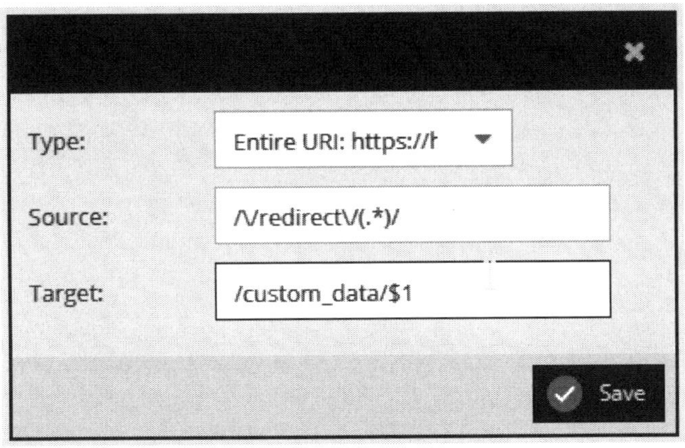

Figure 8.9: Adding a redirect

The **Type** dropdown lets you choose the type of redirection, while **Source** and **Target** allow you to choose the mapping rule that redirects the source to the target URL.

3. Enter `/\/redirect\/(.*)/` in the **Source** box and `/custom_data/$1` in the **Target** box, like in *Figure 8.9*.

4. Open a browser and navigate to `http://localhost/redirect/xxx/`. You will be redirected to `http://localhost/custom_data/xxx/` instead.

In this section, we learned how to create custom web pages using the MVC model. In particular, we covered all the most important topics:

- **Controllers**: We understood how controllers interact with request parameters and pass data to the view. Inside a controller, we can implement our business logic without any limitations.

- **Views**: We learned how the template engine works and how we can use the helpers to implement presentation logic.

- **Routing and URLs**: We learned how to manage the page's URL properly. We didn't limit ourselves to Symfony's standard routing but also covered static routes and redirect options. With all these options, we can choose the right solution based on our use case. The most important thing to know is that this wide set of options give us the power to solve any URL problems that we may face.

In the next section, we will have a deep dive into Pimcore editables and we will learn how to combine them to get results without writing tons of lines of code.

Using editables

As we introduced in *Chapter 4, Creating Documents in Pimcore*, Pimcore's editables are a set of visual components that can be used to enter information in the CMS page and are able to render the output to get the web page ready. You should remember the `pimcore_input` and `pimcore_wysiwyg` components; well, the good news is that Pimcore has a lot of components like that and covers most of your user needs. In this section, we will take a look at these.

> **Important note**
>
> In the **Editables** list, we should have **Area** and **Areablock** components, but we won't discuss these in this chapter. These elements, in conjunction with **Bricks**, are the pillars of code reuse in Pimcore and will be covered in *Chapter 10, Creating Pimcore Bricks*. The motivation is that without discovering what bricks are, the Area, Areablock, and Block components would be hard to understand.

In the next sections, we will discover a list of the editables available. For each one, we will add a snippet of code to show you how to add it to your code and, for the more complex items, we also have some screenshots to explain the interaction.

The process for testing an editable in your live Pimcore environment is the following:

1. Add a document into your CMS and link the document to a template. This process is well described in *Chapter 4, Creating Documents in Pimcore*.
2. Copy the snippets that you find in the following subsections.
3. Enter the page editor and see how the component looks.
4. Open page preview and see the data that is saved inside the editable. Remember that by using `{{ pimcore_xxx('name') }}`, you will print the data, but you can also set it to a variable using `{% set var = pimcore_xxx('name') %}` and then implement your own presentation logic.

All these examples are contained in the `editable.htm.twig` template, used in **The Editable Pages** that you will find in the demo related to this chapter.

Checkbox

The following editable adds a checkbox that can be checked by the page editor:

```
{{ pimcore_checkbox('myCheckbox') }}
```

The value can be used to implement some rendering logic (that is, showing or not showing something basing on the `myCheckbox` value).

Date

This snippet adds a `DateTime` picker to the web page:

```
{{ pimcore_date('myDate', {
    'format': 'd.m.Y',
    'outputFormat': '%d.%m.%Y'
  })
}}
```

When editing the page, you will see an editable `DateTime` picker like the one shown here:

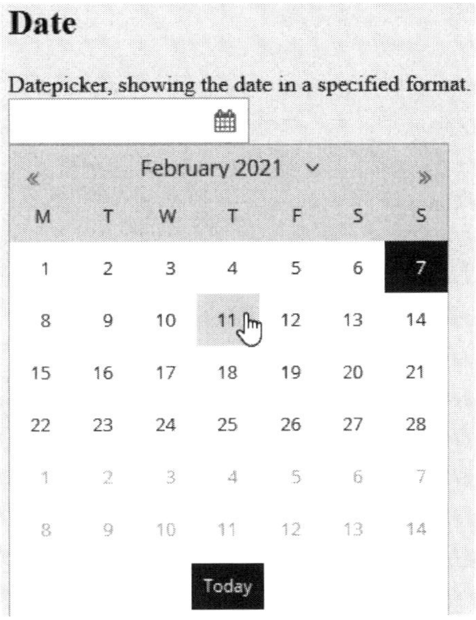

Figure 8.10: The date picker in action

During the page rendering, when you are not in edit mode, the function outputs the value that the user selected in the editor. This value can be displayed or be used for implementing presentation logic.

Relation (Many-To-One)

This editable provides the opportunity to add a `relation` to an object. You can select which types of elements you want to add (for example, `asset` or `object`) and which subtypes. In the following example, we allowed only classes of type `MyObject`:

```
{{ pimcore_relation("myRelation",{
    "types": ["asset","object"],
    "subtypes": {
        "asset": ["video", "image"],
        "object": ["object"],
    },
    "classes": ["MyObject"]
}) }}
```

This component, once added to the page, is displayed as a simple edit box where you can drag the items that you want to show, as in the following screenshot:

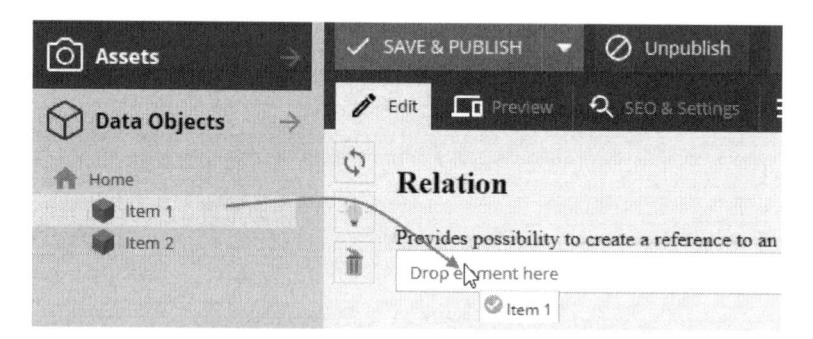

Figure 8.11: Relation configuration

Then the relation named `myRelation` will contain your selection value, and you can use it in the template for rendering data.

In the following example, we will add a **Link** button that navigates to the selected item:

```
<a href="{{ pimcore_relation("myRelation").getFullPath() }}">{{ "Go to" }}</a>
```

The previous snippet will display a link in the text.

Relations (many-to-many relation)

This editable is like the many-to-one relation but allows you to select references to multiple other elements (such as documents, assets, and objects). The following snippet is the same as the previous use case, but because this editable has multiple references, we used a `for` loop to list all the selected options:

```
{% if editmode %}
    {{ pimcore_relations("objectPaths") }}
{% else %}
<ul>
    {% for element in pimcore_relations("objectPaths") %}
        <li><a href="{{ element.getFullPath }}">{{ element.getTitle }}</a></li>
    {% endfor %}
</ul>
{% endif %}
```

Now we can drag and drop multiple items:

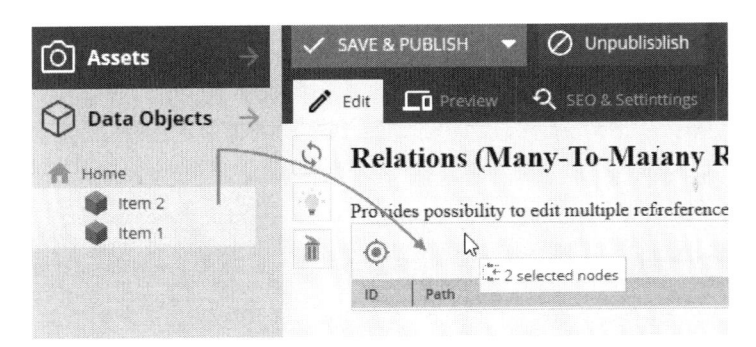

Figure 8.12: Relation configuration

The result of the selection is shown in the following table:

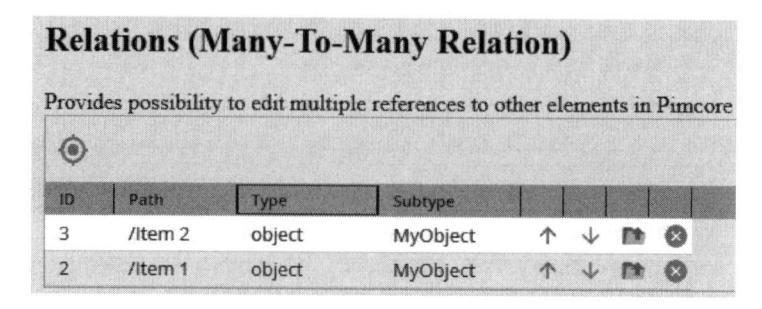

Figure 8.13: Relations in edit mode

With the data in our sandbox, we will have something like this:

- Item 1
- Item 2

Figure 8.14: The output of relations

Image

This editable gives you a widget where you can upload an image. If you drag a file from the asset folder and drop it on the component, the image will be displayed. The advantages compared with the `Relation` component are that the image is easier to use and integrated with the thumbnail system.

The next piece of code allows you to upload an image:

```
{{ pimcore_image("myImage", {
    "title": "Drag your image here",
    "thumbnail": "myThumbnails"
}) }}
```

You can upload images or drag and drop them to the widget as shown in the following screenshot:

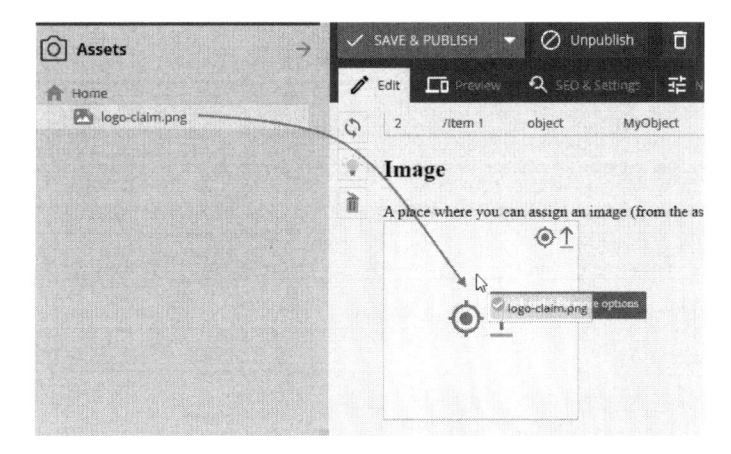

Figure 8.15: Image configuration

Input

`Input` allows the user to input a single line of text, and we can use the input for rendering HTML:

```
{{ pimcore_input("myHeadline") }}
```

We used it in *Chapter 4, Creating Documents in Pimcore*; there isn't anything more to add about this editable.

Link

This is a component for rendering a link:

```
{{ pimcore_link('blogLink') }}
```

The following screenshot shows the link in edit mode:

Figure 8.16 – The link component in edit mode

The component comes out with two buttons: the folder that opens the selected link, and the edit button (pencil icon) that opens the settings form. The next screenshot shows the popup and the parameters available for a link:

Figure 8.17: Link configuration

Once completed, the result is an HTML link with the text and the destination provided.

Select

This snippet adds a `select` component that lets the user choose between a set of items. The following snippet shows how it works:

```
{% if editmode %}
    {{ pimcore_select("myItem", {
        "store": [
            ["option1", "Option One"],
            ["option2", "Option 2"],
            ["option3", "Option 3"]
        ],
        "defaultValue" : "option1"
```

```twig
                }) }}
{% else %}
    Your choice:{{ pimcore_select("myItem").getData() }}
{% endif %}
```

The `store` parameter contains a list of arrays. Each item is composed of an array of two elements: the first is the key, the second is the value. The `defaultValue` setting configures the default value for the selected list item.

This is what is shown in edit mode:

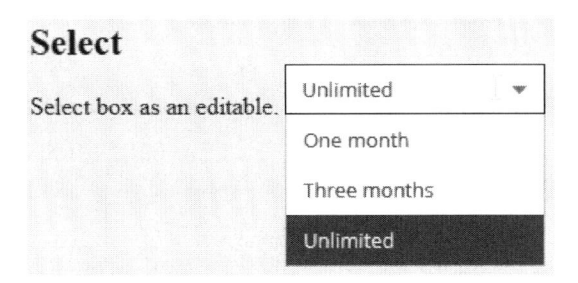

Figure 8.18: Select configuration

Multiselect

The `Multiselect` component is very similar to the `Select` one, but it allows multiple choices:

```twig
{{% pimcore_multiselect("categories", [
        "width" => 200,
        "height" => 100,
        "store" => [
            ["cars", "Cars"],
            ["motorcycles", "Motorcycles"],
            ["accessories", "Accessories"]
        ]
]) %}}
```

This is what is shown in edit mode:

Figure 8.19: Multiselect configuration

Numeric

This editable is like the `Input` one, but specifically for numbers:

```
{{ pimcore_numeric('myNumber') }}
```

This is what is shown in edit mode:

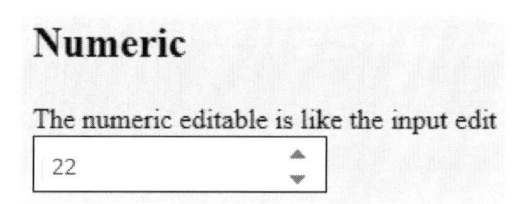

Figure 8.20: Numeric editor

And in edit mode, it returns the number chosen.

Renderlet

The `Renderlet` is a special container that is able to render an object. It uses a controller and an action to process the selected items, and the resulting HTML is provided to the user:

```
{{
    pimcore_renderlet('myGallery', {
        "controller" : "App\\Controller\\CustomController::galleryAction",
        "title" : "Drag an asset folder here to get a gallery",
        "height" : 400
```

```
        })
}}
```

In this case, we need some extra steps to test it. Follow the next steps:

1. Add a template file inside the /app/Resources/views/Default folder called gallery.php, and add the following code to render your data:

   ```
   {% if assets %}
           {% for asset in assets %}
               {% if asset is instanceof(
               '\\Pimcore\\Model\\Asset\\Image') %}
               <div style="border: 1px solid red;
               width:200px; padding 10px;
               margin:10px;">
                   {{ asset.getThumbnail(
                       'MiniIcons').getHTML()|raw}}
               </div>
               {% endif %}
           {% endfor %}

   {% endif %}
   ```

2. Add an action to the default controller with the following code:

   ```
       /**
        * @Template()
        */
       public function galleryAction(Request $request)
       {
           $result=array();
           if ('asset' === $request->get('type')) {
               $asset = Asset::getById($request->get('id'));
               if ('folder' === $asset->getType()) {
                   $result["assets"] = $asset-
                   >getChildren();
               }
           }
   ```

Creating Custom CMS Pages

```
        return $result;
    }
```

3. Then add a `Renderlet` editable into the page with the following configuration:

```
{{
    pimcore_renderlet('myGallery', {
        "controller" : "App\\Controller\\
        CustomController::galleryAction",
        "title" : "Drag an asset folder here to get a
        gallery",
        "height" : 400
    })
}}
```

This configuration tells Pimcore to use the action `galleryAction` from the `Default` controller to render the data.

4. Drag and drop a folder into `Renderlet`; this is what is shown in edit mode:

Figure 8.21:Dragging a folder to Renderlet

View the page as a normal user and see the result of your template:

Figure 8.22: Output with the sample template

Snippet

This component is used to include a document or snippet (a special document type) inside the document; this is useful for reusing scripts or pieces of the website on your page:

```
{{ pimcore_snippet("mySnippet", {"width": 250, "height": 100})
}}
```

Once you have entered the code, this is how to add a snippet to the web page:

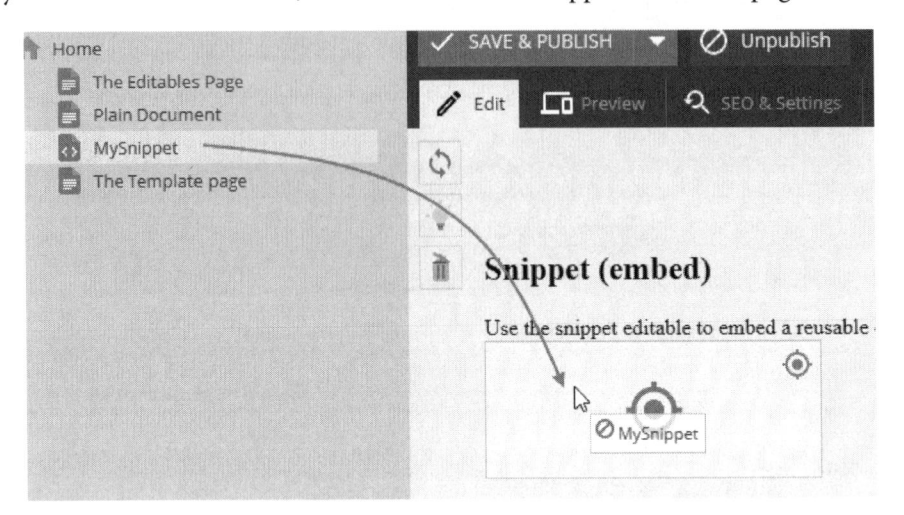

Figure 8.23: Configuration of the snippet control

And this is what you will see as a website user:

Figure 8.24: The output of the snippet control

In the previous screenshot, the text **I'm the default template** comes from the snippet.

Table

This editable creates a table and lets the editor define the data inside of it. You can specify the default number of columns (`cols`) or rows (`rows`). You can also add a matrix of data (array of array) into the `data` parameter. The user will be able to add rows and columns by itself. Here is an example of the editable:

```
{{ pimcore_table("productProperties", {
    "width": 700,
    "height": 400,
    "defaults": {
        "cols": 3,
```

```
        "rows": 3,
    }
})
}}
```

This is the resulting editor interface:

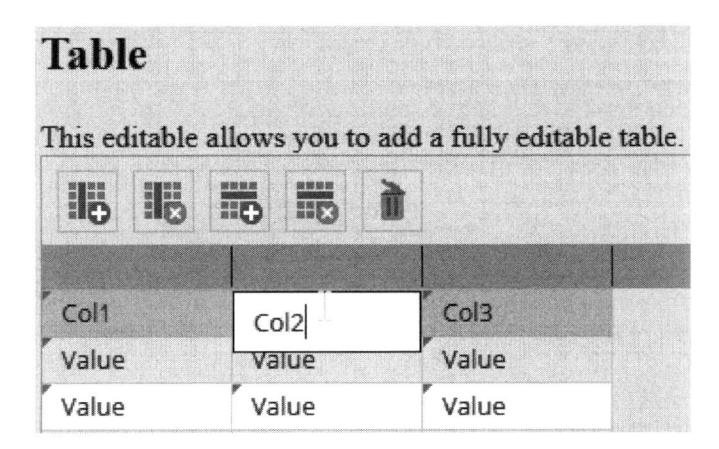

Figure 8.25: Configuration of the table control

And this is the default rendering result:

Figure 8.26: Table output

The previous figure doesn't look nice because the component outputs a simple HTML table without any styles. Of course, based on your CSS theme, you can apply all the styles you want to make it coherent for your website design.

Textarea

This is very similar to the `Input` editable but uses a `Textarea` component instead:

```
{{ pimcore_textarea("myTextarea",
    {"placeholder": "My Description" })
}}
```

Video

This editable allows you to insert movie assets into your page content. It is very similar to the image component but works with video. You will need to add the following snippet to activate it:

```
{{ pimcore_video('campaignVideo', {
    width: 700,
    height: 400
}) }}
```

Then you will be able to define the source (local assets or an external link) and fine-tune some options:

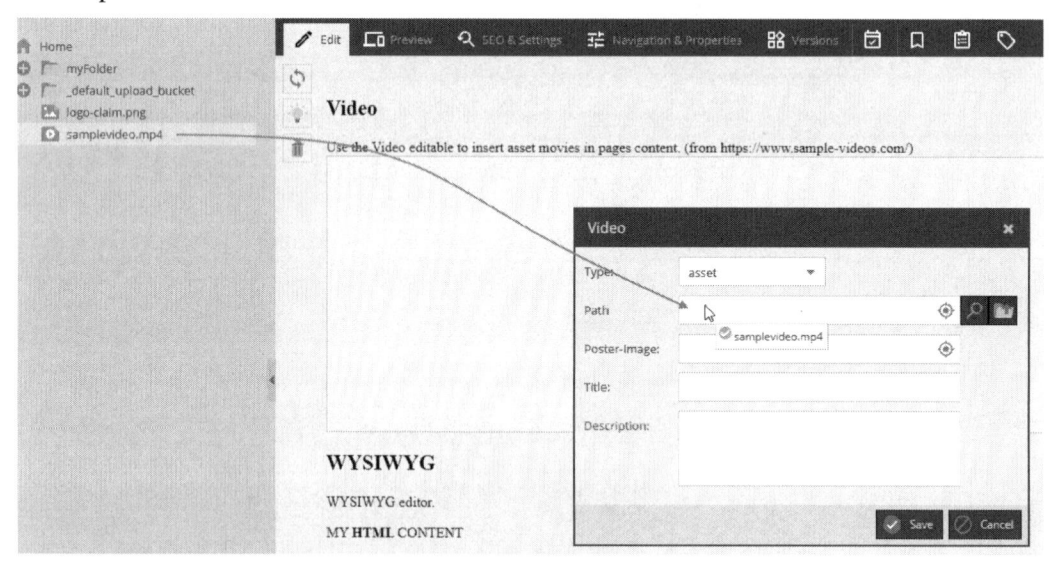

Figure 8.27: Video control

On the web page, you will see it inside a video player as in the following screenshot:

Figure 8.28: Video control output

The video editable is a very powerful solution for letting the user be autonomous in terms of uploading and managing videos without asking for help from a developer.

WYSIWYG

This WYSIWYG editor is used for entering HTML content. In the next piece of code, there is a sample of editable usage:

```
{{  pimcore_wysiwyg("specialContent")      }}
```

We used it in *Chapter 4, Creating documents in Pimcore*; there isn't anything more to add.

In this section, we saw an overview of the most important editables. Using them as base components for the web pages that we create gives us absolute power to customize any aspect of our HTML. Moreover, with this large set of options, cases when you need something more than adding input for the user and then templating the data that you collect are very few. Generally speaking, you do not have to code to satisfy the customer's needs but just template the pages.

For more information about editables, you can consult the official documentation at the following URL: https://pimcore.com/docs/pimcore/current/Development_Documentation/Documents/Editables/.

In the next section, we will discover the usage of blocks, which are simple tools that help to create dynamic pages.

Using blocks

Pimcore blocks are a very clever system for iterating parts of a page. For example, if you have a standard page composed of horizontal bands or titled paragraphs, you can define a piece of HTML that explains how each item should look and let the user add as many items as they want. As another example, you can define a block composed of an H2 title and text, and this will create many titled paragraphs on your web page. Alternatively, you could use a block with an image and create a gallery iterating the blocks. Moreover, you can also manage the visibility of blocks by scheduling their publication.

Regular Blocks

`pimcore_iterate_block` can return the list of blocks. All the code that is wrapped inside the `for` loop can be replicated as many times as the user wants.

The difference between a block iteration and a regular `for` loop is that in the case of a block, the user defines how many items they want, and all the data input inside the editables is persisted.

The syntax for defining a block is very easy and we can see in the next snippet the usage of the previously mentioned functions:

```
{% for i in pimcore_iterate_block(pimcore_block('block name')) %}
    My content
{% endfor %}
```

In the next example, we will see a block in action that iterates over a small template with a header and text that builds a web page with titled paragraphs:

1. Create a page and link the page with a template, as we have done many times before. If you have any doubts, just refer to *Chapter 4, Creating Documents in Pimcore*.

2. Copy the following snippet into the template:

   ```
   {% for i in pimcore_iterate_block(pimcore_block('contentblock')) %}
       <h2>{{ pimcore_input('title') }}</h2>
       <p>{ pimcore_wysiwyg('content') }}</p>
   {% endfor %}
   ```

3. The template part is composed of a `title`, surrounded by a H2 tag and a `paragraph`. In the next screenshot, you will see the result of our code in edit mode before adding the blocks:

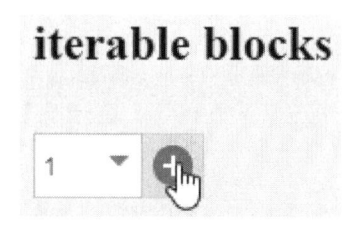

Figure 8.29: Adding a block to the list

4. Go to the page editor and click the green + icon to add one block to the block list. Now the block is visible in the editor and you will be able to enter data. You can add as many blocks as you want; you will be able to edit them one by one in the backend.

5. Now enter data into the editables. In this example, I put **My first item** as the title and **value** inside the long text. The output will be something like the following screenshot:

Figure 8.30: Editing the element in the block list

6. Iterate this for as many blocks as you like.

   The final result will look like this on the web page:

   Figure 8.31: The result after adding more elements

Scheduled Blocks

The scheduled block component is very similar to the block, but it has the option to define an expiration date for the contents. The syntax is the same, as you can see in the next snippet:

```
{% for i in pimcore_iterate_block(pimcore_
scheduledblock('block')) %}
    <h2>{{ pimcore_input('blockinput') }}</h2>
    <p>{{ pimcore_image('myimage') }}</p>
{% endfor %}
```

The process for testing this snippet is exactly the same as the standard block that we saw in the previous section.

In the next screenshot, we will see the edit mode for the scheduled block, where we have a `DateTime` picker near the green + icon that allows the user to define when the content will expire:

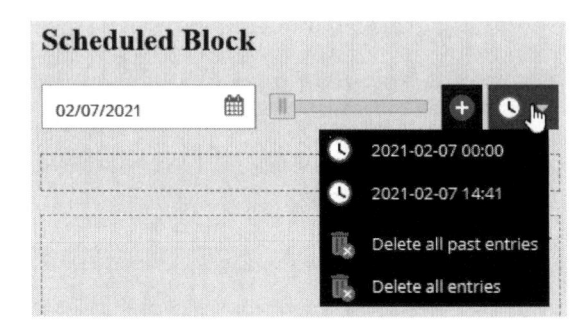

Figure 8.32 – Editing a scheduled block

The block engine is a very powerful system that allows a lot of opportunities for making dynamic pages easily editable by the user. We will appreciate this feature more in *Chapter 10*, *Creating Pimcore Bricks*, when we will use blocks in conjunction with bricks to create fully dynamic templates. Anyway, what we have learned so far is very interesting: we can give the user the opportunity to manage a repetitive template with a well-structured approach.

Summary

In this chapter, we learned all the information needed for creating a custom CMS page. We gained an understanding of the MVC model, and we had a deep dive into the templating engine of Pimcore, discovering all the helpers and how to create our own. We also learned how to write backend code in the controller and make it work by defining routing rules. We saw that there are many ways to manage URLs in Pimcore (Hardcoded, Static Route, and Redirect) and they cover all the use cases for a website. Then we had a complete overview of editables, which left us able to master any custom web page just by templating it. Finally, we discovered the block system that allows the iteration of pieces of a template by giving the user the opportunity to manage repetitive patterns in web pages.

This was an intense chapter that provided us with full knowledge of custom CMS pages. What we learned here will be very useful in the next chapter, *Chapter 9*, Configuring Entities and *Rendering Data*, where we will use it to render web pages for implementing a simple blog engine.

9
Configuring Entities and Rendering Data

In the previous chapter, we learned how the **model-view-controller** (**MVC**) development pattern works and then learned what views and model controllers are. We have also seen how the Pimcore routing system works and how to create relationships between elements. Finally, we saw how to modify the content of our entities, adding images, text, and date fields.

In this chapter, we're going to create a blog, and we will cover the following topics:

- Defining blog classes
- Creating blog Users and Roles
- Routing
- Editing the Controller for our blog
- Rendering blog views
- Differences between Pimcore and WordPress

By the end of this chapter, we will have built our first blog with Pimcore, with articles grouped by categories and authors. We will have also learned how to create suitable templates for each page, inserting the necessary code to display the content created.

Technical requirements

As with the previous chapters, there is a demonstration that you can find on our GitHub repository, which you can access here:

https://github.com/PacktPublishing/Modernizing-Enterprise-CMS-using-Pimcore/

All you need to do to run the demo connected with this chapter is to navigate to the `Full Demo` folder and start the Docker environment.

To read this chapter, the only requirement is to have an up-and-running Pimcore installation and be able to access it via the command line.

If you have installed Pimcore with Docker, just run these simple instructions:

1. Run Docker with the following command:

    ```
    docker-compose up
    ```

2. Restore the local installation settings by running this command:

    ```
    docker-compose exec php bash restore.sh
    ```

3. Navigate to `http://localhost/admin` and log in with your admin/pimcore credentials.

You are now ready to put into practice all the aspects related to this chapter.

Defining blog classes

As we said, a blog is made up of articles and categories, so the first step we need to do is to create two classes relating to these. In addition to these two classes, we have to create a third class: `BlogAuthor`.

All the field types that we are going to use in our classes have already been seen and described in depth in *Chapter 5*, *Exploring Objects and Classes*, so what interests us in this chapter is to define them with their name and type.

The only new element we use is the `slug` field, which for this reason we will briefly describe.

A **slug** is a part of a **Uniform Resource Locator** (**URL**) that identifies a particular page on a website in an easy-to-read way. In other words, it's a part of a URL that explains a page's content—for example, for a URL of `https://demo.pimcore.fun/slug`, the slug simply is `/slug`.

Using a slug thus allows us to identify a page through a readable and more identifiable text, compared—for example—to its numeric **identifier** (**ID**). Furthermore, this improves the indexing of a page by search engines, which prefer text-based URLs rather than URLs with numbers.

Let's take a look at each class we plan to create now.

Defining a BlogArticle class

The `BlogArticle` class is where we will generate articles for our blog. The creation of this class has already been discussed in *Chapter 4, Creating Documents in Pimcore*; the fields in the following list are standard for any article, but nothing prevents you from adding more as needed:

- `Title`: An input field
- `Content`: A **what you see is what you get** (**WYSIWYG**) component
- `Category`: A many-to-one relation of the `BlogCategory` class
- `Slug`: A slug field
- `Author`: A many-to-one relation with the `BlogAuthor` class
- `Image`: An image component

Let's jump directly to what our created class will look like. For convenience, we have grouped the fields in tabs, to make data entry more linear. In the next screenshot, here's what the newly created class looks like:

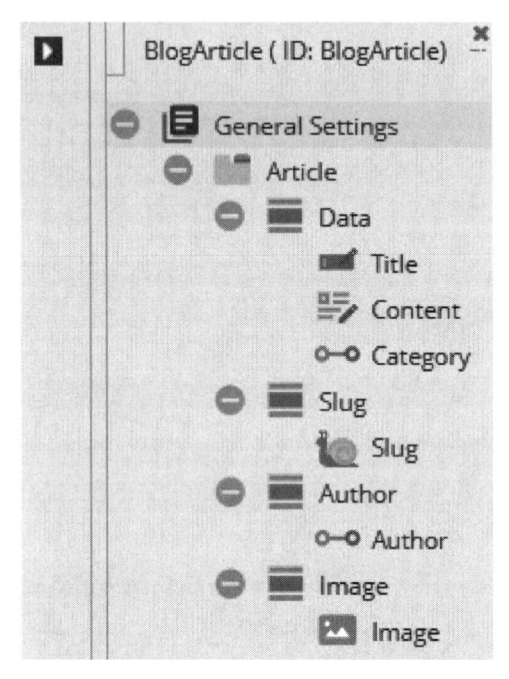

Figure 9.1: BlogArticle class

As you can see in the preceding screenshot, all fields are organized and are easy to recognize thanks to their respective icons.

Defining a BlogCategory class

The category class is relatively simple—it is, as we said, a container of articles. It is used to group articles by topic, so only a few simple fields will be needed, as follows:

- `Title`: An input field
- `Slug`: A slug field
- `Description`: A text-area field
- `Image`: An image component

We will see how to link articles with categories in the *Putting it all together* section.

Defining a BlogAuthor class

As we said, an article is written by a person—or user, in computer terms—so, each article will have an author; that is, it must be associated with the user who wrote it. And in fact, in the `Article` class, we created an `Author` relationship field for just that.

In Pimcore, on the other hand, user management is minimal and does not allow us to extend the user directly. Instead, it allows us to create a relation between a user and one or more Pimcore objects. This can be used to add information to a user or to associate one or more objects directly with a system user.

To do this, we then create an additional class, `BlogAuthor`, so that we can extend the Pimcore user with other properties, such as `FirstName` and `LastName`, a photo, and a biography.

The `BlogAuthor` class is composed of the following fields, whose names are already self-describing:

- `FirstName`: A text field
- `LastName`: A text field
- `User`: A user field
- `Slug`: A slug field
- `Bio`: A text-area field
- `Photo`: An image component
- `User`: A user field

A small clarification should be made for the `User` field. This field uses a component of Pimcore—the `User` type. In the next screenshot, we thus see what the `User` field looks like:

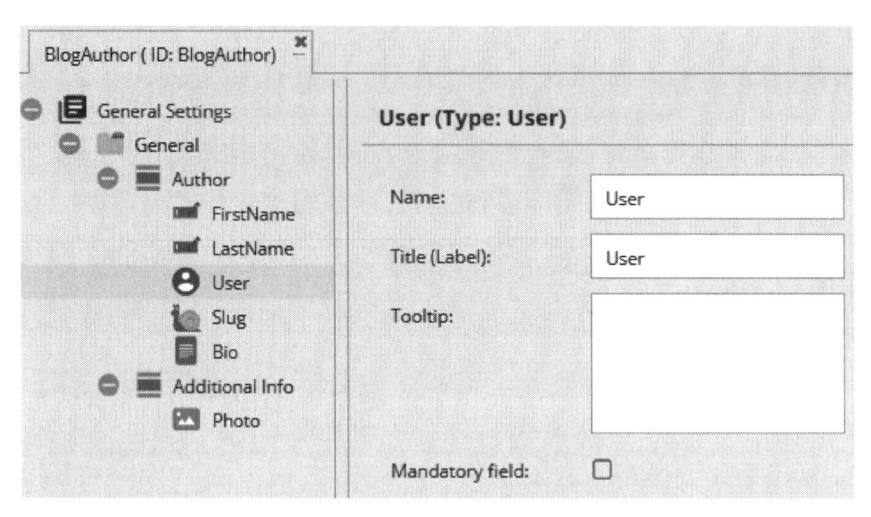

Figure 9.2: User type field

As you can see from the preceding screenshot, the configuration is not particularly complicated, and in fact, the only fields that we can populate will be the name and title of the field itself.

When creating an object instance of the member class, you can see the input widget for the user property. This is a combo box where a user can be selected from all available Pimcore users. Let's see how to associate an author with a Pimcore user. The following screenshot illustrates the process:

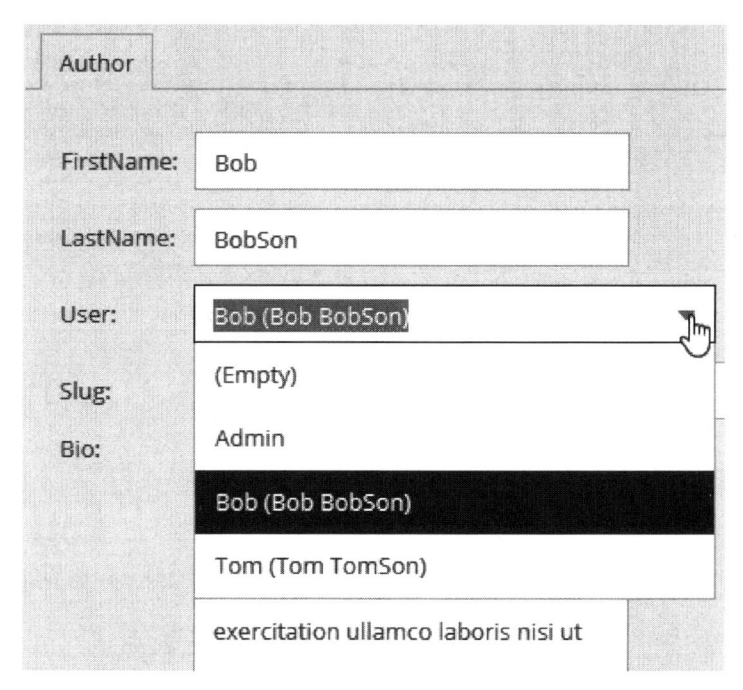

Figure 9.3: Linking author to Pimcore system use

In this example, the user `Bob` was selected.

Now that we have created all the necessary classes for our blog, we still have to configure Pimcore with the users and roles necessary to ensure that the articles can be associated with their respective authors.

Creating blog Users and Roles

The creation of users and roles has already been explained in *Chapter 7, Administrating Pimcore Sites*, so we just have to go back to the notions learned in that chapter to create the necessary users and roles.

For this example, we can create two users, our dear `Bob` and `Tom` (our authors), and an author role to be assigned to our users.

Creating an Author Role

First, we will create a role for the authors. The role configuration is shown in the next screenshot:

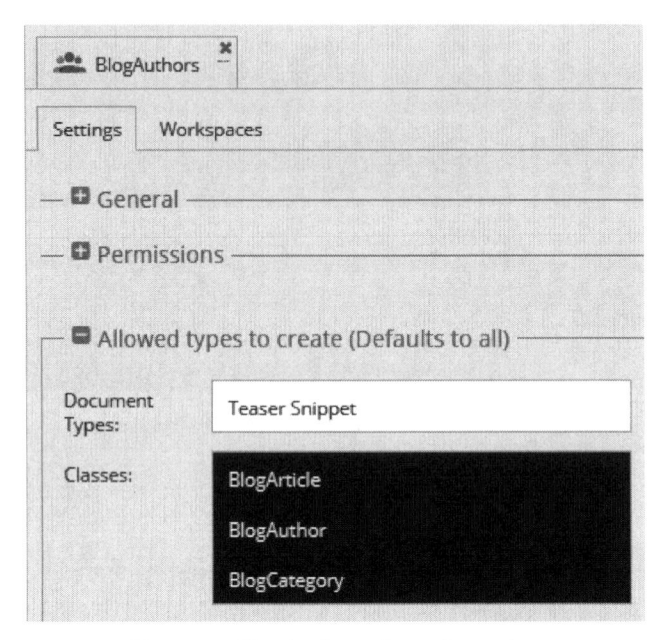

Figure 9.4: BlogAuthor role configuration

As you can see from the preceding screenshot, we have assigned the creation permission for the three classes of the blog: `BlogArticle`, `BlogCategory`, and `BlogAuthor`. This is because we need to allow users who are part of this role to manage these objects. In the **Permissions** section (which in *Figure 9.4* is compressed for reasons of space), we have selected the following items: **Assets**, **Classes**, **Objects**, and **Users**. This will allow users to upload images for their articles, and view the categories and articles created.

A final configuration for the role, as you can see in the next screenshot, is the permissions for each class inside the **Workspaces** tab:

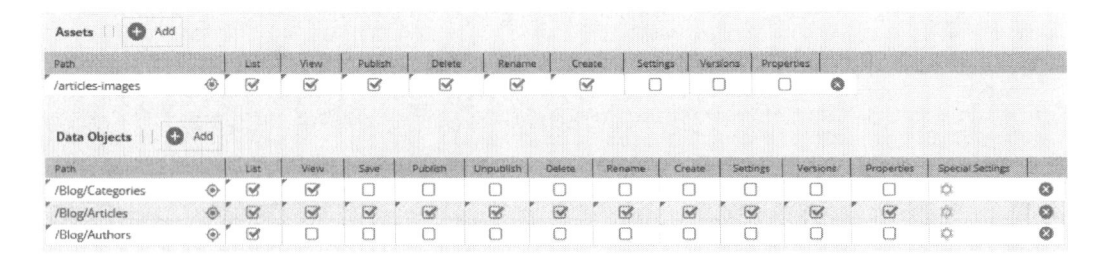

Figure 9.5: BlogAuthors role workspace configuration

As you can see in the preceding screenshot, which represents the configuration of the role for each class, it will be necessary to set the permissions for users—in particular, for the possibility of creating articles, uploading or selecting images, or being able to see a list of authors and categories.

Creating Users

Now that the configuration is complete, we can move on to create the actual entities, based on the classes we created.

First, we need to create users `Bob` and `Tom` and assign them the author role. We have already learned how to create users and roles in *Chapter 7, Administrating Pimcore Sites*, so all we have to do is repeat the same operations already done.

Once that's done, let's create authors. The creation of an author, as well as an article or a category, is done from the Pimcore interface, in the **Data Objects** section.

For convenience, we have grouped the created objects into folders and subfolders, as you can see in the next screenshot:

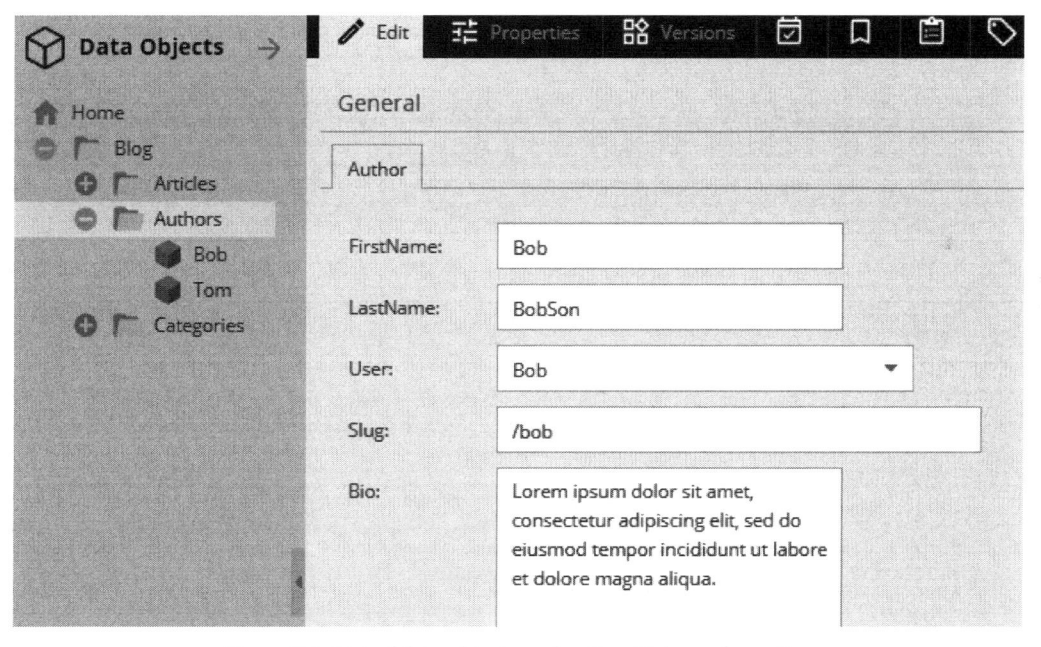

Figure 9.6: List of data objects and author Bob configuration

As you can see in the preceding screenshot, we have created three folders that must contain the objects we are going to create. In particular, the `Blog/Authors` folder will contain all the authors we will create, the `Blog/Categories` folder will contain all the blog categories, and the `Blog/Articles` folder will contain all the articles written by the authors.

In *Figure 9.6*, we can also see that the `User` field is a selection box, where it is possible to associate a user, and in our case, we have selected the system user `Bob`. We then finished filling in the `FirstName`, `LastName`, `Slug`, and `Photo` fields and completed a short biography in the `Bio` field. These fields will be displayed on the author page.

Putting it all together

Once we have created classes for the blog, user, and author, we need to create data objects to represent on the pages: categories and articles. The creation of objects has already been seen in detail in *Chapter 4, Creating Documents in Pimcore,* and *Chapter 5, Exploring Objects and Classes,* so it will not be necessary on this occasion to go into detail on how to do this. For our blog, however, we have created author categories and also uploaded the necessary images for the categories and articles. In the following example screenshot, we see the creation of a first article, with the necessary information and relationships:

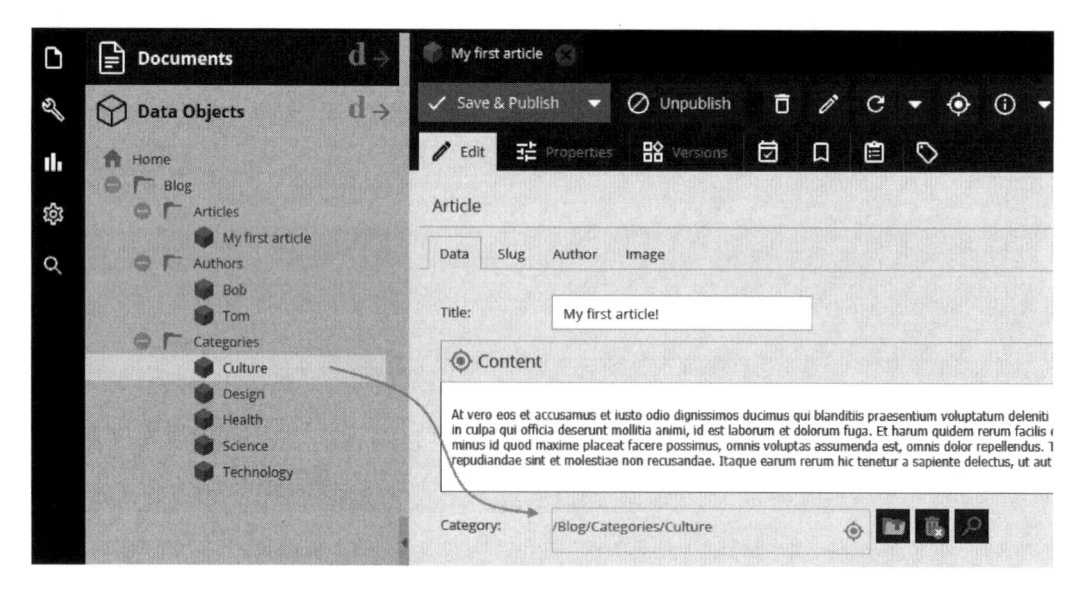

Figure 9.7: Creating our first article

As you can see in the previous screenshot, all the elements have been created, and therefore it is possible to create an article and assign it an author, a category, and an image previously loaded into the asset. The arrow drawn in *Figure 9.7* identifies the drag-and-drop operation of the category in the `Category` field of the article. The same drag-and-drop method can also be used to link the author and image to the corresponding fields in the article.

It is also possible to see how we have grouped objects and assets in different folders. Organizing the directory structure is not mandatory, but it certainly helps to keep the objects we create grouped by type. As you can see from the next screenshot, it is possible to create folders to organize our items by right-clicking on **Home** or any other folder already created:

Figure 9.8: Creating our first article

In the preceding screenshot, you see how we organized our folders, starting from the `Blog` folder, and inside it creating folders for articles, authors, and categories.

The next step we must do is define the rules for navigation around our blog—or, in other words, the routing.

Routing

Routing is a key part of setting up our blog and was discussed in detail in the previous chapter, *Chapter 8, Creating Custom CMS Pages*. We will therefore go on to create hardcoded routes, going directly to the `routing.yml` file to modify this.

Let's create a set of rules that are needed in order to identify articles, categories, and author pages. In addition, we want pages to be accessed by using either our ID or our slug.

As an example, we report the two routing rules related to the article, in this following piece of code:

```
blog_article_by_id:
    path:        /blog/article/{page}
    controller: BlogBundle\Controller\
BlogController:articleAction
    requirements:
      path: '.*?'
      page: '\d+'

blog_article_by_slug:
    path:        /blog/article/{page}
    controller: BlogBundle\Controller\
BlogController:articleAction
    requirements:
      path: '.*?'
      page: '[\w-]+'
```

As you can see in the preceding code snippet, we have defined a path for the display of an article, and we have also set the controller and the parameters needed to identify the article by the ID (`blog_article_by_id`) or by the slug (`blog_article_by_slug`).

By analyzing the two rules, we can see that they differ only in the `path` parameter. In the case of the rule to identify the article by ID, in the path we have to search for an integer, which is the ID of the article. This is possible through the use of **regular expressions** (**regexes**). The regular expression that filters an integer is `\d+`. In the case of the rule that identifies the page through its slug, we must identify a string, and to do this we use the regex defined as `[\w-]+`. This last regex filters all strings composed of words, divided by the minus sign.

> **Important note**
>
> A regular regular expression, also called a regex is a method of matching patterns in text—for example, a regular expression can describe the pattern of email addresses, URLs, telephone numbers, employee identification numbers, social security numbers, or credit card numbers, and of course routes to pages on a site. The use of regular expressions is standard practice in many system and scripting languages. Regular expressions can be simple or very complex. There are hundreds of guides on the subject, easily available on the internet, simply by looking for `regex` on any web search engine.

We have seen how the rules for articles are defined. The `routing.yml` file also contains routing rules for categories and authors, which are defined in exactly the same way, except for the actions to be called on the `BlogController` controller.

Now that we have completed the routing configuration, we must create actions on the controller so that our pages can contain and display the data that interests us.

Let's go now to see how `BlogController` and its actions are written, which we have up to now seen in the routing rules.

Editing the Controller for our blog

Everything about the controller has been explained in the previous chapter, *Chapter 8, Creating Custom CMS Pages*, and therefore in this chapter, we limit the scope to just see which changes we need to make for the blog to work properly.

What we are interested in doing now is to create actions that correspond to the rules we have just finished configuring in the previous section. In fact, if we look at the configuration, we can see that the `Controller` field contains the name of the bundle (`BlogBundle`), followed by the `Controller` keyword, followed by the name of the controller (`BlogController`). The last part is the name of the action (`articleAction`) to be called when the browser URL matches the routing rule.

To clarify these ideas, imagine we write this URL in our browser: `https://myblog.com/blog/article/my-first-article`. We uniquely identify a `blog_article_by_slug` rule. This rule, written in the configuration, indicates that the `articleAction` action is called in the `BlogController` controller of the `BlogBundle` bundle. So, with the URL that we have just written, we have identified an action that is called, which is the `ArticleAction` action. So, let's see how this action is written.

Action for an article (ArticleAction)

As we have just mentioned, this action is called when the URL identifies the route that must display an article, by the ID or the slug. The first thing to do, therefore, will be to retrieve the article, based on the input parameter, as illustrated in the following code snippet:

```
/**
 *  Get detail of article. route: /blog/article/id|slug
 *  @Template()
 */
```

```
public function articleAction(Request $request, $page) {
  if (intval($page)) { // by id
    $article = DataObject\BlogArticle::getById($page);
  }
  else { // by slug
    $slug = UrlSlug::resolveSlug("/$page");
    if ($slug instanceof UrlSlug) {
      $id = $slug->getObjectId();
      if (intval($id) && $id > 0) {
        $article =  DataObject\BlogArticle::getById($id);
      }
    }
  }
  if ( !( $article instanceof DataObject\BlogArticle || $article->isPublished() ) ) {
    // article not found, redirect to blog
    return $this->redirect('/blog');
  }
  return $this->renderTemplate(
    '@Blog/Blog/article.html.twig', array(
      // get all categories for widget
      'categories' => $this->getAllCategories(),
      'article' => $article
  ));
}
```

As you can see from the preceding code snippet, the `articleAction` function takes two parameters: `request` and `page`. The `page` parameter is what interests us, to understand whether we have an ID or a slug in the URL.

First of all, we need to check whether the input parameter in the `$page` variable is of the integer type and retrieve the value it represents. To read an integer from a string, we can use the `intval` function of the PHP language, which gets the integer value of a variable. If the `intval` function returns us an integer value, it means we have an ID. To retrieve an object through its ID, you can use the `getById` function, which Pimcore makes available in all objects. If instead, the `$page` variable is not an integer, then free text has been entered in the URL, which can be the slug of the article. We must then retrieve the object ID via the slug, and once retrieved, we are able to retrieve the object via its ID, exactly as we have just done.

Once the object has been retrieved, we verify that it is an object of type `article`. This is done with the following `if` statement:

```
if ( !( $article instanceof DataObject\BlogArticle || $article->isPublished() ) ) {
```

The first part, the `instanceof` construct, is useful for checking whether an object is of the `BlogArticle` type; the second part of the `if` statement uses a specific Pimcore function, `isPublished()`, which checks whether the document is published. At this point, if everything is correct, we just have to call the `RenderTemplate` function, a function that accepts two parameters: first, the path of the Twig template file, and second, an array of objects to pass to the view. In our example, we passed the path to the article page template (`@Blog/Blog/article.html.twig`) and an array with the two objects necessary for rendering the page view: the article and the list of categories (we will see shortly how to use these variables in the view). For further details on how the MVC pattern works, and about the passage of data from routing to the controller and from the controller to the view, please read *Chapter 8, Creating Custom CMS Pages*.

Other Actions

We have just seen how to write an `ArticleAction` action, linked to the routing rules. The other rules that are present in the `routing.yml` file, which identify the categories and authors, will have their actions, which are written exactly like the action article just seen.

Inspecting the `BlogController` code, we can easily see that all actions have the same structure because they perform the same operations. The purpose of these operations is to identify an object by its ID. The only thing that changes is the object that is recovered, which in one case is the article, in another the category, and in yet another, the author.

Since the code for each action is very similar between actions, it is not necessary to see in detail the other actions, but we only report a list of actions that must be present in the controller, outlined as follows:

- `blogAction`
- `articleAction`
- `categoryAction`
- `authorAction`

All the files used for this demo—such as `routing.yml`, `BlogController.php`, and all the `*.html.twig` files of the views—can be downloaded from our Git repository related to this book: `https://github.com/PacktPublishing/Modernizing-Enterprise-CMS-using-Pimcore/`.

We have seen how routes are defined and what the actions related to them are within the controller. Now, let's go through the files and the code needed to view the data we have recovered in this section.

Rendering blog views

Once we have identified which page a visitor requested, through the routing rules seen before, and after the data has been extracted and passed to the view through the controller, it remains for this to be displayed correctly on the page. In Pimcore, this can be done using a templating system called **Twig**, which as we said in *Chapter 4, Creating Documents in Pimcore*, is the solution with which Pimcore keeps the business logic separate from the presentation logic.

Briefly, Twig is a modern template engine for PHP supported by Symfony (and therefore by Pimcore) that allows you to process code directly in the view page, through its own syntax. The official page of the project, from which it is possible to read the complete documentation, can be reached here: `https://twig.symfony.com/`.

The template is useful and necessary because it is possible to create a single view for different content. In other words, the templating allows us to create a single HTML page to view all the articles of our blog, whether they are a few or in the millions. The view of the page will be the same for everyone—only the content will change. This saves us from having to create a page for each article, which would be a long and useless job.

So, there are four templates we need to create, as follows:

1. `blog`: This is the main page of the blog, which will contain a list of categories.
2. `category`: This is the category page, which will contain all the articles under this category.
3. `article`: The actual article page, where the user can read the article content.
4. `author`: A page containing information about the author, with a name and photo, and a list of their articles.

We will talk about these four templates shortly; however, first, we will mention how the pages were created in HTML and **Cascading Style Sheets** (**CSS**).

Stylization and layout of HTML pages with Bootstrap

Before talking about the blog template page, we need to understand how the pages were made. The pages were written in **HTML**, with some Twig code snippets, while using Bootstrap for graphic styles and layouts. **Bootstrap** is a collection of graphic, stylistic, and layout tools that allow you to have a large number of features and styles that can be modified and adapted according to your needs. You can learn more about this framework on the official project page here: `https://getbootstrap.com/`.

The main component of Bootstrap is the **Grid System**. This component allows you to create layouts, dividing the space into **rows** and **columns**. These layouts will be the starting point for building our template. In addition to the classes for creating a layout, Bootstrap provides a set of CSS classes that stylize the elements of the HTML, such as titles, paragraphs, tables, buttons, and so on. Then, there are the other JavaScript components—that is, elements such as drop-down menus, tab interfaces, tooltips, alerts, accordion menus, sliders, and navigation banners.

After this brief but necessary introduction to Bootstrap, let's get back to our blog. Using the Bootstrap system grid, we have created some layouts, dividing the pages into columns. In the next screenshot, you can see the three types of layouts we used:

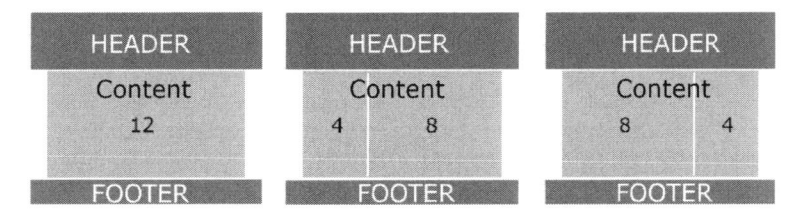

Figure 9.9: Template layouts

As you can see, we have three different layouts for the page, outlined as follows:

- In the first layout, the content has not been divided, and therefore we have a column that occupies twelve-twelfths of the space.
- In the second layout, the content has been divided into two columns—one with four-twelfths of space and the other with eight-twelfths.
- In the third layout, as in the previous layout, the content is divided into two columns of different sizes, but in reverse order compared to the second layout.

We used the first layout with no division for the main blog page, the second with the small column on the left for the author page, and the third for the article and category pages.

Let's see how this was done in the HTML page. To make the layout, we used Bootstrap classes to define the size of the columns. For the first layout, we have the following:

```html
<!-- Page Blog Content -->
<div class="container">
    <div class="row">
        <!-- Post Content Column -->
        <div class="col-lg-12">... here the content
        </div>
    </div> <!-- row -->
</div> <!-- container -->
```

For the second layout, we have the following:

```html
<!-- Page Content -->
<div class="container">
    <div class="row">
        <!-- Post Content Column -->
        <div class="col-md-4">... here the content
        </div>
        <!-- Sidebar Widgets Column -->
        <div class="col-lg-8">... here the content
        </div>
    </div> <!-- row -->
</div> <!-- container -->
```

Finally, for the third layout, we have the following:

```
<!-- Page Content -->
  <div class="container">
    <div class="row">
      <!-- Post Content Column -->
      <div class="col-lg-8">... here the content
      </div>
      <!-- Sidebar Widgets Column -->
      <div class="col-md-4">... here the content
      </div>
    </div> <!-- row -->
  </div> <!-- container -->
```

In this section, we have briefly but clearly seen how the layouts for our template were created. In the next section, we will see how to write the code inside the view files that make up our template.

Templating

The template files are `*.html.twig` files, and with Twig, we are able to insert the data coming from the controller. The layout and graphic style part is done via Bootstrap, as we saw in the previous section. We can report the four templates we have already defined as the following list, with the route to which they respond and the corresponding template file:

1. Blog:

   - Route: `/blog`
   - Twig file path: `BlogBundle/Resources/views/Blog/blog.html.twig`

2. Category:

   - Route: `/blog/category/{page}`
   - Twig file path: `BlogBundle/Resources/views/Blog/category.html.twig`

3. Article:
   - Route: `/blog/article/{page}`
   - Twig file path: `BlogBundle/Resources/views/Blog/article.html.twig`

4. Author:
   - Route: `/blog/author/{page}`
   - Twig file path: `BlogBundle/Resources/views/Blog/author.html.twig`

So, let's see how a complete template is made. As an example, we will take the template of the article.

Inspecting the Article view

In order to understand how the template was made, the best thing is to report the code and describe the parts one piece at a time. So, let's start with the complete template code of the `article.html.twig` file, as follows:

```twig
{% extends '@Blog/Layout/layout.html.twig' %}
{% block content %}
    {% include '@Blog/Layout/header.html.twig' %}
    <!-- Page Content -->
    <div class="container">
        <div class="row">
            <!-- Post Content Column -->
            <div class="col-lg-8">
                <!-- Title -->
                <h1 class="mt-4">{{article.getTitle()}}</h1>
                <!-- Author -->
                <p class="lead">
                    by <a href="/blog/author{{article.getAuthor().getSlug()[0].getSlug()}}">{{article.getAuthor().getFirstName()}}</a>
                </p>
                <hr>
                <!-- Date/Time -->
                <p>Posted on {{article.getModificationDate() | date("F jS \\a\\t g:ia") }}</p>
```

```twig
            <hr>
            <!-- Preview Image -->
            <img class="img-fluid rounded" src="{{article.getImage()}}" alt="">
            <hr>
            <!-- Post Content -->
            {{article.getContent() | raw}}
            <hr>
        </div>
        <!-- Sidebar Widgets Column -->
        <div class="col-md-4">
            {% include '@Blog/Widget/widget.html.twig' %}
        </div>
    </div>
    <!-- /.row -->
</div>
<!-- /.container -->
{% endblock %}
```

Let's start with the first line: the `extends` command indicates to Twig that the page extends the page identified by the `@Blog/Layout/layout.html.twig` path. Extending a page is like saying that the current page is somehow included within the page it extends. In this case, the `layout.html.twig` file contains the definition of the `block content` that we find in the `article.html.twig` file we are analyzing. We've already talked about blocks in *Chapter 4, Creating Documents in Pimcore*, so we can go further and describe the next lines.

Immediately after the start of the content block, we have another `include` statement, which is used to load the content of the `@Blog/Layout/header.html.twig` file. In this file, we find the HTML for the construction of the site header—that is, the image at the top and the title.

Scrolling the file, we see the data relating to the article in the main column: this data is retrieved through the `getTitle()`, `getAuthor()`, `getModificationDate()`, `getSlug()`, and `getImage()` functions. These elements are rendered using Twig commands, which we will see in more detail in the next section of this chapter. However, we can see how all the data is extracted from the `article` variable, which as we recall was passed to the view by the controller in the `RenderTemplate` command.

The other templates differ slightly from this one just seen, and therefore we will not describe them, but all the files are available in the repository related to this book, at `https://github.com/PacktPublishing/Modernizing-Enterprise-CMS-using-Pimcore`.

Rendering the Categories Widget

As we saw in *Figure 9.9*, we have created three types of layouts, two of which have two columns of different sizes. We thought of inserting a component in the narrower columns, called a **widget**, which would contain a list of categories. In the next screenshot, you can see how the **Categories** widget is displayed on the right of the page:

Figure 9.10: Template layouts

As you can see from the preceding screenshot, the **Categories** widget contains a list of all the blog categories, with the number of articles within each category in parentheses.

The **Categories** widget is a recurring element in the various pages, and since it is a recurring element, we have placed it in a separate template under the `Widget` folder. The inclusion of the widget is done through Twig's `include` command. The `include` command expects at least one parameter, which is the path of the file to include, as you can see in the following code snippet:

```
<!-- Sidebar Widgets Column -->
<div class="col-md-4">
```

```
    {% include '@Blog/Widget/widget.html.twig' %}
</div>
```

The function to retrieve the list of categories is written in the `BlogController` controller, as can be seen in the following code snippet:

```
/**
 * get a complete list of categories for blog
 */
public function getAllCategories() {
  $categories = new DataObject\BlogCategory\Listing();
  foreach ($categories as $category) {
    $articles = new DataObject\BlogArticle\Listing();
    $articles->setCondition('Category__id = ' . $category->getId());
    $category->ArticleCount = $articles->getTotalCount();
    if( !empty( $category->getSlug()[0]->getSlug()) ) {
      $category->link = $category->getSlug()[0]->getSlug();
    }
  }
  return $categories;
}
```

Inside the widget file, we created a bulleted list of all the categories through the `for` Twig statement, as illustrated in the following code snippet:

```
<ul class="list-unstyled mb-0">
    {% for cat in categories %}
    <li>
        <a href="/blog{{cat.link}}" >
            {{cat.getTitle()}} ({{cat.ArticleCount}})
        </a>
    </li>
    {% endfor %}
</ul>
```

To get the data, we used the `getTitle()` function, and we read the `ArticleCount` property we created and passed to the view in the controller. We have not used the **Category Description** field, but we leave this as an exercise to you to retrieve this field and display it on the page.

Understanding Twig filters

Filters are functions that change the value of a variable—for example, think of all those PHP functions that transform the value of a string: `strtoupper`, `strtolower`, and so on. In Twig, they are used through the `pipe`, `|`, and some arguments are accepted. Here are some examples:

```
{{textWithsomeCharUpperCase | lower}}
{{arrayOfStrings | join (',')}}
```

The first example converts the value of the string to lowercase, while the second prints the contents of the `arrayOfStrings` array by separating the elements with a comma. You can consult a list of filters in the official documentation here: `https://twig.symfony.com/doc/`.

Now, let's see in detail the filters we used to create our templates.

Formatting dates with the date filter

The `date` filter formats a date to a given format. Here's how we used this filter:

```
<p>Posted on {{article.getModificationDate() | date("F jS \\a\\t g:ia") }}</p>
```

As you can see from the preceding code snippet, we used an `F jS \\a\\t g:ia` date format. The `F jS` part indicates how we want to format the date, while `g:ia` indicates the time format. The middle text, `\\a\\t`, is just there to write "*at*" between the date and time. For all possible formatting types for the date and time, you can consult the PHP online guide at `https://www.php.net/manual/en/datetime.format.php`.

Content ellipsed with the slice filter

In some cases, the text we have to display is too long, such as in the article list, where we want to display only an image of the article and the first two or three lines of the content. What we would like is to truncate the text and replace the cut text with three ellipses, to make the visitor understand that the article is not complete. To do this, we use the `slice` filter. The `slice` filter extracts a slice of a sequence, an array, or a string. Here's how we used this filter:

```
{% set content = cat.getContent() | length > 100 ? cat.
getContent() | slice(0, 100) ~ ' ...' : cat.getContent() %}
...
<div class="card-body">
    ...
   <p class="card-text">{{ content | raw }}</p>
</div>
```

As you can see from the preceding code snippet, we have set a `content` variable, which we will then use in the content of the template, with the value of the article content, applying a condition and a filter on the length. In particular, if the text exceeds `100` characters, we apply the `slice` filter and take the first `100` characters, and concatenate the three continuation points to the string. If instead, the content is not more than `100` characters, we take it in its entirety. We also used the `length` filter to get the length of the string in characters. One last trick: we used the tilde character (~) to concatenate the string.

Rendering text with the raw filter

The `raw` filter marks the value as being "safe," which means that in an environment with automatic escaping enabled, this variable will not be escaped if `raw` is the last filter applied to text. As we have just seen, we used the `raw` filter to view the article content, as illustrated here:

```
<p class="card-text">{{ content | raw }}</p>
```

If you want to see exactly how the `raw` filter behaves, you can try removing the `raw` filter from the content of an article, and see the result.

Filters are very useful tools because they allow us to modify data directly during the presentation phase. In this section, we have seen some of the filters available and how to use them. For all the other filters, it is possible to go to the official page of the Twig project, following this link: `https://twig.symfony.com/doc/`.

Differences between Pimcore and WordPress

We have seen how to create a blog with Pimcore. However, some may wonder whether making a blog using Pimcore is the right choice. There are many **content management systems** (**CMSes**) that already do this job—WordPress, above all.

We mentioned WordPress because, for those who don't know of it yet, this is a powerful open source software solution that you can use easily and freely to create blogs. It is certainly the most popular CMS, due to its ease of installation and configuration. Almost all website-hosting solutions offer the option of having WordPress pre-installed in your domain. Even the use of it does not require any special knowledge—it is very intuitive and comes with a simple and effective administration page. It is also possible to extend its functionality through the installation of plugins, and for the frontend, it is possible to download and install thousands of graphic themes with nothing more than a click. All these features have made WordPress the preferred choice for 40% of the sites currently online on the web.

So, why use Pimcore to create a blog, instead of WordPress? If, as we said, WordPress is the reference blog CMS, what are the reasons that can lead us to use Pimcore? Let's try to analyze the advantages and disadvantages (if any) of this choice.

Unlike WordPress, Pimcore is based on an MVC development pattern, and this allows the decoupling of business logic with presentation logic. In the view part, in addition, Pimcore uses a rendering engine (Twig) that facilitates the insertion of data into the pages, without having to use PHP code. Among other things, this simplifies **user interface** (**UI**) changes (with a much lower development cost) because the data is passed to the view by the controller, rather than extracted and processed inside the view itself.

Another aspect in favor of Pimcore is the fact of being able to have structured data, while in WordPress, the metadata linked to entities (articles, categories, users...) is not typed. In order to have typed data, it is necessary to install one of the many plugins available. The downside is that plugins store data and typing configuration in their metadata, so if—for example—we want to change or remove a plugin, we will also lose the data we saved with it.

Another thing to take into consideration in our choice is that Pimcore is a complete framework, so it is possible to create features inside it. In WordPress, everything is feasible too, but only with the use of plugins.

Someone will rightly think: *But WordPress already has all the elements to create a blog—articles, users, categories, tags.* True. But it is also true that the effort to create the same structure of a blog in Pimcore, seen in this chapter, is minimal. And once you invest the time it takes to create a blog, the rewards become substantial because at this point, we will have the functionality of WordPress, but with the ability to customize and modify every aspect at will to make it suitable for our needs. Let's take an example: if we want to add the `work` field to the user, what should we do? Well, on Pimcore, as we created the other fields, we just have to add one, and we did. On WordPress? It is obviously possible to do this on WordPress, but by installing a plugin.

We have talked several times about plugins for WordPress. We don't need to know how they work, but what we are interested in saying is that there are thousands of plugins, suitable for all purposes. Many of them are paid, almost all will do many more things than needed, and in general, installing plugins on WordPress requires attention to any conflicts between plugins, as well as configuration, updating, and maintenance. Being created by third-party developers, a plugin is not necessarily up to date; maybe it is not compatible with the latest version of WordPress, or a developer may decide to abandon it. In other words, it is always better and more advantageous to do the development directly inside the platform than to use external third-party tools.

Now, let's see the additional features that Pimcore offers. First of all, it is possible to create multilingual sites. WordPress still does not allow this, so to do this it is necessary once again to install a plugin.

Pimcore allows you to create multisites—that is, manage multiple sites and multiple domains in the same Pimcore installation. Even on WordPress, it is possible to create multisites but only on third levels, so not on different domains. For example, in a multisite WordPress installation, it is possible to manage `mysite.domain.com` and `mysite2.domain.com`, but it is not possible to manage `mysite.com` and `mysite2.com` in the same WordPress installation—a limitation that could be annoying for the management of a site with many connected domains.

Pimcore allows you to easily create perspectives, to limit access to parts of the administrative backend, based on the profile or roles of the user who accesses them. On WordPress, this is not possible, and often access to the administrative area by users must be done through ad hoc views, and therefore without being able to reuse the WordPress backend.

The advantages of having Pimcore, regardless of whether we will use it as a blog or not, will still be greater than using WordPress because with Pimcore, we will have support for business functions such as **product information management** (**PIM**), which we will see in *Chapter 12, Implementing Product Information Management,* or **digital asset management** (**DAM**), seen in *Chapter 6, Using Digital Asset Management*.

With this, we are not saying that Pimcore is better than WordPress, but we are just evaluating and comparing the two systems and what they can do. This will surely help the end user in adopting the most suitable platform for their purposes.

Summary

In this chapter, we have seen how to build a blog, which classes we need to create, how to create files for the pages, how they should be structured as HTML, and how it is possible to render the data thanks to the Twig framework. We have also seen how the routes of a site are built and how it is possible to choose which content to display based on the request, through the use of the `routing.yml` file and the `BlogController` controller. Finally, we learned how to build Bootstrap layouts for our site and learned how to create templates with the Bootstrap framework.

In the next chapter, we will learn how to build reusable components called **Bricks** that can be placed in CMS or **Multiple Virtual Storage** (**MVS**) pages and, moreover, can be ported from project to project using bundles.

10
Creating Pimcore Bricks

In the previous chapter, we learned how to use Pimcore to create entities and render custom web pages. Previously, in *Chapter 8, Creating Custom CMS Pages*, we discovered how to create CMS pages using the web interface or custom **Model View Controller** (**MVC**) pages. In both cases, we'd like to have some reusable components that can be defined once and used in every case by changing some settings. Think about a contact form widget that you can drag and drop on any web page. Well, these kinds of reusable components in Pimcore are called **Bricks**.

In this chapter, we will learn how to build reusable components that can be placed in CMS or MVC pages and, moreover, can be ported from project to project using bundles.

This is our roadmap:

- Creating a bundle
- Understanding how a Brick works
- Implementing a simple Brick
- Implementing a contact form Brick
- Implementing a Slideshow brick
- Using bricks and blocks for a general-purpose template

By the end of this chapter, you will have learned how to create custom interactive widgets to compose pages. This is important to cover all the needs of the users on your website.

Let's start to discover bricks!

Technical requirements

As with the previous chapters, there is a demo that you can find on our GitHub repository here: `https://github.com/PacktPublishing/Modernizing-Enterprise-CMS-using-Pimcore/`.

All you need to run the demo connected to this chapter is to clone it, then navigate to the `Full Demo` folder and start the Docker environment.

To do so, just follow these instructions:

1. Run Docker with the following command:

    ```
    docker-compose up
    ```

2. Then, to restore all the settings from on your local machine, type the following:

    ```
    docker-compose exec php bash restore.sh
    ```

3. Navigate to `http://localhost/admin` and log in with your admin/pimcore credentials.

What you will get with this setup is the following:

- A `BlogBundle` where you will find all the assets produced in this chapter
- A fully working Pimcore instance, with data and configuration installed

This project is a good reference, but after all the practice we have had with Pimcore, you could also start a project from scratch and try to replicate all the steps on your own.

Creating a bundle

Before starting our journey into bricks, we have to learn how to create a bundle. In *Chapter 7*, *Administrating Pimcore Sites*, we learned how to install a bundle released from a vendor, but how do we build our own? In this section, we will learn how a bundle is structured and how you can build it. Bundles are very important for creating a portable set of features that you can reuse or distribute across websites. In our demo project, we will create a blog bundle that is self-contained and that you can pick and place on any of your websites.

What is a bundle?

You have used the main application for many examples in previous chapters. This is good for implementing the specific project but it is not portable. Talking simply, a bundle is a folder that contains both source code and templates. You can get this set of files by adding a composer dependency or by using a local folder. This lets you take your code and reuse it in multiple projects, or simply divide a complex application into modules. For simplicity, in this book, we will use a local folder inside the `bundles` path. Each subfolder will host a different bundle. In this chapter, we will cover all that is needed to start a blog, so we will create a `BlogBundle`. This means that we will have the `/bundles/BlogBundle` folder that will contain all the bundle-related files. This set of files is not discovered automatically; you have to add a specific configuration in your `composer.json`. In the next piece of code, there is the configuration for the blog bundle:

```
"autoload": {
    "psr-4": {
        "App\\": "src/",
        "BlogBundle\\": "bundles/BlogBundle/",
        "Pimcore\\Model\\DataObject\\": "var/classes/DataObject",
        "Pimcore\\Model\\Object\\": "var/classes/Object",
        "Website\\": "legacy/website/lib"
    }
},
```

As you can see in the previous snippet, the blog folder is added to the `psr-4` definition, just after the standard `src` that's mapped to the `App` namespace. In our case, we map the `BlogBundle` namespace with the `bundles/BlogBundle/` folder. Of course, you can play with this configuration and create your own setup to fit your needs. Anyway, we recommend keeping the configuration as close as possible to the Symfony standard.

Here is a list of folders and files inside a bundle:

- `/bundles/BlogBundle`: This is the bundle folder that contains all the bundle assets. The bundle is self-contained, so it contains all the resources (config, themes, and so on) and the classes.
- `DependencyInjection`: This contains two important files for configuring the bundle: `BlogExtension.php` (the convention is the name of the bundle without the `Bundle` word and then `Extension.php`) and `Configuration.php`.

- `Document/Areabrick`: This folder is used for `Brick` classes; we will look at it in detail in the next section.
- `Controller`: This folder contains the controllers.
- `Resources`: This contains the following subfolders:

    a) `config`: Where your YAML files are built.

    b) `public`: Here you can load all the assets that will be published under `/bundles/{bundle name}/`, so if you add here a file called `script.js`, you will have it at `http://localhost/bundles/blog/script.js`.

    c) `views`: You can create here a subfolder containing templates for each controller. This folder also contains the `Areas` subfolder, which will have all the `Brick` templates.

Now it's time to create our first bundle!

Creating a bundle from the command line

You could manually create the files and folders by using the naming convention. This is not hard, but it is easy to make some errors while doing it manually. Fortunately, we have a command from Pimcore that does the job for us.

In Symfony 5, this is no longer a built-in feature, so we have to install a bundle from Pimcore and then we can use the console to create a bundle skeleton.

Creating a bundle is very straightforward and will be explained in the next steps:

1. Enter your Docker instance using the following command:

    ```
    docker-compose exec php bash
    ```

2. Install the bundle generator using the following command:

    ```
    composer require pimcore/bundle-generator
    ```

    The previous command will add the bundle and configure it for use as a regular console command.

3. Navigate to `config/bundles.php` and register the bundle using the following piece of code:

    ```
    <?php

    use Pimcore\Bundle\BundleGeneratorBundle\
    ```

```
    PimcoreBundleGeneratorBundle;

return [
    PimcoreBundleGeneratorBundle::class => ['all' =>
    true],
];
```

4. Run the following command:

   ```
   bin/console pimcore:generate:bundle BlogBundle
   ```

   This will create a set of folders and files for your bundle. The result after you run this command is the creation of the bundle with all the basic subfolders.

5. Moreover, in order to make the bundle content available for the application, we need to change our composer definition by adding a namespace mapping, as in the next example:

   ```
   "psr-4": {
       "App\\": "src/",
       "BlogBundle\\": "bundles/BlogBundle/",
       ...
   }
   ```

   After this step, you might need to run `chmod -R www-data.` for a permission fix. In the Docker example we provided, this is mandatory.

6. Now the bundle is available for the system and can be enabled and installed as explained in *Chapter 3, Getting Started with Pimcore Admin UI*.

In this section, we learned how a bundle is composed and how to create a new one. Now that we have our bundle ready, we can start talking about bricks by using some practical examples.

Understanding how a Brick works

In simple words, a Brick is composed of a class that takes the place of the controller and a view. Building a Brick is not so different from implementing an MVC page. The most important exception is that, in this case, we do not have the routing part, as the Brick is added to an existing page (it cannot be run standalone). In the following diagram, we have a schema that explains how Bricks work:

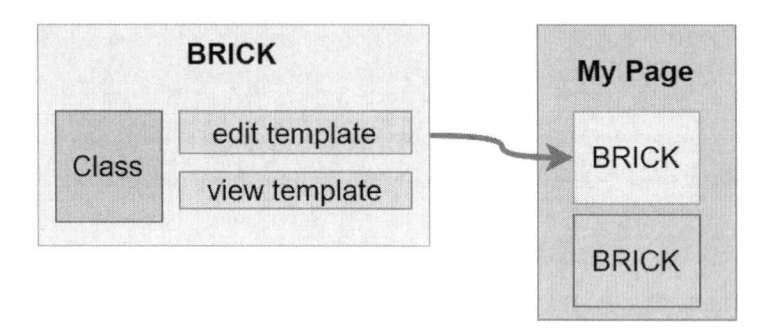

Figure 10.1: Conceptual schema for a brick

In the previous diagram, we can see that a page (**My Page**) can host many bricks. Each one is composed of a **Class** and two templates (**edit** and **view**).

In the following sections, we will learn how to implement every single component, including classes and templates.

The class implementation

A brick is an instance of `Pimcore\Extension\Document\Areabrick\AreabrickInterface`, but for convenience, we always extend the `AbstractTemplateAreabrick` class, which implements the interface and gives us some interesting methods. These classes can be loaded manually or autoloaded using YAML files. Even if adding classes to YAML files is easy, it is always an additional step to do. So, we usually prefer the autoloading scenario, which simply requires us to use a default folder (`Document/Areabrick`) where we place the classes. The namespace of your class must be `namespace BlogBundle\Document\Areabrick`.

The following class implements a simple brick:

```
class MyBrick extends AbstractTemplateAreabrick
{
    public function getName()
    {
```

```php
        return 'The Brick Name';
    }

    public function getDescription()
    {
        return 'The Brick description';
    }
    public function getTemplateSuffix()
    {
        return static::TEMPLATE_SUFFIX_TWIG;
    }
}
```

As you can see in the preceding snippet, there are some methods that have to be implemented to provide the information for your components. These methods, highlighted in the code, are as follows:

- getName: This method returns the name of the brick (it should be unique).
- getDescription: This method returns the long description of the brick and it is shown in the web interface to give the user an idea of what the brick does.
- getTemplateSuffix: This method is used for defining the template extension (Twig or PHP). To adopt Twig templates instead of a PHP template, use static::TEMPLATE_SUFFIX_TWIG.

Now that the class part is ready, we can see how to set up the templating in the next section.

Templating

Usually, for brick classes, the template follows a naming convention. The place where they have to be located is the Areas folder inside the view folder (Resources/views). Each brick must have its own folder, but the folder name must be in spinal case (all lowercase with hyphens between words, so MyBrick will need a folder named my-brick). The name of the view template has to be view.html.twig.

Some bricks are fully WYSIWYG, and you can change the component's behavior just by entering data. Others have the configuration separated by the rendering. In these cases, you can configure an edit popup that will prompt for data. We will see that configuration in detail with the next sections' examples.

In the next schema, we summarized the naming convention, adding a path example for each case. The **Global** scenario is the option where you add the brick to the main project (app folder) and the **Bundle** scenario is where you will add the brick to specific a bundle:

- **View path**:

    a) **Global**:
    ```
    templates/views/Areas/{BrickID}/view.html.(php|twig)
    ```

    b) **Bundle**:
    ```
    {BundleLocation}/Resources/views/Areas/iframe/view.html.(php|twig)
    ```

- **Class**:

    a) **Global**:
    ```
    src/Document/Areabrick/{BrickID}
    ```

    b) **Bundle**:
    ```
    {BundleLocation}/Document/Areabrick/{BrickID}
    ```

In this section, we learn what a brick is composed of. This was important for understanding the naming convention and the principles for using them. Now it's time to go in depth with some examples! In the next section, we will cover the most important use cases, from easy to complex usage.

Implementing a simple brick

In this section, we will implement our first brick. Because the spirit of this book is to learn using real-world examples, we won't limit this to a "hello world" example. In our first example, we will create a widget that could be placed many times on the page and reused. This widget will allow adding text, choosing the header type (h1, h2, and so on), and entering the text.

To complete this goal, we have to follow these steps:

1. Create a document and link it to a controller and a template file. We have done this step many times in *Chapter 4, Creating Documents in Pimcore*, and *Chapter 9, Configuring Entities and Rendering Data*. This document will be used for testing the brick that we are creating.

2. Create a `Heading.php` file inside `/bundles/BlogBundle/Document/Areabrick`. The contents of the file should be like this:

```php
class Header extends AbstractTemplateAreabrick
{
    public function getName()
    {
        return 'Header';
    }

    public function getDescription()
    {
        return 'A component for rendering a Header';
    }

    public function getTemplateLocation()
    {
        return static::TEMPLATE_LOCATION_BUNDLE;
    }
}
```

The code provided declares a brick called `Header` with a specific description. Now that we have the brick definition, we have to add a template for it. This will be our next step.

3. Add a template in `/bundles/BlogBundle/Resources/views/Areas` called `view.html.twig`.

4. Add the following code to the file:

```twig
{% if editmode %}

{{pimcore_select('style', {
        "store" : [
            ['h1', 'H1'],
            ['h2', 'H2'],
            ['h3', 'H3']
        ],
        "defaultValue" : "h1"
```

```
    })}}
```

```
    {{pimcore_input('text')}}
```

```
    {% else %}
```

```
    <{{pimcore_select('style')}}>{{pimcore_
    input('text')}}<{{pimcore_select('style')}}>
```

```
    {% endif %}
```

The code is divided into two branches. The first one is activated in edit mode and displays a select component that lets you choose the heading type (h1, h2, and so on) and the text; the second branch of code displays the data wrapping text in the header. All we need to implement our first brick is done; we just have to test it now.

5. Inside the template that was created in *Step 1*, add the following snippet:

```
    {{ pimcore_areablock("header") }}
```

This editable will display the following component in edit mode:

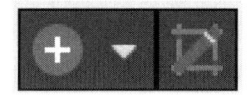

Figure 10.2: Editable components

This component is just a placeholder that will let us choose a brick from the brick list and will put it inside the page. We will do this in the next step.

6. Click on the plus button. It will display the following menu:

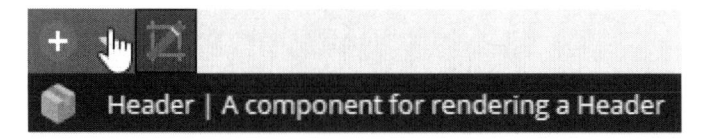

Figure 10.3: The menu for Areablock

As you can see in the preceding screenshot, the data we entered into the class is used to distinguish the component. In fact, we chose **Header** as the brick name and **A component for rendering a Header** as the description.

7. Click on the **Header** item. A component will be added to the page. The Pimcore editable component lets us enter the title and pick the right heading type. Choose **H1** and enter `My H1 text` into the box:

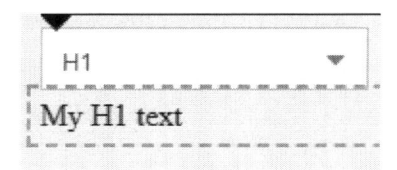

Figure 10.4: The heading brick editing

8. Now click the **Preview** button or navigate to the page. The output will be the following:

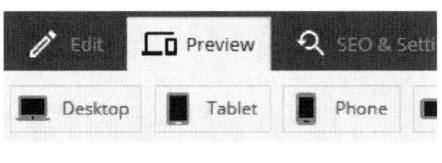

Figure 10.5: The output of the brick

The page displays the text we chose properly.

This first example shows how simple it is to create a reusable component in Pimcore. In fact, we can use the heading brick on every page, giving the user the power of picking it when needed and configuring it. You can use this in conjunction with **blocks** to allow the user to choose a sequence of custom elements or hardcode it in a template. Moreover, we can also use an interactive brick. We will discover all these features in the next sections.

Implementing a contact form brick

In this example, we will discover how to create an interactive component where the user can insert data. For this purpose, we will create a contact form. The behavior of this widget will be straightforward: we will have a form with a subject, name, message, and clickable button. An email will be sent to a fixed recipient address once the details are filled in and the button is clicked. This example will also introduce a working example of opening the brick's editor to get parameters not shown in the view. Follow these steps to implement the example:

1. First, create a document with a template and place an `areabrick` in the editable's template. In the next step, we will have to create the brick.

2. Create the ContactForm.php file in /bundles/BlogBundle/Document/ Areabrick/. The content will be as follows:

```php
class ContactForm extends AbstractTemplateAreabrick
{
    public function getName()
    {
        return 'ContactForm';
    }

    public function getDescription()
    {
        return 'ContactForm';
    }

    public function getTemplateLocation()
    {
        return static::TEMPLATE_LOCATION_BUNDLE;
    }
}
```

3. Now we need to ask the user to add the recipient address for the contact form. In a complex scenario, you may need to add more parameters and organize them. This is possible by implementing a special EditableDialogBoxInterface interface. In the next piece of code, we can see the code that we have to add:

```php
class ContactForm extends AbstractTemplateAreabrick
    implements EditableDialogBoxInterface
{

    public function
    getEditableDialogBoxConfiguration(Document\Editable
    $area, ?Info $info): EditableDialogBoxConfiguration
    {
        $config = new EditableDialogBoxConfiguration();

        $config->setItems([
            'type' => 'tabpanel',
```

```
            'items' => [
                [
                    'type' => 'panel',
                    'title' => 'Contact Form Settings',
                    'items' => [
                        [
                            'type' => 'input',
                            'label' => 'Email Recipient',
                            'name' => 'recipient'
                        ]
                    ]
                ]
            ]
        ]);

        return $config;
    }
}
```

The configuration is, in fact, an array of items that can be grouped in a container. In our case, we used a tab pane, and we placed the input inside it. This array will be used to automatically generate the user's input form. Entered data will be available to the user as regular editables, as in the following snippet:

```
$recipient=$this->getDocumentEditable($info-
>getDocument(), 'input', 'recipient')->getData();
```

4. Create the view.html.twig file. This file will contain all the content that will be displayed to the user. In the next snippet of code, we have a simplified version of the form for brevity (the full bootstrap example is in the source code related to this book):

```
{% if alert is defined %}
    {{ alert }}
{% endif%}

<form id="contact-form" name="contact-form" method="POST">
```

```
<input type="hidden" name="sendEmail" value="true"/>
<input type="text" id="name" name="name" >
<input type="text" id="email" name="email" >
<input type="text" id="subject" name="subject" >
<textarea type="text" id="message" name="message" >
</textarea>
<input type="submit" value="submit" />
</form>
```

The template contains an alert message, which is a message used to confirm sending the email to the user or to display an error. The form contains the input for getting the field from the user and a submit button. The action is not specified, so this form will submit data to the page itself. The input hidden `sendEmail` is a flag that will activate the sending procedure.

5. Now it's time to specify logic in the backend for reading POST data and to send a real email. The next snippet shows the method to add to the brick class:

```
public function action(Info $info)
{
    $request=$info->getRequest();

    $id= $info->getEditable()->getName();
    $info->setParam('id', $id);

    $sendEmail=$request->get("sendEmail");
    if($sendEmail==$id)
    {
        $name=$request->get("name");
        $email=$request->get("email");
        $subject=$request->get("subject");
        $message=$request->get("message");

        //send an email here
        $sent= $this->sendEmail($name,$email,
        $subject,$message, $recipient);
        if($sent)
        {
```

```
            $alert="the message is sent!";
        }
        else
        {
            $alert="there was an error, try later";
        }
        $info->setParam('name',$name);
        $info->setParam('email',$email);
        $info->setParam('subject',$subject);
        $info->setParam('message',$message);
        $info->setParam('alert',$alert);


    }


    $recipient=$this->getDocumentEditable($info->
    getDocument(), 'input', 'recipient')->getData();
    $info->setParam('recipient',$recipient);


}
```

The preceding code implements the logic for getting parameters and sends an email notifying the user about the result. `$request=$info->getRequest();` is used to get the HTTP request that contains the submitted data, and the `get` method is used to obtain the value of the `sendEmail` flag, which activates the sending procedure. You can pass variables to the view by using the parameters, as in the following piece of code:

```
$info->setParam('recipient',$recipient);
```

Now all the components are in place to test our brick.

6. Add the brick to the page by following *Steps 5-6* from the *Implementing a simple brick* section. Now you will have the contact form component on the page and it will be a working one.

7. Open the settings by clicking the pencil icon in the brick's toolbar:

Figure 10.6: Opening the popup

8. By clicking the pencil icon, a popup will be shown:

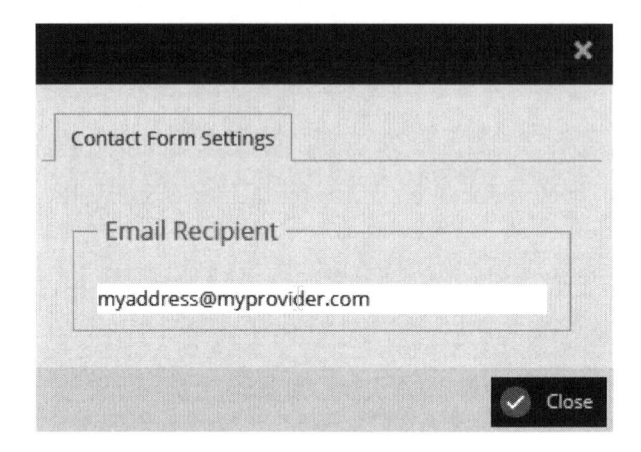

Figure 10.7: The popup for entering the recipient

You can enter an email address to be used as the recipient for the contact form.

9. Save the document and open the document's page you created in *Step 1* of this section. The contact form will be shown.

10. Fill in the form with data (it is a contact form, so the field meanings should be self-explanatory) and click **Send**. You should see a confirmation alert as in the following screenshot:

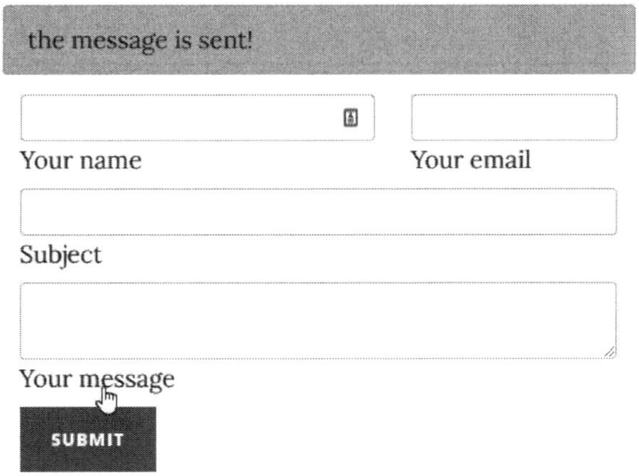

Figure 10.8: The contact form showing the confirmation message after sending

As you have learned from this example, it is quite easy to implement an interactive widget such as a contact form. Anyway, there are some tricks to know to avoid conflicts when you have multiple components on the same page. We will explain this in the next section.

Avoiding conflicts

For the contact form example, we have to raise a point about submitting data on a page with multiple bricks. Using the post approach, we send data to the server and manage the request on the backend. This procedure is very easy but it can lead to some issues. In fact, think about a case where you have many components on the same page.

In our example, if we put two contact form widgets on the same page, clicking send will trigger both actions. The same can happen with different components with similar field names.

To avoid such conflicts, follow these troubleshooting steps:

1. Add a unique prefix (per component) to all the field names. In our case, this could be cf for ContactForm, and the name will be cf-name, cf-sendEmail, and so on.

2. Add the instance name as the trigger value. This is required to make your post unique. The changes to the action method of the brick class (created in *Step 5* of *Implementing a contact form brick*) are the following:

```
...
$id= $info->getEditable()->getName();
$sendEmail=$request->get("cf-sendEmail");
```

```
if($sendEmail==$id)
{
    ...
```

The email sending procedure is now processed only if the name of the component is exactly the same that originates the post. Two different instances of the same brick produce different names, so your action will be triggered only once.

The final step is to make a small change in the view template file (created in *Step 3* of *Implementing a contact form brick*). We will be adding a hidden input with the `cf-sendEmail` name attribute and the ID computed from the action method as `value`. Cut and paste the next snippet to your view file:

```
<input type="hidden" name="cf-sendEmail" value="{{id}}"/>
```

This value will be sent back to our action method with the post argument and we will be comparing it with the one generated on the server side. If they are not equal, the post is not matched to the current component, and we avoid any action.

In this section, we learned how to implement a contact form. The example we have just finished showed us how simple it is to create an interactive brick that can be reused. You are not only able to reuse this component on any page of your website, but you can also copy the bundle to another website and get this feature for free. In the next example, we will discover how to implement a slideshow, mixing controllers and bricks to reuse the code that we might have written for an MVC page.

Implementing a slideshow brick

In this example, we will build a slideshow widget that can be used to display a carousel of images. This will be very easy, and we will use just bootstrap and the tools learned so far. In fact, we will reuse the code used for displaying the image gallery in *Chapter 9, Configuring Entities and Rendering Data*, but we will integrate it into a brick. To do that, follow these steps:

1. First of all, prepare the environment by creating a folder called `Slideshow` and upload a list of images to it. We should use wide images (such as 1920x1080).

2. Open the image settings for each image and add the title and description of the image as metadata. We will use it in the template.

3. Access the properties panel by clicking the **Properties** tab button on the toolbar. Each Pimcore entity (objects, documents, and assets) has a set of key/pair properties that can be used to expand the information dynamically. We will use them to add metadata to our images. In the next screenshot, we can see a valid configuration:

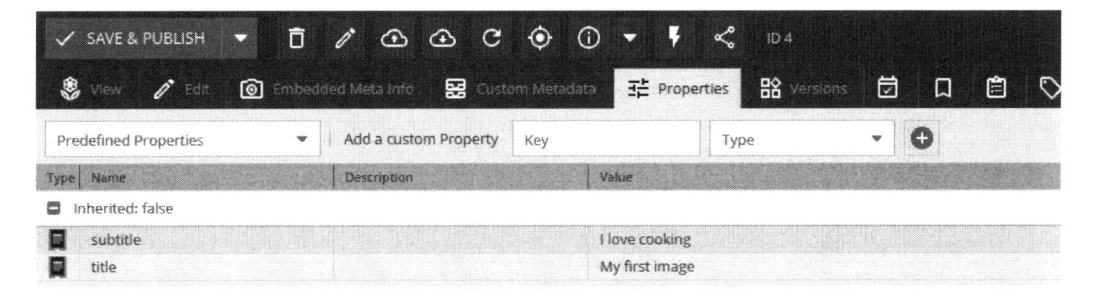

Figure 10.9: Image properties

The previous screenshot shows the properties table. We added a title and subtitle field with some value inside.

4. Create a thumbnail preset. We have to configure the thumbnail engine to resize the uploaded images to match the format that the slideshow component expects. The user could upload images too big or with the wrong proportions (for example, landscape instead of portrait) but we need to make sure that all the images have the same height to show the images properly. We need to crop the uploaded images and make them the same format. In our example, we can use a crop transformation that will produce images that are only 400 px tall. To do that, just enter the **Width, Height** and **X, Y** settings as in the following screenshot:

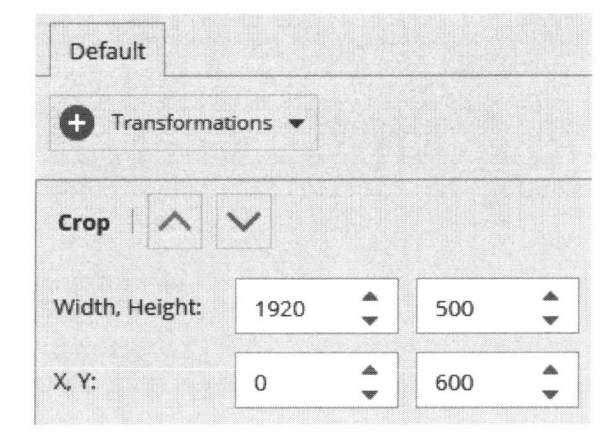

Figure 10.10: The thumbnail configuration

5. Create a brick called `SlideShow` by adding `SlideShow.php` in the brick class folder (for example, `/bundles/BlogBundle/Document/Areabrick/SlideShow.php`).

6. Create the template file in the view folder (for example, `/bundles/BlogBundle/Resources/views/Areas/slide-show`). Pay attention to the folder name – it has to match the brick name, but it's lowercase with the words split with a hyphen, so `slide-show` will be `Slideshow`.

7. Now add the following content to the template:

```
{{
    pimcore_renderlet('myGallery', {
        "controller" : "BlogBundle\\Controller\\SlideShowController::galleryAction",
        "title" : "Drag an asset folder here to get a gallery",
        "height" : 400
    })
}}
```

The preceding code adds a Pimcore renderlet that lets the user drag a folder on it and uses a controller for implementing the rendering logic. In our case, we will use the gallery action from the `SlideShow` controller. We are using a controller in a bundle, so we must specify the bundle name also.

8. Add the `SlideShow` controller to the controller folder (for example, `/bundles/BlogBundle/Document/Controller/SlideShowController.php`). The initial content should be the following:

```
<?php

namespace BlogBundle\Controller;

use Pimcore\Controller\FrontendController;
use Symfony\Component\HttpFoundation\Request;
use Symfony\Component\HttpFoundation\Response;
use Symfony\Component\Routing\Annotation\Route;
use Sensio\Bundle\FrameworkExtraBundle\Configuration\Template;
```

```
use Pimcore\Model\Asset;

class SlideShowController extends FrontendController
{
}
```

9. Now we have to implement the action for rendering the view. This action will take the folder added by the user and will load the image list for passing it to the view. In the following snippet, we have the action implementation; take it and add it to your controller:

```
public function galleryAction(Request $request)
{
    $result=array();
    if ('asset' === $request->get('type')) {
        $asset = Asset::getById($request->get('id'));
        if ('folder' === $asset->getType()) {
            $result['assets'] = $asset->getChildren();
        }
    }
    return $result;
}
```

The code is the same as what we used in the gallery example of *Chapter 9, Configuring Entities and Rendering Data*, so there is no need for more explanation.

10. The last step for rendering it properly is to create a view called `gallery` and place it into the folder relative to the controller (for example, `/bundles/BlogBundle/Resources/views/slide_show/gallery.twig`). The template that we will use is the following:

```
<div id="carouselExampleControls" ...>
    ... omitted bootstrap tags
    {% if assets %}
        {% set active ='active' %}
        {% for asset in assets %}
            {% if asset is instanceof('\\Pimcore\\
```

```twig
                    Model\\Asset\\Image') %}

                    <div class="carousel-item {{ active
            }}">
                        <img src="{{ asset.getThumbnail(
                    'SlideShow') }}" ... />
                        <div ...>
                            <h5>{{ asset.getProperty('title')
                    }}</h5>
                            <p>{{ asset.getProperty(
                    'subtitle') }}</p>
                        </div>
                    </div>
                    {% set active=""%}
                {% endif %}
            {% endfor %}
        {% endif %}
            ... omitted bootstrap tags for navigation
</div>
```

In the preceding snippet, all the tags that are not relevant to our explanation are omitted for brevity. Focusing on the part that really matters, we have a simple `for` loop that prints images following the bootstrap carousel standard. The image thumbnail is extracted from the original image using the `getThumbnail('SlideShow')` function. The `title` and `subtitle` fields are read from the asset properties using the `asset.getProperty` method.

11. Add the brick to a page and drag a folder to it:

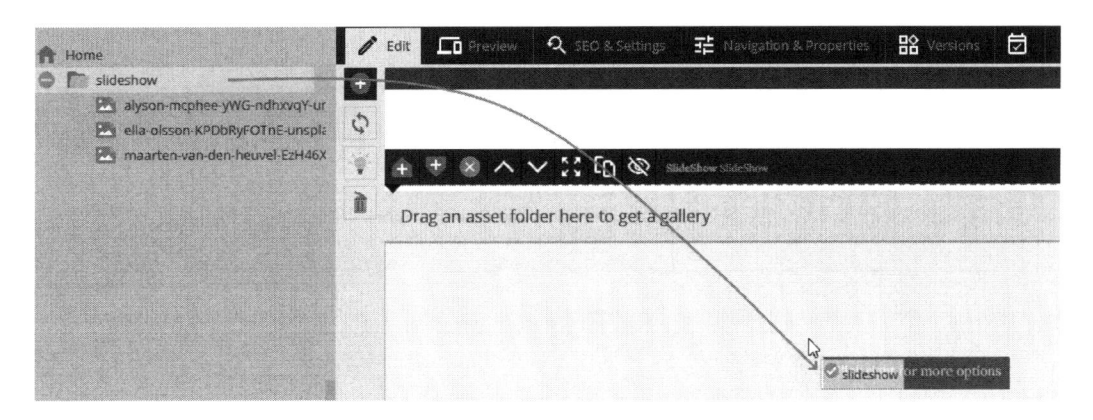

Figure 10.11: Dragging the folder to the component

12. Now you will see a sliding carousel as in the next screenshot:

Figure 10.12: The slideshow in action

In the previous screenshot, we highlighted the navigation buttons and the fields printed over the image.

In this section, we discovered how we can integrate controllers and bricks. The same result can be achieved by using the relation editable covered in *Chapter 8*, *Creating Custom CMS Pages*, and implementing the template inside the brick itself. Now that we have covered all the topics relating to bricks, it's time to learn how to implement a layout that could let us create any kind of page without writing any additional code.

Using bricks and blocks for a general-purpose template

What we want to do in this section is to find a solution for implementing all kinds of layouts without wasting hours creating custom templates. Theoretically speaking, we could have a set of base objects and then mount them together to create all kinds of websites. In practice, this is what we should do with Pimcore:

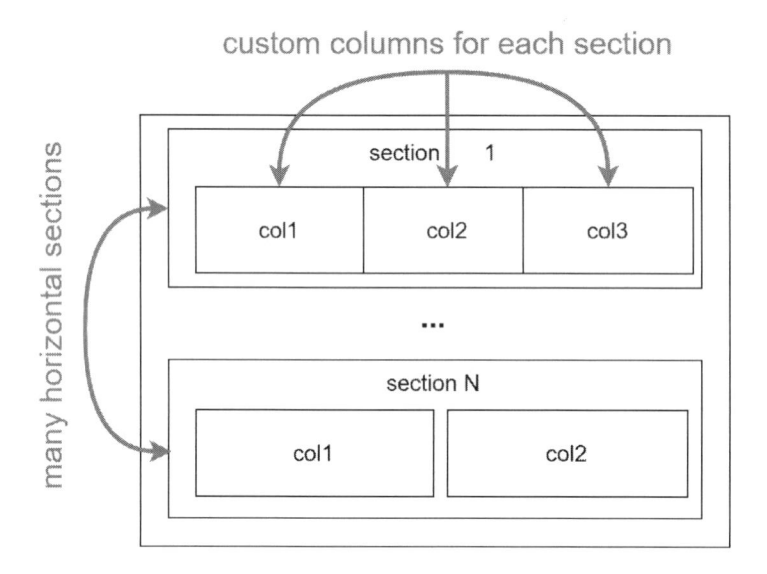

Figure 10.13: General-purpose template

The previous diagram shows how a multipurpose layout is structured. We have many horizontal sections (**Section 1**, ..., **Section N**) that can be divided into columns (**col1**, **col2**, **col3**). In each place, you will be able to add bricks for composing the page in any layout you want.

Theoretically speaking, we need to add a block iteration that will print rows inside another block iteration that will print columns. This lets us create a matrix of elements where we can add an `areablock` that lets us choose any brick we want. This layout is quite easy to implement in words, and feasible by putting into practice what we learned in the last chapters.

In this example, we will create a generic layout like the one that is shown in the following figure:

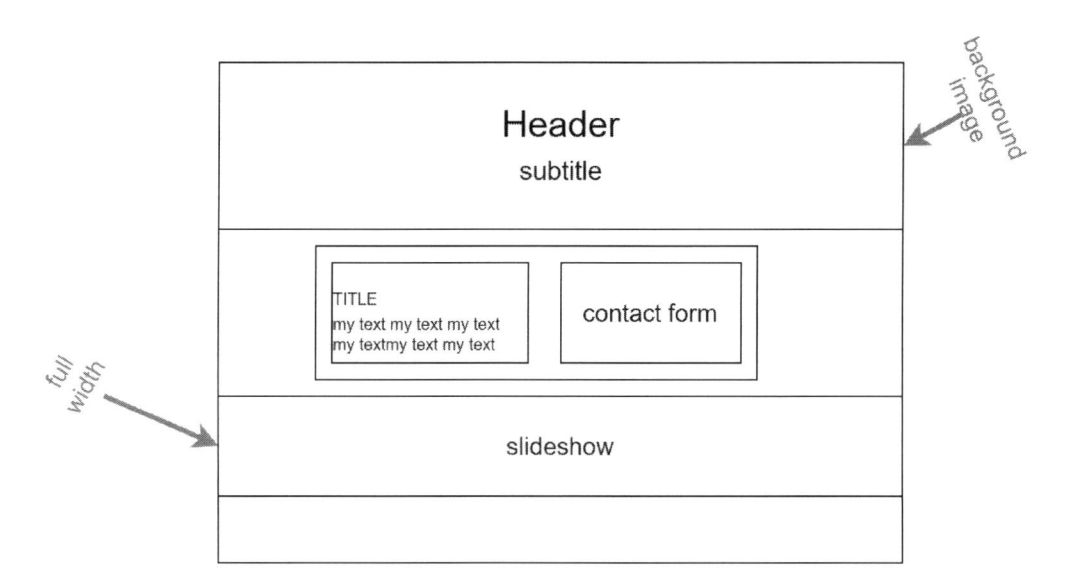

Figure 10.14: Generic website layout

In the preceding figure, we can note the three bands (**Header**, **contact form** with a description on the left side, and then a **full width slideshow**). This is, of course, a very simple use case, but with some imagination, you should understand how you can extend this to any kind of web page. Follow these steps to create a custom layout:

1. The first step is to create an area brick that could implement a Bootstrap container. This area brick will let the user choose the column number and sizes. So, we have to create the brick class in `Document/AreaBrick/Container.php`. The starting code is the following:

```php
<?php

namespace BlogBundle\Document\Areabrick;

class Container extends AbstractTemplateAreabrick implements EditableDialogBoxInterface
{
    public function getName()
    {
```

```
        return 'Container';
    }

    public function getDescription()
    {
        return 'Container';
    }
}
```

2. The second step is to configure the component for exposing the column configuration to the user. In this example, we assume that we can have only three layout options (one column, two columns 30%-70%, and two columns of the same size). In a real-world example, you can prepare any possible combination in terms of the number of columns and sizes to make the user really autonomous in managing any kind of layout. In the next piece of code, there is the configuration for creating a drop-down list with all the layout:

```
public function
getEditableDialogBoxConfiguration(Document\Editable
$area, ?Info $info): EditableDialogBoxConfiguration
{
    $config = new EditableDialogBoxConfiguration();
    $config->setWidth(600);
    $config->setItems([
        'type' => 'tabpanel',
        'items' => [
            [
                'type' => 'panel',
                'title' => 'Column settings',
                'items' => [
                    [
                        'type' => 'select',
                        'label' => 'Layout',
                        'name' => 'layout',
                        'config' => [
                            'store' => [
```

```
                                    ['one.html.twig',
                                    'One column'],
                                    ['two-50-50.html.
                                    twig', 'Two column
                                    50-50'],
                                    ['two-30-70.html.
                                    twig', 'Tre column
                                    30-70'],
                                ]
                            ]
                        ]
                    ]
                ]
            ]]);

            return $config;
        }
```

Note that, for simplicity, we used the names of a file template as values for the select item, so that the item could be simply related to the content.

3. The last step in the class is to read the configuration parameter and pass it to the view. To do this, you can just add the `action` method implementation that you find in the following piece of code to your class:

```
public function action(Info $info)
{
    $layout=$this->getDocumentEditable($info->
    getDocument(), 'select', 'layout')->getData();
    $info->setParam('layout',"@Blog/areas/
    container/templates/$layout");
}
```

As you can see from the source code, the relative filename is transformed into a full path and added to the property bag.

4. Now we have to implement the main view template. Just add to the `view.html.twig` file the following code:

```twig
<div class="container blog-container">
{% include layout %}
{% if editmode %}
    <div class="blog-container-footer">
            CONTAINER
    <div>
{% endif %}
</div>
```

The previous piece of code includes the template based on the variable set in the action and simply wraps it in a bootstrap container. Moreover, when you are in edit mode, it adds a bar to the bottom to help the user identify the layout.

5. Now we have to implement the brick template. As usual, we need to create a `view.html.twig` file, but this time we will also create a folder with many other templates that will be loaded dynamically. So, create the `one.html.twig`, `two-50-50.html.twig`, and `two-30-70.html.twig` files. The final result will be the following:

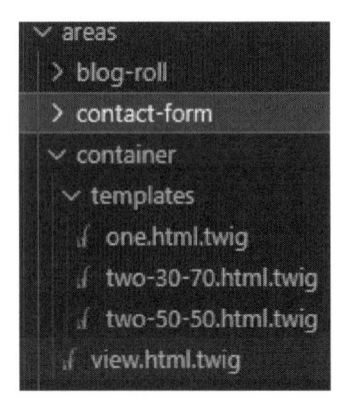

Figure 10.15: Files configuration

6. Now we have to implement the three templates. For brevity, we will report here only one case: the others are very similar and can be found in the repository code. The next piece of code shows the two-column implementation:

```twig
<div class="row">
    <div class="col-6 blog-col">
```

```twig
            {{ pimcore_areablock("content_50501")}}
        </div>
        <div class="col-6 blog-col">
            {{ pimcore_areablock("content_50502")}}
        </div>
    </div>
```

As you can see in the previous piece of code, there is a bootstrap row and two columns (`col-6`; `col-6` means the same width). Inside each column, the `areablock` component will allow you to choose the component to add inside it. Now we are ready to use our general-purpose template in a real-world example!

7. Create the `layout.html.twig` file in `/bundles/BlogBundle/Layout`, and add the following snippet:

```twig
{# SETTING THE IMAGE URL#}
{% set imageurl=null %}
{% if not editmode %}
  {% set image =pimcore_relation("image")%}
    {% if  image.getElement() is defined and  image.getElement() != null %}
      {% set imageurl= image.getElement().getThumbnail("SlideShow") %}
    {% endif %}
{% endif %}
{# PRINT HEADER#}


<header class="masthead" style="background-image: url({{imageurl}})">
    <div class="overlay"></div>
    <div class="container">
      <div class="row">
        <div class="col-lg-8 col-md-10 mx-auto">
          <div class="site-heading">
            <h1> {{ pimcore_input('headline', {'width': 540}) }}</h1>
            <span class="subheading"> {{ pimcore_input('subheading', {'width': 700}) }}</span>
          </div>
```

```twig
                </div>
            </div>
        </div>
    </header>

{# IMAGE INPUT #}
{% if editmode %}
    {{ pimcore_relation("image",{
        "types": ["asset"],
        "subtypes": {
            "asset": [ "image"],
        },
        "classes": ["person"]
    }) }}
{% endif %}
```

This snippet of code will render a parametric header that is put on all our pages. You don't want to have it on all the pages? Not a problem. You can always transform this code into a brick and place it only where you really need it.

8. Now, create a template. Because we want to create a standard layout with horizontal bands, we will allow the use of only the Container brick.

9. To do that, just create a file inside the default folder called generic.html.twig, and add it in the following piece of code:

```twig
{% extends 'BlogBundle:Layout:layout.html.twig' %}
{% block content %}
    {% include 'BlogBundle:Layout:header.html.twig' %}
        {{ pimcore_areablock("content",
{'allowed':['container']}) }}
{% endblock %}
```

The preceding script defines a page structure with a header and an area block that will host the containers for our page layout.

10. Create a web page and use the generic.html.twig template we created during *Step 6* of this procedure.

Using bricks and blocks for a general-purpose template   259

11. Open the web page that you have created in edit mode. You should see the following result:

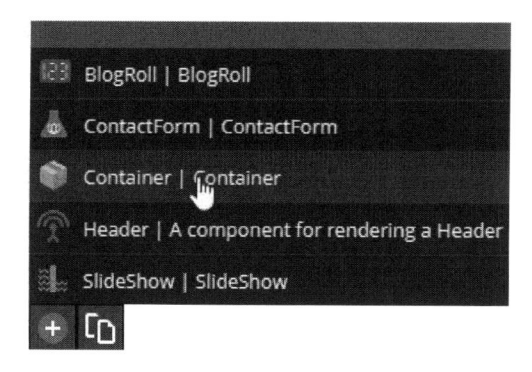

Figure 10.16: Adding the container to the page

12. After this step, the component will be ready on the page. Now click on the configuration button, as in the following screenshot:

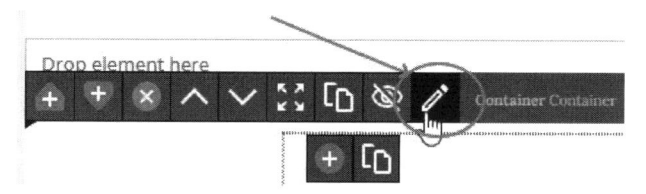

Figure 10.17: Opening settings

13. At this point, the user is able to select a layout using the edit box as in the contact form example that we saw in the previous section. The result of this configuration is the following popup:

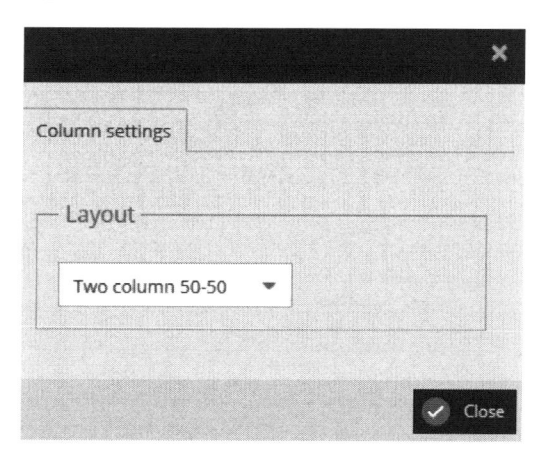

Figure 10.18: Selecting the layout

260   Creating Pimcore Bricks

The following screenshot shows the area brick that lets us create as many bands as we want. After this step, you should get the following result:

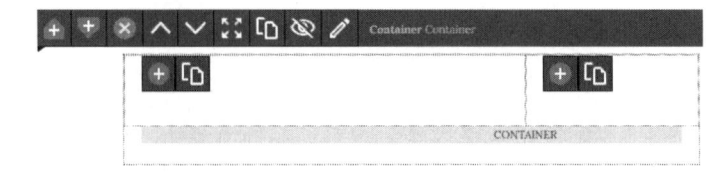

Figure 10.19: The container component on the page

14. Add the columns content into it by clicking the plus button inside the container area (shown in *Figure 10.19*) and choosing the column brick.

15. Add a contact form on the right by clicking the plus button and choosing the item from the component menu.

16. On the left column, add a header component, the one we created earlier in the *Implementing a simple brick* section. Then add a WYSIWYG editor just above the header. You should get the result shown in the following screenshot:

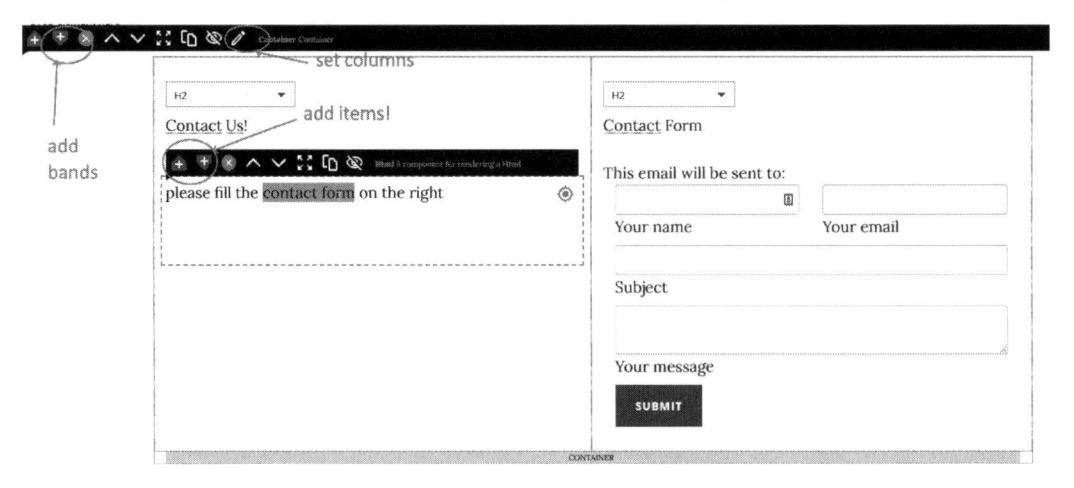

Figure 10.20: The web page with the contact form and data

17. Now add another container just after the previous one by clicking on the top down arrow (*Figure 10.20*). On this component, add a slideshow brick. Configure it by dragging and dropping the images as we have done in the slideshow example in this chapter. The next screenshot summarizes your work in this part of the page:

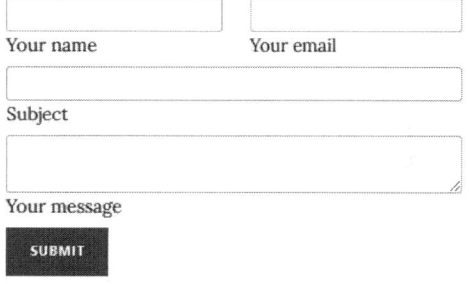

Figure 10.21: The result to obtain in this example

In this section, we learned how to create a template that could suit most situations. The example has been a good opportunity for testing the general-purpose layout in a real-life scenario. This template, in conjunction with all the bricks that you could create, will cover the most common scenarios and will save a lot of time.

Summary

In this chapter, we continued our journey with the Pimcore CMS by discovering the bricks engine, another important tool for creating dynamic websites. By creating bricks, it's easy to prepare reusable components that can be used by web page editors to compose any website without asking the developers for customization. This new way to proceed is very important in reducing the development effort, keeping quality standards high, and increasing the speed of implementing the features that users want.

To be more specific, we discovered how bricks work by implementing real-world examples. The contact form and slideshow are components that you will reuse in your projects for sure. Moreover, we also learned how to create a general-purpose template that enables us to produce any layout of a page without writing a single line of code.

In the next chapter, we will learn how to finalize our website by discovering some important details and solutions for everyday Pimcore usage. To list the most important ones, we will learn how to create a bundle's installers to easily recreate our classes and contents after the setup, and we will learn how to create a multisite instance of Pimcore.

11
Finalizing the Website

In the last chapter, we finalized the building of our blog using Pimcore. Thanks to the capabilities of CMS and the data management engine, we were able to achieve complex goals such as creating custom unstructured content (the website's pages) and structured content (blog articles). It was a pleasant journey that makes us autonomous regarding the implementation of any kind of website or portal. Moreover, there are many additional steps that we may need to take to make our work reusable, extensible, and easy to deploy. As the title states, in this chapter we will learn how to finalize our website.

The points that we will cover will be the following:

- Making a Multisite in Pimcore
- Making the bundle installable
- Using a multi-environment configuration
- Using environment variables

Technical requirements

As for the previous chapters, there is a demo in our GitHub repository that you can find here: https://github.com/PacktPublishing/Modernizing-Enterprise-CMS-using-Pimcore.

All you need to do to run the demo connected with this chapter is to clone it and navigate to the `Full Demo` folder to start the Docker environment.

To do so, just follow these instructions:

1. Run Docker with the following command:

   ```
   docker-compose up
   ```

2. Then, to restore all the settings on your local machine, type the following:

   ```
   docker-compose exec php bash restore.sh
   ```

3. Navigate to http://localhost/admin and log in with your admin/pimcore credentials.

Making a Multisite in Pimcore

Each time you create a website, you need to take time to create the environment, install plugins, and configure all the other Pimcore settings. Moreover, we also need a hosting space, which means extra costs. This is an activity that we have to do each time we are going to create a website, but we would reduce the impact of this activity on each website creation.

For example, think about a scenario where a customer has 10 websites, maybe one for each brand of the company. With the digital exposure that each company has nowadays, it is a plausible use case. Even if we can create a bundle that can be used to port the common components between websites, having separate websites still involves overhead. From the user's point of view, having 10 different websites to admin is very hard to manage.

The solution for this common situation is still Pimcore itself. The **Multisite** feature lets us manage multiple websites in the same instance, reducing hosting costs and using the same resources (themes, bricks, custom code) in all the websites. With the power of scaling that the cloud provides, we do not expect server load problems, and we can follow this method without side effects.

To cover all the possible scenarios you may have with a real-world website, we will implement a test case where we will transform a branch of a website tree in a standalone website. This will allow users to reach the web pages as if they were browsing an independent website. This is the basic tenet that will let you manage multiple websites in the same Pimcore instance (for example, `product1.mywebsite.com` and `product2.mywebsite.com`) and website alias (for example, `www.mywebsite.com` and `mywebsite.com`).

In the next example, we will create a generic subsite called **subsite1**, and we will make it available using a different domain than the default. Moreover, we will use different kinds of domain mapping to cover all the most common scenarios (addresses, aliases, and wildcards):

1. Add a document to the page tree. Call it **subsite1**. The name of the page doesn't affect the behavior of the site. In our case, we used our full demo setup, and we have got a web page like the one shown in the following screenshot:

Figure 11.1: The page used for the test

266   Finalizing the Website

2. Navigate through the tree menu and right-click on the **subsite1** item. Then click on **Use as site**:

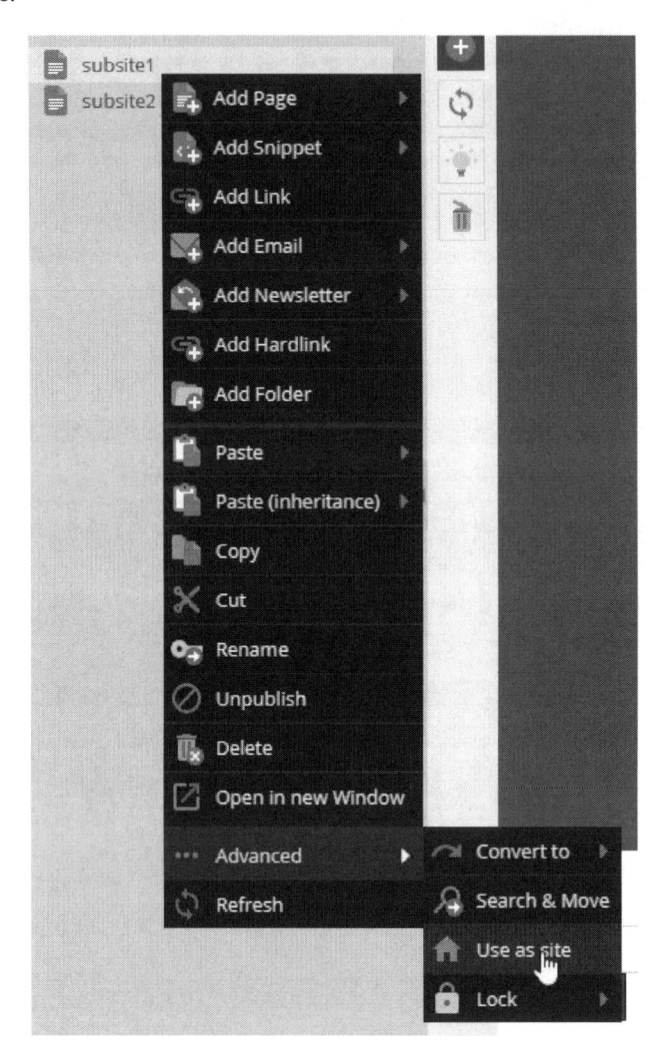

Figure 11.2: The menu used to convert a web page into a website

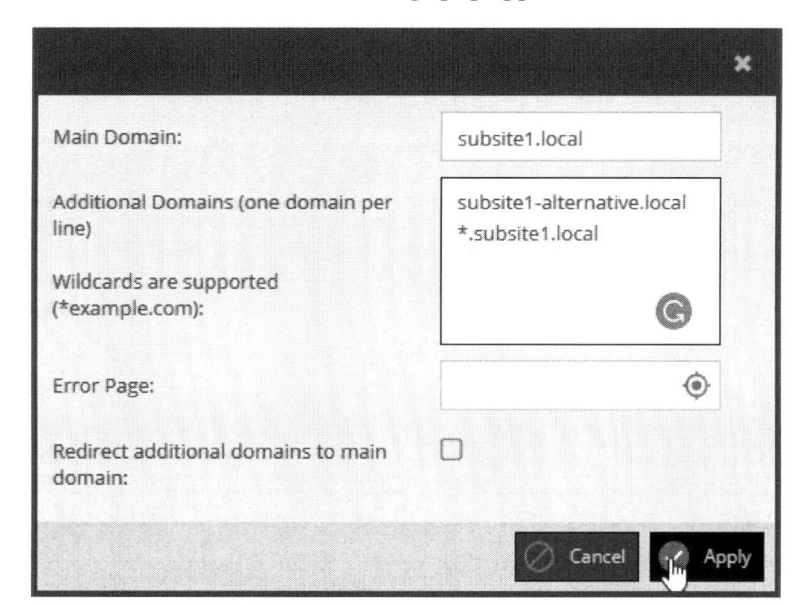

If you click on the **Use as site** button, a popup appears:

Figure 11.3: The form for configuring a website

3. Fill in the form with the following information:

- **Main Domain**: `subsite1.local`.
- **Additional Domains**: `subsite1-alternative.local` and `*.subsite1.local`. These values have to be put on two different lines. This setting applies to the item that we have selected and all its children. This configuration tells Pimcore to serve requests using the pages under the one that we have promoted to a site in *step 2*. This means that if you navigate to one of the added domains, the pages under this page will be served. So, if you navigate to `subsite1.local` and `subsite1-alternative.local`, you will see the converted page; if you look for a path inside the domain (such as `subsite1.local/xxx`), a page with the same relative path under the page site will be served. The same goes for all the third-level domains of `subsite1.local`, such as `mysubsite.subsite1.local`, because we entered a wildcard address.

4. Edit your hosts file to reach these fake URLs. Open the hosts file and add the following lines:

```
127.0.0.1 subsite1.local
127.0.0.1 subsite1-alternative.local
127.0.0.1 test.subsite1.local
```

5. Go to these URLs: `http://subsite1.local`, `http://subiste1-alternative.local`, and `http://test.subsite1.local`. You will always get the same results, which proves that the multisite is well configured.

In this section, we learned how to transform a part of the page tree into a standalone website. This is very useful for hosting multiple websites and reusing themes and components from the same code base. This is a big help for reusable code that can work in conjunction with bundling and sharing the source code. In the next section, we will learn how to create installation processes for creating data and settings during our bundle's installation.

Making the bundles installable

In *Chapter 10, Creating Pimcore Bricks*, we created all the assets in a single bundle to make them self-contained and portable. The opportunity to start our next Pimcore project by installing a bundle means we don't have to redo certain tasks, making this an attractive option. Anyway, there are some steps that we have done manually through the user interface that have to be replicated. Think back to the class generation in *Chapter 9, Rendering Data*—they were created manually, but you do not want to replicate this step in every new blog you will create. Even if you only take a few minutes creating them, there is always the risk of entering the wrong field name or making a mistake; they will transform your 5-minute task into a small nightmare.

But never fear! The Pimcore installation system lets you add a special class that can manage the installation process. Some common use cases are as follows:

- Creating or updating the class definition
- Entering seed data (such as standard categories)
- Updating the database schema (add tables, columns, indexes, and so on)
- Importing translations

Installers are, in fact, classes that are used by Pimcore when a bundle is installed.

This topic is covered by two different approaches:

- **Installer**: A class that manages the installation process that gives you the power to customize all the phases (installation and uninstallation).
- **Migrations**: This part is designed for managing the database changes and supporting both upgrade and downgrade options.

Let's examine the two options in the next sections.

Installers

While the installer takes care of the initial configuration, migrations keep the database updated. When you install the bundle, an installation process will be run. Then, on each bundle update, you can apply some changes to the database to implement a data migration.

An installer class can inherit `AbstractInstaller` and has the following anatomy:

```
class MyInstaller extends AbstractInstaller
{
    public function install()      {}
    public function uninstall()    {}
    public function isInstalled(){
        return true;
    }
    public function canBeInstalled(){
        return false;
    }
    public function canBeUninstalled(){
        return false;
    }
    public function needsReloadAfterInstall() {
        return false;
    }
}
```

`AbstractInstaller` has an instance of `BufferedOutput` that integrates with the console tool and the web UI. That means that if you use it to write logs, the logs will be prompted to the user. The `BufferedOutput` instance can be accessed by the `getOutput()` method.

Now we will create an installer that automatically installs the classes related to our project. This is very easy, and we just need to complete the following steps:

1. Create a class definition with one or two fields. Call it `test`. To keep it simple, the class complexity is not relevant for our goal. If you have any doubts about how to create classes, just look at *Chapter 5, Exploring Classes and Objects*, where this topic is covered.

2. Download the class definition by clicking the **Export** button on the class definition page:

Figure 11.4: Menu bar for class export

3. Now create a folder named `class_sources` inside `/bundles/BlogBundle/Resources/install/`, making the final path `/bundles/BlogBundle/Resources/install/class_sources`.

4. Copy the JSON file you exported into this folder.

5. Create a folder called `Setup` in your bundle and add the `BlogInstaller` class inside it. The content should include the following:

```
<?php
namespace BlogBundle\Setup;
... usages
class BlogInstaller  extends AbstractInstaller
{
}
```

6. Now we have to register the installer class to make it available for dependency injection. Add the following configuration to the `service.yml` file:

```
services:
    BlogBundle\Setup\BlogInstaller:
        public: true
        autowire: true
```

Now the dependency injection knows your installer and can create instances of it.

7. Open the `BlogBundle.php` bundle file and add the following method:

```php
public function getInstaller() {
    return $this->container->get(
    BlogInstaller::class);
}
```

This function will tell Pimcore that your bundle has its installer and will use it. What happens when you install your bundle is that the event of your installer will be triggered, and you will be able to do all the stuff you need. In the next steps, we will implement the initial configuration.

8. The next snippet of code implements the class restore, so add this function (logs and output messages are omitted for brevity):

```php
public function install(){
    $files = $this->getClassesToInstall();
    foreach ($files as $file) {
        $data = file_get_contents($file);
        $json= json_decode($data);
        $name= $json->id;
        $class = ClassDefinition::getById($name);
        if($class) continue; // do not overwrite

        $class = new ClassDefinition();
        $class->setName($json->id);
        $class->setId($json->id);

Service::importClassDefinitionFromJson($class, $data,
false, true);
    }
}
```

The installation procedure is composed of a few simple steps. First of all, we read the filesystem and fetch all the files in the `classes` folder (`files = $this->getClassesToInstall();`). Then, for each one, we check whether the class exists; if it doesn't exist, we create and import the class. If the class exists and we override it with a different definition, we may experience data loss and we do not want that.

9. The next snippet contains the `getClassesToInstall` procedure. Copy it to the installer class:

```
protected function getClassesToInstall()
{
    $realpath = realpath(__DIR__."/../
    Resources/install/class_sources/");
    $files=glob($realpath.'/*.json');
    return $files;
}
```

The preceding piece of code reads all `*.json` files in the `class_sources` folder and returns them to the caller to be installed.

10. Now it's time to test the bundle. To make a rigorous test, we should create a new environment, move the bundle to the environment, and test it. However, this way requires time and effort, and it is not relevant for this explanation, so we will use a shortcut.

    Because we do not have any database migrations or unreversible activities, we will use the current installation. The first operation is to delete the classes you have exported. That is mandatory because our procedure will otherwise skip the creation (see *step 7*). You can do that by right-clicking on the class name and then hitting **Delete**, as shown in the next figure:

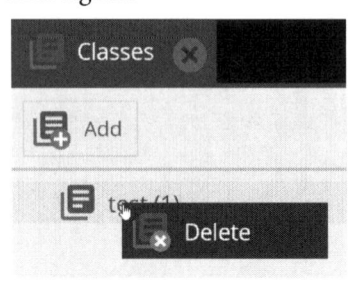

    Figure 11.5: How to delete a class

11. Now we have to trick Pimcore by telling it that our bundle is installable. To do this, implement the `canBeInstalled` method in the installer class, returning `true` (which means "yes, it can be installed!"). Copy the following piece of code and paste it to your file:

```
public function canBeInstalled(){
    return true;
}
```

Making the bundles installable 273

The next screenshot shows the change before and after the method is implemented:

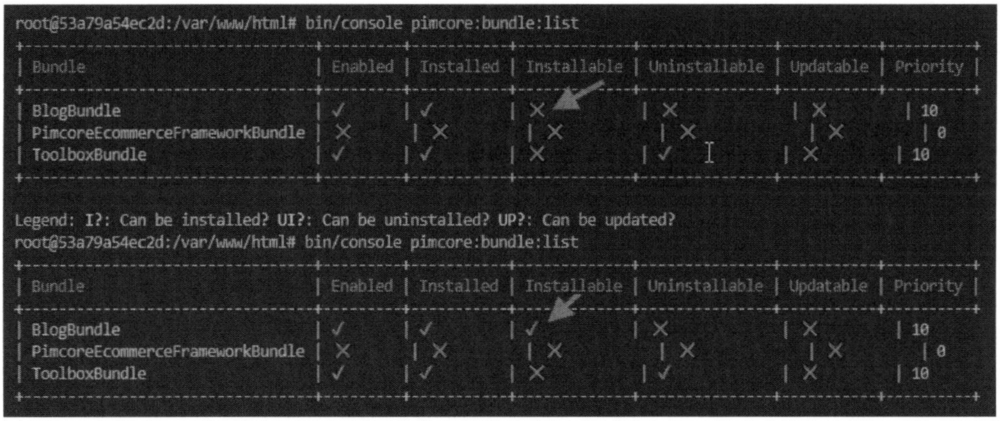

```
root@53a79a54ec2d:/var/www/html# bin/console pimcore:bundle:list
+--------------------------------+---------+-----------+-------------+---------------+-----------+----------+
| Bundle                         | Enabled | Installed | Installable | Uninstallable | Updatable | Priority |
+--------------------------------+---------+-----------+-------------+---------------+-----------+----------+
| BlogBundle                     | ✓       | ✓         | ✗           | ✗             | ✗         | 10       |
| PimcoreEcommerceFrameworkBundle| ✗       | ✗         | ✗           | ✗             | ✗         | 0        |
| ToolboxBundle                  | ✓       | ✓         | ✗           | ✓             | ✗         | 10       |
+--------------------------------+---------+-----------+-------------+---------------+-----------+----------+
Legend: I?: Can be installed? UI?: Can be uninstalled? UP?: Can be updated?
root@53a79a54ec2d:/var/www/html# bin/console pimcore:bundle:list
+--------------------------------+---------+-----------+-------------+---------------+-----------+----------+
| Bundle                         | Enabled | Installed | Installable | Uninstallable | Updatable | Priority |
+--------------------------------+---------+-----------+-------------+---------------+-----------+----------+
| BlogBundle                     | ✓       | ✓         | ✓           | ✗             | ✗         | 10       |
| PimcoreEcommerceFrameworkBundle| ✗       | ✗         | ✗           | ✗             | ✗         | 0        |
| ToolboxBundle                  | ✓       | ✓         | ✗           | ✓             | ✗         | 10       |
+--------------------------------+---------+-----------+-------------+---------------+-----------+----------+
```

Figure 11.6: Comparing bundle settings before and after changing the flag

The previous screenshot shows how the installation status changes as we alter the `canBeInstalled` method. The first flag matrix is the output of the `pimcore:bundle:list` command, and you can see that the bundle is marked as not installable. After the change in the installer class, the installable flag becomes active and Pimcore will let us install the bundle again.

12. Finally, it's time to test the bundle's installer. Go to the **Admin UI**, navigate to **Tools | Bundles**, and then click the green plus icon, or run `bin/console pimcore:bundle:install BlogBundle` from the command line:

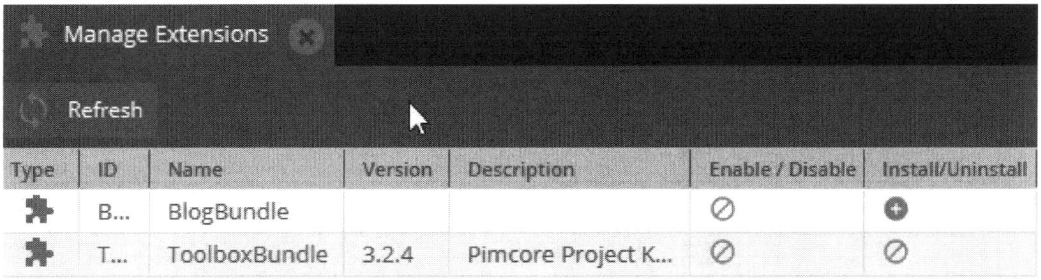

Type	ID	Name	Version	Description	Enable / Disable	Install/Uninstall
🧩	B...	BlogBundle			⊘	⊕
🧩	T...	ToolboxBundle	3.2.4	Pimcore Project K...	⊘	⊘

Figure 11.7: The extension panel now lets you install the bundle again

As you can see in the previous screenshot, the options available in the UI reflect the information gathered from the console.

13. Navigate to the class list. You will find the `test` class that you deleted on the menu again because it was recreated by the install process:

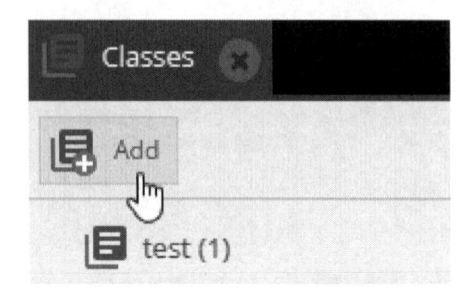

Figure 11.8: The created class

In this section, we covered how the installation process works. In the next section, we will take care of the schema update and data seeding using migrations.

Migrations

The purpose of migrations is to manage data migration and schema updates. This is very useful if you are working with a custom database structure. The basic concept of migration is that it starts with an existing version that can be incremented by applying a delta of changes. The migration can be reversed by implementing a rollback function. To be more concrete, a migration in Pimcore is a class implementation that has two methods: up (to apply changes) and down (to revert changes).

The migration process is explained in the following diagram:

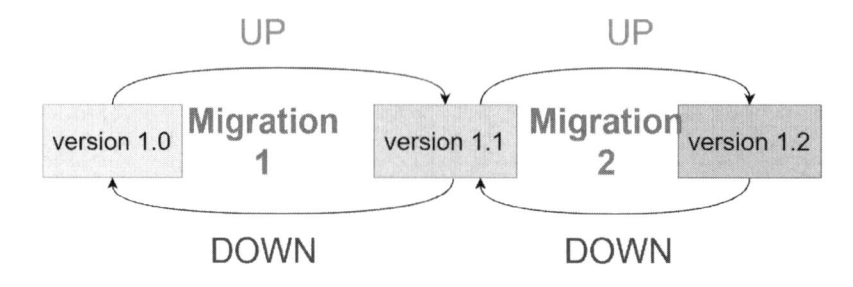

Figure 11.9: The migration process

As you can see in the previous figure, after an update, version 1.0 is updated to 1.1, but if there is a rollback, the down method brings it back to the initial version.

The first step of adding the ability to manage migrations to your application is to map a folder for the migration files to your namespace. To do so, just open the `/config/config.yml` file and add the following snippet:

```yaml
doctrine_migrations:
    migrations_paths:
        'App\Migrations': 'src/Migrations'
```

The previous piece of code maps your namespace with the related folder.

For creating a migration class, the best method is to invoke the `console` command:

```
bin/console doctrine:migrations:generate --namespace=App\\Migrations
```

The preceding command creates a file inside the migration folder of the main application. Each version has a generated name, such as `/src/Migrations/Version20210227065641.php`, where the `Version` prefix of the filename is followed by a timestamp.

The created file will look something like the following:

```php
<?php
namespace App\Migrations;
... uses
class Version20210227065641 extends AbstractMigration
{
    public function up(Schema $schema)    {
        //do things here
    }

    public function down(Schema $schema)    {
        //do things here
    }
}
```

The `Schema` object is a doctrine element that lets you manipulate the database structure. The following examples show the most important use cases, such as creating a table, adding fields, and dropping them:

```
$table = $schema->createTable('foo');
$table->addColumn('title', 'string');
$table->addColumn('description', 'string');
$schema->dropTable('foo');
```

> **Important Note**
>
> For a complete overview of the Schema object's capabilities, take a look at the Symfony documentation: `https://www.doctrine-project.org/projects/doctrine-dbal/en/latest/reference/schema-representation.html`.

In this section, we learned how to create an installer to manage the setup of a bundle and manage data migration. This topic is very useful when you want to create a portable bundle or product based on Pimcore. Think, for example, of a bundle with all the bricks and utilities that you can use as the basis for your projects. In the next section, we will cover another important topic when we work with multiple environments in the same code base.

Using a multi-environment configuration

In any modern deployment workflow, we have four environments: `local`, `dev`, `test`, and `production`. Each of these environments may have different configurations and tunings. Your production environment will probably have to face tons of users and a heavy load in a clustered system, while your local environment will just need to fight with the amount of RAM. What we see is that each environment has different needs, and consequently, needs different configurations. The approach that we want to follow is to keep all the data in a single code base and keep all the settings in the same place. If you are thinking that you'll need to manage a lot of files and complicated logic to switch them, you are wrong.

Fortunately, Pimcore is based on Symfony and extends its very powerful configuration system. Pimcore manages `dev`, `test`, and `prod` environments natively (while others can be added with an additional configuration). To switch the environment, you have to specify the `PIMCORE_ENVIRONMENT` environment variable. Because our Pimcore instance runs in a container, this setting doesn't have any impact on our PC, as the configuration is limited to the container.

Once the variable is set, Pimcore will load the files following this order:

1. `config/pimcore/system_{env}.yml`
2. `var/config/system_{env}.yml`
3. `config/pimcore/system.yml`
4. `var/config/system.yml`

The configuration files can include other configuration files and inherit properties. The default setup that comes with a fresh Pimcore installation has an incremental configuration from `dev` to `prod` of the `config.yml` file (`prod` includes `test`, which includes `dev`). This mechanism is very useful for sharing settings and overriding them when needed.

If you omit `PIMCORE_ENVIRONMENT`, the base files will be taken following the next escalation:

1. `config/pimcore/system.yml`
2. `var/config/system.yml`

When you are running Pimcore from the console, you can pass the environment as an argument, like in the following example:

```
./bin/console --env=dev ...
```

In a Pimcore environment, it is very important to have different configurations of Pimcore to match the different specifications of the environments where we will work. By the way, not all the configurations can be saved into the settings files for security reasons. In the next section, we will learn how to manage sensitive data, such as passwords and API keys, safely with Pimcore.

Using Environment variables

The modern approach of using containers makes heavy use of environment variables for injecting values into applications. This approach is very convenient because it makes your application agnostic to the environment in which it will be deployed. This process implies that some part of the configuration is pulled from outside the application code.

Moving all the configuration outside the application makes developers unaware of everything going on internally, and this creates misunderstandings between the developer and operations teams when problems occur. You have your local code and you can see it working, but you will have no idea what can happen in the production environment when other settings will be applied. Often, those who manage the operations don't know much about the meaning behind configurations because they are not experts on the applications and usually are not developers. Developers know how the application works and are aware of the impact of settings changes but know little about the infrastructure and cannot make tests to fix the problems that the application may have (they don't have access to the production environment).

What we are going to explain in this section is a solution that can keep production settings safe, share configurations between developers and operations, and is easy to implement with Pimcore. A good compromise is to keep all the configuration in the source code but remove sensitive information that is injected during the deployment. Keeping the sensitive information separate from the configuration lets us share settings with the entire team and makes everybody aware of the configuration chosen but does not open us to security issues. This approach creates a clean division of responsibility and makes our repository safer. In that way, the developers are aware of the configuration in each environment, and operations can manage system settings independently.

This solution has the positive side effect that the developers can test different configurations on their local PCs (but without accessing the production system) and the result is more predictable. But how is it possible to configure Pimcore to separate configurations from sensitive data? In the next example, we will create a configuration that will work in all environments but without adding sensitive data to the source code files.

Using environment variables for managing database connections

We aim to have a Pimcore instance with the same configuration for the local, test, and production environments. The configuration will all be stored in the **YAML** files, but the right settings will be injected using an environment variable that will change based on the stage (dev, test, prod). The piece of configuration that we want to manage in that way is the configuration string. We will remove the hardcoded connection string of Pimcore, making it parametric. This data is usually set in the config/local/database.yml file, and it is generated by Pimcore at the first installation; it is not usually committed. As we are using a Dockerized environment, all the developers that download the source code work locally in a separate environment, so there isn't any problem with sharing this information.

We can now start work in these settings:

1. Delete or rename the database.yml file (we won't need it anymore).

2. Add the following code to docker-compose.yml. This configuration will add the settings as environment variables:

```yaml
services:
  ...
  php:
    ...
    environment:
      - PIMCORE_ENVIRONMENT=dev
      - PIMCORE_HOST=db
      - PIMCORE_DB=pimcore
      - PIMCORE_USERNAME=pimcore
      - PIMCORE_PASSWORD=pimcore
      - PIMCORE_PORT=3306
```

The next figure shows a bare copy of the MySQL settings on the same file:

```
db:                                        php:
  ...                                        ...
  environment:                               environment:
    - MYSQL_ROOT_PASSWORD=ROOT                 - PIMCORE_ENVIRONMENT=dev
    - MYSQL_DATABASE=pimcore                   - PIMCORE_HOST=db
    - MYSQL_USER=pimcore                       - PIMCORE_DB=pimcore
    - MYSQL_PASSWORD=pimcore                   - PIMCORE_USERNAME=pimcore
                                               - PIMCORE_PASSWORD=pimcore
                                               - PIMCORE_PORT=3306
```

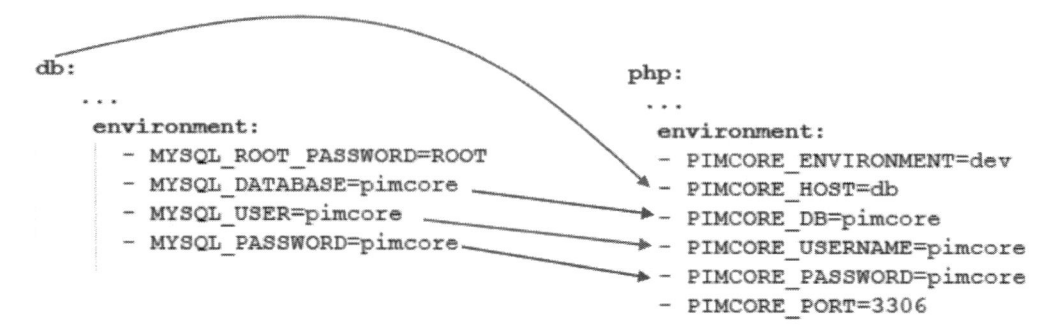

Figure 11.10: Field mapping between containers

3. Now we have to tell Pimcore to use this variable's configuration. The chain of dependencies is that `config_prod.yml` includes `config_test.yml` and `config_dev.yml` includes `config.yml`. So, adding the proper configuration to the `config` or `config_dev` file will make it available for all the environments.

4. Open `config.yml`. The first change to make is to disable the import of the database configuration. Just comment out the following line:

```
#  - { resource: 'local/' } removed... it users
  environments now!
```

The import of the `local` resource set is disabled (otherwise, you can just drop the `database.yml` file).

5. Then add the following configuration to the file:

```
doctrine:
    dbal:
        connections:
            default:
                host: '%PIMCORE_HOST%'
                port: '%PIMCORE_PORT%'
                dbname: '%PIMCORE_DB%'
                user: '%PIMCORE_USERNAME%'
```

```
                       password: '%PIMCORE_PASSWORD%'

parameters:
    PIMCORE_ENVIRONMENT: '%env(PIMCORE_ENVIRONMENT)%'
    PIMCORE_HOST:    '%env(PIMCORE_HOST)%'
    PIMCORE_DB:   '%env(PIMCORE_DB)%'
    PIMCORE_USERNAME:    '%env(PIMCORE_USERNAME)%'
    PIMCORE_PASSWORD:    '%env(PIMCORE_PASSWORD)%'
    PIMCORE_PORT: '%env(PIMCORE_PORT)%'
```

The configuration is the same as `database.yml` but parametric. We define internal parameters that import the environment variable from the container. We used a 1:1 map, reusing the same name of the environment variables for the parameters. This makes the configuration easier to read.

Then we use the parameter in the `doctrine\dbal\connection\default` section of the file. This makes sure that Pimcore will activate a connection with this configuration, using the parameters that get values to form the host environment (the `docker-compose` file in our case).

After this step, we fully decouple the configuration from the data so we can set them separately. You can commit any configuration (`dev`, `test`, `prod`) without the fear that someone will steal sensitive data, and during the deployment, the right values will be injected into the environment (virtual machine or container).

6. Open Pimcore and check whether you can log in. Because our changes are about the connection to the database, if we are able to log in, our new settings have been successful.

In this section, we learned how to manage sensitive information in the Pimcore configuration and how to make variables without replicating the settings. Using containers is a useful solution because the container can be deployed as a standalone virtual machine, PC, or cloud service, meaning the solution covers most use cases. Moreover, having all the configurations on the source code makes it available to the developers, sharing a deeper awareness of how the platform will work in production. All the configurations can be easily tested locally and then committed.

Summary

In this chapter, we learned some details of the Pimcore developer that are very important for finalizing our website.

The multisite configuration allows us to use only one Pimcore instance to manage all the company's websites. This is a very interesting feature for saving time and money, using only one Pimcore installation to manage all the company websites.

The installers give us the power to execute installation steps to recreate the configuration needed by our bundle. We can create data assets and perform updates on them. This means that we can take our bundle, install it on another Pimcore instance, and add all the classes and data that the bundle needs to work on. We also learned that we can manage the database changes at a low level.

The multi-environment feature lets UX specify different configurations based on the environment we are using. This is very useful for keeping all the features in one code base. Moreover, we discovered how the powerful inheritance system of the configuration works.

Environment variables can help make the configuration agnostic from the environment, and we learned how to remove sensitive data from files.

Now our journey with the CMS part is almost completed, and we can move to the enterprise solutions that Pimcore has out of the box. In the next chapter, we will learn how to properly collect and store products in Pimcore and spread the information to all other applications. This is very important in enabling a company to use Pimcore as a PIM solution.

12
Implementing Product Information Management

In previous chapters, you learned about some key features of the Pimcore environment presented in *Chapter 1, Introducing Pimcore*. In particular, in *Chapter 6, Using Digital Asset Management*, you discovered the Pimcore **Digital Asset Management** (**DAM**) feature and all aspects related to images and asset management. Then, in *Chapter 4, Creating Documents in Pimcore*, and in *Chapter 8, Creating Custom CMS Pages*, you learned about the concept of **content management systems** (**CMSes**) and how to create documents and site pages.

In this chapter, we will go in-depth through the concept of **Product Information Management** (**PIM**), putting into practice the concepts of Pimcore classes learned in *Chapter 5, Exploring Objects and Classes*, to define a `Product` entity. The chapter is organized as follows:

- What is a PIM?
- Defining the `Product` entity
- Creating Product Variants

- Creating a Bundle Product
- Managing different Product Types
- Working with Workflows

Starting with the explanation of what a PIM system is, we will implement an example of a `Product` class. After having defined the class attributes, you will learn how to create product variants and bundle products, and how to manage different product types using Objectbricks. In the last section of the chapter, you will learn how to define a workflow to fill in the product information step by step.

Technical requirements

As you have done in previous chapters, all you need to do is run the demo connected to this chapter by navigating to the `12. Implementing Product Information Management` folder of the official book repository and start a Docker environment.

To do so, just follow these instructions:

1. Run Docker with the following command:

   ```
   docker-compose up
   ```

2. Then, to restore all the settings on your local machine, just open a new shell and type the following command:

   ```
   docker-compose exec php bash restore.sh
   ```

3. Navigate to `http://localhost/admin` and log in with your admin/pimcore credentials.

You can access the official book repository to get the source code through the following link:

`https://github.com/PacktPublishing/Modernizing-Enterprise-CMS-using-Pimcore/tree/main/12.%20Implementing%20Product%20Information%20Management`

Now you are ready to navigate through the demo to discover all the aspects related to this chapter.

What is a PIM?

In *Chapter 1*, *Introducing Pimcore*, we briefly introduced the concept of **Product Information Management (PIM)**. In this section, we will better explain this concept, which we will put into practice throughout the following sections of this chapter.

The concept of PIM encompasses a set of technologies and procedures that allow centralized management of product data and their distribution across different channels. In many common scenarios, information relating to products may come from multiple sources, potentially with different data structures, both due to different needs dictated by their distribution channels and through the provision of different technologies in distinct areas within the same company.

The use of a PIM allows you to integrate information from different sources into a single platform and organize it all coherently, with the possibility of redistributing this information in different ways to e-commerce platforms, websites, paper catalogs, and so on. It also allows complete and dynamic management of the product data, including customizing and filtering information related to different types of products to manage prices and currencies, different units of measurement, multilingual translations, multimedia content, and much more.

The ability to centralize all this information in a single platform allows you to manage products completely independently of any distribution channel; the PIM will be responsible for sending only the information it needs to each channel. This centralized management gives consistency to product information, avoiding the need to replicate data in different platforms and keeping them aligned, reducing design errors. This also brings benefits in terms of the management cost of any catalogs, price lists, and online platforms.

The use of a PIM is essential for companies that need to sell or present their products in different platforms and media, but also for business scenarios in which it is necessary to share information relating to products in different departments or development areas, always keeping the production of such information centralized. The need to have a PIM increases even more as the number of products to manage increases, as the cost of managing and maintaining data is drastically reduced, limiting it to a single platform.

PIM technologies also make it possible to integrate information relating to products alongside them with the management of multimedia content associated with them and to send such content to the various distribution channels.

All these aspects regarding the concept of PIM and its usages are summarized in the following diagram:

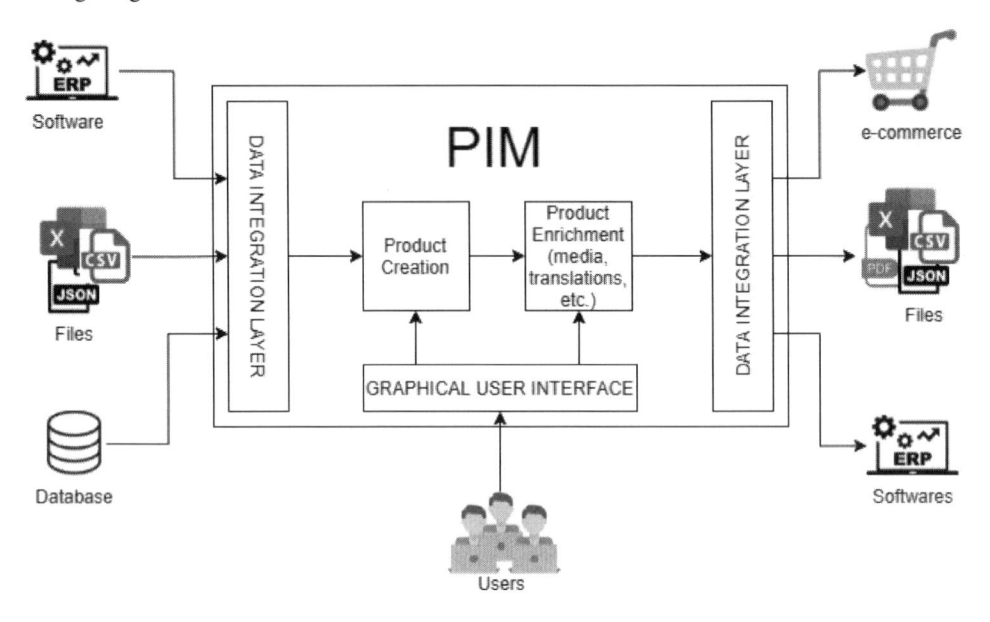

Figure 12.1: PIM Architecture

As you can see in the previous diagram, products can be imported into a PIM system by uploading files or implementing specific flows to establish an integration with other software or databases. Products can also be created and enriched directly in the PIM environment, through the **graphical user interface** (**GUI**).

Product data can then be exported to e-commerce or other software, or properly exported to files. In *Chapter 14*, *Data Integration*, you will learn different ways to import and export products in Pimcore.

To summarize, in this section, you learned about the concept of PIM and the benefits that a PIM system brings as regards to product data management and distribution. In the following section, we will build a `Product` entity step by step, defining a Pimcore class that will represent the product concept.

Defining the Product Entity

In the previous section, you learned about the concept of Product Information Management. As the name suggests, in a PIM system, it's mandatory to create a class that represents the products, and this is what we are going to do in this section.

Defining the Product Entity   287

Pimcore does not set any constraints as far as the concept of products is concerned, so we can simply create a class named `Product` and define all the attributes that reflect our needs. So, as you learned in *Chapter 5, Exploring Objects and Classes*, just go through **Settings | Data Objects | Classes**, and create a new class named `Product`.

If you followed the instructions provided in the *Technical requirements* section, you should find an already defined `Product` class. Please note that this is just a typical example of the concept of a product and that you can add or remove class attributes according to your needs. You can see what this class looks like in the following screenshot:

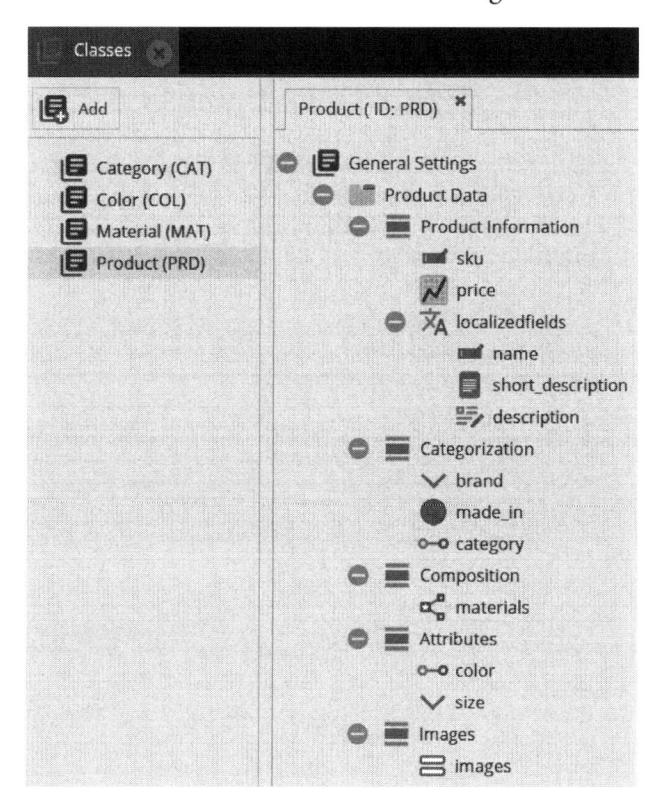

Figure 12.2: Product class

Let's describe the various class components that are shown in the previous screenshot. The class is composed of five panels that enclose different attributes representing common concepts for products, and these are outlined here:

- **Product Information**: In this panel, you can find the **Stock-Keeping Unit** (**SKU**), which is a unique identifier for products and the product price. Then, we added the product name and description as localized fields so that you can provide translations.

- **Categorization**: In this panel, you can see some attributes defined to categorize the product. The `brand` attribute is a custom-defined single select field with common brands as options; there's also a predefined options list to choose the country where the product was made. The last attribute is a many-to-one relation with another class added to describe categories.
- **Composition**: In this panel, you can find an advanced many-to-many relation component to relate the product to the materials that compose the product. In this relation, you can set the percentage of the various materials to define the composition.
- **Attributes**: In this panel, we have defined attributes that can be used to represent the product variants, such as `color` and `size`. For the `color` attribute, we have defined a relationship with a dedicated class.
- **Images**: As the name suggests, this panel is designed to contain the product images. In particular, we used a **Fieldcollection** to administer an undefined number of images.

For the sake of completeness, in the following screenshot, you will see the other class definitions:

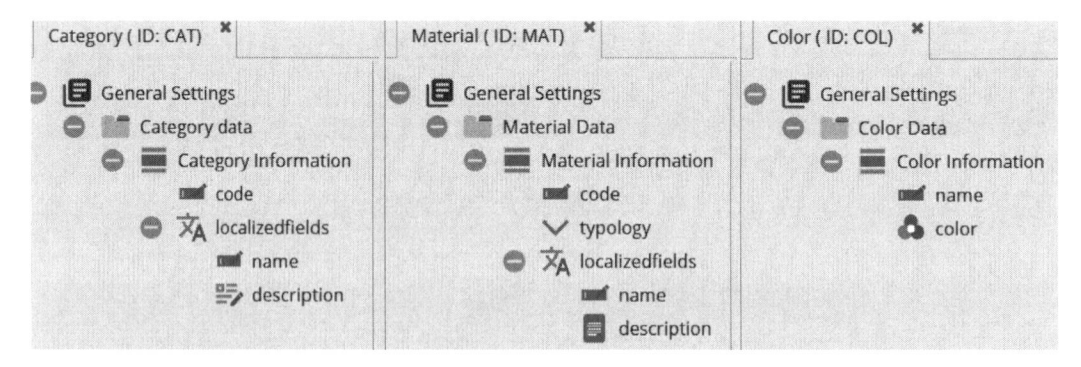

Figure 12.3: Class definitions

In the previous screenshot, you can see the definitions for the `Category`, `Material`, and `Color` classes. For the `Category` class, we have defined a unique `code` attribute and a couple of localized fields, called `name` and `description`. The same structure is made for the `Material` class, with the addition of another field to define the material typology. For the `Color` class, an attribute to set the **hexadecimal** (**hex**) value was added.

As previously mentioned, you should already find these classes after the installation process described in the *Technical requirements* section of this chapter, but you can import them at any time by selecting the files that you can find in the `src/classes` folder of the chapter repository, as you have seen in *Chapter 7, Administrating Pimcore Sites*.

As you have learned in *Chapter 5, Exploring Objects and Classes*, you can easily perform data entry to create products and other entities. In the following screenshot, you can see an example of a created product:

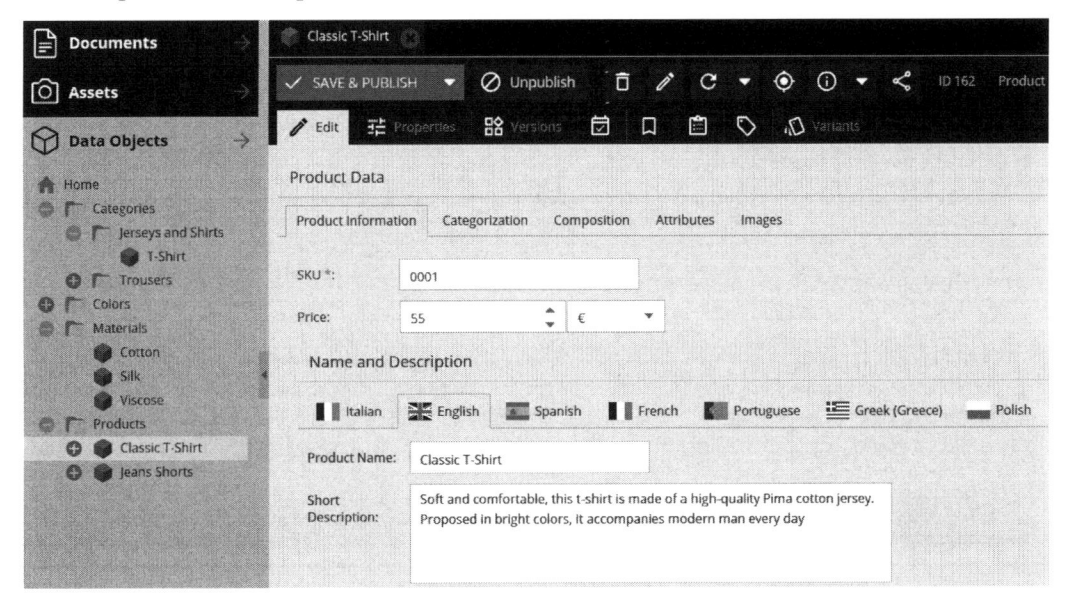

Figure 12.4: Product entity

As you can see in the previous screenshot, the structure of the created product reflects the class definition. To better organize the contents, objects of the various classes are divided into the corresponding subfolders.

To summarize, in this section, we have seen how to define a `Product` entity. We have presented a possible implementation of the product concept, but this concept has no fixed definition in terms of attributes, so you can choose to create attributes that better reflect your needs. Beside from this, we have defined other secondary classes to relate the products to other concepts such as categories, materials, and colors. This is useful for keeping this information linked to a product without the need to replicate them in all products.

In the following section, you will learn how to create product variants in order to create configurable products.

Creating product variants

In the previous section, you have seen how to define a `Product` entity and an example of product object creation. In this section, you will learn how to enable the inheritance for the `Product` class to create product variants and define configurable products. Later in this section, we will see some **PHP: Hypertext Preprocessor** (**PHP**) code examples that will show how to practically use variants during development.

To enable inheritance for the `Product` class, open the class definition and select the **General Settings** root element. You can enable class inheritance and allow the variants' creation by selecting the checkboxes that you see in the following screenshot:

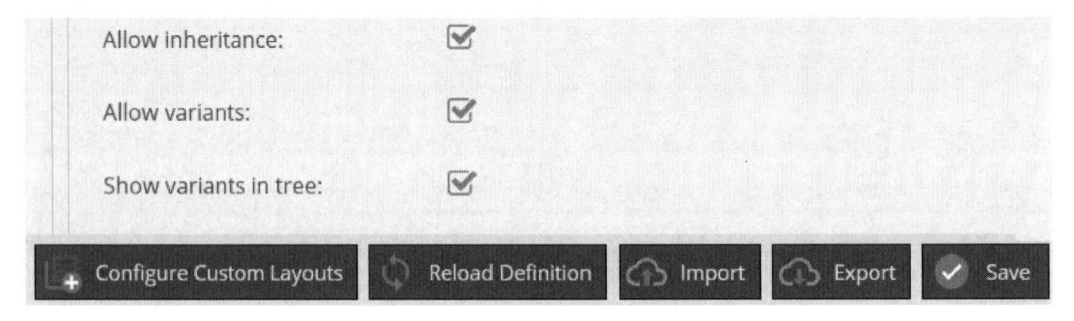

Figure 12.5: Enabling inheritance

As you can see in the previous screenshot, three checkboxes can be enabled, as follows:

- **Allow inheritance**: If checked, this property enables inheritance among objects in a tree-structured way. The child objects can be instances of the same class or may belong to a different class.

- **Allow variants**: If checked, this enables the possibility to create object variants. The variant definition is a particular kind of inheritance. The variant class cannot be chosen, but the class is forced to be the same as the parent object.

- **Show variants in tree**: If enabled, this property allows you to see the variants in the object tree.

Once you have enabled these checkboxes, you must click on the **Save** button to apply the changes. After having enabled variants for the class, variants can be created for products. To create a variant, just right-click on a previously created product, select **Add Variant**, and type the variant name.

In the following screenshot, you will see an example of a configurable product with variants defined:

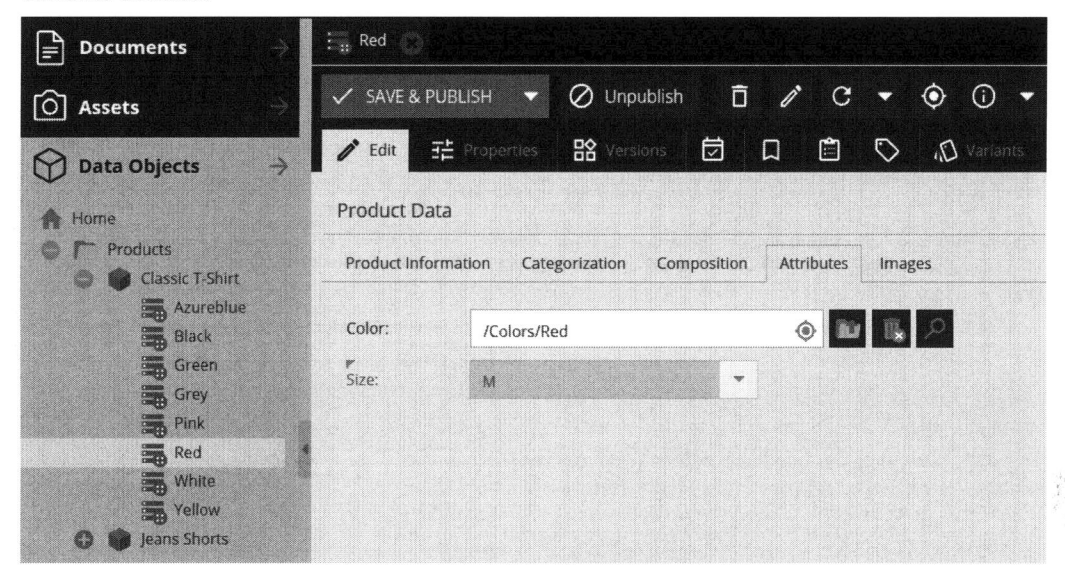

Figure 12.6: Product variant example

As you can see in the previous screenshot, enabling the corresponding property lets the product variants be shown in the object tree. You can recognize product variants by the different specific icons in the tree structure.

The variants inherit all property values from the parent, but it's possible to override those properties in each variant. In this specific example, we have used the `Color` attribute to create a configurable product with different variants.

Now that you have learned how to create product variants in the Pimcore interface, let's see how to practically use variants in code, looking at some coding examples.

A key aspect concerning variants is the object **type**. This is a system property defined for objects of all classes; this property cannot be filled manually, but it's automatically defined when we create an element. There are three different object types, outlined as follows:

- `folder`: This type is assigned when we create a folder in the **Data Objects** section.
- `object`: This type is assigned when we create an object instance of a class.
- `variant`: This type is assigned when we create an object variant.

When coding in Pimcore, it's important to know that all native methods that perform searches for lists of objects always consider only `folder` and `object` types, so it's necessary to explicitly specify that you want to retrieve variants. Through the following examples, we will see how to do this.

Parent PHP class

In this first example, you will learn how to create a parent PHP class for the `Product` class and how to create a method to retrieve the product variants. The creation of this class is not strictly related to the concept of variants, but it's a feature that is worth discovering and that can be useful in different scenarios.

As we briefly introduced in the *Creating and Editing a Class Definition* section of *Chapter 5*, *Exploring Objects and Classes*, for each class, there is the possibility of defining a custom parent PHP class. This can be any PHP class that directly or indirectly extends the `Pimcore\Model\DataObject\Concrete` class.

The `Concrete` class is a PHP class that is originally extended by all Pimcore classes and that contains all the common methods for all the classes, such as the `save` and `getById` operations, to cite a couple of them.

In the following code snippet, you will see an example `product` parent class with a defined method to retrieve product variants:

```php
<?php

namespace App\Model;
use Pimcore\Model\DataObject;

class AbstractProduct extends DataObject\Concrete
{
    /**
     * @return self[]
     */
    public function getVariants(){
        $variantType = self::OBJECT_TYPE_VARIANT; //variant
        $variants = $this->getChildren(array($variantType));
        return $variants;
    }
}
```

As you can see in the previous code snippet, this class extends the previously mentioned `Concrete` class. In this class, we have created a `getVariants` method that invokes the original `getChildren` method, specifying the need to retrieve objects of the type `variant`. This is necessary because, as we said in the previous section, all listing methods consider only objects and folders if no types are directly specified.

Once the PHP class is created, we must properly set the corresponding property in the `Product` class, as you can see in the following screenshot:

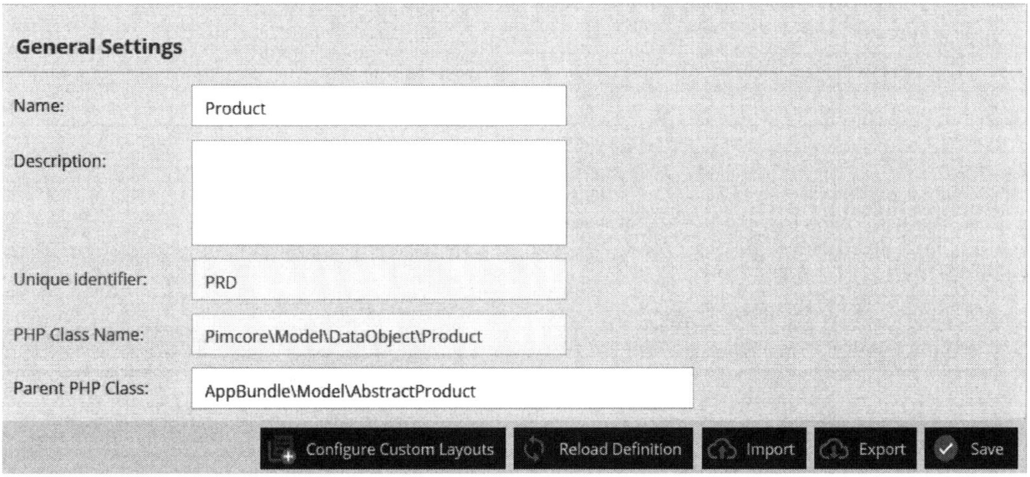

Figure 12.7: Configuring the parent PHP class

As you can see in the previous screenshot, you may write the complete class namespace in the **Parent PHP Class** input. Once you have filled that in, you must click on the **Save** button to apply the changes.

After having defined the parent PHP class, you can call the `getVariants` method for each product object instance, as you can see in the following code snippet:

```php
<?php
    use Pimcore\Model\DataObject;

    $product = DataObject\Product::getById(1);
    $variants = $product->getVariants();
?>
```

In the previous code snippet, you can see that since the `Product` class extends the previously created `AbstractProduct` class, every product object can use the defined `getVariants` method.

The `getChildren` method that we have seen in this example is just one particular case of object listing. In the following example, we will see how to retrieve variants in common listing methods.

Object Listing

In the previous example, we have seen how to retrieve the variants of a specific product, using the methods that retrieve the product children. In this example, we will see how to retrieve variants in generic listing methods.

In the following code snippet, you can see how product variants can be retrieved on listing queries:

```php
<?php
    use Pimcore\Model\DataObject\Product;
    use Pimcore\Model\DataObject\AbstractObject;

    $list = new Product\Listing();
    $list->setObjectTypes([AbstractObject::OBJECT_TYPE_VARIANT]);
    $variants = $list->load();
?>
```

In the previous code snippet, you can see how to initialize a product listing. For listing objects, there is a specific method to set the object types that you want to retrieve. This method is the one that is used internally by the `getChildren` method you have seen in the previous example. The `load` method returns an array of objects that respect the listing conditions.

In these first two examples, you have learned how to retrieve existing variants. In the following example, you will see how to create a new variant instead.

Creating a new Variant

In the previous examples, you learned how to query for existing variants. In this example, you will learn how to create a product variant.

In the following code snippet, you will see how to create a variant for an existing product:

```php
<?php
    use Pimcore\Model\DataObject\Product;
    use Pimcore\Model\DataObject\AbstractObject;

    $tshirt = Product::getByName("Classic T-Shirt", "en", 1);

    $orange = new Product();
    $orange->setKey("Orange");
    $orange->setParent($tshirt);
    $orange->setType(AbstractObject::OBJECT_TYPE_VARIANT);

    $orange->save();
?>
```

As you can see in the previous code snippet, first of all you have to get the product object. The retrieved product must be declared as the parent of the new product variant. Then, it's necessary to explicitly set the product type to declare that the created product is a variant.

In the example, you will note the use of the `getByName` method. This kind of method is automatically generated for each class attribute at class-definition save. The first argument is the value to search for, the second one is for localized fields (the language for which the value must be searched), and the third one is the limit parameter. If the limit is 1, a single object is returned; otherwise, the return type is an instance of the class listing.

To summarize, in this section, you learned how to enable variants for the `Product` class and how to create product variants. Then, through some code examples, you learned how to retrieve existing variants and how to create new ones.

In the following section, you will learn how to create bundled products and how to create a service that listens to events fired after certain operations are made—for example, to automatically calculate one or more product field values when a product is saved.

Creating a Bundle Product

In the previous section, you learned how to enable and create product variants and how to practically use them in code examples. In this section, you will learn how to define bundle products.

In marketing, the concept of **Product Bundling** is the practice of offering a set of individual products or services together as one combined product or service package. Typically, bundle products are intended to be kits or, more generically, a group of coherent products, with the advantage of a discounted price if bought together instead of buying them separately.

Through this chapter, we will first see how to modify our previously created `Product` class to define bundle products. Then, we will discover how to automatically perform operations once the product is saved to calculate the bundle price.

Defining bundle products

In this section, you will learn how to modify the `Product` class to be able to define bundle products. The easiest solution is to create a self-referenced relation attribute with the `Product` class itself. This will let you choose the products that will form the bundle from the previously created products.

To add this attribute, you need to perform the following instructions:

1. Open the `Product` class definition.
2. Right-click on the **Product Information** panel and select **Add Data Component | Relation | Many-to-Many Object Relation**.
3. Write `bundle_products` as the attribute name and `Bundle Products` as the attribute title.
4. In the **Allowed Classes** list, select the `Product` class.
5. In the **Visible Fields** list, select the class fields that you want to show in the relation—for example, `sku` and `name`.
6. Click on the **Save** button to apply the changes.

In the following screenshot, you can see what the `Product` class should look like after these operations:

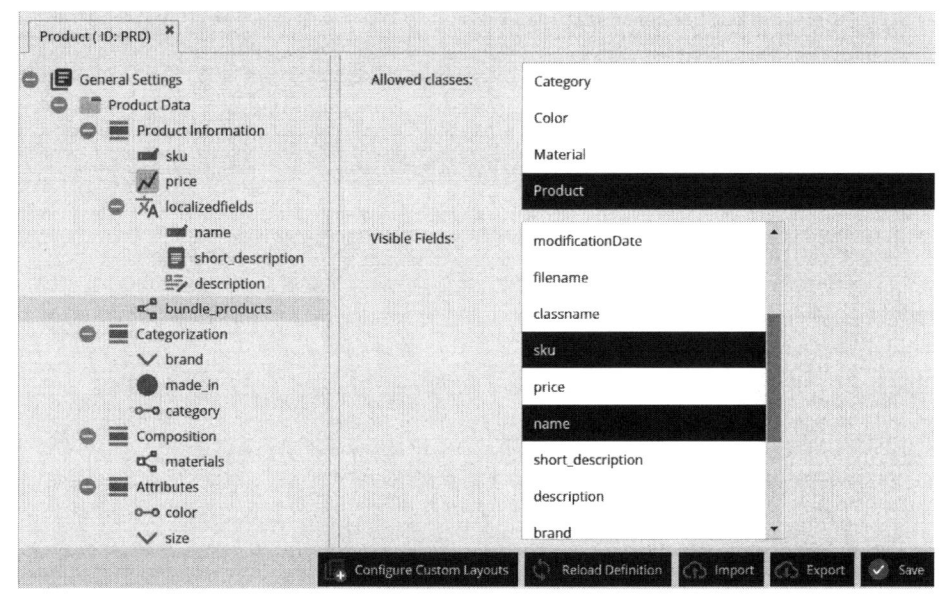

Figure 12.8: Bundle_Products Attribute

As you can see in the previous screenshot, the new attribute is added at the bottom of the panel, and the desired visible fields are selected.

Now that we have created this attribute, we can create a bundle product. To do that, simply create a new product object, then use the previously created relation attribute to select a couple of products that will compose the bundle product. Once you have selected these products they will appear in the relationship, as you can see in the following screenshot:

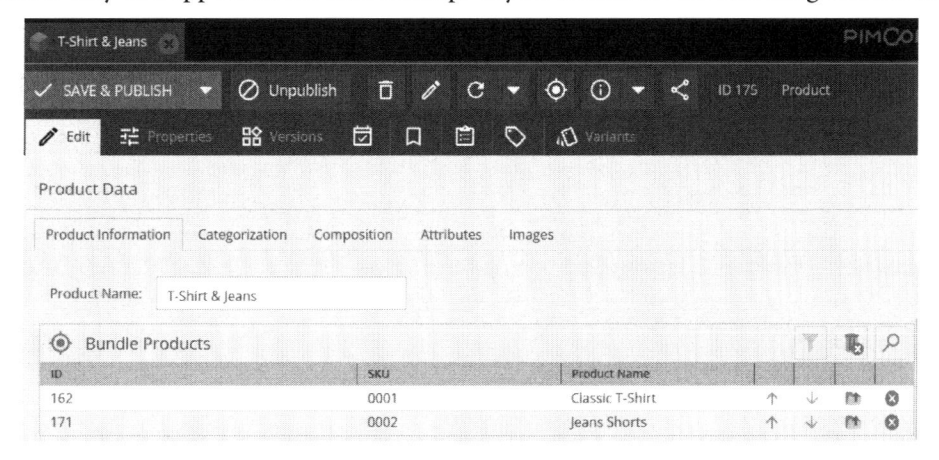

Figure 12.9: Bundle Products relation

As you can see in the previous screenshot, only the previously selected product fields are visible in the relation attribute.

Now that we have defined which are the products that compose our bundle, we may want to automatically calculate the bundle price based on the price of the selected products. So we need to open the class definition and add a new numeric attribute to store the bundle price, as you can see in the following screenshot:

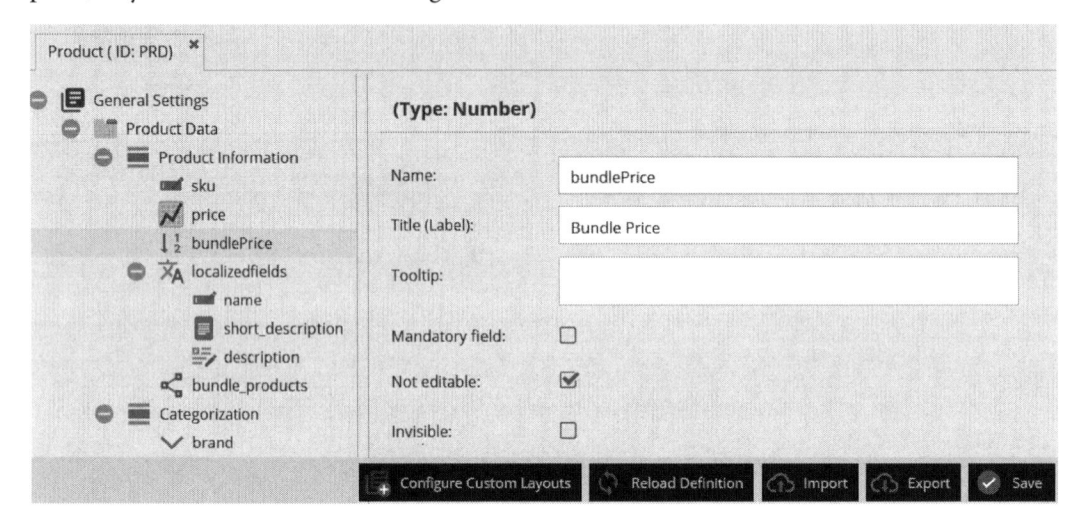

Figure 12.10: Bundle price attribute

In the previous screenshot, you can see that this attribute is marked as **Not editable**, and this means that we need a method to calculate the bundle price.

To summarize, in this section, you learned how to alter the `Product` class to define bundle products. In the following section, you will learn how to create a listener class that listens for an event fired by the product save operation, which will allow you to automatically calculate the bundle price.

Creating an Event Listener

In the previous section, you learned how to define bundle products. In common scenarios, the price of a bundle product is less than the sum of the individual price of the products it's composed of. It may be useful to automatically calculate the price of a bundle product with a predefined rule, instead of manually inserting this value.

In this section, you will learn how to create an event listener to capture events fired once the product is saved. The saving of an object is just one of the events that could be listened to in Pimcore, which includes all **create, read, update, and delete** (**CRUD**) operations on objects, assets, and documents, operations on users, the opening of search or grid lists, and many others.

To create an event listener, you first need to register a new class in the `app/config/services.yml` file, as you can see in the following code snippet:

```yaml
services:
    App\EventListener\DataObjectListener:
        tags:
            - { name: kernel.event_listener, event: pimcore.dataobject.postUpdate, method: onObjectPostUpdate }
```

As you can see in the previous snippet, a new service can be defined by adding the class namespace. In the `tags` attribute, we must define one or more tags of our service. Each tag is composed of three properties, outlined as follows:

- `name`: The name of the tag. We must provide the `kernel.event_listener` fixed value to let the service be correctly recognized as an event listener.
- `event`: Used to specify which event we want to listen to. In our case, we are interested in listening to the `postUpdate` event for objects. This event, as the name suggests, is fired after an object is saved.
- `method`: In this property, we must put the name of the method of our class that will be called automatically when an event is fired.

For event listeners, each defined tag represents a specific event, so you must add one tag for each event that you want your service to listen to.

Let's now see how to implement the defined service to calculate the price of our bundle product. In the following code snippet, you will see a possible implementation:

```php
<?php
namespace App\EventListener;
use Pimcore\Event\Model\DataObjectEvent;
use Pimcore\Model\DataObject\Product;
class DataObjectListener
{
    public function onObjectPostUpdate (DataObjectEvent $e)
    {
```

```
            $obj = $e->getObject();
            if($obj instanceof Product)
            {
                $bundleProducts = $obj->getBundle_products();
                $currentPrice = $obj->getBundlePrice();
                if(count($bundleProducts) >0)
                {
                    $bundlePrice = 0;
                    foreach($bundleProducts as $product)
                    {
                        $price = $product->getPrice()
                            ->getValue();
                        $bundlePrice += $price;
                    }
                    //substract the 20% of the sum
                    $bundlePrice = round($bundlePrice*0.8,2);
                    //Add this check to avoid circular saves
                    if($bundlePrice != $currentPrice)
                    {
                        $obj->setBundlePrice($bundlePrice);
                        $obj->save();
                    }
                }
            }
        }
    }
}
```

Let's analyze the previous code snippet, to understand the key aspects. First of all, you may note that we have defined a method named `onObjectPostUpdate`, which is the name defined in the `services.yml` file.

This method takes the fired event as an argument, and from this event, we can extract the object that fired the event itself. As you may note, we must check for the object class to do the operations part only if the object is a product.

For each product that composes the bundle, we add up the product prices, and in the end, we decrease this sum by 20%. Please note that this is just an example and that you can define your own rule.

To avoid a circular loop on product saves, we save the product only in cases where the new calculated price is different from the previous one. If we omit this check, the save operation made on this service will fire the event again.

To summarize, in this section, you learned about the concept of product bundling and how to change the `Product` class by adding attributes that allow you to define bundle products. Later, you learned how to create an event listener service to capture events fired by operations on objects, such as the saving of a product. In the provided example, you have seen how to automatically calculate the price of a bundle product.

In the following section, you will learn how to extend the `Product` class to manage different types of products without the need to create a specific class for each product.

Managing different Product Types

In the previous section, you learned how to define bundle products. In this section, you will learn how to manage different types of products without creating a different class for each product type. If you need to manage a heterogeneous set of products, such as shirts and shoes, you will probably need specific attributes to better represent these concepts.

Surely, we could create two different classes for shirts and shoes, but we will need to define redundant fields for both classes to describe properties that are shared between them—for example, the title, price, description, and so on.

In *Chapter 5, Exploring Objects and Classes*, we introduced the concept of **Objectbricks**. With Objectbricks, we just need to create little sets of attributes to describe specific fields and allow our class to dynamically add these bricks. As the name suggests, class objects can be composed of one or more bricks added to the common attributes.

Before creating Objectbrick definitions, we need to create an attribute in the `Product` class to accommodate the various bricks. To create this attribute, just right-click on a panel component inside the class definition and select **Add Data Component | Structured | Objectbricks**, fill in the attribute name, and click on the **Save** button to apply the changes. In the following screenshot, you can see an example of this:

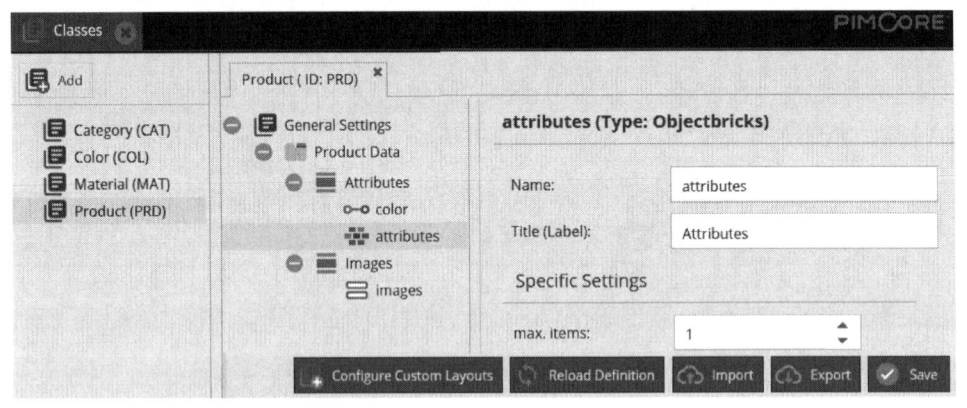

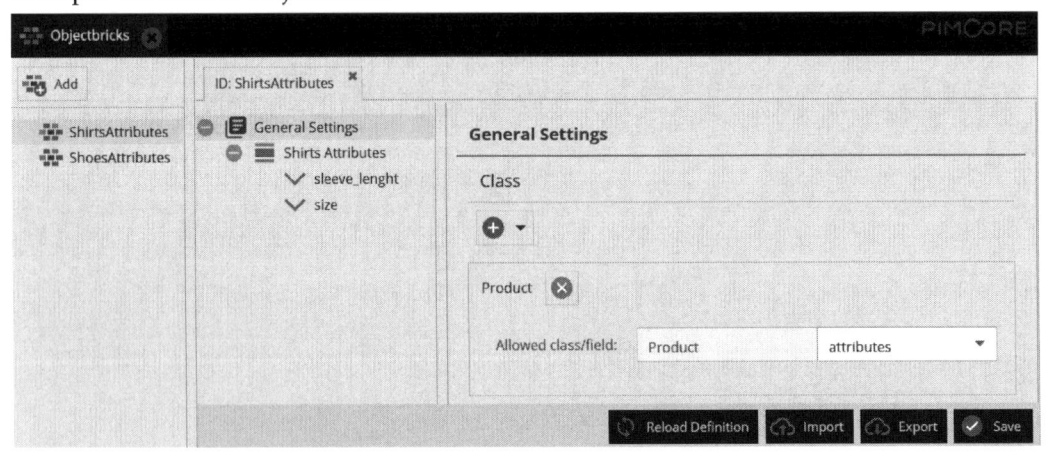

Figure 12.11: Objectbricks attribute

As you can see in the previous screenshot, we have created an attribute of the **Objectbricks** type. As an optional property, we can set the maximum number of bricks that can be attached to each object.

Now that we have defined the attribute in the `Product` class, we can define one or more Objectbricks. To do that, just go through **Settings | Data Objects | Objectbricks**. To add a new Objectbricks definition, you just need to click on the **Add** button, write the name of your brick, and click on the **OK** button. In the following screenshot, you can see an example of a created Objectbrick:

Figure 12.12: Objectbrick definition

As you can see in the previous screenshot, the Objectbricks definition panel is the same as the class creation one. Besides, for Objectbricks, we can select the classes and the specific attributes to attach the Objectbrick to. In this example, we have attached the Objectbrick to the `Product` class, and we have selected the previously created attribute.

Once the Objectbricks are defined, we can attach them to the product objects. In the following screenshot, you can see what the Objectbrick looks like in the product object:

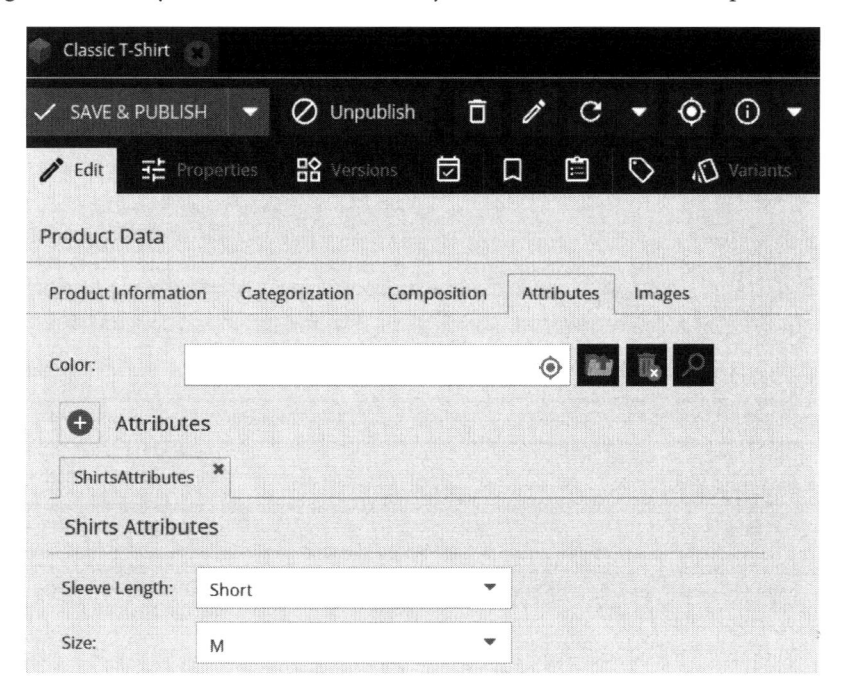

Figure 12.13: Objectbrick instance

As you can see in the previous screenshot, in the product objects, the Objectbricks appear as a specific section. You can attach one or more Objectbricks to every object since the defined limit is reached, and every kind of Objectbrick can be attached once within the same objects.

To summarize, in this section, you learned how to manage different types of products using Objectbricks. Objectbricks can be considered as subsets of attributes that can be attached to classes to extend the class concept with extra attributes. For the `Product` class, for example, we can think about creating specific attributes for shirts, shoes, and so on.

In the next section, you will learn how to configure a workflow that will let you control the completeness of the product information, step by step.

Working with workflows

A workflow consists of a sequence of processes and tasks that represent the work that must be done to reach a common goal. Typically, we may think about workflows as a graph.

Pimcore Workflow Management provides configurations of multiple workflows on assets, documents, data objects, to support data maintenance processes, element life cycles, and various other processes. Pimcore workflows are based on the Symfony workflow component and extend it with specific features. Before starting the configuration of a Pimcore workflow, let's describe the basics concepts of the Symfony workflow component, as follows:

1. **Workflow Type 'Workflow'**: This is the default type of workflow and allows you to model a workflow net that is a subclass of a petri net. For this kind of workflow, an element can be in several states of the workflow at the same time.
2. **Workflow Type 'State Machine'**: A state machine is a subset of a workflow and its purpose is to hold a state of your model. A state machine cannot be in more than one place simultaneously.
3. **Place**: A place is a step in a workflow and describes a characteristic or status of an element. Depending on the place, an element may appear in a specific view—for example, to have a focus on translations only. We will have a look at how to create a custom layout for a Pimcore class in the following section.
4. **Marking Store**: The marking store stores the current place(s) for each element.
5. **Transition**: A transition describes the action that is performed to move from one place to another. Transitions may be allowed or not, depending on additional criteria, and may require additional notes and information entered by the user.
6. **Transition Guard**: Defines a criterion that defines whether a transition is currently allowed or not.

By reading the following sections, you will learn how to properly configure a Pimcore workflow. We will start by defining a custom layout for the `Product` class and will then see how to set up a workflow that will guide the completion of product information.

Configuring a Custom Layout

As mentioned before, in the various places of a workflow we can show a custom view for the element. This is made possible by configuring custom layouts on the corresponding class.

To create a custom layout, just open the class definition and click on the **Configure custom layouts** button. When that button is clicked, a new modal window is opened, and you can add a new custom layout or load a previously created one. To create a new layout, just click on the **Add** button. In the modal that will open, you can write the new layout name and **identifier** (**ID**), as you can see in the following screenshot:

Figure 12.14: Creating a Custom Layout

As you can see in the previous screenshot, to add a new custom layout you just need to fill in the **Name** and **Unique identifier** fields and click on the **OK** button to confirm.

Once you have initialized the custom layout, you can specify which attributes you want to show in the layout itself. In the following screenshot, you can see how this configuration can be done:

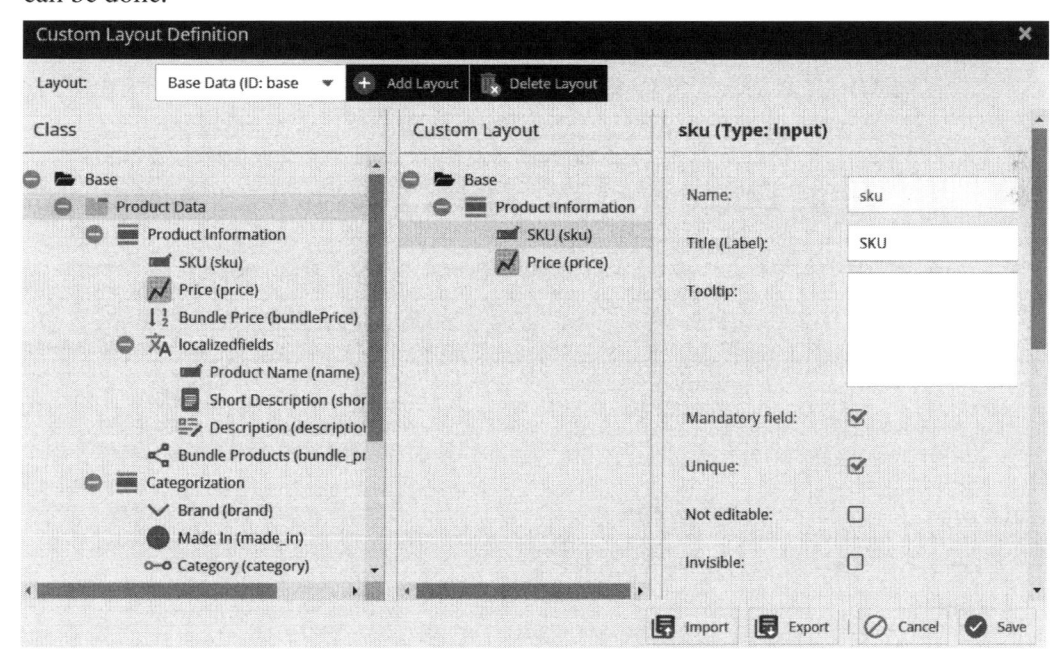

Figure 12.15: Custom Layout Configuration

As you can see in the previous screenshot, the configuration modal is composed of two main panels. In the left panel, you will find the previously defined class structure, while in the right panel, you can drag and drop the attributes you want to show in the custom layout from the left panel.

For each attribute, you can decide to change some properties, such as the possibility to edit the attribute itself. Once you have configured the custom layout, you can click on the **Save** button to apply the changes.

Now that you have seen how to configure custom layouts, let's see how to use them in a workflow configuration.

Configuring a Pimcore workflow

In the previous section, you learned how to configure custom layouts for Pimcore classes. In this section, you will learn how to configure Pimcore workflows and how to use the previously created custom layouts.

As with many other services, Pimcore workflows must be defined in the `config.yaml` file of the Pimcore project or the same file of a specific bundle. In this section, you will learn how to properly configure a workflow.

In the following code snippet, you will see how to initialize the workflow configuration:

```yaml
pimcore:
    workflows:
        product_workflow:
            label: 'Product Workflow'
            type: 'state_machine'
            supports:
                - 'Pimcore\Model\DataObject\Product'
            marking_store:
                type: single_state
                arguments:
                    - marking
```

As you can see in the preceding snippet, to initialize a workflow you must add the `workflows` keyword under the `pimcore` keyword. Then, you must add a unique ID for the workflow, which is `product_workflow` in our example.

At the lower level, you can define some parameters, which are provided here:

1. `label`: The workflow title.
2. `type`: The workflow type, which can be `workflow` or `state_machine`, as described in the chapter introduction.
3. `supports`: One or more classes to which the workflow is applied.
4. `marking_store`: For `state_machine` workflows, you can specify which attribute of the class must be used to store the workflow state. If that attribute is a picklist attribute, you can let the class dynamically create the picklist options by reading the workflow states by defining the options provider, as you can see in the following screenshot:

Options Provider Class or Service Name:	@pimcore.workflow.place-options-provider
Options Provider Data:	product_workflow

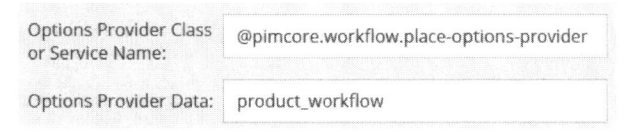

Figure 12.16: Workflow states options provider

As you can see in the previous screenshot, you can fill in the **Options Provider Class or Service Name** and specify the workflow name as the **Options Provider Data**. The options provider class will automatically read the workflow states, which you can configure with the `places` keyword, as you can see in the following snippet:

```
pimcore:
    workflows:
        product_workflow:
            places:
                base_data:
                    label: 'Base Data'
                    color: '#ffd700'
                    permissions:
                        - objectLayout: basedata
```

As you can see in the previous code snippet, you can add one or more states behind the `places` keyword. For each state, you must specify a unique ID and define a label and a color that will be used to highlight the label text. If you want to restrict the visible class attributes for a particular state, you may specify a previously defined custom layout in the `objectLayout` keyword behind `permissions`.

The last step in the workflow configuration is to define transitions between different states. You can see how to define transitions in the following code snippet:

```yaml
pimcore:
    workflows:
        product_workflow:
            transitions:
                product_images:
                    from: [ translations, enrichment ]
                    to: images
                    guard: subject.checkTranslationsCompleted()
                    options:
                        label: 'Edit Images'
                        notes:
                            commentEnabled: true
                            commentRequired: false
                            iconClass: 'pimcore_icon_image'
```

As you can see in the previous snippet, the transitions must be defined behind the `transitions` keyword. For each transition, you must define a unique ID; then, you must specify one or more states from which the transition can start and one destination state only. In the following screenshot, you can see how a transition can be invoked:

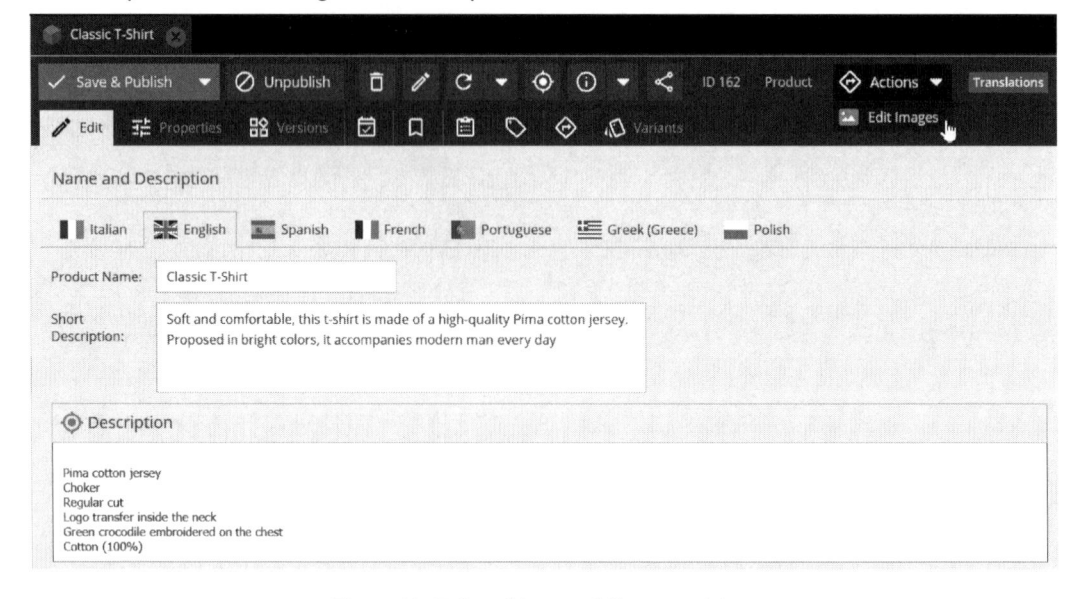

Figure 12.17: Invoking workflow transitions

As you can see in the previous screenshot, a grouped button is automatically injected into the object editor to let you select the available transitions.

If needed, you can also specify a `guard` function that is automatically invoked when the workflow is placed in one of the `from` states. If the `guard` function does not pass, it will not be possible to apply the transition and move to the destination state. In this specific example, you can let the user edit the images only after the transitions are completed. A transition guard must be a function of the object, so the best solution is to create this function in the parent PHP class that we mentioned in the *Creating product variants* section of this chapter.

Optionally, you can also specify some extra options on a transition, such as setting up a custom icon for the transition or letting the user write a note when the transition is invoked, as you can see in the following screenshot:

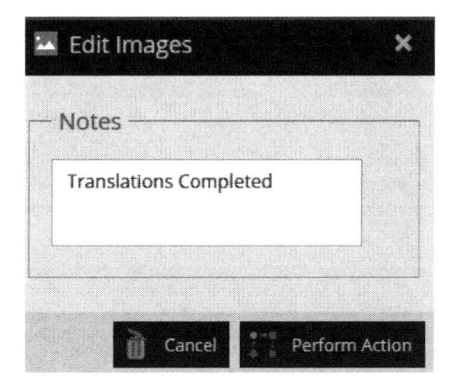

Figure 12.18: Notes on transition

As you can see in the previous screenshot, when the user clicks on the transition action, a modal will open and the user can write a comment that will be stored in the **Notes & Events** section inside the object, and then click on the **Perform Action** button to complete the transition.

To summarize, in this section, you learned how to configure a Pimcore workflow. By defining custom layouts, you can force users to fill in product information step by step, to ensure data completion. In particular, you learned how to define places for the workflow and how to configure workflow transitions.

Summary

In this chapter, you learned about the concept of **Product Information Management** by defining a `Product` entity and providing practical examples. In the first section of the chapter, you learned what a PIM is and what its main features are. Then, you learned how to create and configure a `Product` class, according to your needs.

After having defined the `Product` class, you learned how to enable inheritance for the class and how to define product variants for an existing product. Through practical code examples, you also learned how to retrieve variants on listings and how to create new product variants.

Later in this chapter, you learned about the concept of product bundling and how to add new fields to the `Product` class to let you define bundle products. Then, you learned how to create an event listener service to listen to events fired by the objects—for example, to catch once the product is saved. In particular, you have seen a code example showing how to calculate the price of a bundle product.

After that, you learned how to use Objectbricks to extend the `Product` class, attaching groups of attributes useful to define specific concepts. This is useful if you want to represent different kinds of products without creating a class for each kind, to avoid the redundancy of common attributes.

In the last section, you learned how to configure custom layouts for Pimcore classes and how to use them in Pimcore workflow configurations. Through a concrete example, you learned how to configure a workflow to fill in product information step by step.

In the next chapter, you will learn how to expose products and other entities to the outside through the Pimcore Datahub bundle and how to turn Pimcore into a **Master Data Management** (**MDM**) platform.

13
Implementing Master Data Management

In the previous chapter, you learned about the concept of **Product Information Management** (**PIM**), and how to properly create a Pimcore class to represent products. Through some coding examples, you learned how to create product variants and bundle products, and how to define different types of products by extending the defined class with Objectbricks.

In this chapter, we will present the concept of **Master Data Management** (**MDM**), and how to expose Pimcore objects to third-party applications using the **Datahub** Pimcore bundle. The chapter is organized as follows:

- Turning Pimcore into MDM
- Activating the Pimcore Datahub bundle
- Exposing entities
- Using mutation queries
- Creating a custom mutation
- Defining custom reports

Starting with a definition of **Master Data Management**, we will see how to turn Pimcore into MDM. Then, we will present the Pimcore Datahub bundle and explain how to install it. After that, we will see how to expose created objects, how to use mutation queries to create new objects, and how to create custom mutations. Last but not least, we will see how to define custom reports.

Technical requirements

As you have done in previous chapters, all you need to do to run the demo connected with this chapter is to navigate to the `13. Implementing Master Data Management` folder in the official book repository and start a Docker environment.

To do so, just follow these instructions:

1. Run Docker with the following command:

   ```
   docker-compose up
   ```

2. Then, to restore all the settings on your local machine, just open a new shell and type the following command:

   ```
   docker-compose exec php bash restore.sh
   ```

3. Navigate to `http://localhost/admin` and log in with your admin/pimcore credentials.

You can access the official book repository to get the source code through the following link:

https://github.com/PacktPublishing/Modernizing-Enterprise-CMS-using-Pimcore/tree/main/13.%20Implementing%20Master%20Data%20Management

Now you are ready to navigate through the demo to discover all aspects related to this chapter.

Turning Pimcore into MDM

In *Chapter 1*, *Introducting Pimcore*, we briefly introduced the concept of Master Data Management. MDM is a fundamental process used to manage, centralize, organize, categorize, locate, synchronize, and enrich critical data based on your company's sales, marketing, and operational strategies. In this section, we will explain this concept better to let you understand how easily you can put into practice the learnings from the previous chapters to turn Pimcore into an MDM system.

We have already seen in *Chapter 12, Implementing Product Information Management,* the potential that Pimcore has in terms of data management, but it has one big limitation: it's strictly related to the concept of products.

In many company scenarios, products are not the only kind of data that needs to be defined, managed, and shared through the company users or distributed in different channels. For example, if we think in terms of e-commerce purposes, we may want to store orders and customers or define the details of our physical shops to create a store locator page on an e-commerce site.

To provide a completely different example, the classes created in *Chapter 9, Configuring Entities and Rendering Data,* to store articles and categories can be intended, in a certain sense, as a possible implementation of MDM.

That said, the first step that we must do to turn Pimcore into an MDM system is to create a class for each concept that we need to represent, and we can easily do this through the Pimcore class-definition interface. This alone is not sufficient, but think about how easy it is to create Pimcore classes through the out-of-the-box interface, as you learned in *Chapter 5, Exploring Objects and Classes,* and how this produces a strong and easy-to-maintain structure without writing a single line of code.

Since you have already learned how to create Pimcore classes in the previous chapter, we will not repeat the process in this chapter as well. If you followed the instructions provided in the *Technical requirements* section, you should find some already defined classes.

Once the structure is defined, we can take advantage of Pimcore potentials to implement the data management processes, among which we can cite the following:

- **Data validation**: For class attributes, we can define a few validation rules—for example, we can decide whether each attribute is mandatory for a class and, for text attributes, add a regular expression to validate the content. This can be useful, but it does not permit defined complex validation scenarios such as (for example) cross-attribute validation. This can be done by implementing event listeners, as you learned in the previous chapter.

- **Data quality**: Data quality consists of a set of tools and processes needed to give qualitative and quantitative consistency to our data—for example, we may want to check whether translations for our objects are complete or not. We can accomplish this by creating specific kinds of attributes that are **Calculated Value** and **Dynamic Text Label** attributes (we will see an example of these in the next section).

- **Versioning**: One of the main characteristics of **PIM**, **DAM**, and **MDM** is the possibility to share objects. Every user that has write permission can edit products and other objects, and different users may access and save the same object. For this reason, it's important to keep track of object versions to have a clear view of which user has made changes.

Now that we have defined the main characteristics of an MDM system, let's see an example of a Data Quality implementation.

Implementing Data Quality

In the previous section, we introduced the definition of Master Data Management, and you learned what the main characteristics of an MDM system are.

In this section, through an example, we will see how to implement **data quality**. As we mentioned in the previous section, we can accomplish this using two different kinds of attributes, which are **Calculated Value** and **Dynamic Text Label** attributes.

These particular kinds of attributes require the development of a **PHP: Hypertext Preprocessor** (**PHP**) class whose methods are automatically called when an object is opened. Once this class is developed, we must write the class namespace in the attribute configuration, as you can see in the following screenshot:

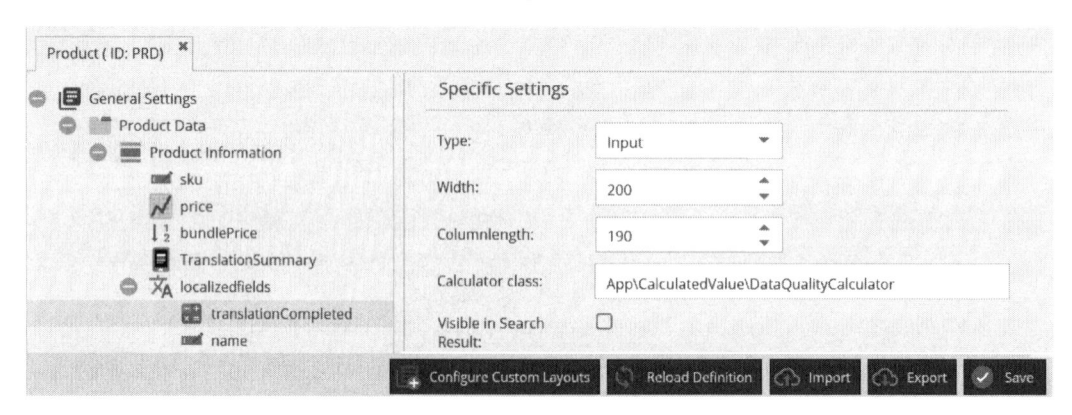

Figure 13.1: Calculated value configuration

As you can see in the previous screenshot, we can put the class namespace in the **Calculator class** input in the attribute configuration. Once the input is filled, you can click on the **Save** button to apply the changes to the class. The same configuration can be done for the **Dynamic Text Label** attributes.

Now that we have seen how to configure the attributes, in the following code snippet, we will see how to implement the `Calculator` class:

```php
<?php
namespace App\CalculatedValue;

use Pimcore\Model\DataObject\ClassDefinition\
CalculatorClassInterface;
use Pimcore\Model\DataObject\Concrete;
use Pimcore\Model\DataObject\Data\CalculatedValue;
use Pimcore\Model\DataObject\Product;
use Pimcore\Tool;

class DataQualityCalculator implements CalculatorClassInterface
{
    public function compute(Concrete $object, CalculatedValue
    $context): string
    {
        return $this->getCalculatedValueForEditMode($object,
        $context);
    }

    public function getCalculatedValueForEditMode(Concrete
    $object, CalculatedValue $context): string
    {
        if ($object instanceof Product) {
            $language = $context->getPosition();
            if(empty($object->getName($language))
                || empty($object->getShort_
                description($language))
                || empty($object->getDescription($language))){

                return "no";
            }
            return "yes";
        }
        return '';
    }
}
```

In the previous code snippet, you can see how to realize a PHP class suitable for **Calculated Values**. As you can see, this class must implement the `CalculatorClassInterface` interface, which involves implementing the following two methods:

- The `compute` method is called on the object save, to store the calculated value in the database.
- The `getCalculatedValueForEditMode` method is invoked to display the value in the object edit modal.

These two functions are typically expected to return the same value, so it's a best practice to let one function return the value of the other one to avoid code duplication.

These functions take the object instance and the attribute context as input that contains useful information such as the `fieldname` attribute. For localized fields, the current language is defined in the `position` property of the context.

In this specific example, we first check whether the object is a product, which is the class for which we have set the **Calculated Value** attribute. Then, we check whether for each language all the localized fields are empty or not.

In the following code snippet, we will see how to implement a method needed to render the dynamic text label:

```php
<?php
namespace App\CalculatedValue;

use Pimcore\Model\DataObject\ClassDefinition\Layout\DynamicTextLabelInterface;
use Pimcore\Model\DataObject\Concrete;
use Pimcore\Model\DataObject\Data\CalculatedValue;
use Pimcore\Model\DataObject\Product;
use Pimcore\Tool;

class DataQualityCalculator implements DynamicTextLabelInterface
{
    public function renderLayoutText($data, $object, $params)
    {
        if ($object instanceof Product) {
```

```php
            $htmlTable = '<table style="border: 1px solid black">';
            $htmlTable .= '<thead><tr>
<td style="border: 1px solid black">Language</td>
<td style="border: 1px solid black">Translation Status</td>
</tr></thead>';

            foreach (Tool::getValidLanguages() as $language) {
                $htmlTable .= '<tr>';
                $htmlTable .= '<td style="border: 1px solid
                black">'.$language.'</td>';
                $htmlTable .= '<td style="border: 1px solid
                black">'.($object-
                >getTranslationCompleted($language) == "yes" ?
                "completed" : "not completed").'</td>';
                $htmlTable .= '</tr>';
            }
            $htmlTable .= '</table>';

            return "<h2 style='margin-top: 0'>Translations
            Summary</h2>" . $htmlTable;
        }
        return '';
    }
}
```

As you can see in the previous code snippet, the class is similar to the previously created one. To render the dynamic text label, the class must implement the `DynamicTextLabelInterface` interface. This interface presents the `renderLayoutText` method, which we must implement.

In the `renderLayoutText` method, we can return **HyperText Markup Language** (**HTML**) text that will be rendered in the label. In this specific example, we have realized a simple HTML table that shows whether the localized fields are completed for each language, using the previously created calculated value.

In the following screenshot, you can see what these attributes look like:

Product Data

Product Information | Categorization | Composition | Attributes | Images

Translations Summary

Language	Translation Status
it	completed
en	completed
es	not completed
fr	not completed
pt	not completed
el_GR	not completed
pl	not completed

Name and Description

Italian | English | Spanish | French | Portuguese | Greek (Greece) | Polish

Translations Completed: yes

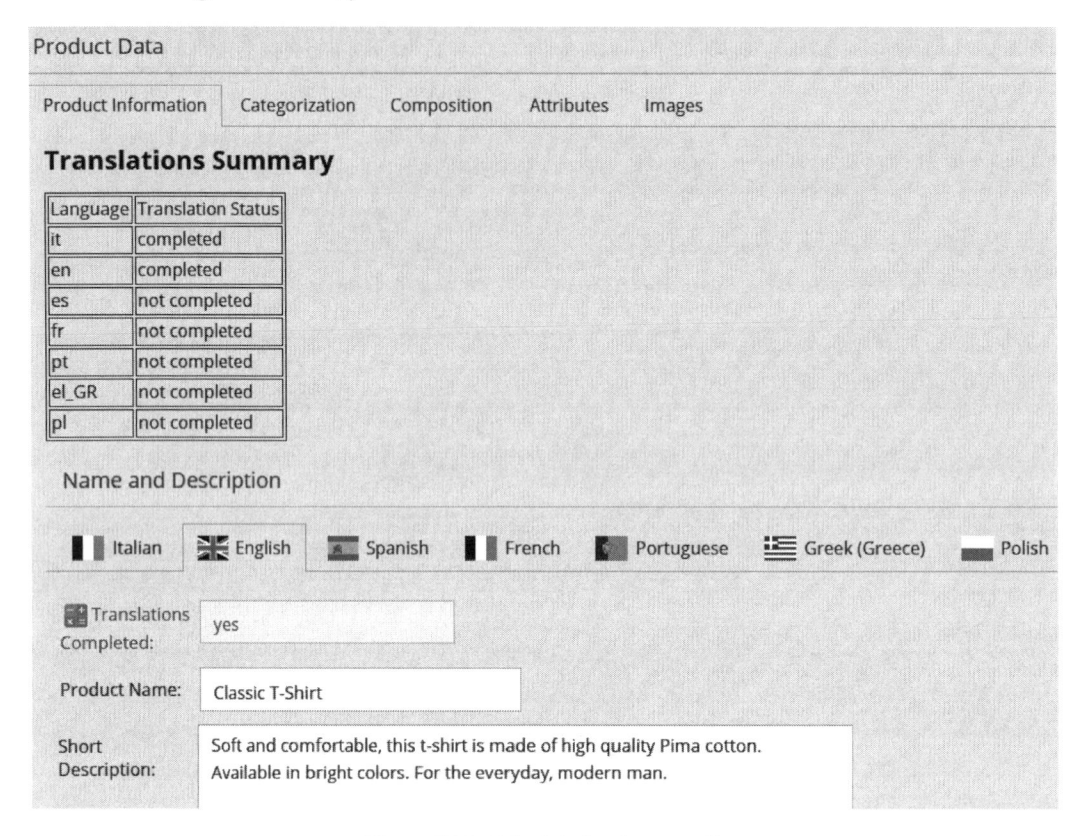

Product Name: Classic T-Shirt

Short Description: Soft and comfortable, this t-shirt is made of high quality Pima cotton. Available in bright colors. For the everyday, modern man.

Figure 13.2: Calculated values result

As you can see in the previous screenshot, the dynamic text label shows the completeness status for each language, while the calculated value shows whether the selected language fields have been completed.

To summarize, in this section, you learned about the concept of **Master Data Management** (**MDM**), and how you can take advantage of Pimcore potentials to implement the data management processes, turning Pimcore into an MDM system. Later, you learned how to implement calculated values to realize data quality.

In the following section, you will learn how to activate the Pimcore Datahub bundle that you can use to expose Pimcore objects to third-party applications.

Activating the Pimcore Datahub bundle

In the previous section, you learned how to implement data management processes, such as the data quality process. These processes, the name of what? unclear, are key aspects of the MDM concept. Another fundamental feature for MDM systems is the possibility to expose entities to third-party applications and sites.

In this section, you will learn how to activate the Pimcore **Datahub** bundle and how to configure that bundle properly. Later in this chapter, you will learn how to use this bundle to expose Pimcore objects and let external applications create new objects.

As you learned in the *Installing a Bundle* section of *Chapter 7, Administrating Pimcore Sites*, Pimcore bundles can be downloaded through the `composer` package manager; to download the Datahub bundle, you just need to follow these instructions:

1. Open a shell and point to the chapter folder of the book source code.
2. Run the following command to jump inside the Docker container:

   ```
   docker-compose php bash
   ```

3. Run the following command to download the Datahub bundle:

   ```
   composer require pimcore/data-hub
   ```

Once the bundle is downloaded, it must be enabled and installed to be able to use it. You can do this through the **Tools | Bundles** menu, as shown in the following screenshot:

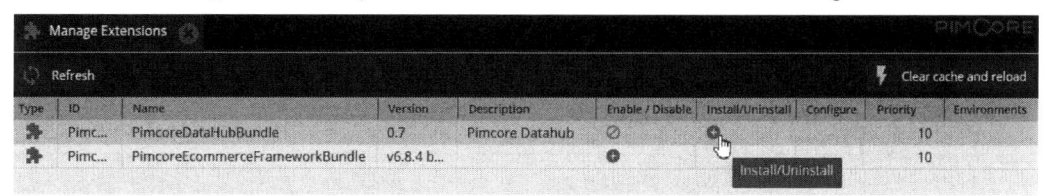

Figure 13.3: Datahub Bundle Installation

As you can see in the previous screenshot, the Datahub bundle must first be enabled and then installed. The installation of the bundle will create additional tables inside the database structure.

These operations can be accomplished alternatively through the following Bash commands:

```
php bin/console pimcore:bundle:enablePimcoreDatahubBundle
php bin/console pimcore:bundle:installPimcoreDatahubBundle
```

Please note that running these commands is just an alternative to the operations made through the extension manager interface; only one method should be used.

Now that you have learned how to install the Datahub bundle, let's see how to create Datahub configuration models.

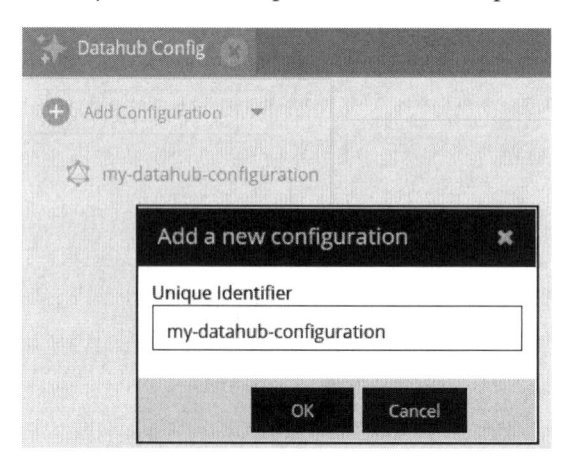

Creating a Datahub configuration

In the previous section, you learned how to install and activate the Pimcore Datahub bundle. In this section, you will learn how to create configurations for Datahub. These configurations will govern how third-party applications can interact with Pimcore to retrieve, create, or update objects.

To open the Datahub configuration panel, just go through **Settings | Datahub Config** in the Pimcore menu. To create a new configuration, just follow the next instructions:

1. Click on the **Add Configuration** button.
2. Write the configuration name inside the window that appears.
3. Click on the **OK** button to confirm the creation.

In the following screenshot, you can see a representation of the previous instructions:

Figure 13.4: Creating a Datahub configuration

As you can see in the previous screenshot, once the configuration is created it is visible in the left-side menu. If you click on the created configuration, the configuration will open in the edit mode. The setup of the configuration can be made through three different panels, as we are about to see.

The **General** panel contains general information about the configuration, such as the configuration name. We can see what this panel looks like in the following screenshot:

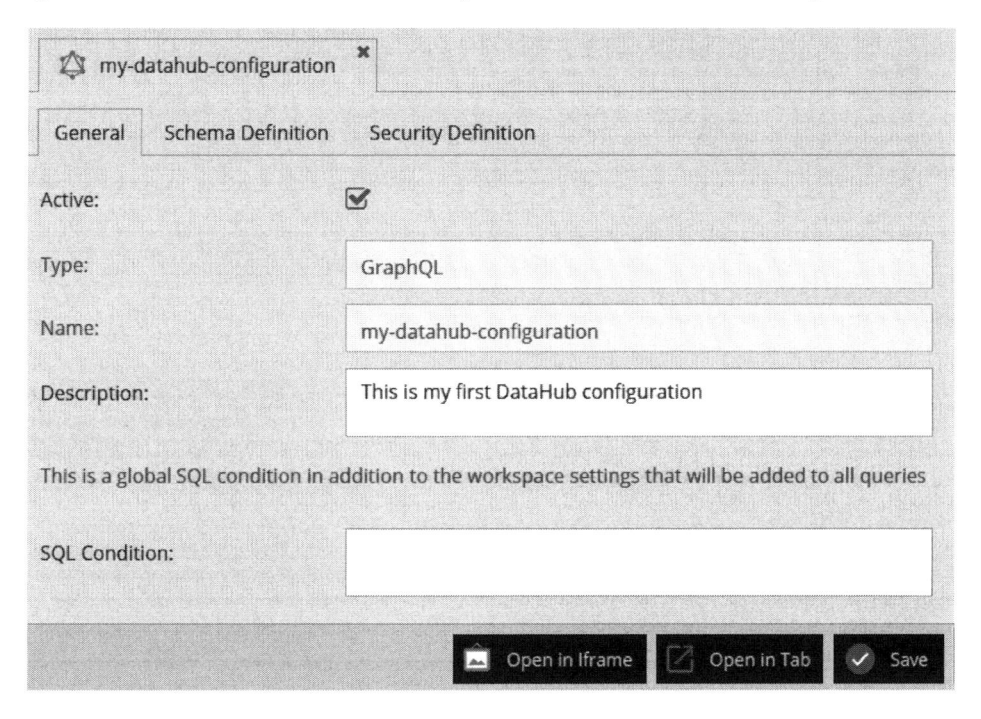

Figure 13.5: General panel

Let's now describe each property that we see in the preceding screenshot, as follows:

- **Active**: If enabled, the configuration is active and can be exposed to external applications.
- **Type**: The configuration type. In the current version, only the GraphQL typology exists.
- **Name**: The configuration name, defined during the configuration creation. This may not be changed.
- **Description**: This lets you write a textual description for the configuration.
- **SQL Condition**: In this property, you can add a **Structured Query Language** (**SQL**) condition that will be used to do a pre-filtering of all the queries.

In the **Schema Definition** panel, we can define which classes are enabled for queries and mutations. We can see what this panel looks like in the following screenshot:

Figure 13.6: Schema Definition panel

Let's now describe each property that we see in the preceding screenshot, as follows:

- **Query Schema**: In this section, we can select one or more classes, with objects that will be available for queries. For each selected class, it's possible to define which attributes must be exposed in queries. We will see this concept in the *Exposing entities* section.

- **Mutation Schema**: Similar to the **Query Schema** section, in this section we can select classes that could be available for mutation queries. For each class, we can define whether objects can be created, updated, and deleted. We will see more on mutation queries later in this chapter, in the *Using mutation queries* section.

- **Generic Types**: Here, we can define whether assets, documents, and folders must be exposed for queries and mutations. For example, if we enable the **Read** option for object folders, we can retrieve all the objects that are contained in one folder.

In the **Security Definition** panel, we can manage authentication rules and restrict the visibility of entities to specific folders. We can see what this panel looks like in the following screenshot:

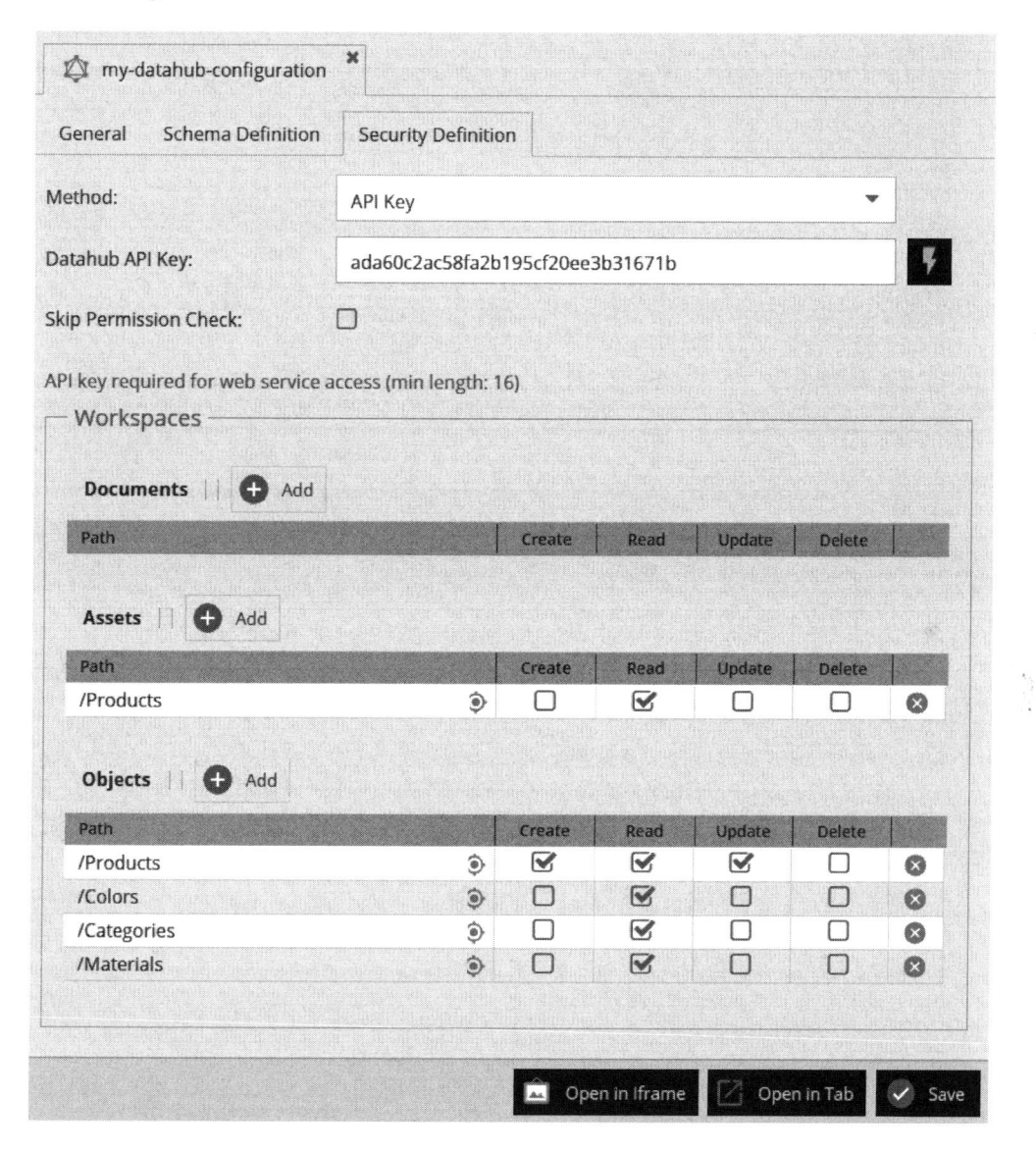

Figure 13.7: Security Definition panel

Let's now describe each property that we see in the preceding screenshot, as follows:

- **Method**: The authentication method. In the current version, only authentication through an **Application Programming Interface** (**API**) key is available.
- **Datahub API Key**: The API key that will be required for authentication. This can be generated by clicking on the lightning bolt icon on the right.
- **Skip Permission Check**: If enabled, the check for mandatory fields' completeness is skipped when performing a mutation query.
- **Workspaces**: In this section, we must specify specific **Documents**, **Assets**, and **Objects** folders to which we want to expose queries and mutations.

Once you have completed the configuration, click on the **Save** button to apply the changes.

After the configuration is saved, queries can be tested in two different ways, as follows:

- Through an integrated **inline frame** (**Iframe**), which could be opened in a new panel in the Pimcore interface by clicking the **Open** in **Iframe** button
- In a new browser tab, which could be opened by clicking the **Open in Tab** button

For third-party applications, queries can be made by performing **HyperText Transfer Protocol** (**HTTP**) calls to the following endpoint:

```
/pimcore-graphql-webservices/
{configurationname}?apikey={yourApiKey}
```

In the previous endpoint, you can see that the configuration name and the API key are variables, so you must substitute the placeholders with the values defined in the configuration.

All the defined configurations are stored in a `var/config/Datahub-configurations.php` file. If you want to share the same configuration between different environments, you can commit this file in the code base and rebuild the Datahub configurations running the following Bash command:

```
php bin/console Datahub:graphql:rebuild-definitions
```

To summarize, in this section, you have learned how to download and activate the Pimcore Datahub bundle and how to create a configuration for that bundle. In the following section, you will learn how to expose entities and how to perform queries on Datahub, testing them through the integrated Iframe.

Exposing entities

In the previous section, you learned how to activate a Datahub bundle and how to create a new configuration. In this section, you will learn how to set up the configuration to expose entities and how to perform queries on Datahub.

As we mentioned in the previous section, in the **Schema Definition** panel of the Datahub configurations, we must select which classes should be available for queries, and add them in the **Query Schema** section.

For each class, we must define which fields can be exposed for queries. This can be done by clicking on the **Settings** icon for each added class. In the following screenshot, you can see how to select the fields to expose:

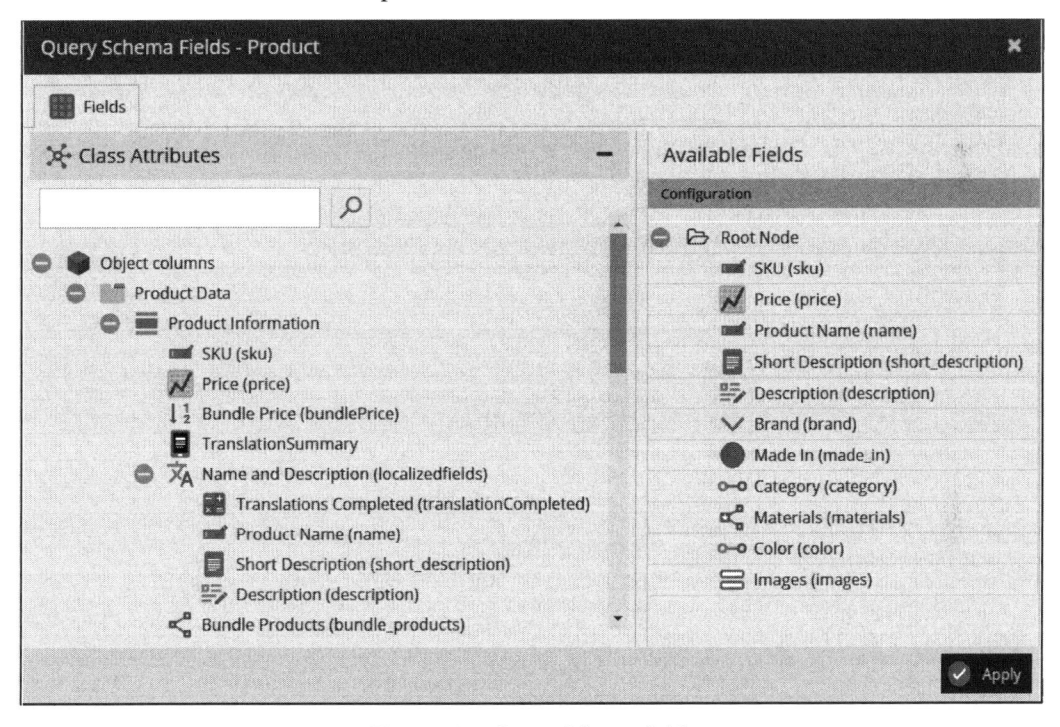

Figure 13.8: Query Schema fields

As you can see in the previous screenshot, on the left side you can find a list of the class fields. If you double-click one of these fields or drag and drop a field on the right column, that field will be exposed and will be available for queries. Once you have selected all the fields you want to expose, just click on the **Apply** button to confirm your choice.

Now we have learned how to configure a query schema, in the following section, you will see how to perform GraphQL queries on Datahub.

Performing GraphQL queries

In the previous section, you learned how to expose classes and fields to let them be queryable. In this section, you will learn how to perform queries for your created configurations, seeing some query examples.

As we previously mentioned in the *Creating a Datahub configuration* section, the only supported configuration type is GraphQL. GraphQL is a query language for building APIs and a tool for serving these APIs with real data. GraphQL provides a complete and understandable description of your API data, giving clients the power to request only what they need and nothing else. This allows easy integration with external software and allows you to easily maintain and evolve the APIs over time.

GraphQL queries always return a predictable result, and therefore applications that use GraphQL are fast and reliable because they are in control of the data they require, not the server.

GraphQL queries, in addition to accessing the data of a resource, can follow references with other entities. This eventually allows you to retrieve all the data needed by an application in a single call, unlike a typical **REpresentational State Transfer** (**REST**) API, which typically requires multiple calls to get data.

GraphQL APIs are therefore organized in terms of types and not endpoints; all data can be accessed with a single endpoint and the use of types ensures that external applications can only request what is allowed, which allows you to provide clear and useful error messages.

Now that we have introduced what GraphQL is, let's have a look at the Pimcore Datahub Iframe environment. In the following screenshot, you can see what this environment looks like:

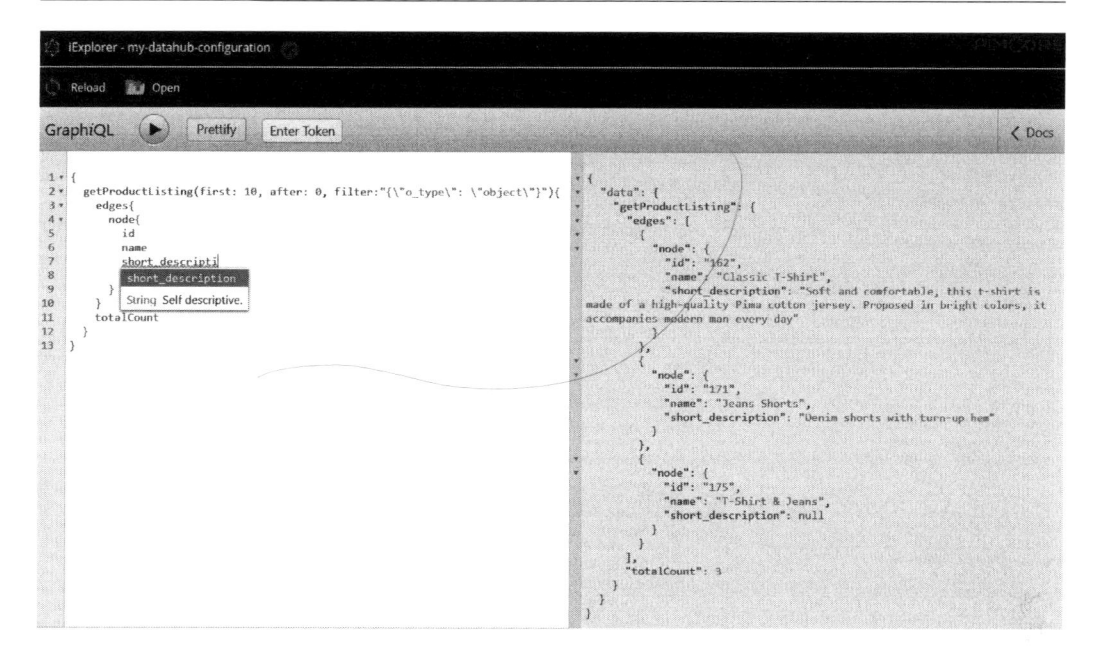

Figure 13.9: Datahub Iframe Environment

As you can see in the previous screenshot, the Iframe is divided into two panels. In the left panel, we can write a query that we want to run, while in the right panel, the query results are shown. As you can see, in the left panel, suggestions are shown when we write field names, giving the possibility to have auto-completeness. Once a query is ready, you can run it by clicking the **Play** button.

Now that we have seen how to perform queries, let's have a look at some query examples that cover the various field types.

Getting an Object Listing

In this example, you will learn how to perform object listing. In the following code snippet, you can see how a listing query is formed:

```
{
    getProductListing(first: 10, after: 0, filter: "{\"o_type\": \"object\"}") {
        edges {
            node {
                id
                name
                short_description
```

```
            }
          }
        totalCount
      }
}
```

As you can see in the previous code snippet, the query statement is composed of a `get` prefix, the class name, and a `Listing` suffix. The listing function has the following input attributes:

- `first`: The number of results to retrieve.
- `after`: The number of objects to skip. Combined with the previous parameter, this can be used to perform pagination.
- `ids`: A list of the **identifiers** (**IDs**) of objects to retrieve. If omitted, all products that respect the other filters are retrieved.
- `fullpaths`: Similarly to the previous property, we can specify the paths of the objects to retrieve.
- `filter`: One or more composed filters that will be applied to filter the objects to retrieve.
- `published`: Specify whether the query must include unpublished objects.
- `defaultLanguage`: Specify the default language for localized fields.
- `sortBy`: The field to sort the results by.
- `sortOrder`: The sorting order for the specified field.

The query content consists of an `edges` component, in which you can specify a list of fields to retrieve for each `node`, and a `totalCount` component, which always retrieves the total number of results despite the current page parameters.

In the following examples, we will see how to retrieve a single object and how to retrieve values for different kinds of fields.

Getting a single object

In this example, we will see how to retrieve a single object. You can see how to perform this query in the following code snippet:

```
{
getProduct(id: 162, defaultLanguage: "en"){
    name
    name_it: name(language: "it")
    price{
        value
        unit{
            abbreviation
        }
        toString
    }
}
}
```

As you can see in the previous code snippet, the query statement is composed of the `get` prefix and the class name. In the query function, we must define the object `id` or the object `fullpath`.

Then, we can optionally define the default language for localized fields. In the query content, you can see that for localized fields we can define a different language despite the default one.

In this example, you can also see how to query for `QuantityValue` fields. As you can see in the previous code snippet, you can require the field value, the unit of measure, and the composition of value and unit by the `toString` property.

In the following example, you will learn how to retrieve details of object relations.

Getting relation details

In the following code snippet, you can see how to get details for standard relations and advanced relations:

```
{
    getProduct(id: 162){
        category{
            ... on object_Category{
```

```
                    id
                    name
                }
            }
            materials{
                element{
                    id
                    name
                }
                metadata{
                    name
                    value
                }
            }
        }
    }
}
```

As you can see in the previous code snippet, for standard relations, as category one, we must specify the related class. In GraphQL syntax, this can be made by adding three dots, followed by the `on object_` keyword and the class name. For the related class, you can specify the fields to retrieve.

For advanced relations, in the `element` component, you can specify the fields to retrieve for the related object, while in the `metadata` component, you can retrieve the name and the value for each relation metadata.

In the following example, you will learn how to retrieve values for Fieldcollections and how to require image details.

Getting Image Details

In this example, we will see how the same syntax can be used for **Fieldcollections**, and you will learn how to retrieve image details. In the following code snippet, you can see how to perform this kind of query:

```
{
    getProduct(id: 162){
        images{
            ... on fieldcollection_ImageInfo {
                image{
```

```
                    id
                    filename
                    fullpath
                    filesize
                    data
                }
            }
        }
    }
}
```

As you can see in the previous code snippet, the syntax is quite similar to the previous one that we have seen for object relations. For each image, we can require image details such as filename and file size, but we also can get Base64 image content by the `data` attribute.

Getting Object Variants

In this example, you will learn how to get object variants. In the following code snippet, you can see how to get object children:

```
{
getProduct(id: 162){
    children(objectTypes:["variant"]){
        ... on object_Product{
            id
            color{
                ... on object_Color{
                    name
                }
            }
        }
    }
}
}
```

As you can see in the previous code snippet, you can retrieve the object variants using the `getChildren` function. To get variants, you must specify that you require them by using the `objectTypes` property.

To summarize, in this section, you learned how to expose entities for Datahub configurations. After having seen what an integrated Iframe looks like, through some query examples you learned how to perform queries to retrieve object listing and details for different kinds of attributes.

In the following section, you will learn how to perform mutation queries to create, update, and delete objects.

Using mutation queries

In the previous section, you learned how to expose entities for Datahub configurations and how to perform queries to retrieve object data. In this section, you will learn how to expose entities for mutations and how to perform queries to create, update, and delete objects.

As we mentioned in the *Activating the Pimcore Datahub bundle* section, in the **Schema Definition** panel of Datahub configurations, we must select which classes should be available for mutations and add them to the **Mutation Schema** section.

As we did for classes in the **Query Schema** section, we can define which fields can be exposed for mutation queries by clicking on the **Settings** icon for each added class. Besides, for each class, we can decide whether we want to make it available for creation, update, or deletion.

Throughout this section, we will learn how to perform mutation queries for creating, updating, and deleting objects.

Creating Objects

In this section, you will learn how to perform a mutation query to create a new object. In the following code snippet, you will see the query syntax for mutation queries, and a specific one that creates a new object:

```
mutation{
    createProduct(path:"/Products", key:"Running Shoes",
    input:{
        sku: "0003"
        name: "Runner Shoes"
        category: {id: 177}
    }){
```

```
            success
            message
            output {
                id
                sku
                name
            }
        }
}
```

As you can see in the previous snippet, all mutation queries must start with the `mutation` keyword. Then, the query function is composed of the desired operation as a prefix, which is one of `create`, `update`, or `delete`, followed by the name of the class.

In the function arguments, you can specify the following attributes:

- `key`: The key of the object. This will be shown in the object tree.
- `path`: The path in which the object is created. This could be a folder or a parent product.
- `parentId`: This can be used as an alternative to the `path` argument to define the parent folder or object.
- `published`: If `false`, a product is created in the unpublished status.
- `omitMandatoryCheck`: If `true`, an object is created even if all the mandatory fields are not filled.
- `type`: We can specify if a created object must be an object or a variant.
- `input`: In this attribute, we can specify the field values for an object that we want to create.

The query content consists of three components, outlined as follows:

- `success`: A Boolean flag that will be `true` if the query runs successfully and `false` otherwise.
- `message`: A successful message if the query runs successfully.
- `output`: If an object is created successfully, this will show the object fields requested in the query.

Running the previously defined query will return the following result:

```
{
  "data": {
    "createProduct": {
      "success": true,
      "message": "object created: 178",
      "output": {
        "id": "178",
        "sku": "0003",
        "name": "Runner Shoes"
      }
    }
  }
}
```

As you can see in the previous code snippet, if the object is created correctly, the object `id` is returned. This can be used to perform queries to update or delete an object.

Now that we have seen how to create a new object, let's see how to perform a query to update a previously created object.

Updating objects

In the previous section, you learned how to create new objects using mutation queries. In this section, you will learn how to update previously created objects.

In the following code snippet, you can see the syntax for an update mutation query:

```
mutation{
    updateProduct(id:178, input:{
        short_description: "The classic model of low
        sneakers is certainly very comfortable and
        practical and defines a personal style"
    }){
        success
        message
        output{
            id
            sku
```

```
                name
            short_description
        }
    }
}
```

As you can see in the previous code snippet, the mutation query function starts with the `update` keyword. The object `id` must be passed as a function argument, and an error message will be returned if an object with the provided `id` does not exist.

Now that we have seen how to update a previously created object, let's see how to perform a query to delete that object.

Deleting Objects

In the previous section, you learned how to update objects using mutation queries. In this section, you will learn how to delete an object.

In the following code snippet, you can see the syntax for a delete mutation query:

```
mutation{
    deleteProduct(id:178){
        success
        message
    }
}
```

As you can see in the previous code snippet, the mutation query function starts with the `delete` keyword. The object `id` must be passed as a function argument, and an error message will be returned if an object with the provided `id` does not exist.

To summarize, in this section, you learned the syntax of mutation queries. In particular, we have seen how to create, update, and delete objects through specific queries. In the following section, you will learn how to create a custom mutation query function.

Creating a custom mutation

In the previous section, you learned how to use mutation queries to create, update, and delete objects. These kinds of queries work well for simple scenarios but present some limitations in terms of the kinds of attributes that we can update or for the interdependence of multiple attributes. For example, on standard mutation queries, the `QuantityValue` fields cannot be filled.

In this section, you will learn how to create a custom mutation function and how to use that to update values that cannot be updated through standard mutation queries.

To create a new custom mutation function, we need to add a function definition to the Datahub configuration schema. This can be made by implementing a listener for the `pimcore.Datahub.graphql.mutation.preBuild` event.

In *Chapter 12*, *Implementing Product Information Management*, you learned how to implement an **EventListener**. In the following code snippet, you will see an example that will show how to implement a listener that will affect the Datahub configuration schema:

```php
<?php
namespace App\EventListener;

class DatahubListener {
    public function onMutationEventsPreBuild (MutationTypeEvent $event) {
        $config = $event->getConfig();
        $opName = "updateProductPrice";

        $inputType = new \GraphQL\Type
            \Definition\InputObjectType([
            'name' => "priceType",
            'fields' => [
                'priceValue' => ['type' =>Type::float()],
                'unit' => ['type' =>Type::string()]
            ]
        ]);

        $operation = [
            'type' =>Type::string(),
            'args' => [
                'id' => ['type' =>
                    Type::nonNull(Type::int())],
                'input' => ['type' => $inputType],
            ], 'resolve' => function ($source, $args, $context,
                ResolveInfo $info) {
                $id = $args['id'];
```

```
            $product = Product::getById($id);

        if(empty($product)){
            throw new \Exception("Product with id '$id'
            does not exists.");
        }
        $value = $args['input']['priceValue'];
        $uom = $args['input']['unit'];
        $unit = Unit::getByAbbreviation($uom);

        if(empty($unit)){
            throw new \Exception("Unit of measure
            '$uom' does not exists.");
        }

        $price = new QuantityValue();
        $price->setValue($value);
        $price->setUnitId($unit->getId());

        $product->setPrice($price);
        $product->save();

        return "Price updated for product with id
        '$id'";
        }
    ];

    $config['fields'][$opName] = $operation;
    $event->setConfig($config);
    }
}
```

In the previous code snippet, we have implemented a simple function that will set the product price. As you can see in the example, the listener function has an input argument of type `MutationTypeEvent`. That event variable has a `config` property that contains the Datahub configuration schema. To add a new mutation function, we must add a new operation to this configuration.

The first step is to create an object of type `InputObjectType`. This object must contain a `fields` property, which has to be an array that must define the name and the type for each property that must be filled in the `input` argument of the mutation query function.

We must then create an array that will define a new operation. This array must contain the operation arguments, such as the object `id` and the previously defined `input` argument, and must define a `resolve` function that, in our case, will set up the product price given the price value and unit.

Once you have defined this operation, you must add that to the configuration attribute. As a result, the created function will be selectable in the Iframe, as you can see in the following screenshot:

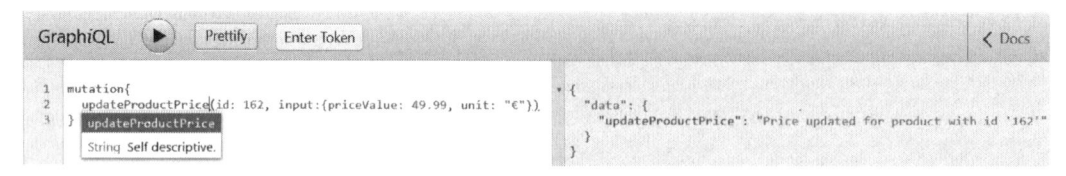

Figure 13.10: Custom Mutation Query

As you can see in the previous screenshot, in the left panel you can select the previously defined function and fill in the value and the unit for the product price. In the right panel, you can see the result message that was defined for the mutation query.

To summarize, in this section, you learned how to create a custom mutation query. This can be useful to set up object attributes for complex scenarios. As an example, you learned how to implement an event listener to create a custom mutation query that will set the product price.

In the next section, you will learn how to define custom reports to create tabular or chart reports with filtering and export functionalities.

Defining custom reports

Custom Reports is a report engine that is integrated directly into Pimcore. These reports are based on direct SQL queries on the database, and it's possible to render them both as tables and charts. To define or generate a new custom report, follow these steps:

1. To create a new report, go to the **Marketing** menu and click on the **Custom Reports** menu option.

2. Then, click on the **Add** button and insert the report name. After having created the report, you can start configuring it. In the following screenshot, you can see how to set up a report's general settings:

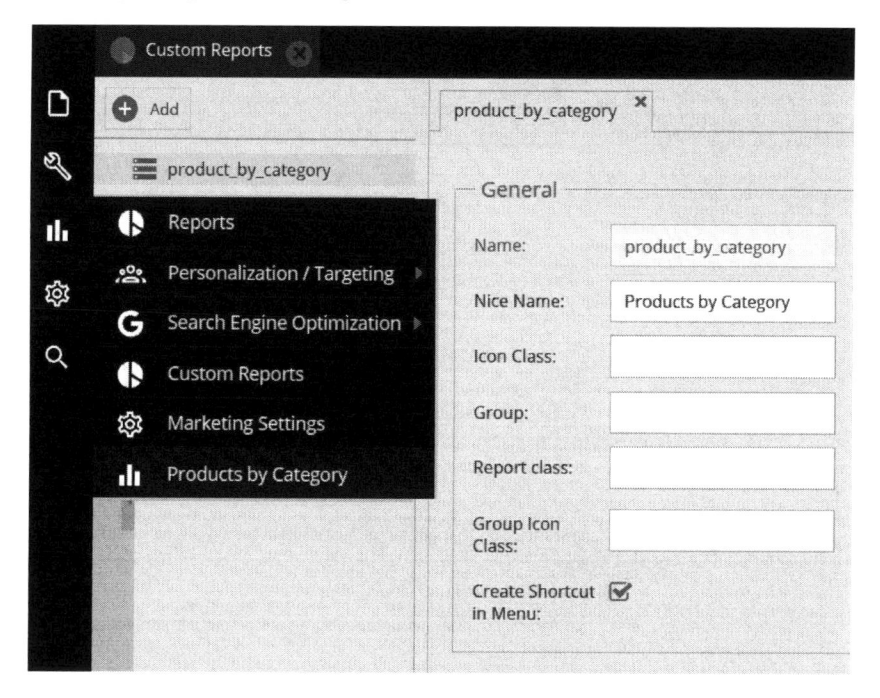

Figure 13.11: General settings

As you can see in the previous screenshot, the report **Name** is the one that was inserted before.

3. Then, add a user-friendly label and eventually group the reports in folders.
4. Click on the **Create Shortcut in Menu** checkbox, and the report will be directly available in the **Marketing** menu.

5. After having configured the general settings, the next step is to configure the data source. This can be done by directly defining an SQL query, as you can see in the following screenshot:

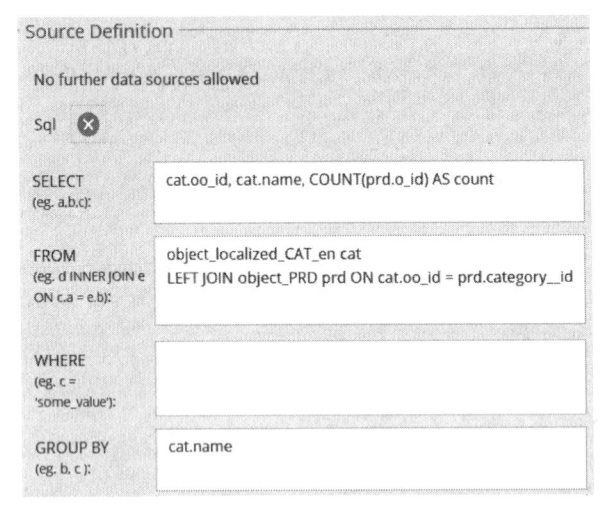

Figure 13.12: Source definition

As you can see in the previous screenshot, you can add a direct SQL query as a source definition. This gives you the possibility to design complex scenarios but requires advanced knowledge of the database structure. In this specific example, we want to count the number of products per category.

6. After having defined a data source, define how to render data. You can see how to manage the column configuration in the following screenshot:

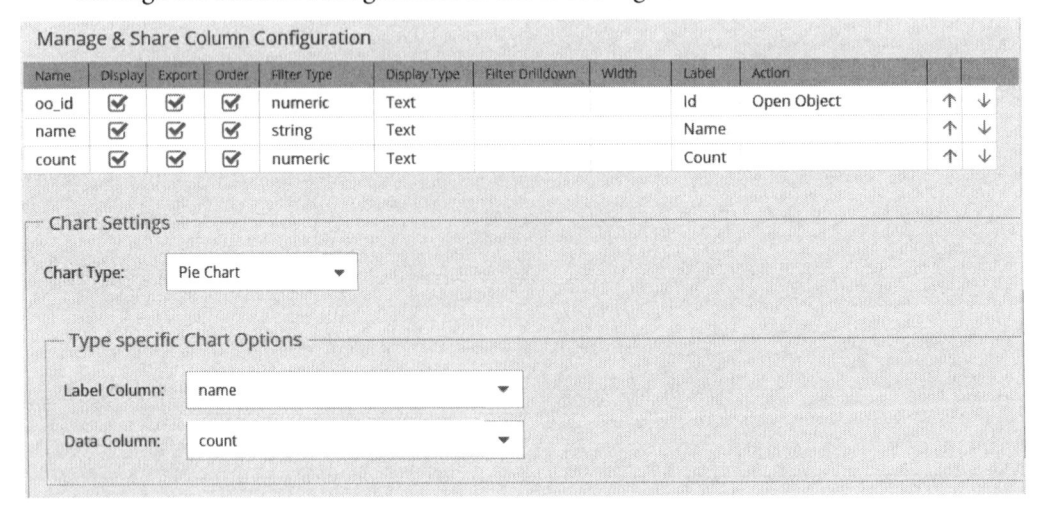

Figure 13.13: Managing the Column Configuration

As you can see in the previous screenshot, if a query is well formed, the columns are automatically detected. For each column, we can specify whether the column must be shown in the report and whether the column can be exported and sorted. Then, we can also define whether each column can be filterable, along with the filter type to apply, and then specify the width and the label for them. If a column contains an object `id`, we can also specify an **Open Object** action. As we will see in the next step, this will add a button that lets you open the corresponding object by the report table.

After having defined the column configuration, you can define the chart type, choosing from **Pie Chart**, **Bar Chart**, and **Line Chart**. For pie charts, you must then specify which column must be used to define the values list, and which one contains the data count.

7. Once the configuration is completed, go to the **Marketing | Reports** menu to see how the report is rendered. You can see what a defined example looks like in the following screenshot:

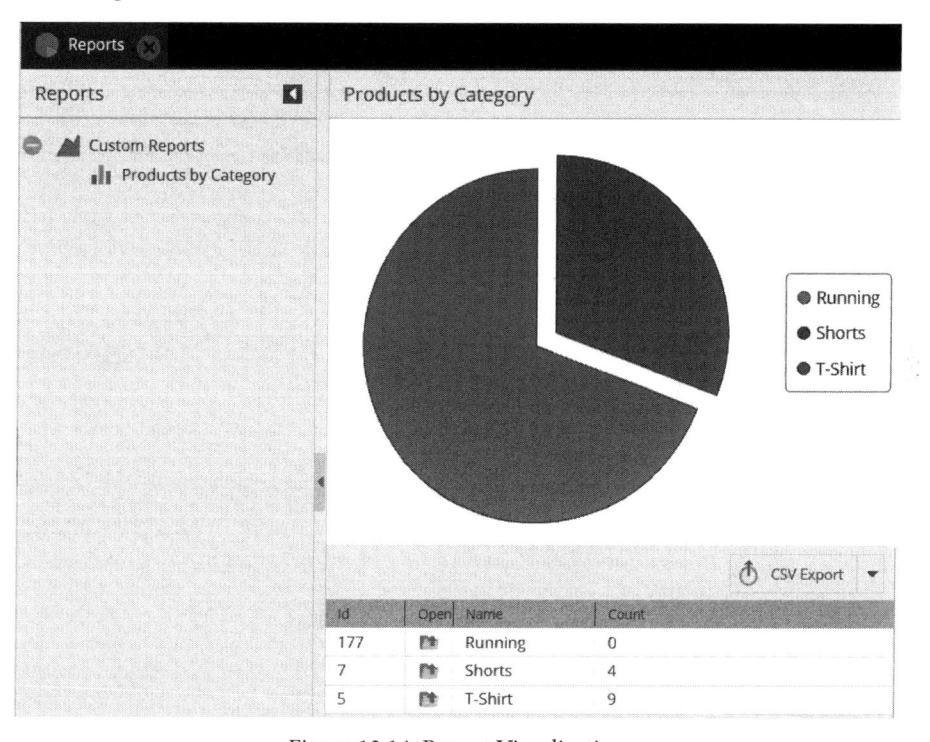

Figure 13.14: Report Visualization

As you can see in the previous screenshot, the report is shown as a pie chart as we defined, with categories' names, a list of the different values, and a count of the products that form the pie slices.

At the bottom, you can see the report in a tabular version. In particular, you can see the **Open** button, which lets you open the linked category object. If you don't specify a chart type, only the tabular version is shown. The report table can be exported in a **comma-separated values** (**CSV**) file.

To summarize, in this section, you learned how to configure and render reports using the **Custom Reports** engine. Starting from the general settings, you learned how to configure a data source and how to properly render data in the report.

Summary

In this chapter, you learned the concept of Master Data Management and how to expose Pimcore objects to third-party applications using the Datahub Pimcore bundle.

After having defined that concept, you have seen an example of how to implement the concept of data quality, which is a key feature of MDM systems.

Later in the chapter, you learned how to activate a Datahub Pimcore Bundle and how to create a configuration for that bundle, and how to set up the configuration to expose objects and other entities with external applications.

After having introduced the GraphQL query language, you learned how to perform queries to retrieve object data through some query examples, as well as how to create, update, and delete objects through mutation queries. Then, you learned how to implement a custom mutation query function, which is useful for defining complex scenarios.

In the last section, you learned how to configure and render custom reports, which let you present and export the data.

In the next chapter, you will learn how to perform Data Integration in Pimcore, with a specific focus on how to import and export objects and on when the standard functionalities are supposed to be used, and otherwise when they have limitations that make the implementation of a custom solution necessary.

14
Data Integration

In the previous chapter, you learned about the concept of **Master Data Management** (**MDM**), and how to expose Pimcore objects to third-party applications using the **Datahub** Pimcore bundle. After defining how to install and activate that bundle and how to configure it, you learned how to perform GraphQL queries to retrieve object data and to create, update, or delete objects.

In this chapter, you will learn how to perform data integration in Pimcore through standard import and export functionalities, when these standards are supposed to be used, and, otherwise, when the implementation of custom solutions is necessary.

The chapter is organized as follows:

- Importing Data
- Exporting Data
- Limitations of Standard Functionalities
- Implementing Custom Solutions
- Configuring the Data Importer

We'll start by presenting how to perform simple CSV data importing and exporting using standard solutions. Then, we will explain the limitations you may encounter on using these standard solutions for importing and exporting, and we will explain how to implement a custom data operator that can be used in import configuration. Later in this chapter, we will present how to implement custom solutions for importing and exporting.

Technical requirements

As you have done in previous chapters, all you need to do is run the demo connected to this chapter by navigating to the `14. Data Integration` folder of the official book repository and start a Docker environment.

To do so, just follow these instructions:

1. Run Docker with the following command:

    ```
    docker-compose up
    ```

2. Then, to restore all the settings on your local machine, just open a new shell and type the following:

    ```
    docker-compose exec php bash restore.sh
    ```

3. Navigate to `http://localhost/admin` and log in with your admin/pimcore credentials.

You can access the official book repository to get the source code through the following link:

`https://github.com/PacktPublishing/Modernizing-Enterprise-CMS-using-Pimcore/tree/main/14.%20Data%20Integration`

Now you are ready to navigate the demo to discover all the aspects related to this chapter.

Importing Data

In this section, you will learn how to import data through a standard Pimcore CSV import. We will see how to configure the import of a simple CSV file, looking at the details of each step of the configuration, and how to save this configuration to use it in future imports.

Although this feature is deprecated in PimcoreX, we must consider that the Pimcore 6 version still has widespread usage, so the explanation of this feature is still quite important. In the *Configuring the Data Importer* section of this chapter, we will then explain how to configure the new Pimcore Data Importer.

To start a new CSV import, just right-click on the folder in which you want to import the objects, select **CSV Import**, and select the object class of the objects you want to import. This operation will open an **Upload** dialog, through which you can upload the CSV file to import.

Once the file is uploaded, a new modal will be opened, and you can start to configure the import. In the following sections, we will analyze each step of this configuration.

CSV File Preview

In the first panel of the imported configuration, a preview of the uploaded CSV file is shown. In the following screenshot, you can see how this panel looks:

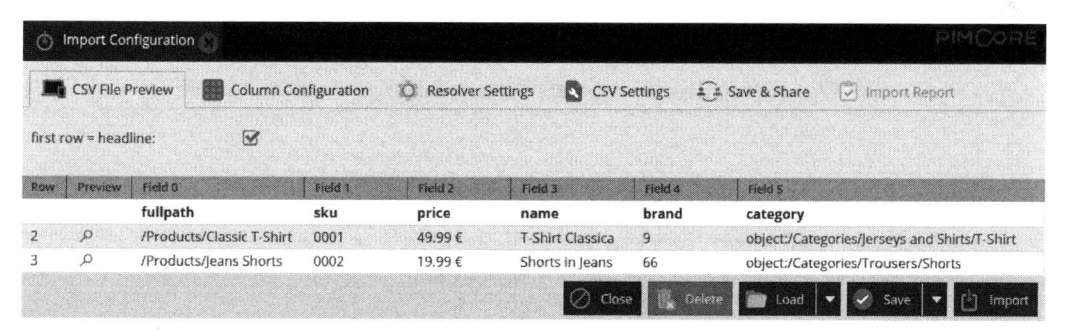

Figure 14.1: CSV File Preview

As you can see in the previous screenshot, the CSV file rows are rendered as a table. If the checkbox at the top is enabled, the first CSV row is intended to contain the headers.

In the next section, we will see how to perform column configuration, to associate every CSV column with the corresponding class attribute.

Column Configuration

In the **Column Configuration** panel, we can associate every CSV column to the corresponding class attribute, so that for each CSV import, we can affect only a subset of the class fields. You can see how this panel looks in the following screenshot:

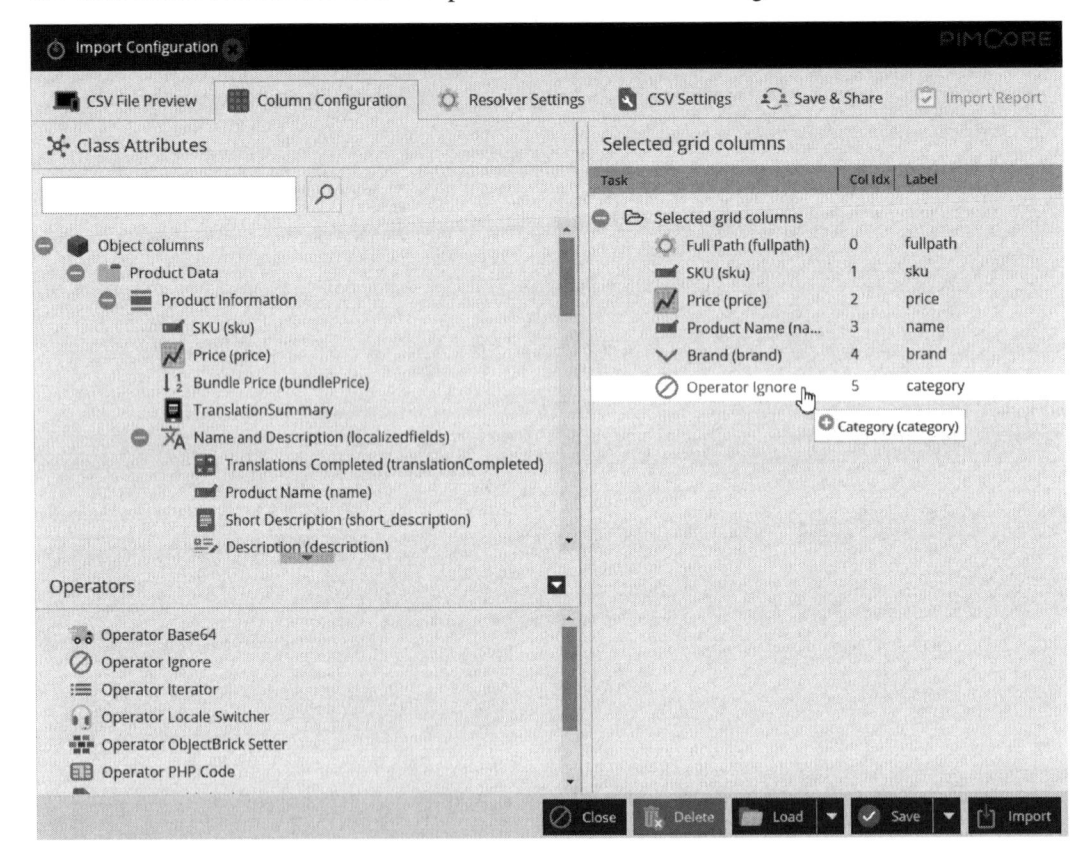

Figure 14.2: Column Configuration

As you can see in the previous screenshot, in this panel there are two distinct areas. In the left region, you will find the class attributes, and you can drag and drop each attribute to the corresponding CSV columns, which are disposed of in the right region.

In the left region, you can also see the **Operators** section. These operators can be used to change the way the data is processed. Let's describe how each of these operators works:

- **Operator Base64**: This operator performs a Base64 encode or decode on the CSV data.

- **Operator Ignore**: This operator just lets the importer skip the corresponding CSV column.

- **Operator Iterator**: This operator lets you import the same CSV cell to multiple class attributes, by dragging and dropping these attributes as operator children.

- **Operator Locale Switcher**: This operator is useful to select the language for each localized field, allowing the import of text in different languages within the same CSV file.

- **Operator ObjectBrick Setter**: This operator lets you import a specific attribute of an **ObjectBrick**.

- **Operator PHP Code**: This operator type does not do anything on its own. It requires you to develop a PHP class to manage the CSV data, and pass the class namespace as a parameter of the operator. You will learn how to create a custom PHP operator in the *Creating a Custom Operator* section of this chapter.

- **Operator Published**: This operator just lets you publish or unpublish the imported objects, based on the CSV column value.

- **Operator Splitter**: This operator can be used to split the value of the CSV column into multiple attributes, given the separator character.

Now that we have defined how to map each object attribute, in the next section we will show the criteria that permits us to resolve each row, to recognize whether each object already exists.

Resolver Settings

In the following screenshot, you can see how the **Resolver Settings** panel looks:

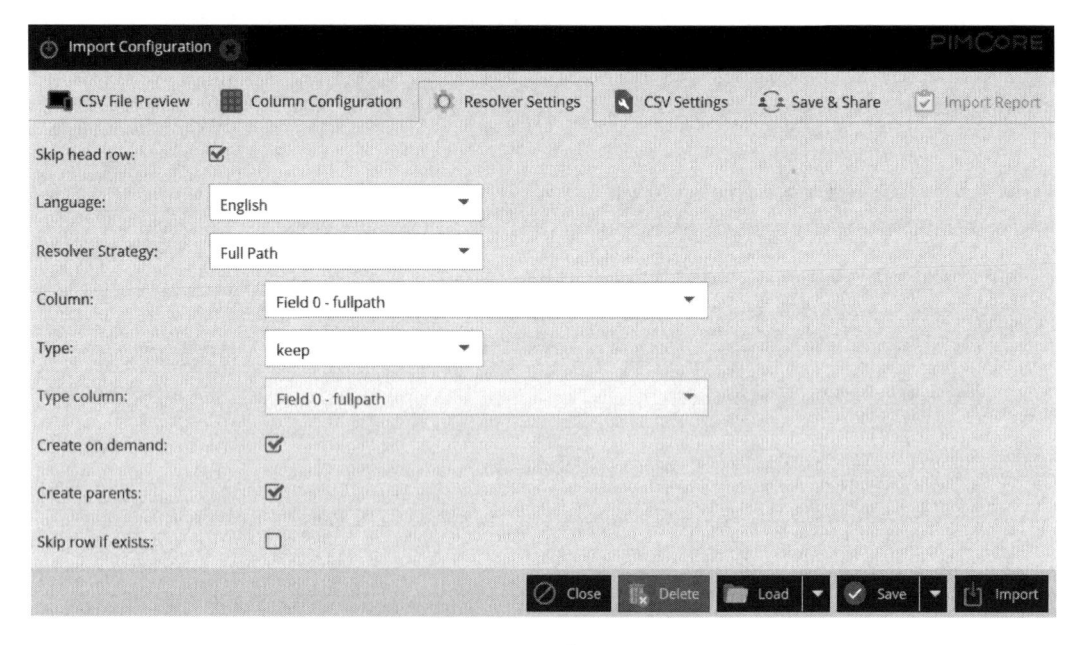

Figure 14.3: Resolver Settings

As you can see in the previous screenshot, there is a set of properties to configure, which we are going to describe here:

- **Skip head row**: Defines whether the first row must be skipped. This must be checked if the first row of the CSV contains column headers.
- **Language**: The language of the import. All the values for localized fields will be imported for the specified language. If you need to import localized values for different languages within the same CSV import, you must use a **Locale Switcher** operator.
- **Resolver Strategy**: This property is the one that specifies the strategy rule to recognize whether objects already exist. Based on the selection, different properties must be filled. The following options are choosable:

    - **ID**: Resolves the objects via the object ID. If the object does not exist, an error will be thrown.

    - **Filename**: Resolves the objects via the object key within the import folder. If the object does not exist, it will be created.

- **Full Path**: Resolves the objects via the object's full path.

- **Get by Attribute**: Resolves the objects via one of the class attributes. That attribute must be specified as a property if this option is selected.

- **Code**: This option lets you create a custom resolver. This can be done by implementing a PHP class that extends the `Pimcore\DataObject\Import\Resolver\AbstractResolver` class and passes the class namespace as an attribute.

- **Column**: This property lets you select the CSV column that contains the value that must be used by the resolver strategy.

- **Type**: This property lets you define whether the imported rows must be objects or variants. It's possible to force this type, to let the importer keep the current type, or to dynamically set the type for each row, specifying the **Type column** property.

- **Create on demand**: If checked, not existing objects will be created.

- **Create parents**: If checked, subfolders on the object path will be created if they don't exist.

- **Skip row if exists**: If checked, the row is skipped if the object already exists.

Now that we have seen how to set up the resolver strategy, in the next section we will see how to change the CSV settings.

CSV Settings

Here, you can see how the **CSV Settings** panel looks:

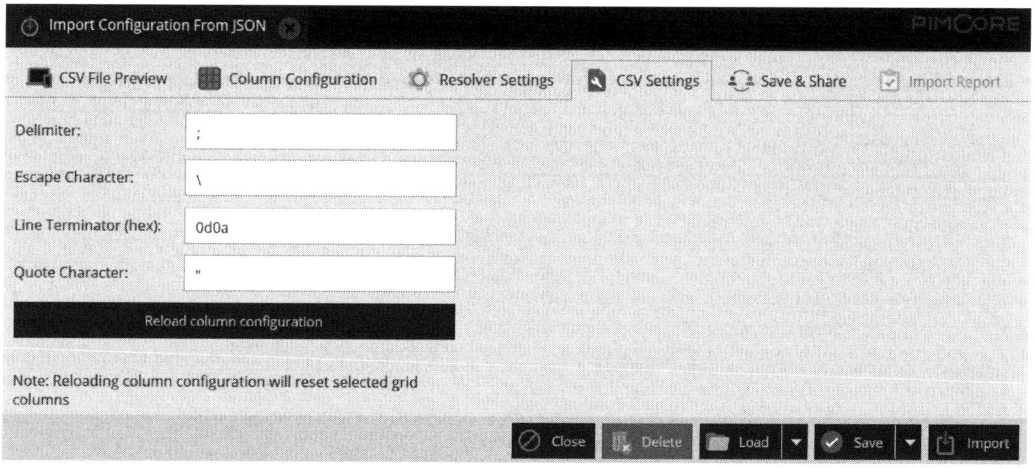

Figure 14.4: CSV Settings

As you can see in the previous screenshot, in this panel you can change the CSV parsing settings, which include **Delimiter**, **Quote Character**, and so on. These settings are automatically detected during the file upload, but you can change them manually. After having changed these values, you must click on the **Reload column configuration** button to apply the changes.

In the next section, we will see how to save and share the defined configuration.

Save & Share

In the following screenshot, you can see what the **Save & Share** panel looks like:

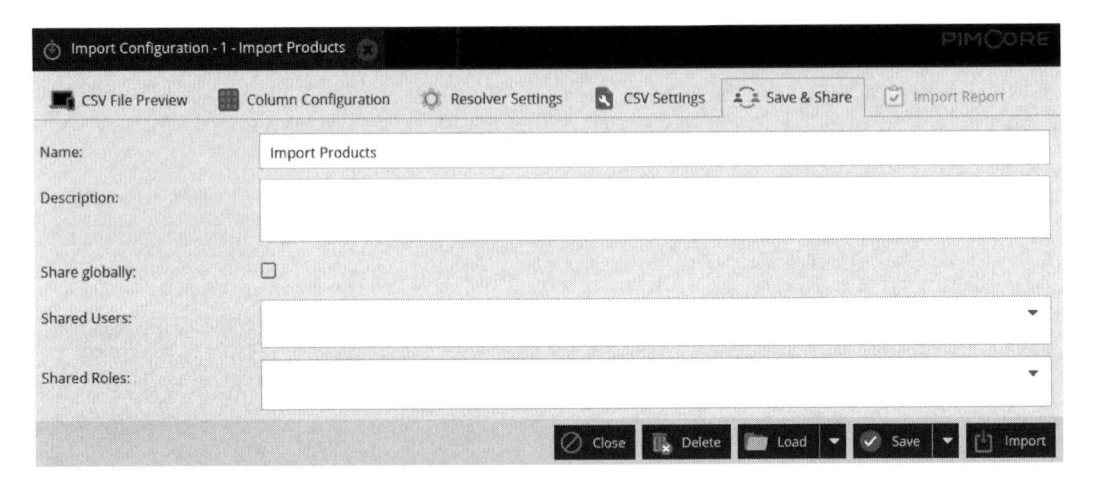

Figure 14.5: Save & Share

As you can see in the previous screenshot, you can set the configuration name, and click on the **Save** button to save the configuration in the database. All the saved configurations can be restored by clicking the **Load** button and selecting the chosen configuration. The import configurations can be shared globally to all users, or to a restricted set of users and roles.

Once the configuration is done, you can run the import by clicking the **Import** button. In the following screenshot, you can see the **Import Report** panel:

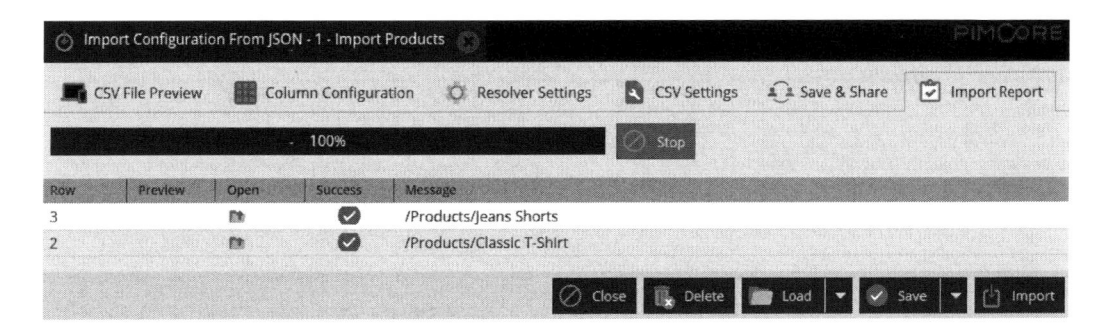

Figure 14.6: Import Report

As you can see in the previous screenshot, for each row we can see whether the row was imported successfully and, if not, the error message for the row. For each imported row, the imported object can be opened.

To summarize, in this section you learned how to configure and run CSV imports. In the following section, you will learn how to export data in Pimcore.

Exporting Data

In the previous section, you learned how to configure and run CSV imports. In this section, you will learn how to export data. Similar to what we saw in the previous section on data importing, we can set up and save export configurations.

The first step to start a data export is to open an object grid by clicking on an object folder. When the grid is opened, the grid will contain only the class attributes that were marked as **Visible in Grid View** in the class configuration, as you learned in *Chapter 5*, *Exploring Objects and Classes*.

To add or remove the fields that are shown in the grid, you must click on the **Grid Options** button to open the configuration modal. You can see how this configuration modal looks in the following screenshot:

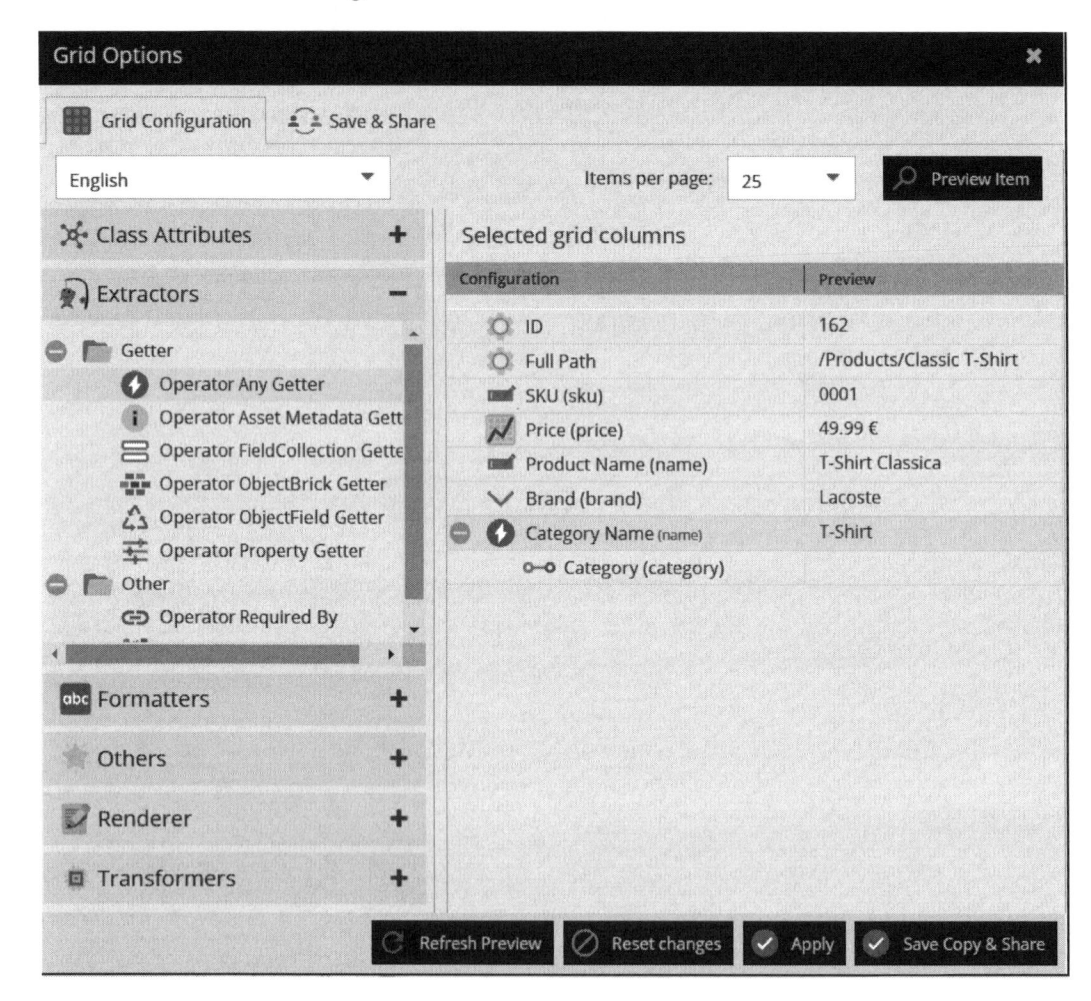

Figure 14.7: Grid Options Configuration

As you can see in the previous screenshot, the configuration modal structure is quite similar to the one that we saw in the column configuration panel of the import configuration.

In the left region, you can find the list of the class attributes and some sets of operators to format, render, and transform object data and to extract values from object relations. We can drag and drop class attributes and the operators in the right region so that these attributes will be shown in the grid.

In the previous screenshot, you may note that we used **Operator Any Getter** to extract a specific property from a relation. To do this, we just need to drag and drop the relation attribute as a child of the operator and specify the property that we want to extract for that relation.

Once the grid configuration is completed, you can click on the **Apply** button to confirm the changes, and you can also save the configuration to reuse it in the future by clicking the **Save Copy & Share** button.

In the following screenshot, you can see how the object grid looks after the changes:

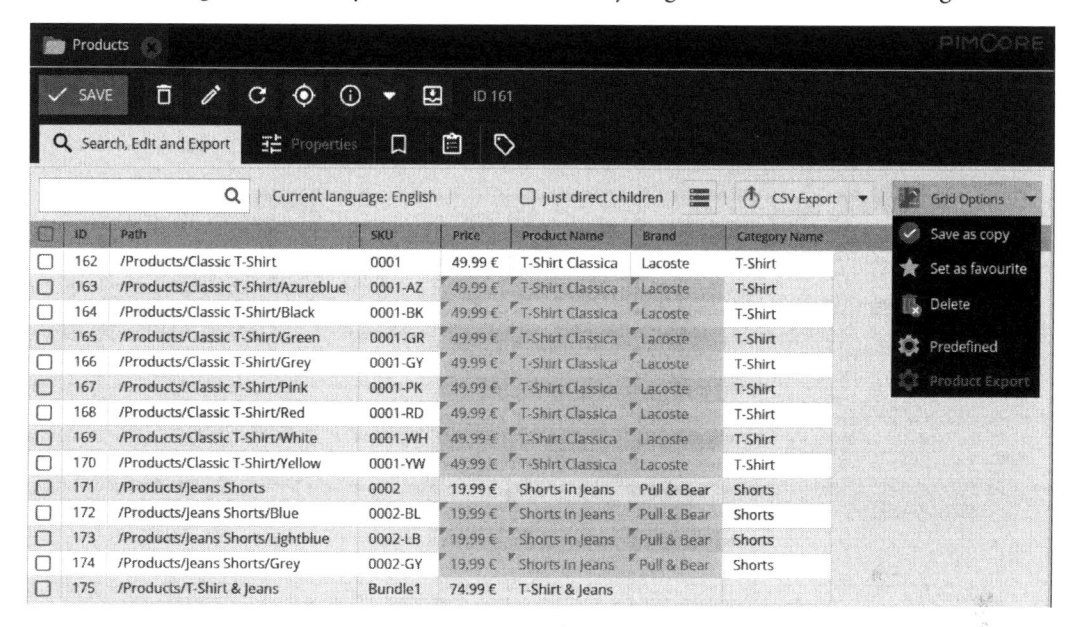

Figure 14.8: Object Grid

As you can see in the previous screenshot, in the object grid the previously defined columns are shown. In the screenshot, you can also see that, if we open the **Grid Options** submenu, we can switch from different configurations, save a copy of the current configuration, set that configuration as favorite, or delete the current configuration.

The object grid shows all the objects and variants created inside the opened folder and, eventually, in existing subfolders. If you want to limit the objects shown to the first level of the hierarchy, you can enable the **just direct children** checkbox, as you can see in the following screenshot:

Figure 14.9: Object Grid

As you can see in the previous screenshot, only direct children objects are shown. The objects in the grid can be exported both in CSV and in XLSX files. For CSV exports, you will be asked to choose the delimiter character.

To summarize, in this section you learned how to configure object grids, and how to perform data export. In the following section, you will discover which limitations you may encounter using standard import and export functionalities, and how to create custom operators for importing.

Limitations of Standard Functionalities

In the previous sections, you learned how to perform data importing and exporting through standard functionalities. As you learned, these functionalities are easy to configure and work well for simple scenarios.

In this section, you will learn what the main limitations of these standard functionalities are, and you will learn how to implement a custom PHP operator to be used in CSV importing. Let's start by presenting the limitations of the previously seen export functionality.

Limitations of Data Export

In the *Exporting data* section, you learned how to configure object grids to export object data. When using these configurations, you may encounter the following limitations:

- **Showing complex field values**: The grid configuration is quite similar for simple textual and numeric fields, but it could be difficult to extract information for structured fields, such as for `Fieldcollections` attributes. The `Fieldcollections` can present a different cardinality for each object class, and it's very difficult to represent these kinds of attributes in a flat structure such as a CSV or an XLSX file.

- **Parent-child relation redundancy**: Another limitation given by the file format is the fact that the parent-child relations cannot be explained without avoiding data redundancy because each object variant will be placed in a different row, and in the exported file there will not be any information about the fact that a row represents an object or a variant.

- **Excluding variants**: In the previous section, in terms of data filtering, you learned that you can use the **just direct children** checkbox to filter objects only and exclude object variants. This works only in the case that all the objects are directly created inside the opened folder, because if objects are created in subfolders, they will be skipped by clicking the checkbox. The only way to filter just for objects is to add a direct SQL condition, as you can see in the following screenshot:

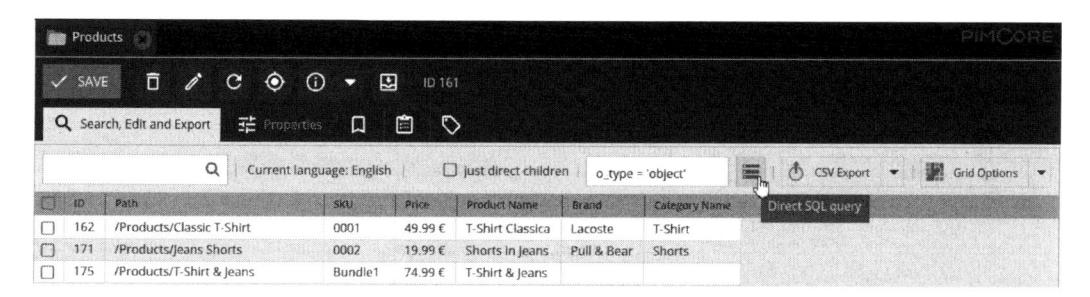

Figure 14.10: Direct SQL query

As you can see in the previous screenshot, clicking on the **Direct SQL query** icon will open a textual input in which you can write a valid SQL condition. This is quite useful, but it requires knowing the database structure.

- **Server timeout**: Last but not least, there could be a problem related to timings. The export operation is done through an HTML call to a controller, so for thousands of objects to export, this operation may require a lot of time, and there could be a timeout depending on the server settings.

Now that you have learned about the limitations of the standard data export, let's see which limitations you may encounter on data import.

Limitations of Data Import

The main problem with importing CSV files is the standard required format for the different types of attributes. For example, for the following kinds of fields, we have the following limitations:

- **QuantityValue**: To import the value for this kind of field, you have to put the numeric value in the CSV cell, followed by the unit of measure.
- **Select**: The CSV cell must contain a valid value for the selection and not the option label. This can be a problem in cases in which the created select has numeric IDs or, in general, not mnemonic values.
- **Multiselect**: Different values on multiselect fields must be only separated by the comma character.
- **Relations**: For relation fields, the CSV cell must contain the `object:/` prefix, followed by the full path of the related object.
- **Advanced Relation**: Metadata for advanced relations cannot be imported.
- **Fieldcollection**: Values for Fieldcollection cannot be imported.
- **Media**: Images and videos cannot be attached to objects through a CSV import.

These limitations make the compilation of CSV files quite complex because it's difficult for non-expert users to create a CSV file that respects all the format rules. These limitations can be circumvented by creating custom PHP operators, as we will see in the following section, but of course, we will lose the advantage of importing data without the need to write any lines of code.

Another limitation related to CSV files is the format itself. Although the CSV format is a widespread standard, there could be dated external applications that cannot produce exports in the CSV format. That said, to import any other kind of file, a custom solution must be developed.

As for what concerns the importation process itself, the whole process cannot be run as a background process. Once the import is started, the import modal cannot be closed until the end of the import process because closing the modal will cause the import to be stopped. For each imported line, the frontend interface is refreshed, and for thousands of rows to be imported, the entire process can last some hours.

Due to these timings, it is not possible to schedule an automatic importation flow between external software and Pimcore because, as said, the import cannot be run as a background process and requires maintaining an open browser for a lot of hours.

Now that you have learned about the limitations of a standard data import, let's see how to create a custom PHP operator to be used on CSV imports. The use of these PHP operators can circumvent some of the previously mentioned limitations.

Creating a Custom Operator

In the previous section, you learned which limitations you may encounter in the standard data import process. One of these limitations is the strict format required for some attribute types. This limitation can be circumvented by creating custom operators to manage CSV cell data.

In this section, you will learn how to create these custom operators, and how to use them within CSV imports. In particular, we will see an example operator that will search for the option of a select field by the option label and not by its value. In the following code snippet, you can see how this operator can be created:

```php
<?php
namespace App\Import\Operators;

use Pimcore\DataObject\Import\ColumnConfig\Operator\AbstractOperator;
use Pimcore\Model\DataObject\ClassDefinition;

class SelectOperator extends AbstractOperator{

protected $additionalData;

    public function __construct(\stdClass $config, $context = null){
parent::__construct($config, $context);
        $this->additionalData = json_decode($config->additionalData, true);
    }

    public function process($element, &$target, array &$rowData, $colIndex, array &$context = array()) {
```

```php
            $value = $rowData[$colIndex];
            $field = $this->additionalData["field"];
            $target->set($field, $this-
>getValueByDisplayName($target->getClass(), $field, $value));
        }
    public function getValueByDisplayName(ClassDefinition
$class, $field, $displayName){
        $fieldDefinition = $class->getFieldDefinition($field);

        if(in_array($fieldDefinition->getFieldtype(),
array("select", "multiselect"))){
            $options = $fieldDefinition->getOptions();
            $option = array_search(strtolower($displayName),
array_map('strtolower', array_column($options, "key")));
            return $option !== false ? $options[$option]
["value"] : null;
        }
        return null;
    }
}
```

As you can see in the previous code snippet, the operator must extend the `AbstractOperator` class. In the class constructor, we can parse the additional data that is defined in the operator configuration, and the implementation of the business logic must be done in the `process` function, which will be automatically called by the import flow.

In this specific example, we use the `getFieldDefinition` method of the object's class to retrieve the field definition. If the field is a select or a multiselect attribute, we can use the `getOptions` function to retrieve the select options and search the value that corresponds to the given label.

Once the operator is created, we must use it on CSV import configurations. To do this, just drag and drop the **Operator PHP Code** operator in the CSV column to which you want to apply the operator to. In the operator configuration panel, you must put the operator namespace, as you can see in the following screenshot:

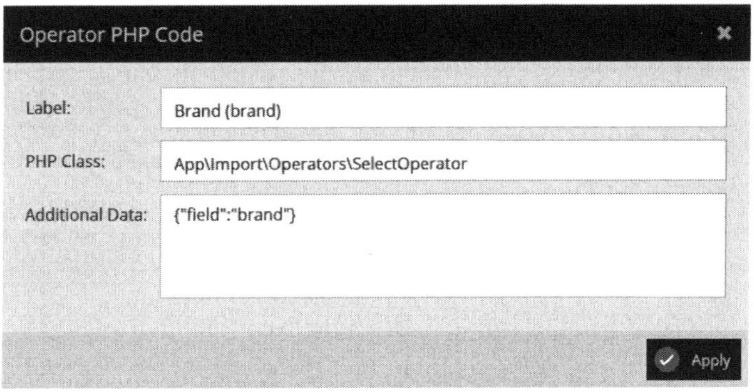

Figure 14.11: Operator PHP Code

As you can see in the previous screenshot, in the operator configuration we must put the PHP class namespace in the **PHP Class** input. Then, in the **Additional Data** text area, we can put some data to pass to the operator. In our example, we are passing this additional information as JSON, which will be parsed by the operator.

To summarize, in this section you learned about which limitations you may encounter on performing standard import and export processes. Then, you learned how to create custom PHP operators that can be used on the CSV import processes. In the following section, you will learn how to implement custom solutions for importing and exporting.

Implementing Custom Solutions

In the previous section, you learned about the limitations of standard import and export functionalities. Then, you learned how to create a custom operator to be used on CSV import processes.

In this section, you will learn how to implement custom solutions for importing and exporting. In particular, you will learn how to add additional buttons to the object and folder editor in the Pimcore backend interface, which will call custom controllers on clicking, and how to create commands that could be scheduled and run as a background process.

Adding custom buttons

In this section, you will learn how to add custom buttons to the Pimcore backend interface, and how to let these buttons call for custom controllers to perform imports and exports.

To add these buttons, we need to implement the `postOpenObject` function inside the `Resources/js/Pimcore/startup.js` file of a previously created Pimcore bundle. In the following code snippet, you can see an example of how to create two buttons to upload and download files:

```js
postOpenObject: function (object, type) {
    if (object.data.general.o_type === 'folder') {
object.toolbar.add({
            text: t('Export'),
iconCls: 'pimcore_icon_download',
            scale: 'medium',
            handler: function (obj) {
pimcore.helpers.download("/admin/export-objects?folderId=" + object.id);
            }.bind(this, object)
        });

object.toolbar.add({
            text: t('Import'),
iconCls: 'pimcore_icon_upload',
            scale: 'medium',
            handler: function (obj) {
pimcore.helpers.uploadDialog("/admin/import-objects?folderId=" + object.id, "Filedata", function (response) {
pimcore.layout.refresh();
object.reload();
}.bind(this), function () {
Ext.MessageBox.alert(t("error"), t("error"));
                });
            }.bind(this, object)
        });

pimcore.layout.refresh();
    }
}
```

As you can see in the previous code snippet, we first check whether the opened object is a folder, to add two different buttons in the folder editor toolbar. For each button, the `handler` function is the one that is called when the object is clicked.

In the first button, we are using the `pimcore.helpers.download` function to let the browser download the file returned in the response. In the second button, the use of `pimcore.helpers.uploadDialog` will render an upload modal; the uploaded file will be passed to the controller.

Let's now have a look at how to implement the controller actions that will be called by the created buttons. In the following code snippet, you can see an example of controller implementation:

```php
<?php
namespace App\Controller;

use Pimcore\Bundle\AdminBundle\Controller;
use Symfony\Component\Routing\Annotation\Route;
use Symfony\Component\HttpFoundation\Request;
use Symfony\Component\HttpFoundation\Response;
use Symfony\Component\HttpFoundation\ResponseHeaderBag;

/** @Route("/admin") */
class AdminController extends Controller\AdminController {
    /** @Route("/export-objects") */
    public function exportObjectsAction(Request $request) {
        $folderId = $request->get("folderId");

        //Add business logic here
        $response = new Response();
        $response->setContent($jsonResponse);

        $disposition = $response->headers->makeDisposition(
ResponseHeaderBag::DISPOSITION_ATTACHMENT,
            "export_".date("YmdHis").".json";
        );

        $response->headers->set('Content-Type', 'application/json');
```

```
            $response->headers->set('Content-Disposition',
$disposition);

            return $response;
    }

    /** @Route("/import-objects", methods={"POST"}) */
    public function importObjectsAction(Request $request) {
        $folderId = $request->get("folderId");

        $tmpName = $_FILES['Filedata']['tmp_name'];
        $fileContent = file_get_contents($tmpName);
        //Add business logic here
        $response = $this->adminJson(['success' => true]);
        $response->headers->set('Content-Type', 'text/html');

        return $response;
    }
}
```

As you can see in the previous code snippet, a specific function is created for each controller action. The HTTP request object is passed as an input argument for each action, and the request attribute values can be accessed by the `get` function.

On the `exportObjectsAction` function, we have configured the response to accept the download of a JSON file by setting the response header properly. The chosen file format is just an example and can be changed to the required one. On the `importObjectsAction` function, we read the uploaded file content from the `$_FILES` global variable, so that depending on the business logic, we can import the objects.

To summarize, in this section you learned how to add custom buttons to the Pimcore backend interface, and how to specifically realize controllers to import and export files. In the following section, you will learn how to create a command that can be invoked by the Pimcore console and that, eventually, can be scheduled to be executed as a background process.

Creating Pimcore Commands

In the previous section, you learned how to create custom controllers to perform imports and exports of any kind of file, by creating additional buttons to place in the Pimcore backend interface. In this section, you will learn how to create commands that can be invoked by the Pimcore console.

To create a new command, you just need to create a class that extends the `Pimcore\Console\AbstractCommand` class, as you can see in the following code snippet:

```php
<?php

namespace App\Command;

use Pimcore\Console\AbstractCommand;
use Pimcore\Console\Dumper;
use Symfony\Component\Console\Input\InputInterface;
use Symfony\Component\Console\Input\InputOption;
use Symfony\Component\Console\Output\OutputInterface;

class ImportCommand extends AbstractCommand
{
    const IMPORT_FOLDER = PIMCORE_PROJECT_ROOT."/var/imports";

    protected function configure() {
        $this->setName('import-file')
            ->setDescription('Import a file in background');

        $this->addOption("filename", null, InputOption::VALUE_REQUIRED, "The name of the file to import");
    }
    protected function execute(InputInterface $input, OutputInterface $output) {
        $this->dump("The execution is starting!", Dumper::NEWLINE_AFTER);

        $filename = $input->getOption("filename");
```

```
        $fileContent = file_get_contents(self::IMPORT_
FOLDER."/".$filename);
```

```
        //Add business logic here
        $this->writeError('Please implement this command with
business logic...');
    }
}
```

As you can see in the previous code snippet, in the command configuration you can specify a name and a description for the command, and a list of optional or required arguments and options for the command.

The business logic for the command must be implemented in the `execute` function. We can use command native functions such as `dump` and `writeError` to print messages in the console.

Once the command is developed, it must be declared as a service, as is shown in the following code snippet:

```
services:
    App\Command\ImportCommand:
        tags:
            - { name: 'console.command', command: 'import-file' }
```

You may note that, in the previous code snippet, the `command` tag reports the name of the created command. To invoke the command, you just need to run the following instruction:

```
php bin/console import-file --filename=my-import-file.csv
```

When running the command, the filename must be specified as an attribute. You can see the command result in the following screenshot:

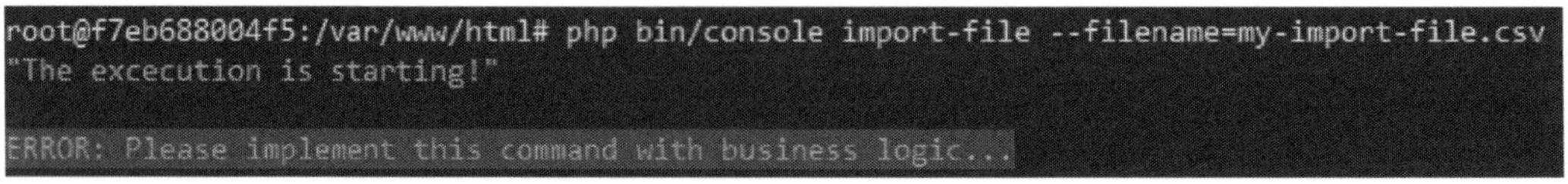

```
root@f7eb688004f5:/var/www/html# php bin/console import-file --filename=my-import-file.csv
"The excecution is starting!"
ERROR: Please implement this command with business logic...
```

Figure 14.12: Command execution

As you can see in the previous screenshot, messages and errors are dumped in the console.

To summarize, in the first part of this section you learned how to add custom buttons to the Pimcore backend interface, and how to let these buttons call for controller actions to upload and download files. Then, you learned how to create and run Pimcore commands through the Pimcore console.

In the next section, you will learn how to configure the new Pimcore Data Importer, which will let you import data from different sources and schedule imports in the background.

Configuring the Data Importer

In the previous section, you learned how to implement custom solutions, and in particular, how to add custom buttons to the object interface and how to create executable commands.

In this section, you will learn how to install and configure the new Pimcore Data Importer, which in the PimcoreX version will replace the standard CSV import that we described in the *Importing Data* section.

The Data Importer plugin is an extension of the Datahub bundle, which we described in *Chapter 13*, *Implementing Master Data Management*. To install Data Importer, you just need to run the following script:

```
docker-compose exec php bash
composer require pimcore/data-importer
./bin/console pimcore:bundle:enable PimcoreDataImporterBundle
```

As you can see in the preceding script, the Data Importer can be downloaded through Composer and can be enabled like every other Pimcore bundle, with the `pimcore:bundle:enable` command.

Once you have enabled the bundle, you can open the **Datahub** configuration panel by accessing the **Settings | Datahub Config** option in the Pimcore menu. To create a new import configuration, you just need to click on the **Add Configuration** button, as you can see in the following screenshot:

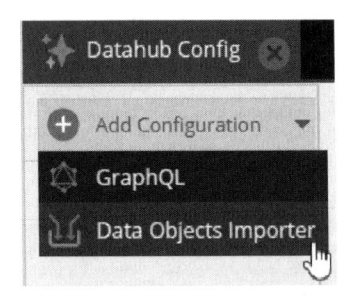

Figure 14.13: Add import configuration

As you can see in the previous screenshot, in addition to the GraphQL configuration, you can select the **Data Objects Importer** option and fill in the configuration name.

To configure and run the import, you must follow these steps:

1. In the **General** tab, enable the **Active** checkbox and add an optional description, as you can see in the following screenshot:

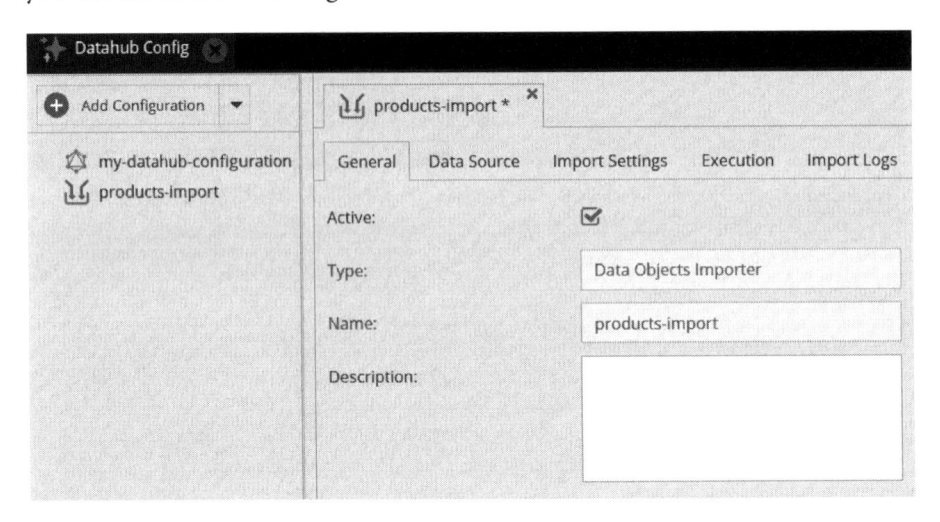

Figure 14.14: General settings

As you can see in the previous screenshot, the defined configuration name is shown in the settings.

2. In the **Data Source** tab, define the kind of import that you want to perform. In the following screenshot, you will see an example of data source configuration:

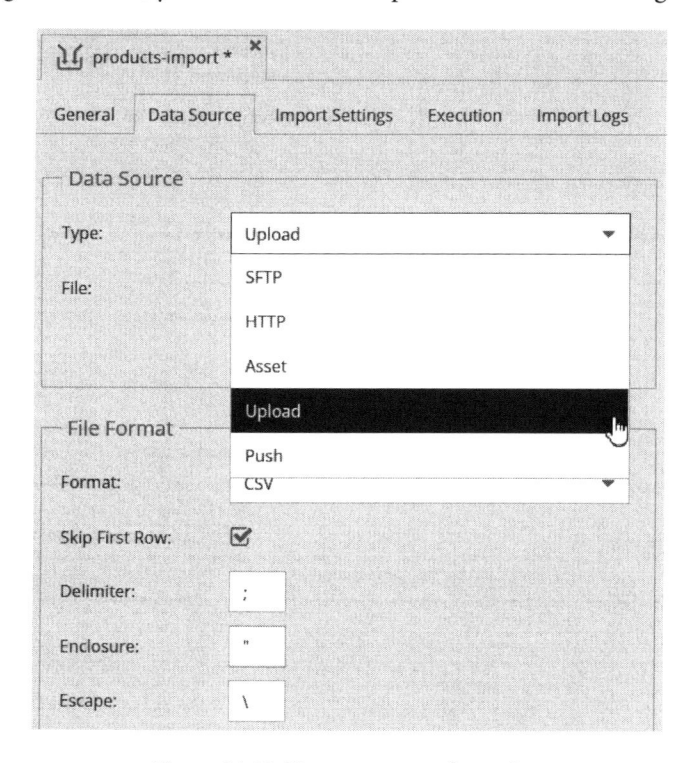

Figure 14.15: Data source configuration

As you can see in the previous screenshot, you can select different source types:

- **SFTP**: If this option is selected, you must fill in the SFTP connection credentials such as **Host**, **Port**, **Username**, and **Password**, and the remote file location inside the SFTP server.

- **HTTP**: This option lets you define an HTTP or HTTPS URL that points to the remote file.

- **Asset**: With this option, you can select the file to import from the previously uploaded Pimcore assets.

- **Upload**: If this option is selected, you must upload a file from your local sources.

- **Push**: This option lets you define an API key and generate a URL that an external application can invoke to pass the file to import with a `POST` call to the generated URL.

Once you have defined the data source, you can specify the file format, choosing from CSV, JSON, XLSX, and XML, and fill in the specific configurations.

3. In the **Import Settings** panel, configure the resolver and the mapping for each field in the uploaded file. In the following screenshot, you will see how to configure the resolver:

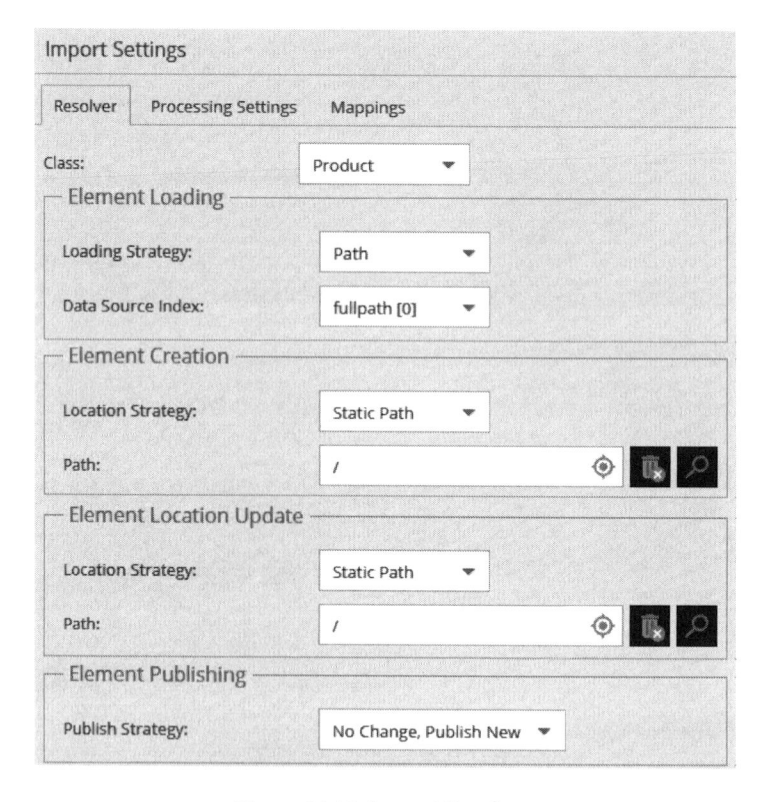

Figure 14.16: Import Resolver

As you can see in the previous screenshot, you can define the class involved in the import and the loading strategy, choosing from **Path**, **Id**, **Attribute**, or **No Loading**. This last option will let the importer always create new objects, without looking at these objects' existence. Then, you can choose where created and updated objects must be located, by defining an existing folder path, and how the published status must be affected.

In the **Processing Settings** tab, you can define whether the configured import can be run multiple times in parallel or whether every importation run must be sequential.

4. In the **Mappings** tab, define a mapping for each attribute of the uploaded file that you want to import. In the following screenshot, you will see how to add a new mapping and how to map a simple text field:

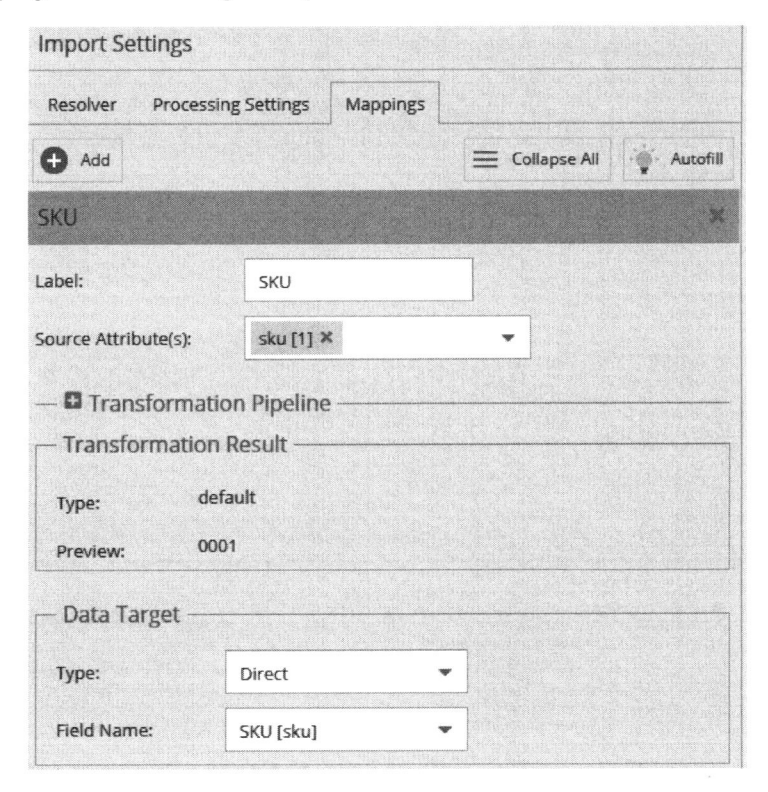

Figure 14.17: Import Mappings

As you can see in the previous screenshot, you can add a new field mapping by clicking on the **Add** button. To map a simple text field, you just need to select the correct field from the auto-detected source attributes and select the corresponding class field in the **Field Name** picklist.

For different kinds of fields, you may need to add one or more transformations using the **Transformation Pipeline**. You can see an example in the following screenshot:

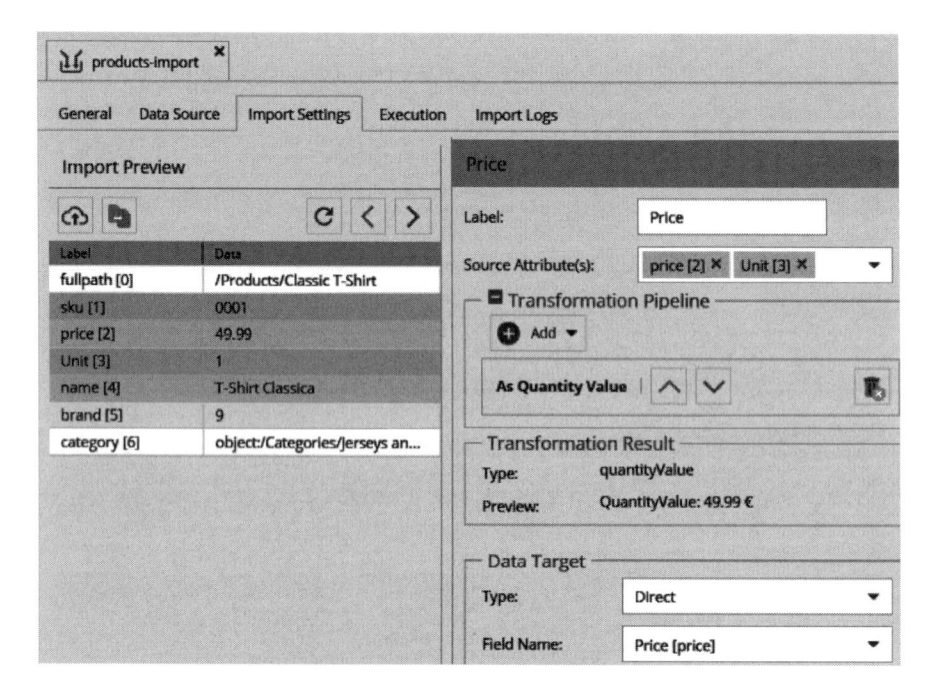

Figure 14.18: Import Mappings

As you can see in the previous screenshot, for **QuantityValue** attributes we can add a specific transformation. This requires selecting two source attributes, one containing the value and one containing the unit of measure.

These pipelines can be used to import dates and numeric fields, or mode complex fields such as, for example, images and other kinds of assets, or the relation with other objects.

In the left panel, you can see that the already defined fields are highlighted.

5. In the **Execution** panel, run the import that you have configured. You can manually run the import by clicking on the **Start** button, as you can see in the following screenshot:

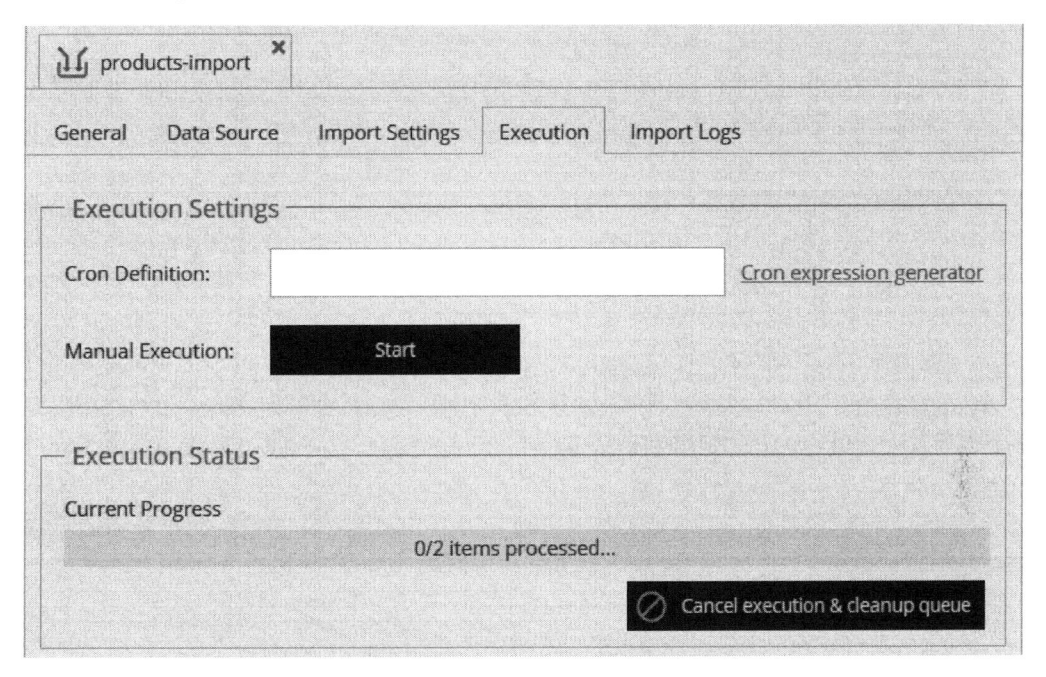

Figure 14.19: Import Execution

As you can see in the previous screenshot, the import status is shown in the progress bar, and you can stop the import at any time.

If you want to schedule the import to be run in the background, you just need to fill in the **Cron Definition** rule.

6. To enable the cron execution, you just need to schedule the execution command as shown in the following script:

```
* * * * * php /home/project/www/bin/console datahub:data-importer:execute-cron
```

Scheduling the cron execution, as shown previously, will let Pimcore check which import configurations must be run every minute. These configurations will be run according to the cron definition of every single configuration.

To summarize, in this section you learned how to install and enable the Data Importer plugin. Through a step-by-step configuration, you learned how to create and execute an import configuration.

Summary

In this chapter, you learned how to import and export data using the standard Pimcore functionalities, which let you import and export CSV files after having defined the respective import and export configurations.

After having described how to properly set up these configurations, you learned which limitations you might encounter when performing these standard functionalities, and how to implement a custom operator to be used in the CSV import process.

Later in this chapter, you learned how to implement custom solutions for importing and exporting. In particular, you learned how to add custom buttons to the Pimcore backend interface, which lets you upload and download files, and how to create commands that can be invoked by the Pimcore console and, eventually, scheduled as background processes.

In the last section, you finally learned how to enable the Data Importer plugin to create import configurations from different kinds of sources, which you can execute manually or schedule to be executed in the background.

As this is the last chapter, let's try to summarize the whole book's content. In the first part of the book, we talked about the Pimcore basics, introducing Pimcore and its features, showing how to set up a development environment, how to move inside the Pimcore menus and functionalities, and how to administrate Pimcore sites.

In the second part, you learned how to implement a blog, step by step, using the Pimcore CMS engine, starting by learning how to create custom CMS pages and how to render data for the blog, and then how to create reusable components and how to finalize the website.

In the last chapters, we described how to use Pimcore for enterprise solutions, with a focus on the PIM and MDM Pimcore features and the data integration processes, providing concrete examples of how to connect Pimcore to external systems.

Now that you have reached the end of this book, we hope it has been an inspiring read, and that this book will be a useful guide for you to develop your projects with Pimcore.

Packt.com

Subscribe to our online digital library for full access to over 7,000 books and videos, as well as industry leading tools to help you plan your personal development and advance your career. For more information, please visit our website.

Why subscribe?

- Spend less time learning and more time coding with practical eBooks and Videos from over 4,000 industry professionals
- Improve your learning with Skill Plans built especially for you
- Get a free eBook or video every month
- Fully searchable for easy access to vital information
- Copy and paste, print, and bookmark content

Did you know that Packt offers eBook versions of every book published, with PDF and ePub files available? You can upgrade to the eBook version at packt.com and as a print book customer, you are entitled to a discount on the eBook copy. Get in touch with us at customercare@packtpub.com for more details.

At www.packt.com, you can also read a collection of free technical articles, sign up for a range of free newsletters, and receive exclusive discounts and offers on Packt books and eBooks.

Other Books You May Enjoy

If you enjoyed this book, you may be interested in these other books by Packt:

Drupal 9 Module Development - Third Edition

Daniel Sipos

ISBN: 978-1-80020-462-1

- Develop custom Drupal 9 modules for your applications
- Master different Drupal 9 subsystems and APIs
- Model, store, manipulate, and process data for effective data management
- Display data and content in a clean and secure way using the theme system
- Test your business logic to prevent regression

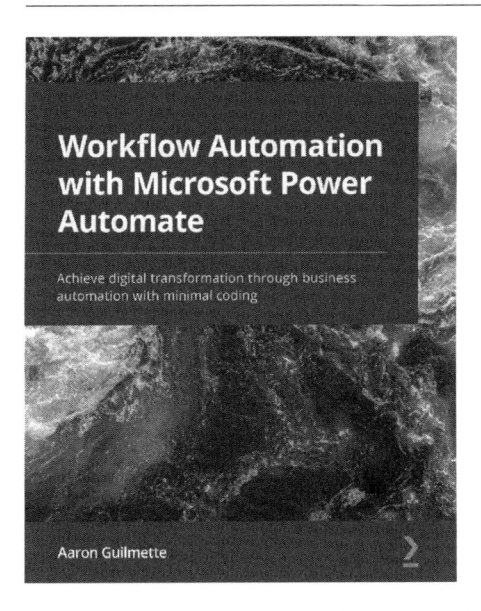

Workflow Automation with Microsoft Power Automate

Aaron Guilmette

ISBN: 978-1-83921-379-3

- Get to grips with the building blocks of Power Automate, its services, and core capabilities
- Explore connectors in Power Automate to automate email workflows
- Discover how to create a flow for copying files between two cloud services
- Understand the business process, connectors, and actions for creating approval flows
- Use flows to save responses submitted to a database through Microsoft Forms
- Find out how to integrate Power Automate with Microsoft Teams

Packt is searching for authors like you

If you're interested in becoming an author for Packt, please visit `authors.packtpub.com` and apply today. We have worked with thousands of developers and tech professionals, just like you, to help them share their insight with the global tech community. You can make a general application, apply for a specific hot topic that we are recruiting an author for, or submit your own idea.

Hi!

We are Daniele, Marco and Francesco, authors of this book. We really hope you enjoyed reading this book and found it useful for mastering the Pimcore platform and deliver modern enterprise solutions.

It would really help us (and other potential readers!) if you could leave a review on Amazon sharing your thoughts on Modernizing Enterprise CMS Using Pimcore.

Your review will help us to understand what's worked well in this book, and what could be improved upon for future editions, so it really is appreciated.

Best Wishes,

DANIELE FONTANI    MARCO GUIDUCCI    FRANCESCO MINÀ

Index

A

Accordion component 86
action columns 135
assets
  organizing 112, 113
  relating 110
  relating, to data objects 113-115
  uploading 110-112
assets metadata
  defining 117, 118

B

bin folder 38
Block component 95
Blocks
  about 61
  regular block 197, 198
  scheduled block 199, 200
  using 197
  using, for general-purpose
    template 252-261
blog
  article, creating 210, 211
  Author Role, creating 208, 209
  routing 211-213
  users and roles, creating 207
  users, creating 209, 210
BlogArticle class
  defining 203, 204
BlogAuthor class
  defining 205-207
BlogCategory class
  defining 204
blog classes
  defining 202, 203
blog views
  Article view, inspecting 220-222
  Categories widget, rendering 222, 224
  HTML pages, stylization and layout
    with Bootstrap 217-219
  rendering 216
  templating 219
Bootstrap
  about 217
  URL 217
  used, for stylization and layout
    of HTML pages 217-219
Bricks
  about 229
  class implementation 234, 235
  implementing 236-239
  templating 235, 236

380 Index

using, for general-purpose
    template 252-261
  working with 234
bundle
  about 130, 231
  creating 230
  creating, from command line 232, 233
  files 231
  folders 232
  installing 131-135
bundle installation
  installers 269
  installers, creating 270-273
  migrations 274-276
  processes, creating 268
bundle products
  creating 296
  defining 296-298
  event listener, creating 299-301
Business to Consumer (B2C) channel 14
Button component 87

C

Cascading Style Sheets (CSS) 217
checkbox editable 182
class
  about 78
  defining 79
  no code 79
class definition
  creating 80-83
  editing 80-83
Classification Store component 95
Column Configuration panel 346, 347
command line
  bundle, creating from 232, 233

Composer
  Pimcore, installing from 28-30
config folder 38
configurable routes 178-180
contact form brick
  conflicts, avoiding 245, 246
  implementing 239-245
Content Management System (CMS)
  about 2, 11, 226
  change in requirements 2
controller actions, examples
  data, passing to view 160
  HTTP headers, setting 160, 161
  JSON output, generating 161
  other cases 162
  template path, specifying 161
controller, for blog
  ArticleAction 213-215
  authorAction 216
  blogAction 216
  categoryAction 216
  editing 213
controllers 159
create, read, update, and
  delete (CRUD) 299
CRM components 92
crontab 155
CSV File Preview panel 345
custom buttons
  adding 359-362
custom layouts
  configuring 305, 306
custom mutation
  creating 335-338
custom operators
  creating 357-359
custom reports
  defining 338-342

custom solutions
  implementing 359

D

DAM system
  assets distribution 108
  characteristics 107
  content enrichment 107
  organization 107
  sharing and access control 108
  versioning 108
data
  decoupling, from UI 7
  exporting 351-354
  importing 344, 345
database connections
  managing, with environment variables 279-281
data components 88, 89
data export
  limitations 355, 356
Datahub 5
Datahub configuration
  creating 320-324
data import
  limitations 356
Data Importer
  configuring 365-371
data management 10
data objects
  assets, relating to 113-115
data quality
  implementing 314-318
Date component 91
date editable 183
date filter
  used, for formatting dates 224

Decoupled CMS 7
Digital Asset Management (DAM) 4, 15, 16, 106, 107
Digital eXperience Platform(DXP) 3-5, 11
Docker
  need for 26
  used, for installing Pimcore 31
  used, for starting Pimcore 35, 36
docker-compose file 32, 33
document
  about 56, 57
  creating, with Pimcore CMS 58-60
  editing 66-70
  inheriting 71-75
  types 57
document tree 56

E

editables
  about 65
  checkbox 182
  date 183
  image 186
  Input 187
  link 187, 188
  Multiselect 189
  numeric 190
  relation (many-to-one) 184
  relations (many-to-many relation) 185, 186
  Renderlet 190-193
  select 188, 189
  snippet 193
  table 194, 195
  testing 182
  Textarea 195
  using 182

video 196
WYSIWYG 197
enterprise e-commerce solution
　features 18
Enterprise Resource Planning (ERP) 13
entities
　exposing 325, 326
environment variables
　using 278
　using, for database connections
　　management 279-281
event listener
　creating 298-301

F

Field-Collection component 93
Field Container component 86
Fieldset component 86
field types 83
file menu 52
File Transfer Protocol (FTP) 2
focal point
　on thumbnails 123
　setting up, in Pimcore images 119
folder conventions 36
formatting types for date and
　　time, PHP online guide
　reference link 224

G

Geographic components 92
glossary module 165, 166
GraphQL queries
　image details, obtaining 330, 331
　object listing, obtaining 327, 328
　object variants, obtaining 331, 332
　performing 326, 327
　relation details, obtaining 329, 330
　single object, obtaining 329
grid component
　first tab bar 49
　opened document 51
　second tab bar 50, 51
　toolbar 49
　working with 48
GridSystem 217

H

hardcoded routes 176, 177
headless CMS 7
helpers
　about 163
　glossary 165, 166
　include 170
　instance of 171
　navigation 169
　pimcore_asset 164
　pimcore_cache 164, 165
　pimcore_device 165
　pimcore_document 163
　pimcore_head_link 167
　pimcore_head_meta 167
　pimcore_head_script 168
　pimcore_head_style 168
　pimcore_head_title 168
　pimcore_inc 169
　pimcore_inline_script 169
　pimcore_object 163
　pimcore_placeholder 167
　render controller output 164
　request 165
　thumbnails 172-174

Index

translations 170
website config 171
hexadecimal (hex) 288
HTML pages
  stylization and layout, with
    Bootstrap 217-219

I

identifier (ID) 203, 305
Iframe component 87
image editable 186
image editor 116, 117
imported configuration
  about 344, 345
  Column Configuration panel 346, 347
  CSV File Preview panel 345
  CSV Settings panel 349, 350
  Resolver Settings panel 348, 349
  Save & Share panel 350, 351
include helper 170
information columns 134
Input component 89, 187
installation file 33-35
installers
  about 269
  creating 270-273
instanceof construct 171

L

layout
  about 61
  implementing 62-65
layout components
  about 84
  Accordion 86
  Button 87

Field Container 86
Fieldset 86
Panel 85
Preview / Iframe 87
Region 86
Tabpanel 85
Text 87
left sidebar 46
link component 187, 188
LocalizedFields
  component, moving to 103
Localized Fields component 94
Long Term Support (LTS) 22

M

main frame 46
marketing menu 53
Master Data Management (MDM)
  about 4, 13-15, 312
  Pimcore, turning into 313
Media components 91
menu items
  file menu 52
  marketing menu 53
  search menu 54
  settings menu 54
  tools menu 53
menus
  inspecting 51, 52
migrations
  about 269
  process 274-276
  purpose 274
mixed components 92
Model View Controller (MVC) 7
multi-environment configuration
  using 276, 277

Multiselect component 189
Multisite
  creating, in Pimcore 264-268
mutation queries
  objects, creating 332-334
  objects, deleting 335
  objects, updating 334, 335
  using 332
MVC (Model View Controller) model
  using 158

N

namespaces 154
navigation helper 169
Number component 90
numeric component
  text component, converting into 103
numeric editable 190
numeric value
  converting, to quantity value 103

O

Objectbricks 93
object data entry
  classes, editing 102
  folders, creating 100, 101
  objects, editing 102
  object variants, adding 101, 102
  performing 100
Object-Relational Mapping
    (ORM) tool 20
object types 291
opened document 51
open source software, benefits
  about 20
  agility 21

community 22
cost-effectiveness 22
shared maintenance costs 21
speed 21
transparency and security 21

P

Panel component 85
parent PHP class
  creating 292, 293
Password component 90
permissions
  about 138
  assigning, to users 138
perspectives
  about 142
  fields 145
  managing 143-148
PHP: Hypertext Preprocessor (PHP) 290
Pimcore
  about 5, 6
  advantages 18-20
  capabilities 313, 314
  characteristics 6
  company, readying for cloud 8, 9
  data, decoupling from UI 7
  document types 57
  folders 37
  installing, from Composer 28-30
  installing, with Docker 31
  licensing 22, 23
  manual installation 27
  Multisite, creating 264-268
  starting, with Docker 35, 36
  turning, into MDM 313
  user experience, unifying 7, 8
  versus WordPress 226-228

Index   385

Pimcore Architecture 42, 43
pimcore_asset helper 164
Pimcore bundle management page 134
pimcore_cache helper 164, 165
Pimcore CMS
  used, for creating document 58-60
Pimcore commands
  creating 363-365
Pimcore Commercial License (PCL) 22
Pimcore Console
  using 152-155
Pimcore DAM, features
  about 109
  asset organization 109
  image and video conversion 109
  users rights and permissions 110
Pimcore DataHub bundle
  activating 319, 320
pimcore_device helper 165
pimcore_document helper 163
Pimcore Enterprise Subscription 22
Pimcore Experience Portals 22
Pimcore, features
  CMS 11
  DAM 15, 16
  data management 10
  digital commerce 17, 18
  discovering 9
  DXP 11
  MDM 13-15
  PIM 12, 13
pimcore_head_link helper 167
pimcore_head_meta helper 167
pimcore_head_script helper 168
pimcore_head_style helper 168
pimcore_head_title helper 168
Pimcore images
  focal points, setting up 119

pimcore_inc helper 169
pimcore_inline_script helper 169
Pimcore Marketplace
  URL 131
pimcore_object helper 163
Pimcore page design process
  working 61
pimcore_placeholder helper 167
Pimcore settings
  exporting 148-150
  importing 148-151
Pimcore workflow
  configuring 306-309
Platform as a Service (PaaS) 9
Preview component 87
Product Bundling 296
Product Data Syndication 22
product entity
  defining 286-289
Product Information Management
    (PIM) 4, 12, 13, 285, 286
product types
  managing 301-303
product variants
  creating 290-295
  parent PHP class, creating 292, 293
  retrieving, in object listing 294
public folder 39
public folder, subfolders
  bundles 39
  var 39

Q

quantity value
  numeric value, converting to 103

R

raw filter
  text, rendering 225
redirects
  about 180
  creating 180, 181
Region component 86
regular block 197, 198
regular expressions (regexes) 212
Relation components 91
relation (many-to-one) 184
relations
  about 96, 97
  example 98, 99
  Generic Relations field 97
  Object Relations 98
relations (many-to-many relation) 185
render controller output 164
Renderlet editable 190-193
request 165
Resolver Settings panel 348, 349
right sidebar 47, 48
roles
  exploring 136
  setting 137
  using 141, 142
routing 176, 211-213

S

Save & Share panel 350, 351
scheduled block 199, 200
Schema object's capabilities
  reference link 276
search menu 54

second tab bar 50, 51
select component 91, 188, 189
Service-Level Agreements (SLAs) 22
settings menu 53, 54
sidebar menu 45, 46
silos 4
Single-Page Application (SPA) 7
slice filter
  using, for content ellipsed 225
Slider component 90
slideshow brick
  implementing 246-251
slug 203
snippet component 193
Software as a Service (SaaS) 17
src folder 38
standard functionalities
  limitations 354
Stock-Keeping Unit (SKU) 287
structured components
  about 92
  Block component 95
  Classification Store component 95
  Field-Collection 93
  Localized Fields 94
  Objectbricks 93
  Table component 95
Symfony 19
system permissions 139, 140

T

Table component 95
table editable 194, 195
Tabpanel component 85

Index 387

template
  creating 60
  Pimcore page design process 61
template helper
  implementing 174, 175
templates folder 38
templating 219
Textarea component 89, 195
text component
  converting, into numeric
    component 103
Text components 87, 89, 90
thumbnail feature 172-174
thumbnails
  about 120-123
  downloading 126, 127
  focal point 123
  usage examples 124-126
  using 120, 124
tools menu 53
Total Cost of Ownership (TCO) 17
translations 170
Twig 216
Twig filters
  about 224
  date filter 224
  raw filter 225
  reference link 224
  slice filter 225

U

UI
  data, decoupling from 7
UI Components
  exploring 43-45

left sidebar 46
main frame 46
right sidebar 47, 48
sidebar menu 45, 46
URLs 176, 203
user permissions
  about 138
  managing, on data elements 140
users
  exploring 136
  permissions, assigning to 138
  setting 137
  using 141, 142
user settings
  configuring 138, 139

V

var folder 38
var folder, subfolders
  application-logger 38
  cache 39
  classes 39
  config 39
  email 39
  installer 39
  logs 39
  recyclebin 39
  tmp 39
vendor folder 39
video editable 196
views 163

W

web portals 7
website config 171
What You See Is What You Get
    (WYSIWYG) interface 11, 65
widget 222
WordPress
  versus Pimcore 226-228
workflow
  custom layouts, configuring 304, 306
  Pimcore, configuring 306-309
  working with 304
WYSIWYG component 90
WYSIWYG editor 197

Printed in Germany
by Amazon Distribution
GmbH, Leipzig